POLITICS IN PUBLISHING

POLITICS IN PUBLISHING

JAPAN AND THE GLOBALIZATION OF
INTELLECTUAL PROPERTY RIGHTS,
1890s – 1971

MAJ HARTMANN

Leuven University Press

Published with the support of the KU Leuven Fund for Fair Open Access

Published in 2024 by Leuven University Press / Presses Universitaires de Louvain / Universitaire Pers Leuven. Minderbroedersstraat 4, B-3000 Leuven (Belgium).

© 2024, Maj Hartmann

This book is published under a Creative Commons Attribution Non-Commercial Non-Derivative 4.0 Licence. For more information, please visit https://creativecommons.org/share-your-work/cclicenses/

Attribution should include the following information:
Maj Hartmann, *Politics in Publishing: Japan and the Globalization of Intellectual Property Rights, 1890s – 1971*. Leuven: Leuven University Press, 2024. (CC BY-NC-ND 4.0)

ISBN 978 94 6270 429 9 (Paperback)
eISBN 978 94 6166 584 3 (ePDF)
eISBN 978 94 6166 585 0 (ePub)
https://doi.org/10.11116/9789461665843
D/2024/1869/34
NUR: 697
Layout: Crius Group
Cover design: Jason Anscomb

TABLE OF CONTENTS

ACKNOWLEDGEMENTS	7
NOTE ON JAPANESE NAMES AND TRANSLATION	9
ABBREVIATIONS	11
INTRODUCTION. POLITICS IN PUBLISHING	13

CHAPTER 1. BEFORE BERNE: THE ESTABLISHMENT OF THE BERNE CONVENTION AND THE OPPOSITION OF JAPAN'S PUBLISHING INDUSTRY — 29

The Development of Copyright Protection in Japan — 31
Japan's Early Internationalists and the Institutional Foundations for State-Society Cooperation — 34
The Emergence of an Opposition Movement — 39

CHAPTER 2. AN UNPREDICTED DEMAND: JAPANESE PUBLISHERS BETWEEN THE ACCESSION TO THE BERNE CONVENTION AND WORLD WAR I — 47

The Copyright Conference of 1900 and the Double Standard of Japanese Publishers — 48
The 1908 Berlin Revision Conference and Japan's Proposal for Free Translation Rights — 55
Japanese Publishers and the Berne Convention During World War I — 62

CHAPTER 3. DEFENDING THE EXCEPTION: COPYRIGHT NEGOTIATIONS BETWEEN THE FOUNDING OF THE LEAGUE OF NATIONS AND THE 1928 ROME REVISION CONFERENCE — 71

The League of Nations and New Structures of International Intellectual Cooperation — 72
The Re-emergence of the Copyright Problem — 76

Japan's National Committee on Intellectual Cooperation 79
Business-State Cooperation in the Preparations of the 1928 Rome
    Revision Conference 82
The 1928 Rome Revision Conference and Japan's Request for an
    Exemption from the Translation Right Regulations 95

CHAPTER 4. EXPANDING GLOBAL VISIBILITY: JAPANESE COPYRIGHT EXPERTS AND THE STATE DURING THE 1930S COPYRIGHT NEGOTIATIONS 103
Intensifying Cultural Cooperation Versus International Isolation 105
The Establishment of Copyright Advisory Councils 112
The Paris Committee of Experts and the Second General Meeting of the
    National Committees 122
Preparations of the Brussels Revision Conference and the Second Expert
    Meeting 132
Reactions by the Transnational Copyright Community 137
Outbreak of World War II 140

CHAPTER 5. TOWARDS INDEPENDENCE: PUBLISHERS, TRANSLATORS, AND UNESCO IN THE POSTWAR PERIOD 145
The Continuation of International Copyright Negotiations under SCAP
    and UNESCO 147
Japan's Reentry into the Transnational Copyright Community 153
Post-Occupation Changes and the Universal Copyright Convention 159
The Return of the Publishers 168
The 1967 Stockholm Revision Conference and the Promotion of the
    Publishing Sector in Developing Countries 173

CONCLUSION 181

NOTES 189

BIBLIOGRAPHY 239

INDEX 253

ACKNOWLEDGEMENTS

This book is the culmination of a long journey and I feel I owe an enormous debt of gratitude to the people who accompanied me on my way, whether for just a part of the road or for the entire journey.

The core of this book originates from my PhD dissertation, and I would like first to thank my PhD supervisor Jan Schmidt who has become a close friend. He opened the world of history to me and shared with me his keen insights and extended personal networks from which this book has profited. During my time as a PhD candidate at KU Leuven with research visits at Keiō University and Sophia University, I also received extensive input and guidance from the other members of my PhD defense committee including Dimitri Vanoverbeke, Shimizu Yu'ichirō, Regine Mathias, and Martin Kohlrausch.

At Sophia University, I would like to thank Shibano Kyōko for opening her personal archives to me during my fieldwork stay in Japan. She also introduced me to Shirai Tetsu and Ichihara Tokurō who shared their insights about their personal experience working in the postwar Japanese publishing industry. I would also like to thank my other teachers in Japan, Tamai Kiyoshi at Keiō University and Tosh Minohara at Kōbe University, for allowing me to join their respective seminars and giving me the opportunity to present and discuss my research on numerous occasions. Furthermore, I thank Aurel Baele, Betto van Waarden, Daniel Wollnick, Fujiwara Hirosumi, Jorinde Wels, Lieven Sommen, Morohashi Eiichi, Tarō Nishikawa, and Tsuruoka Satoshi for their support, constructive comments and help with revisions over the years. I owe particular thanks to my dear friend Jason Butters who has challenged and inspired my research from the first day we met in Kōbe. I am also extremely grateful for the valuable input and advice I received from Sheldon Garon at Princeton University. I genuinely enjoyed the conversations we shared about Japanese History at conferences from Leuven to Tel Aviv. Lastly, I would like to express my sincere gratitude to two anonymous reviewers who provided me with many useful comments that helped me see the forest again and not just the trees.

The transnational scope of my research has led me to many archives across Europe and Japan and I would like to express my gratitude for the wonderful support I received from the archivists and librarians at the UNESCO Archives, the United Nations Archives, The Archive of British Publishing and Printing Reading Sources, the Monacensia, the Bundesarchiv, the Mohr-Siebeck Archiv, the National Diet library of Japan, the National Archives of Japan, The National Archives of England, Wales and the United Kingdom, as well as the KU Leuven East Asian Library. I also had the opportunity to present part of this work at international conferences and seminars at the Asian Studies Conference Japan, the East Asian Translation Studies Conference, the Initiative zur historischen Japanforschung, the Israeli Association for Japanese Studies, Aoyama Gakuin University, Keiō University, Kōbe University, Oxford University, the University of Buenos Aires, and the Shuppan Gakkai (Publishing Society) in Tōkyō.

I was able to conduct the research upon which this book is based with the generous financial support I received as a PhD Fellow of the Research Foundation Flanders (FWO), an FWO long stay abroad grant, and, initially, as part of a Starting Grant that was provided to Jan Schmidt by the KU Leuven in 2016. Here, I would also like to thank the entire Research Group Japanese Studies in the East Asian and Arabic Studies Research Unit at KU Leuven, as well as my students in the graduate seminar on Transnational Actors in Japanese History who inspired and challenged my research in this field.

Over the course of preparing this book project, I was extremely lucky to have been surrounded by my wonderful friends and family. My parents Monika and Matthias, to whom I dedicate this book, who remain a rock in my life, taught me never to stop wondering, and motivated and supported me throughout the oftentimes lonely years of my early studies.

Finally, while this journey began as a single journey, today I no longer travel alone. There is no one who experienced the daily difficulties of completing this book more closely than my husband Felix who alongside this research project shared with me the joys and challenges of raising Nao and Eleas while trying to make deadlines and building an (academic) career. Coordinating academic and family life is not always easy and certainly requires much endurance and many sleepless nights. I therefore thank from the bottom of my heart my wonderful husband who has been supporting me in every feasible way to make sure this book project came to life.

Maj Hartmann

Brussels, 2024

NOTE ON JAPANESE NAMES AND TRANSLATION

Japanese names are given in the traditional order—family name then given name. In case of Japanese scholars whose names are well known in general Western-language scholarship, e.g., Akira Iriye, the names will be treated in the Western convention, with the given name followed by the family name. Japanese names and terms are transliterated according to the Revised Hepburn system. All quotations from Japanese, French, and German texts were translated into English by the author of this book. Committees and institutions will be introduced in their English translation, followed by the original name at the first mention. For important concepts, partial quotes, or individual terms, the Japanese transliteration will be added following the translation. Translations of Japanese titles will be provided in the notes.

ABBREVIATIONS

ALAI	Association Littéraire et Artistique Internationale (International Literary and Artistic Association)
BIRPI	Bureaux internationaux réunis pour la protection de la propriété intellectuelle (United International Bureaux for the Protection of Intellectual Property)
CIE	Civil Information and Education Section
DA MoFA	Diplomatic Archives of the Ministry of Foreign Affairs (Gaimushō Gaikō Shiryōkan)
GHQ	General Headquarters
ICIC	International Committee on Intellectual Cooperation
IIIC/Paris Institute	International Institute of Intellectual Cooperation
IPA	International Publishers' Association
JACAR	Japan Center for Asian Historical Records (Ajia Rekishi Shiryō Sentā)
NAJ	National Archives of Japan (Kokuritsu Kōbunshokan)
NDL	National Diet Library (Kokuritsu Kokkai Toshokan)
SCAP	Supreme Commander of the Allied Powers
UCC	Universal Copyright Convention

INTRODUCTION
POLITICS IN PUBLISHING

Intellectual property rights are one of the most powerful legal instruments of modern capitalist society. This is because, in a global and knowledge-based economy, power resides not only in those who have access to certain resources and knowledge but also in those who decide what falls under the scope of its protection. Today, individuals, companies, and national governments seek to protect intellectual property, and with it the valuable knowledge and access to resources, globally through treaties adopted within the framework of international organizations and international law. At the core of this system of intellectual property rights is the Berne Convention, an agreement for the "Protection of Literary and Artistic Works" established in 1886 by a federation of mainly European states at the request of various authors' and publishers' associations.[1] Since its inception, governments expanded the scope, geopolitical reach, and length of protections guaranteed by the convention.

To understand the principles that underlie today's intellectual property rights system, we will need to turn back a century and a half to the founding days of the Berne Convention and the subsequent efforts to update and modernize the treaty to be in line with the needs of the time. The mid-nineteenth century was a time of rapid transformation where new ways of travel and communication moved politics, culture, trade, and education into the "transnational" sphere—that is, beyond the borders of nation states or an empire leading to new questions about how to manage and govern the world across national borders not only within Europe but also beyond. For example, for those affected by the globally expanding book trade, the existing bilateral copyright agreements were outdated and no longer capable of protecting authors' and publishers' rights. With these complaints, states in cooperation with private interest associations founded international organizations and other international bodies in the second half of the nineteenth century, reflecting a growing trend towards intensified communication and cooperation beyond national borders. Changes in education, infrastructure or technology needed to be governed and managed, they argued, and this monumental task should be taken on by dedicated civil servants and experts engaged in collaboratively discussing these matters at international conferences. It was during these official and unofficial gatherings that they worked to formulate and draft the international treaties with which to regulate specific domains.

What do we know about the history of the international copyright system that today claims authority across most of the world? Much has been written about making international copyright law. Nevertheless, few have considered the contributions by actors outside the European context—such as by the Japanese actors on which this book is focusing. Most of the North and South American countries including the United States were governed by a different multilateral copyright system, the Pan-American Union, throughout the first half of the twentieth century and became relevant to globalizing intellectual property rights only from the 1930s by when discussions about a unification of existing multilateral treaties were taken up.[2] The limited perspectives on non-Western actors involved in the making of international copyright law should come as little surprise considering that the administration and political activities of the Berne Convention, first handled by the International Secretariat of the Berne Union, a de facto international organization which became generally known as the "Berne Bureau"[3], was then largely appropriated by the two subsequent organizations dominated by European and North Atlantic powers and their interests: League of Nations and, after World War II, by the United Nations (UN). When it comes to the history of international organizations, for a long time, scholars have focused on the emergence of these two international governance bodies. In their studies, many scholars reflect the focus of their subjects on the interests of the League of Nations and the UN in an Anglo-American imperial order. In this way, much of the extant work on international law neglects the fact that the global norms diffused by these organizations were in fact the outcome of developments at the local and regional levels and were impacted by practices and ideas that originated outside the Anglo-American world. As Natasha Wheatley has pointed out, scholars of international law "have barely begun to look beneath the surface of international politics to the substratum of assumptions and preconditions" that lie beneath juridical transformation.[4] Questions about intellectual property rights are questions about sovereignty, authority, and power dynamics within and between nations or entities. The norms these rights seek to establish are asserted to supersede local laws and therefore national sovereignty. It is therefore a problem that, in a world of international law dominated by Western ideas and within an international copyright system that was founded on the initiative of an association of French authors, scholars have neglected the constructive role of actors outside the core founding nations in shaping international copyright norms. While the geopolitical power struggle concerning international copyright law has been subject to previous studies, this book looks not only at the official revision conferences where state leaders represented their country on an international stage to include actors who, though at first not visible, nevertheless shaped the modern international system and contributed to global rule-setting in the field of copyright.[5] Only by amending the Western, Eurocentric perspectives which have dominated the history of international law can we begin to illuminate the true regional and cultural diversity of the histories of these institutions and practices.

This book outlines the globalization of intellectual property rights from outside this familiar frame. It does so by examining Japan from the 1890s until 1971. The term globalization here can be understood as the intensifying process of linking distant places by an increase in communication, the flow of goods and the migration of persons, and by consent to the binding rules of international law. The time starts with the years preceding Japan's accession to the treaty in 1899 and ends with the last major revision of the Berne Convention in 1971, a moment by which one could speak of having achieved a global system for the protection of copyrights. Throughout this period of 70 years, aligning with the first era of international copyright from the treaty's creation in 1886 until 1971, state representatives and international lawyers at several international revision conferences and expert meetings amended the treaty's conditions. While the role of "the Japanese state" as an analytical abstraction in the international copyright negotiations has at least been acknowledged in previous scholarship, until now it remained unclear how those acting in the name of the state towards the transnational copyright community reached their decisions, upon whose initiatives they made those decisions, whose opinions and ideas their decisions reflected, and who was actually part of this broader decision-making and international policy formulation process.[6]

Historians of international copyright have focused largely on two issues: first, the European context of the making of the international copyright agreements; and second, the state as primary actor in charge of the political decisions concerning this agreement.[7] A new generation of scholars has emphasized instead the need to look beyond the core founding states of the Berne Convention and the main literary export nations of the time like France, England, or Germany. Insisting on the inclusion of other regions as well as actors that contributed to the global history of copyright, they shed a light on the need to focus also on non-state activity as it related to the formal enactment of the treaty.[8] By approaching the "still largely unwritten history" of international copyright from a more transnational perspective as well as from the perspective of the full complexity of state and non-state actors domestically, these scholars focused less on traditional state-to-state relations and instead began to include actors who have hitherto been considered peripheral. This means including international organizations and non-governmental organizations (NGOs) as well as individual "brokers" as units of analysis in the development of international copyright.[9] This shifting of the field itself has a history related to its subject of analysis: it developed as a response to the gradual increase of participation of non-state actors like NGOs, political party associations, advocacy networks or multinational corporations in "global governance" that could be observed over the second half of the twentieth century and has been expanding especially since the 1980s.[10] By shedding light on how non-state actors, cooperating and interacting with high-ranking state actors, influenced the decision-making process and international relations, transnational approaches to international copyright history thereby provide a means to understanding local history in relation to global history. By including both networks and connections at a local and those at an international and transnational level, these approaches reveal previously obscured hidden continuities and connections, and, in turn, allow the consideration of the true complexity of historical change in the *longue durée*.[11]

This book ties together the activities of Japanese state and non-state actors and their decisions into the making of an international copyright system while considering the simultaneous ways that the international structure impacted changes in Japan's domestic institutions. It thereby pursues two strands of analysis that are closely intertwined.

The book shows, first, how over the course of more than 70 years the changing international order led to domestic administrative transformations in Japan. It argues that these external changes led to a growing dependency of Japan's ministerial bureaucrats on private experts. This dependence facilitated and intensified cooperation between these actors in the administration and judicial handling of international copyright questions. In the copyright negotiations, these ties incorporated a small circle of involved individuals who frequently interacted with each other over decades, accumulating knowledge and making themselves indispensable in the decision-making process. This dynamic led to a common grammar: a rhetoric of Japanese exceptionalism that was developed, adapted, and applied over decades, across all political shifts and upheavals, and from which it became increasingly difficult to part. The choices that Japanese officials made in international fora from the late nineteenth century onwards depended on the domestic situation and were heavily impacted by the institutions that were put in place such as advisory councils to enable the state leaders to take the best-informed decisions for their nation. It has been argued by scholars of modern Japan that Japanese leadership was "extraordinary sensitive" to external developments and a changing international system, that its strength would have been based on a "tradition of adaptability" to rapid changes.[12] In this book, the author argues that in the case of Japan's lengthy process of fully adhering to the Berne Convention without holding on to any special reservations, those most notably sensitive to external developments—those that helped create policies and institutions to take advantage of the new conditions—were in fact non-state actors. These included academic experts in copyright law and private members of the publishing industry driven by capitalist interests, rather than those high-ranking bureaucrats who, as will be shown, more often proved either disinterested, insufficiently informed, or hesitant to act on their own. This does not contradict the predominance of the state in the history of international copyright law. Rather, this study reveals that state leaders, in their pursuit of national power grounded in realism, closely cooperated with and relied upon the opinions of a small group of experts. These experts, despite working outside of official state roles in the private sector of publishing and research, were ultimately part of an emerging internationalist elite. In this circle, they shared a common background, having come of age during the early Meiji era (1868-1912) when the state rapidly imported Western technology and ideas. Often—like their counterparts within the higher echelons of the state bureaucracy—from the best universities in the country and usually with some experience studying abroad, these men had embraced an "international mindset," a term which, as will be shown, was not a static idea but rather a flexible concept that was adapted according to the changing circumstances and that did not at all exclude nationalism or adherence to an ever-expanding Japanese empire.

The second strand of analysis relates to the agency of this small circle of internationalists in the global copyright system. It follows the evolution of their internationalist activities and rhetoric to pursue Japan's national as well as private capitalistic goals within the international organizations involved and demonstrates how Japanese legal scholars, publishers, and translators in close cooperation with Japan's diplomats and ministerial bureaucrats shaped the global norms which undergird international copyright law to this day. A main area in which these actors stirred up the transnational copyright community was in the issue of translations. Japanese publishers, scholars, and government officials made a substantial contribution to one of the major conflicts in modern—and still ongoing—international copyright being fought between "minor and major languages, users and producers, importers and exporters, developed and developing nations."[13] The 1899 version of the Berne Convention stated that an author of a work only had full protection rights on translations of his work within 10 years after the original publication. This section led to controversies within the transnational copyright community and especially between nations that primarily either imported or exported literature. As the first non-Western member of the Berne Convention and a nation which heavily profited from the import of foreign literature for its development and economic gain, Japanese publishers, but also officials and academic scholars were therefore highly invested in this conflict. At the same time, they fiercely used the same rules to protect their own publications sold on the Asian continent in the expanding reach of the Japanese empire. Central to the translation rights conflict and to Japan's role in the international copyright negotiations were the changing forms of internationalism that connected prewar, wartime, and postwar Japan. The term internationalism must be understood as a "soft, flexible concept whose very usefulness lies in its capacity to be molded to various, even opposing ends."[14] As Jessamyn Abel has shown, the practice of participating in multilateral fora never fully disappeared even in times of war. International cooperation did not stay the same, it was adapted and at times abused, but it is possible to trace the ideas and international activities of Japan's internationalists of the late nineteenth century into the postwar period. Their rhetoric used in the international copyright negotiations shifted from the Meiji period with the spread of Western norms and "civilization," to the 1920s era of international collaboration and attempted collective security. This period was characterized by cultural exchange and intercultural harmony, symbolized by institutions like the League of Nations and its sub-institutions or, for example, the Institute of Pacific Relations. During the 1930s and 1940s, they adopted a different rhetoric of internationalism to legitimize imperialist expansion and regional hegemony over Asia, only to again change in the postwar period to center their arguments on cultural diplomacy and the importance of Japan's special reservations for "the people" of Japan. With the goal to achieve the most advantageous outcome for Japan in the international copyright revisions, the small group of Japanese internationalists adapted its arguments in favor of Japan's special conditions according to the trend of the times.

Together these two strands of analysis reveal a hidden history of the importance of domestic and international struggles and power relations, administrative and cultural transformations, but also of generational continuity in the formation of the modern international system.

To analyze Japan's involvement in international copyright negotiations while drawing conclusions on both continuities and change across the period, this book traces the evolution of the Berne Convention through its revision process, covering the international revision conferences and their preparatory stages. It takes as its point of departure the first revision of the treaty in 1896. Thereafter, it proceeds to examine Japan's subsequent entry in 1899, the Berlin revision of 1908, the Rome revision of 1928, the 1930s preparations for the Brussels revision of 1948, and the postwar revisions of Stockholm in 1967, and Paris in 1971. Only in 1970 did Japanese officials give up their reservations regarding the old copyright law since 1899 and, simultaneous with the last major revision, still valid today, of the Berne Convention in 1971, introduced a new copyright law. Furthermore, by this time, the globalization of intellectual property rights envisioned had achieved an important milestone with the introduction of the Universal Copyright Convention in 1952. The revision conferences that took place over this 70-year period offer insights into the transnational collaboration in the field of copyright, into the social spaces in which the participants interacted, into the ideas that were exchanged, and they reflect the general changes in international (power) relations from the late nineteenth century until the post-Second-World-War period as well as the hitherto often overlooked substantial role by non-state actors directly or (domestically) indirectly involved.

These conferences and their often yearly administrative preparations also demonstrate the rise of experts which started to be increasingly visible at the conferences through personal attendance or through their opinions being integrated into the official proposition catalogues shared among member states ahead of the respective conference.[15] These "professionally qualified individuals who were recognized as such by their peers and/or by a wider public" gained importance during the scientification of the economy, society, and politics during the late nineteenth century as conditions became increasingly complex and policymakers relied on the opinions and support of those new knowledge bearers on topics beyond their fields of expertise.[16] The expert status was often linked with internationalism. However, experts rarely acted independently. In their activities and status, they depended on and served the interests of their respective nation states.[17]

Simultaneous to the rise of the experts, national governments also began sending their own delegations to private international congresses, a political strategy which emerged in the late nineteenth century and is described by historian Madeleine Herren-Oesch as "governmental internationalism."[18] During this time, traditional forms of diplomacy and international relations were changing to involve more private actors, a development that was closely connected to the increasing inability of the governments to acquire sufficient knowledge on all aspects of foreign relations without the engagement of non-state experts or advisors. The foreign ministries were eager to modernize and acknowledged that the exchange across borders played a major part in the process of the intended internationalization.[19] To achieve this goal, nation states interested in the multilateral, international society needed a close collaboration with the newly forming international organizations behind the revision conferences at the heart of this study.[20]

The first organization in charge was the international Bureau of the Berne Union, or Berne Bureau. From the time of the founding of the Berne Convention in 1886 until the emergence of the League of Nations' institutional framework in the early 1920s, it managed the political activities surrounding the international copyright agreement as well as its administration. Historian Isabella Löhr described its function as a "superordinate authority" that brought together state and non-state actors alike to coordinate and institutionalize the development of international legal norms between different nation states.[21] While the Berne Bureau continued to oversee administrative tasks, from 1922 the League of Nation's newly founded International Committee on Intellectual Cooperation (ICIC) supported the work of the Bureau by collaborating with state and non-state actors to adopt a global copyright law. Its primary goal was to improve intercultural collaboration on behalf of the League of Nations. In its work the ICIC was supported by its executive organ, the International Institute of Intellectual Cooperation (IIIC or Paris Institute[22]). Cooperating with the Berne Bureau, from 1928 the ICIC planned to amalgamate the Pan-American Union, a different multilateral copyright system that governed the majority of the North and South American states including the United States, into a new convention with a global standard for the protection of intellectual property. World War II interrupted these efforts until, in 1946, the United Nations Educational, Scientific and Cultural Organization (UNESCO) as successor to the ICIC continued the work of the Berne Bureau and the ICIC, concluding a Universal Copyright Convention (UCC) in 1952. The UCC became effective also in non-member states of the Berne Convention. The Berne Convention, on the other hand, simultaneously continued to exist with its last major revision taken place in 1971.[23] As the three major institutions in charge of governing the Berne Convention, the Berne Bureau, the ICIC, and UNESCO were closely intertwined with the political decision-makers while also sharing the tradition of granting a significant value to the voices of transnational actors—private interest groups and academics—in the international copyright negotiations.[24]

Research on the role and work of these organizations has increased since the turn of the present century, demonstrating the growing interest in "internationalism" and the roles of international state and non-state organizations in shaping the international system.[25] Of particular importance are the efforts by Madeleine Herren and contributing scholars in *Networking the International System: Global Histories of International Organizations* in which attention is raised to the fact that as yet a truly *global* history of international organizations is still missing.[26] In addition, many of the individuals who played a decisive role in establishing global regulations have been overlooked because they were not officially part of the organizations. Only recently have scholars concerned with international relations begun to shift attention to those experts, NGOs, academics, think tanks and private consultants who supported the work of international organizations from the outside, but many aspects remain vastly unresearched—especially regarding supporting actors to the pre-World War II organizations.[27] A closer look into the informal communities of experts which existed in Japan from the late nineteenth century show that they were an integral part in the broader discussions around copyright law and in their function resemble the "outside-insiders" that, according to Thomas G. Weiss, Tatiana Carayannis, and Richard Jolly, are so vital in today's policy process.[28] There is still little known about the groups of actors directly impacted by the copyright revision process such as publishers, authors, translators, and legal practitioners regarding their agency in shaping the development of copyright, especially about the actors outside Europe.[29]

While scholars have started to fill the "missing histories of Asian networks" within the history of international organizations, much of the involvement and contribution of non-Western actors to the work of international organizations remains unclear.[30] One reason is that prior research focused less on intellectual cooperation and more on the political and economic activities of these institutions with the aim of finding answers to prevent a future war.[31] Only recently have scholars of international relations like Tomoko Akami, Saikawa Takashi, Goto-Shibata Harumi, Hirobe Izumi, Jessamyn Abel, or Terada Kuniyuki begun to analyze Japan's intellectual cooperation and interaction with the League of Nations and later with the UN.[32] Japan makes a particularly interesting case in the history of the League of Nations due to its paradoxical existence within the League's institutional framework during the 1930s. Although the country officially withdrew from the League in 1933, links with many of the technical committees were maintained. Communication around the harmonization of international copyright was among the fields of international cultural cooperation that the Japanese state remained committed to until the end of 1939.

Another reason for the comparatively little research on the network of Japan's supporting non-state actors to the work of international organizations is that—as historian Sheldon Garon observed—many scholarly works on late nineteenth and twentieth century Japan have tended to sharply divide society from a powerful state.[33] For a long time, the state was perceived as the exclusive catalyst for progress and change, a viewpoint which was heavily influenced by the modernization theories prevalent in the 1950s and 1960s.[34] During the 1980s, this one-sided portrayal of the Japanese state was challenged by scholars like Carol Gluck or Miles Fletcher who turned to society instead and succeeded in demonstrating the large impact of civil actors in shaping the Japanese state.[35] Research in the area of state-society relations was further advanced by the works of Sheldon Garon who, rather than focusing on either the state or society, concentrated on the cooperation and interaction between the two groups. Garon showed that the groups and public discourses that fell into neither of the above categories, but instead existed in a space between them, did not develop independently from the state, but in many cases were closely connected to it.[36] Some specific studies in this field have since focused on the so-called new bureaucrats (*shin-kanryō*) of the 1920s and 1930s who strived to create strong ties with society and include the "ordinary people" in their actions to achieve their political ideas. The above works, however, focus on social policy, while the cooperation between private actors including their intermediate representatives and the state in the cultural and media sector is still at an elementary stage.[37]

Prior to World War II, although the 1889 Meiji Constitution of Japan designated matters of state as the prerogative of the Privy Council and the emperor, whom the council advised, the actual authority over decisions regarding the international copyright treaty, including drafting a new copyright act domestically, primarily lay with the bureaucrats of the Home Ministry and the Ministry of Foreign Affairs where the negotiations were prepared and overseen. Meanwhile, debates within the Cabinet or in the National Diet played only a minor role for the treaty negotiations regarding intellectual property rights. However, while in theory a Weberian bureaucratic organization existed and ministerial bureaucrats had the legal authority to carry out the task of handling Japan's membership in the international treaty, ministerial bureaucrats faced limitations in their authority and responsibilities due to a lack of knowledge. As we shall see, this lack of knowledge manifested itself at times in the attendance of non-governmental international conferences and congresses to gain insight into topics that went beyond their knowledge capacities, at other times in idleness or bureaucratic "inefficiency" which repeatedly led to the distribution of certain responsibilities to informal contacts within a trusted circle.[38] This circle was made up of a small elite of two groups: The first group included the publishing entrepreneurs and their interest groups whose institutions and activities are still vastly unresearched. The second group included academic experts or legal scholars who were affiliated with an institution of higher learning, in the case of this study primarily with the Faculty of Law of Tōkyō Teikoku Daigaku, of the Tōkyō Imperial University (today's University of Tōkyō).

This book bases itself on the assumption that Japan's contribution to the globalization of intellectual property rights was situated in a middle ground between the following three groups: a strong state that provided the initial networks and contacts to the foreign institutions and held the ultimate realist power to pursue Japan's national interests, academics who were specialized in this new field of law, and a private publishing industry which brought with it the entrepreneurial motivation and expertise that the decision-makers were lacking. It proposes that to understand the political process in its full dimension focus needs to be on all the actors involved. This approach meanwhile reveals the integral dependency on one another that these groups shared. This dependency and the motivation to cooperate with each other in the international negotiations were fuelled by the overlapping goal to achieve terms that were advantageous to Japan, although what these goals looked like differed from actor to actor and were subject to change depending on the political situation. The above groups were not always clearly separated and they often intertwined, closely interacted with each other and took on different mediating roles in the global extension of copyright.

The symbiosis between the actors involved becomes clear when looking at the decision-making process from the time of Japan's entry into the international copyright agreement in 1899 until the introduction of a new copyright law and the related last major revision of the Berne Convention in 1971. According to the decision-making approach by Richard Snyder, H.W. Bruck, and Burton Sapin, which was developed for the field of international politics in the early 1960s, those acting in the name of the state undoubtedly are the decision-makers on the international stage. However, in their actions these actors respond to external conditions and factors which are not part of the organization to which they belong.[39] These factors which may affect state action include the "external setting" which are the actions or reactions of other states that lay beyond the state boundaries, and the "internal setting" referring to domestic politics, public opinion, mass media, organizations, or interest groups.[40] In the history of international copyright and the international revision conferences of the Berne Convention, little has been written in Japanese let alone in English about the "internal setting" that influenced the Japanese decision-makers, in other words, little information exists about the role of publishers, translators, and their private interest groups or about the academics involved in the international copyright negotiations. How were the decisions concerning the treaty reached that were then introduced as official "state decisions" to the international community? Who were the individuals and organizations involved and what did this process look like? Answering these questions contributes not only to our understanding of Japan's involvement in the making of global governing norms, but, in addition, also contributes to Japanese political history and to a global history of publishing.

In 1980, sociologist Herbert Passin contributed an insightful chapter on "Intellectuals in the Decision-Making Process" to Ezra Vogel's seminal edited volume on *Modern Japanese Organization and Decision-Making* in which he identified three main positions from which the intellectuals, who are defined as people who "devote themselves to cultivating and formulating knowledge," can exert influence on the government. Passin described an intellectual as follows:

> (1) as an insider, a civil servant holding a nodal position in the international decision-making process (including high-ranking administrators, scholars in government institutions, policy planners, and even middle-ranking bureaucrats);
> (2) as a consultant called in to provide advice, information, critical review, or new ideas; (…)
> (3) as an independent, very likely an opponent, exerting his influence through the mechanisms available in a democratic polity—the mass media, civil movements, and political parties.[41]

In a similar vein, in 1984 the political scientist John Kingdon defined the advocates of policy change as so-called "policy entrepreneurs": "[They] could be in or out of government, in elected or appointed positions, in interest groups or research organizations. But their defining characteristic, much as in the case of a business entrepreneur, is their willingness to invest their resources—time, energy, reputation, sometimes money—in the hope of a future return."[42]

Although the concepts of both Passin and Kingdon focus on the postwar era, the type of influence on political decision-making that is described here could already be seen in the late nineteenth century and, even more so, from the 1920s onwards. The selected Japanese publishers, translators, and academics in the center of this study not only made use of all three positions described by Passin, but in their devotion to the making of an international copyright agreement, they also showed the characteristics of a successful "policy entrepreneur".

Especially relevant for the inclusion of extra-governmental opinions into the policymaking process was the institution of the "advisory bodies" or "deliberate councils" which in Japan are collectively referred to as *shingikai*. The system was established in 1893 for non-state actors like businessmen or academics to provide advice to the government, also to align the country's governance more with "Western" structures.[43] In the postwar period, this system was reformed by the US occupation authorities, who saw it as an institution that had been appointed by the bureaucracy and whose power needed to be limited. While it is contested whether the same term should be applied both to the pre- and the postwar institution, scholars agree that these fora have greatly changed over time with differences in their "nomenclature, legal basis, membership and function."[44] However, they also agree that regardless of the changes, both prewar and postwar types shared certain key characteristics, most notably, their endeavor to incorporate opinions and voices from outside government in the decision-making process.

In the history of international copyright, advisory bodies played a key role in bringing together publishers, academics, and translators with state officials to discuss policies related to the Berne Convention. For the professional and academic experts, they functioned as an entry point to carry forward their ideas and requests which were then taken to the international stage by state actors who were involved and officially represented Japan during the Berne Convention revision conferences across Europe. The advisory councils were thus an important part of the "internal setting" influencing the international negotiations between the late 1890s and 1971. By assessing these processes across an almost 80-year period, not only do the many changes in international copyright-related cooperation come into view but so too do the existing continuities. Successive advisory councils tied the state to private actors and provided a channel for the continual discussion of copyright-related policies.[45] This dependency became especially problematic when, in the 1930s, the state's representatives decided to use the same rhetoric for their ultranationalist propaganda and plans of imperial expansion. While the wartime years from 1940 to 1945 are largely irrelevant for this study in that the main international organization in charge of handling the planning and administration of the international treaty discontinued its work in 1940, the book still sheds light on the reasons why a number of the major publishing houses collaborated so effectively with the government ministries that they had worked so closely with for decades before the war.

Many of the primary sources used in this book have so far received little to no attention. Japan's handling of copyright and the changes that occurred throughout history regarding the concept of international copyright remain almost completely absent from Western scholarship.[46] In Japan, literature on copyright history seldom crosses the boundaries of studies within the field of literature— let alone national boundaries. Among the sources of this book that give insight into the transnational participation of Japanese actors are the documents of the Ministry of Foreign Affairs. The Diplomatic Archives of the Ministry of Foreign Affairs of Japan, which include many records of internal communication with the Home Ministry, and the National Archives of Japan include, for example, protocols of mutual advisory bodies between publishers and bureaucrats, but also the laws and their drafting process which provide information on the viewpoint of the government and on the importance of the opinion of businessmen and academics on the revision drafts.

Another hitherto overlooked valuable source, especially in connection with the interaction between publishers and bureaucrats during the respective preparation processes for the revision conferences, are publications of different publishers' associations, including a collection of papers of the Tōkyō Booksellers and Publishers' Association (Tōkyō Shosekishō Kumiai) which was published in 1937 after the associations' main sources were destroyed in the Great Kantō Earthquake in 1923, and the (self-)history of the Tōkyō Publishers' Association (Tōkyō Shuppan Kyōkai) first printed in 1929.[47] Without the study of these sources, the influence of individuals like publisher Oyaizu Kaname (1844-1922), who was head of the Tōkyō Booksellers and Publishers' Association at the time of Japan's accession to the Berne Convention, on the early international copyright negotiations would remain invisible. Today, still little is known of the influence of these publishers' organizations on the policies of the state or in a larger global context within the history of international organizations and of the actors in charge as their main agents. Of special relevance to this study are the preserved petitions and written opinions addressed as stakeholders to the bureaucrats in charge of representing Japan on the international stage, a great number of which is included as part of the associations' self-histories. The study of the involved expert networks and their arguments reveals that Japanese publishers, authors, lawyers, and bureaucrats did not always follow a unitary national foreign policy uncontested. The formation of expert communities was accompanied by contestations among the different actors, between state and non-state actors, but at times also within the community of professional publishers and academic experts itself. Thus, while this history with Japan's eventual complete integration into international copyright norms could be read as a linear history of global cooperation, the study presented here likewise emphasizes the areas of conflict and rifts in mutual understanding which led to new differences and fragmentation both within Japan and in relation to its international contacts.

The individual chapters of this book are organized chronologically according to different stages of cooperation between the state and society and the international organizations involved. The relationship between the different actors and Japan's integration into the international copyright system did not follow a linear development but was subject to constant changes influenced by the developments on a national and international level from the late nineteenth century until the 1970s.

Chapter 1 traces the transformation of intellectual property rights protection during the late nineteenth century and the circumstances leading up to Japan's accession to the Berne Convention in 1899 including early forms of cooperation between individuals outside the government and the state. In Chapter 2, we consider the time from Japan's entry to the international copyright treaty until the end of World War I. This period includes the Berlin Revision Conference of 1908 and questions regarding the validity of the law and the impact it had on the Japanese publishing industry during the Great War. Chapter 3 explores new and more extensive forms of cooperation between publishers and governmental actors following World War I until the early 1930s. The chapter also examines the League of Nations and its institutional framework as the new administrative locus in charge of international copyright and associated political activities in connection with regulating authors' copyrights in an increasingly globalized world. It then investigates the involvement of the Japanese private sector in collaboration with the ministerial bureaucracy to prepare the 1928 revision conference of the Berne Convention in Rome. Chapter 4 focuses on the 1930s and the developments surrounding the preparations of the next revision conference originally planned for the mid-1930s in Brussels. For numerous reasons the conference was repeatedly postponed until the outbreak of World War II in Europe brought the negotiations to a close altogether. As mentioned above, closing the doors on the Paris Institute as the main international organization in charge of coordinating the revision process resulted in the wartime years having played no significant role in the revision of the Berne Convention. Accordingly, the wartime years are largely left out in this study. International consultations were resumed in the years immediately following the war and the planned conference was finally held in 1948. While during the previous decades, the cooperation between private actors and bureaucrats involved in the publishing industry was still conducted rather unofficially, the 1930s saw the expansion of official forums for interaction which further facilitated the business-state exchange and added to the global visibility and increasing participation by individuals from Japan's publishing industry. The final chapter centres on the postwar developments, beginning with the revival of the copyright movement under US occupation and the conclusion of the Universal Copyright Convention in 1952. In light of the postwar decolonization in many parts of the world, the second part of Chapter 5 concentrates on the changing role of Japanese publishers and translators in the international debate on how to accommodate the needs of developing nations, in particular, to the newly independent states that were looking for options to replace their colonial judicial systems with laws that would allow their states to prosper and not hinder their development. By the 1967 Stockholm Revision Conference, questions on translation and access of knowledge—that Japanese publishers and other private industry actors had already been inquiring about from the late nineteenth century—had risen to the top of the agenda of the copyright community, challenging the existing historical narratives of the international copyright system. The book shows that the role of individuals from the Japanese publishing industry was central throughout the entire process leading to the final revision of the now truly globalized Berne Convention in 1971.

CHAPTER 1
BEFORE BERNE
The Establishment of the Berne Convention and the Opposition of Japan's Publishing Industry

The rapid technological developments from the second half of the nineteenth century opened new forms of communication through the invention of the telegraph and the telephone as well as faster modes of travel through the locomotive or the steamship that connected the world in unprecedented ways. These new structures brought with them the need to establish international organizations that dealt with the movement of people, items, capital, or information across state boundaries.[1] One of the sectors affected by this rapid increase in flow of information and items was the book market. To respond to the fast movement of literary works from one country to another, in the late nineteenth century this sector saw a radical transformation from the bilateral protection of copyrights to a new form of copyright protection internationally with the introduction of the Berne Convention as the world's first multilateral copyright treaty.

While the idea of copyright protection had already developed as early as in the 15th century with the invention of Johannes Guttenberg's printing press and the simplification of producing copies in great numbers, it was in 1710 that a first modern Copyright Act of Parliament was introduced in the United Kingdom. By 1850 national copyright laws had been implemented in many countries. From around the same time, new printing techniques transformed the industry: metal parts replaced wood, the rotary cylinder press replaced hand presses, and stereotyping helped accelerate the printing process, allowing for more efficiency and for the mass production of texts. With the simultaneous rise in literacy rates, new consumers were targeted, reaching "a market of unprecedented scope."[2] Through the simultaneous development of new ways of travel and communication, the book trade quickly expanded globally which led to widespread copying and spreading of texts without notification to or permission from the original author. As a result, the existing copyright agreements could no longer meet the requirements of sufficiently protecting authors' and publishers' rights. With the aim to counteract this trend of free reproduction of works, publishers and authors across Europe gathered in Brussels for a first international congress for literature in 1858.[3] In the following years, further congresses on the topic were held until in 1878 the newly established authors and publishers' interest group Association Littéraire et Artistique Internationale (International Literary and Artistic Association; ALAI) managed to persuade the Swiss government to invite several countries to come together and discuss the option of forming a multilateral copyright agreement that would protect intellectual property across national borders.[4] Their efforts were rewarded with the Swiss government decision to hold an international conference on the topic resulting in a federation of states that included Belgium, France, Germany, Haiti, Italy, Liberia, Spain, Switzerland, Tunisia, and the United Kingdom. In 1886, these states would sign what would be called the Berne Convention.[5] The protection was also extended to colonies and protectorates of the respective signatory states. The Convention itself was anchored in a union of its signatory states, the so-called Berne Union, which had a permanent office in Berne and, in its role as an international organization represented its member states at international conferences and prepared and contributed to revising the convention depending on the technical and political developments over the next 80 years until it integrated into the World Intellectual Property Organization (WIPO) in 1967.[6]

This chapter traces the formation and development of the opposition against part of the regulations of the Berne Convention in Japan during the late nineteenth century. It follows the internal protest by publishers and academics that arose amid international pressure to have Japan join the treaty in the late 1890s. It will be argued that these protests led to the creation of new forms of cooperation with the state that would later influence the globalization process of intellectual property rights. To construct this argument, the chapter is divided into two parts. Part one gives a historic overview of the development of copyright and the Japanese publishing industry prior to joining the Berne Convention and thereby situates the key actors involved, their activities, and their views in the historical context of the late nineteenth century. It then looks at the formation and first activities of a network opposing parts of the Convention. The groups of actors involved shared a similar background belonging to a small internationalist elite with early exposure to Western culture and languages. Although they also pursued different interests, an overarching goal they shared was prosperity for the Japanese nation. The early negotiations surrounding international copyright functioned as a rallying point where ministerial bureaucrats, publishers, and academics came together and developed a common rhetoric to represent Japan on the international stage.

THE DEVELOPMENT OF COPYRIGHT PROTECTION IN JAPAN

During the above developments and time of rapid acceleration and change during the latter half of the nineteenth century, the new government in Japan, which had been established in the aftermath of the Meiji Restoration of 1867/1868, began promoting the import of European and US technologies and culture, including many books and translations of foreign works. But the development of print culture in Japan had begun long before the import of modern printing technologies from Europe and the connected mechanization of production, with the production of Buddhist invocations dating back to as early as the eighth century. Even movable type already existed prior to the Meiji Restoration and Japan's so-called "opening" in 1868, having been brought to Japan independently by both Jesuit missionaries and by the armies the warlord and de facto ruler of Japan, Toyotomi Hideyoshi, had sent it to Korea in the late 16th century.[7] However, this technology did not manage to establish itself as the dominant printing form and—likely because of the large capital outlay required—was largely abandoned in favour of traditional woodblock printing techniques until experiments with movable type were taken up again with the aim of printing Western books and newspapers in the mid-nineteenth century.[8]

At least since the early Tokugawa period (1603-1868), printed texts were already seen as commercial goods that were bought and sold and had a material value.[9] There are said to have been around 5000 working publishers throughout this period who were organized in booksellers' guilds which protected their members' works from piracy and controlled the observance of censorship regulations imposed by the state.[10] By the time of the Meiji Restoration, Japan thus already had a highly developed and capital-driven print culture.[11]

The Restoration brought with it not only the technological advances from traditional xylography to movable type technology and rotary cylinder presses which greatly facilitated and sped up the printing process.[12] The political and social changes also created a new thirst for foreign news and Western education which resulted in the *bakufu*, the military government in Edo[13], beginning to translate Western newspapers into Japanese. After the mid-1860s, private citizens were allowed to subscribe to these early type newspapers, and an ever-increasing number of publishers joined the business of translating foreign news publications.[14] In 1871, Japan's first daily newspaper, the *Yokohama mainichi*, appeared. It was also the first paper to use metal type. Both the government and private companies were competing for the print market and pushed the industrialization of print forward with the result that by the 1880s, the price of movable type had fallen by 85% since the 1870s. The number of newspapers rose from 225 in 1877 to 470 a decade later. By 1900, the daily circulations of many newspapers reached numbers between 50,000 and 100,000.[15] In comparison, the circulation of the eight main dailies in Britain went through a similar acceleration, rising from 1800 in 1801 to 2775 in 1850 to an average of the main dailies of over 200,000 by 1900.[16]

But not only newspapers flourished as part of this Meiji era "printing revolution."[17] The yearly number of 6,000 newly issued books and magazines in 1879 rose to 26,000 publications per year in 1897, shortly before Japan joined the Berne Convention.[18] The rapid technological advancements in combination with improved literacy created new audiences which contributed to the emergence of a new generation of Japanese publishing entrepreneurs who saw in the growing print market new business opportunities such as the open access to Western published sources.[19] Besides several bilateral agreements, before the Berne Convention of 1886, no laws protected the mainly European authors across national borders, so the reproduction and translation of foreign works was free. It did not take long until in 1871 a British diplomat first issued complaints about the free copying and translating of European works, but the Meiji government at first did not show great interest in drafting an international treaty for the protection of foreign copyright. From the 1880s, increased pressure from Europe persuaded Japan, and with it the Japanese publishing industry, to enter the newly created treaty, and official conferences started being held to discuss the problem of protecting foreign property.[20]

The concept of copyright was not completely new to Japan at the time, even though no such law was yet enshrined in formal legislation. The idea of copyright protection had long been recognized with the first successful petitions written in 1698 by Ōsaka booksellers to city authorities to issue a ban on copyright fraud which was implemented in 1699.[21] For the protection of their rights, booksellers began to form guilds, the first of which were recognized by the *bakufu*, in 1716 (Kyōto), 1721 (Edo) and 1723 (Ōsaka). The guilds were serving the town magistrate in the control of publications, worked for the protection of its members' copyrights, and helped with the exchange of its members' publications.[22]

However, as book historian Peter Kornicki has demonstrated, the matter of copyright protection in the Tokugawa period was closely intertwined with the commercial interests of the publishers, and while the author had some rights by having their names mentioned in the title of the book or being asked for permission before their work was reprinted, their intellectual property right was not yet formalized in legislation. In most cases, an author's name was mentioned when the same had provided the capital investment for the publishing himself.[23] The recognition of copyright until the late Tokugawa period had thus less to do with the commitment of the *bakufu* to the concept of protecting intellectual property per se than with the aim to settle disputes among publishers concerned with protecting the financial investment in the works they published.[24] Kornicki accumulated some evidence according to which by the 1840s the interest of the authors received greater attention by the *bakufu* which had hitherto alone been concerned with the publishers' commercial interest, and by 1843, it ordered that works could no longer be published without the permission of the author.[25]

After the Meiji Restoration in 1868, a time when Japan looked closely to Europe and the United States for direction, the enlightenment thinker Fukuzawa Yukichi was campaigning to establish a copyright law like the ones he had encountered in Britain and France, the major literary nations of the time. Fukuzawa had a personal interest in the establishment of a copyright law as he himself had experienced the pirating of his commercially very successful works *Seiyō jijō* (Conditions in the West) and *Gakumon no susume* (An Encouragement of Learning) published in 1866 and 1872.[26] Furthermore, he had begun translating foreign works and official documents for the government at the beginning of the 1860s and had started his own translations in connection with an expanding private collection of foreign books which he purchased from old bookstores and during government sponsored business trips to Europe and the United States in 1862 and 1867.[27] From the beginning, his profession as a translator and his large output of books as an independent publisher allowed him to pay great attention to crediting the original author in the translations he published. Thus, Fukuzawa was convinced that a copyright law would protect independent publishers like himself from piracy and copyright fraud, regardless of their affiliation with a publishers' guild.[28]

On Fukuzawa's initiative, in 1868 at the time of the Meiji Restoration, an edict for the control of publishing was issued which for the concept of copyright meant a first legal incarnation like the ones Fukuzawa had observed on his travels to Europe and the United States. A year later, in 1869, Japan's first Publication Ordinance (Shuppan Jōrei)[29] was introduced which already contained passages on the protection of literary works that, however, were still only granted to the publisher and not to the individual author of the work. Furthermore, these clauses did not apply to the translations of the works of foreign authors.[30] This lack of protection of foreign works reflected the general problem with copyright protection of the time: The national copyright laws could not keep up with the rapid development in international trade and the expansion of international relations which led to increasingly faster ways of exchanging works. These books were mainly being shipped from the leading book producing countries like England, France, and Germany to foreign countries, where they were duplicated and translated without any form of compensation to the original author.

Domestically, the protection of intellectual property rights in Japan made progress through the revision of the Publication Ordinance[31] in 1875 which, at Fukuzawa's demand, had added a new article which stated that exclusive rights in books (including those of translations) lasted for 30 years. The rights, however, still only protected the publisher and not the author of the work which meant foreign authors' copyright was not protected in Japan.[32] The 1875 Ordinance introduced the literal translation for the term "copyright" (*hanken*) for the first time. Furthermore, in 1887 three statutes on printed works, dramatic scripts and sheet music, and photography were enacted that explicitly focused on the protection of copyright—in contrast to the statutes of previous years that had focused on censorship regulations.[33] These three statutes eventually formed Japan's first Publication Law (Shuppan Hō)[34] in 1893.

JAPAN'S EARLY INTERNATIONALISTS AND THE INSTITUTIONAL FOUNDATIONS FOR STATE-SOCIETY COOPERATION

With the growing discontent among European private authors' and publishers' associations about Japan's unauthorized copying of foreign intellectual property, the Western industrialized nations began to recognize the importance of having Japan join the treaty as a potential new member of the new international copyright treaty. In partly to counter the uncontrolled copying of foreign works and guarantee British citizens their intellectual property rights, in 1894 Great Britain and Japan concluded an Anglo-Japanese Treaty of Commerce and Navigation. The treaty offered an end to the system of consular jurisdiction that had been imposed on Japan as part of the so-called "unequal treaties" in the 1850s and 1860s, on condition that Japan would agree to join the Berne Convention and the Paris Convention for the Protection of Industrial Property created in 1883.[35] Japanese leaders accepted this proposition and signed the treaty as seeking to be part of the international community meant joining international laws, and, as media scholar Kerim Yasar stated: "Acceding to the Berne Convention seemed like a small price to pay for eliminating the far more humiliating concession of extraterritoriality."[36] The British government, however, requested that Japan implement its civil and commercial codes before the treaty came into force.[37] The problem with this task was that the Berne Convention was a completely new form of international law, created by a union of states that had come together as an organization for the specific reason of passing a multilateral agreement. Thus, the Japanese government did not yet have an expert to consult in this new field of international politics. Consequently, in 1896 just after the end of the First Sino-Japanese War which had interrupted the government's plans, Mizuno Rentarō (1868-1949), a young graduate from the Faculty of Law of Tōkyō Imperial University, was asked to look into joining the international copyright system and to draft a new Copyright Act for Japan that complied with the Berne Convention.

Mizuno had graduated with a degree in English Law in 1892 and had launched his bureaucratic career in the Ministry of Agriculture and Commerce in 1893 before being transferred to the Home Ministry a year later.[38] Here, Mizuno worked in several key positions, for example as head of the Bureau for Shrine Affairs or as head of the Construction Bureau. His work at the Ministry did not, however, remain limited to administrative tasks.[39] As one of the best in his field, he was made responsible for copyright matters soon after he had entered the Ministry, and because of his contributions to the accession to the Berne Convention, is considered a pioneer of the first Japanese Copyright Law (Chosakuken Hō).[40] The urgency of the demand to draft a new Copyright Act was the result of yet another trade agreement, this time the German-Japanese Treaty of Commerce and Navigation (Nichi-Doku Tsūshō Kōkai Jōyaku), that had been negotiated in 1896 under the same conditions as the 1894 agreement with Great Britain.[41]

In the midst of the government's legal reform project, in May 1897, Yamada Saburō (1869-1965), a young scholar in private international law at Tōkyō Imperial University from the same generation as Mizuno, published an article in the renowned law magazine *Hōgaku Kyōkai zasshi* (Journal of the Jurisprudence Association) in which he advised the ministerial bureaucracy to urgently study the Berne Convention and the Berne Bureau as the international organization behind its creation onsite in Europe.[42] Born in 1869 to wealthy farmers in Nara, Yamada had studied at Tōkyō Senmon Gakkō (today's Waseda University) and at Tōkyō Imperial University where he specialized in English law. After completion of his studies in 1893, he had to return to Secondary School, which he had not attended during the still tumultuous years of the creation of a modern education system in the first decades after the Meiji Restoration, but which was required of him if he wanted to enter graduate school.[43] However, Yamada's knowledge in the field of international law was quickly recognized and considered so valuable to the Meiji state that while obtaining the secondary school credits he needed to be able to enter graduate school, he began consulting for the government on questions related to international law from shortly after the signing of the 1894 Treaty of Commerce and Navigation. He even assisted with the drafting of Japan's Civil Code.[44]

The fact that Yamada began his career during the 1890s when the Japanese government was in the process of establishing its legal framework in accordance with European standards of international law, contributed to his adoption of "European civilization" and to his desire to raise Japan to the same "standard of civilization," which was seen by the leading Meiji thinkers as essential in succeeding to gain equality with the Western powers.[45] In the mid-1890s, Yamada also began to share his advice in the form of written articles which appeared in the newly emerging expert magazines. This type of consultation was new and came as a result of the increasingly commercialized publishing industry that was opening up a new market for magazines which saw not only the appearance of profit-oriented general interest magazines like *Kokumin no tomo* (Nation's friend) or *Taiyō* (The Sun), but also an increase in special expert magazines in various genres including law. Whereas before, anyone interested in politics and political decision-making shared their opinions in opinion-orientated political debate magazines, the new times enabled a new brand of public intellectuals, private experts, entrepreneurs, and university professors specialized in certain political areas to influence the political debate with their expertise shared in expert magazines.[46] The political debate magazines of the previous decades that had targeted only a small and specific audience disappeared from the mainstream. In 1897, Yamada Saburō who had advised Mizuno to study the Berne Convention onsite in Europe was himself about to leave for Germany as part of the "recruitment pattern" for future faculty members at the Tōkyō Imperial University Faculty of Law. In this pattern, young graduates were selected to study a certain period abroad in Europe on a government scholarship that they received by their professors.[47]

The Faculty of Law of Tōkyō Imperial University, which was educating some of the brightest young men in the country, became known for its close relationship with the Meiji state with many of its graduates filling ministry posts. Expectations of the academic institutions and the experts it employed were high and the state frequently reached out to the Tōkyō Imperial University professors to serve as advisors in government commissions and share their valued knowledge and opinions on increasingly complex conditions in the economy, society, and politics.[48] Historian Byron Marshall showed that until the 1930s the University's intellectuals took on roles as official advisors, or using John Kingdon's words—as "policy entrepreneurs," and that these academics had a broad influence on shaping national policy, especially in the fields of social legislation and the drafting of legal codes.[49] Similarly, sociologist Herbert Passin wrote:

> When a distinguished professor of Tokyo University's Faculty of Law writes a book or an article, or makes a statement on some public issue, the decision-makers may not leap to obey him, but they are not entirely unresponsive; his work often strikes an echo. Most of the key civil servants, and even many of the leading politicians and businessmen may have been his students or classmates. In any event, he will be a respected sensei (teacher) whose works they will have studied and who has had a role in shaping their thought. They will therefore reverberate to his views, his language of thought, his posing of the issues, even if they do not agree with his specific political position.[50]

Whether Mizuno directly followed Yamada's advice is difficult to reconstruct, but in November 1897, 30-year-old Mizuno travelled to the United States, England, Germany, France, and Italy to study the Berne Convention and upon his return began drafting a Copyright Act (Chosakuken Hō, literally Author's Right Act).[51] Japan's entrance into the international copyright treaty was thus carefully planned and implemented by the government and, unlike in Western Europe, did not result from publishers' and authors' endeavors to have their work protected on an international level. By contrast, in Japan, the planned accession to the Berne Convention was heavily opposed by the publishing industry and the media which centered around hindering the conclusion of the treaty. Resistance came especially from the Tōkyō Book Publishing Businessmen's Association (Tōkyō Shoseki Shuppan Eigyōsha Kumiai)[52] and its president at the time: Oyaizu Kaname.[53]

Oyaizu Kaname, born in 1844, was the oldest son of a vassal to the Okazaki feudal domain in Mikawa province in today's Aichi prefecture.[54] At 19, he left for Edo, attending the private school of Ōtori Keisuke, a military leader and diplomat who would fight for the Tokugawa Army in the Boshin War, the short civil war in 1868 that ended in the defeat of the Tokugawa and their allies in the Restoration. Shortly after, Oyaizu transferred to the Kaiseijo, a school for Western learning that had been established by the *bakufu* in 1863. Mastering English, French, and German, Oyaizu became well-versed in Western knowledge during a pivotal period marked by the Boshin War in 1868. Despite potential backlash, he defended his principles—including his openness to the West—and the *bakufu*, going to Hakodate but getting wounded in May.[55] After escaping to Matsumae, he stayed until the *bakufu*'s surrender to the imperial troups in June 1869. Oyaizu faced house arrest upon returning to Okazaki but left in March 1870 to resume his studies.[56] He had private lessons in Numazu and secured a study loan from a former lord, allowing him to enroll in the Daigaku Nankō, a forerunner of the Tōkyō Imperial University. From there, he transferred to Fukuzawa Yukichi's private Keiō Academy.[57] Fukuzawa himself had roots in the former samurai class and in general bore a striking resemblance to Oyaizu whose interest in the learning and publication of Western knowledge was just one of the many traits that he shared with Fukuzawa. Their engagement in the publishing industry combined an economic mind with a growing interest in Western ideas.[58]

In 1872 the abolishment of the feudal domains and the establishment of prefectures as modern administrative units led to the suspension of Oyaizu's scholarship which he took as an opportunity to start his professional career. After briefly working as an English teacher at the English School of Yanagawa, in January 1873, he decided to join the publishing house Yokohama Maruya Shōsha (since 1880 Maruzen Shōsha, hereafter Maruzen). Maruzen had been co-founded by Fukuzawa Yukichi in 1869 and in just four years' existence had become renowned for its imports and translations of Western literature and books on enlightenment.[59] For Oyaizu, this publishing house provided an ideal platform for combining his gift for the English language with Meiji Japan's rapidly expanding trade business. His skills as a young publisher were quickly recognized, as shortly after, in 1877, he was promoted to lead the Ōsaka branch office. Five years later he was put in charge of the

Tōkyō head office where he devoted himself entirely to the import of works from Europe and the United States.[60] As will be shown, both academic scholar Yamada Saburō and publisher Oyaizu Kaname were among Japan's early internationalists who constituted a small elite of influential figures significantly shaping copyright negotiations in the subsequent years.

About a decade after Oyaizu had joined Maruzen and the turmoil of the Restoration had calmed down, the Japanese government began actively promoting certain key domestic industries, amongst others by encouraging the founding of private interest organizations. Individual prefectural governors were given a mandate by the government to advertise and authorize the establishment of new associations in various fields of industry. By providing assistance in the form of subsidies and benefits, the state tried to secure itself an important position within the different organizations with the intention of hindering the autonomous development of the respective associations to include them in their official policymaking.[61] The publishers in and around Tōkyō used this opportunity to join forces to strengthen their stance and founded the Tōkyō Book Publishing Businessmen's Association (Tōkyō Shoseki Shuppan Eigyōsha Kumiai, later renamed Tōkyō Booksellers and Publishers' Association (Tōkyō Shosekishō Kumiai) in 1902, hereafter abbreviated as (Tōkyō) Booksellers' Association) in November 1887 with initially 131 members. Oyaizu Kaname was one of the five main contributors involved in the founding process. The Tōkyō Booksellers' Association stated its initial task as "to act as a mediator between the publishers and the state as well as society in order to promote culture," and to contribute to the diffusion of education and to the development of Japanese society, two areas which had gone through great changes in the years leading up to its foundation.[62] A committee made up of an elected leader and two vice-leaders oversaw sharing the concerns of the members with the state representatives, usually in the form of written petitions (*chinjōsho*). While some petitions were addressed directly to one of the ministries, many others were first handed to the Tōkyō Chamber of Commerce (Tōkyō Shōgyō Kaigijo) which acted as a mediator between the small and medium sized companies, including the publishing houses, and the state.[63]

The Chambers of Commerce[64] were first established in 1878 in the cities of Tōkyō, Ōsaka, and Kōbe with the goal of developing and promoting the trade and industries. In the next four years new chambers emerged all over the country and by 1882, the number of chambers had risen from three to 36 with further steep growth in numbers in the following decades. The chambers were the first business associations of their kind in Japan and served as a forum for communication and interaction among its members with the aim to facilitate the solution of conflicts. Another main strength of the chambers was the ability to exert pressure on the ministries and on political decisions in the form of petitions. While they did receive financial aid from the state, the founding of the chambers had not been the result of an ordinance "from above," but had been the initiative of influential merchants and industrials, among them Shibusawa Eiichi.[65]

From the time of its founding, the Tōkyō Booksellers' Association worked in close cooperation with the Tōkyō Chamber of Commerce. Regulations regarding the Chamber's predecessor, the Tōkyō Association of Commerce and Industry, had even been codified in the official Statute of the Booksellers' Association.[66] These regulations included the election of members to represent the booksellers within the Chamber. When in 1890 the chambers were legally mandated, the new Tōkyō Chamber of Commerce made the two existing associations obsolete. The Tōkyō Booksellers' Association helped to financially sponsor the new chamber and left the Tōkyō Association of Commerce and Industry in 1891. The publisher Kobayashi Yoshinori, who like Oyaizu was one of the main founders of the Booksellers' Association, was chosen to be the promoter of the publishers within the Tōkyō Chamber of Commerce which strengthened the link between both organizations from which the publishers would greatly profit in the following years.[67]

THE EMERGENCE OF AN OPPOSITION MOVEMENT

When Japan's planned entrance to the international copyright treaty drew closer with bureaucrat Mizuno Rentarō's imminent departure for Europe to study the treaty, the publishers, united through their publishers' association, decided to take action. In June 1897, Oyaizu Kaname who had been leading the Booksellers' Association since 1892, wrote a petition addressed to the president of the Tōkyō Chamber of Commerce, Shibusawa Eiichi. Shibusawa had held this post ever since the establishment of the Chamber, so that the Booksellers' Association had already cooperated with him on different juridical matters related to publishing regulations.[68]

Referring to the two trade agreements that Japan had concluded with Britain and Germany in 1894 and 1896, Oyaizu shared the following request of the publishers which consisted of two main points:

> (1) Members of a signatory state should have the right to freely translate and publish the works of members of other signatory states,
> (2) works that have already been translated by a citizen of the Japanese empire should be unaffected by the new treaty.[69]

The latter point was of special importance and was included by the publishers, as the Berne Convention did not differentiate between works that were written before a state's accession to the treaty and those that were written under the new laws which in Japan's case meant having to deal with a great number of illegal copyright frauds in retrospect. In an attached writing Oyaizu listed the reasons for the petition, arguing that Japan had only developed so fast in the past 30-40 years since the opening of the country due to the import of knowledge from Western countries and that the planned accession to the treaty would "hinder the spread and development of general knowledge" (*bun'un no hattatsu shinpo o gai su*) as well as the circulation of new academic theories, made available through translations of research excerpts.[70] Oyaizu further wrote: "(Intellectual) Property is of a global, universal character [sekaiteki uchūteki no seishitsu], and it should not be in the power of the so-called international code to sell the protection of an author's right."[71] He added that translations were harming the author's rights only to a very small extent, which would also be the reason why the Berne Bureau would have defined the duration of translation right protection to only 10 years after the work was first published.[72] The publishers argued that while in Europe free translations would be harming authors' rights and had a negative impact on the sales of the original publication, the same was not the case in Japan. As a "convenient" reason, they argued that the Japanese language was so different from European languages. In their opinion, Japanese publishers had never intended to damage any copyright holder and used the knowledge they gained for the purpose of "civilizational progress" (*bun'un no hattatsu*) in Japan as well as for diplomatic purposes, an area, which would now be under threat by the plans of the Japanese government to join the international treaty.[73] Oyaizu furthermore claimed that the state should compensate the publishers for the extra financial burden that would arise in connection with copyright reimbursement, in other words, the sum that the Japanese publisher had to pay to the original author of a work for granting him the right to translate.[74]

The "civilization" argument in the debates around reproduction and translation rights was not new and had been used by other importer nations, most notably by the United States and Sweden. As early as the 1840s, a debate arose between American and British opponents and proponents of authorial property that centered around fundamental questions of what knowledge meant to a "modern culture as that culture came into being."[75] While British authors criticized the losses they made due to unauthorized reprinting of their works, the opponents of transatlantic copyright, most importantly the American economist Henry C. Carey, argued that Britain held a monopoly on book manufacturing which needed to be broken. Future progress would depend on independence from copyright, and knowledge should be available to all.[76] According to Carey, what was at stake if Britain succeeded in its intent to protect copyright on a universal level, was "civilization" which, as he argued, depended on a decentralized circulation of information and knowledge.[77] Likewise, during the discussions around the establishment of Sweden's first copyright law in 1876, the Swedish Supreme Court advised against limiting free translations: "For a people whose language is so small and geographically limited as the Swedish, any restriction on freedom of translation could not but have a negative impact on the dissemination of knowledge and education."[78]

The Japanese publishers' argument that the treaty hindered the progress of Japan was chosen to spark an interest among the bureaucrats who represented Japan at the negotiating table. Even though these reasons were also of concern to publishing entrepreneurs like Oyaizu who were schooled in Western learning and had a sincere interest in modernizing Japan, it can be assumed that their primary interest lay in the profit they gained from translating foreign works, a field of business that judging from their actions, they now saw endangered by the new international law. Giles Richter focused on this new generation of "aggressive" publishing entrepreneurs in the Meiji era, and emphasized the new business opportunities in the world of print that were essential for their emergence in the 1870s.[79] According to Richter, these included "the dissolution of the Tokugawa booksellers' guilds, open access to Western published sources, the creation of a national textbook market, and the expansion of more effective means to advertise and distribute publications to remote locations."[80] The result was an increasingly commercialized industry.[81] For the publishers who specialized in the publication and translations of Western works without any remuneration to the original author, the Berne Convention was threatening to take away part of their foundation as successful publishing entrepreneurs. For the new Meiji state, however, whose primary goal was to gain recognition by the major powers and to raise its own status, both the knowledge gained through translations of foreign works and economic development through the thriving publishing industry were compelling reasons not to ignore Oyaizu's petition.

As a direct response to the petition, on October 8, 1897, at a meeting between the Tōkyō City Council (Tōkyō Shikai)[82] and the Tōkyō Chamber of Commerce an investigation committee (*chōsa iinkai*) was formed that would function as a direct intermediary between the different actors involved from the state and the industry. The aim of the committee was to investigate Oyaizu's petition and give recommendations to the afore-mentioned Mizuno Rentarō as the main person in charge of drafting the copyright bill. This form of interaction between members of the state and society was new at the time. The forum of "advisory bodies" or "councils of deliberation" that would bring together experts from the industry or academia with ministerial bureaucrats in charge of certain political agendas, had only been established in 1893 to facilitate the exchange and consultations between members of business and the government on topics that concerned both. The results of these bodies were then included in the form of reports and recommendations in the process of bill drafting.[83] The type of committees was usually formed by the prime minister, by the cabinet, ministers, or high-level bureaucrats. However, in some instances, they were formed because of a request that came from outside the government, in this case from the publishers.[84] Realizing the rapid changes on the international political scene, the bureaucrats responsible in the Japanese ministries were open to the extra-governmental consultations they received, as the laws they were dealing with were unprecedented, and the bureaucrats were struggling to school themselves in the various new fields of expertise. Through the mutual interest in the topic of international copyright protection, a new form of cooperation developed between the actors involved that shared the common goal of achieving terms that were advantageous to Japan and its nation-building process.

The chosen committee members included several publishers that were closely acquainted with Oyaizu like Kobayashi Yoshinori, the promotor of the Tōkyō Chamber of Commerce, and Sakuma Teiichi, founder of Tōkyō's largest printing company Shūeisha (now Dai-Nippon Insatsu). Like Oyaizu and Kobayashi, Sakuma also belonged to the group of pioneers of the flourishing Meiji publishing industry. Additionally, he had strong political connections and was an active member not only of the Tōkyō Chamber of Commerce, but also of the Tōkyō City Council.[85] Thus, when on October 8 it was decided to designate Oyaizu's petition as urgent and make it also a matter of the City Council, Sakuma here as well became one of the five members elected to be in charge.[86] In addition to members from the business side, the investigation committee also directly involved high-ranking ministerial bureaucrats: With Ume Kenjirō as one of the selected members, who at the time was the head of the Cabinet Legislation Bureau (Naikaku Hōseikyoku) and engaged with drafting the Japanese Civil Code, an internal bridge was built toward the state delegates in charge of handling juridical decisions. Ume had been a teacher of Mizuno Rentarō whose task was to study and collect information on the Berne Convention onsite in Europe.[87] Unfortunately, the content of these committee meetings and thus the position of the individual members as well as the final recommendation of the committee remain unknown.

The opposition movement by publishers, writers, and private scholars continued in 1898 with newspaper and magazine articles warning the Meiji state of joining the treaty.[88] Despite the uproar, upon his return to Japan in June 1898, Mizuno Rentarō began drafting a copyright bill together with his colleagues Akashi Taka'ichirō and Ōgura Masatsune, both graduates of the class of 1897 of the Tōkyō Imperial University Faculty of Law. The question of whether Japan should enter the treaty or not was not easily answered and led to many discussions among the ministerial bureaucrats involved.[89] They had to weigh up supporting the requests by the publishers as its citizens on whom the state increasingly depended and gaining international respect and status by joining the international treaty. Joining the conference would put Japan, or so its leaders hoped, on par with the Western nations in terms of joining international laws which was understood as a rule of conduct for "civilized nations".⁹⁰ Nonetheless, the Meiji leaders realized and acknowledged the concerns of the publishers that Japan would be hindered to import and translate "Western knowledge" the same way that they had been able to over the previous decades.⁹¹ Administration of their ministerial departments and access to relevant knowledge about the newest developments were among the main concerns for the bureaucrats at the time. The men in charge knew their duties, but lacked the technical expertise and knowledge needed to make decisions in the rapidly changing international politics.⁹² As political scientist and historian of Modern Japanese politics Shimizu Yu'ichirō has remarked, in general the level of knowledge of Japanese bureaucrats in specialized fields before World War I was becoming insufficient of which they were aware.⁹³ However, unlike politicians who were elected, bureaucrats needed to gain political legitimacy through their special expert knowledge that was to contribute to the making of new policies.⁹⁴ Through the forum of advisory bodies, here in the form of a small copyright committee, the bureaucrats were able to receive consultation from private actors. Thus, when from the late 1890s questions related to the international copyright agreement and its effects on the industry emerged, the bureaucrats now had institutionalized contacts with a few high-ranking publishers, including Oyaizu Kaname and Ōhashi Shintarō, to ask for advice and expand their expertise. At the same time, this new cooperation was also beneficial for the publishers who were trying to convince the bureaucrats of their own political interest. The two groups of actors had basically become partners in the nation-building process, but only to an extent where the publishers did not interfere with the plans of the Meiji state. Any ongoing opposition was muted following a plea by Home Minister Itagaki Taisuke to accept the government's decision to be "on par with the great powers."⁹⁵ Itagaki described the entrance into the Convention as the state's duty, and a matter of its reputation.⁹⁶ Prefectural governors throughout the country were instructed to control anyone who still opposed the law which for the moment resulted in a decline of resistance.⁹⁷ Eventually, in December 1898, Mizuno's draft, which in the end comprised 50 paragraphs, was completed and handed to the Imperial Diet.⁹⁸

Throughout the disagreements between the state and the publishing industry on Japan's entrance to the international copyright treaty, the investigation committee continued actively to replace only a few of its candidates. Ume Kenjirō was replaced by yet another ministerial bureaucrat, Ozaki Saburō, who like Ume had been head of the Cabinet Legislation Bureau from 1891-1892 and was now a member of the House of Peers.⁹⁹ Two other new members were the publishers Ōhashi Shintarō, founder of the publishing house Hakubunkan (est. 1887) and Hara Ryōichirō. Ōhashi also shared Oyaizu's interest in Western publishing, having started a business for the sale of Western paper in 1897 alongside his existing publishing enterprise. The two publishers were united in their common ambition to combine their business interest with seeing a need to educate the Japanese people, for which Ōhashi in 1901 established Japan's first private library, the Ōhashi Library, which was open for use by the public.[100] But Ōhashi was also active in politics: In 1902, he was elected into the House of Representatives for the Jin'inkai, in 1926 he became a member of the House of Peers. His case proves that already in the late nineteenth century the dichotomy between state and non-state actors is difficult to maintain, and that the interests and actions of actors from different backgrounds and social affiliation intertwined with one another. Regardless of whether Ōhashi was directly influenced by his work in the investigation committee to review Oyaizu's petition, or had held the same opinion from the beginning, in the years to come, he would join his colleague Oyaizu in petitioning for looser translation rights.

With time running out to stop the government's negotiations and an entire industry relying on his success, Oyaizu wrote another petition on January 7, 1899, this time addressed straight to Home Minister Saigo Tsugumichi. In his writing, Oyaizu expressed the great impact that the treaty would have on himself and other members of the publishing industry. The publishers needed to prepare a written consent and would further have to analyze the legal validity of the scheduled accession. The international correlations in this matter would be highly complex, so that it would be necessary for the publishers to analyze the main points and causes of the treaty and visit the Home Ministry to advise the delegates and cooperate with each other.[101]

It only took a few days until the meeting Oyaizu had requested was held between several unnamed publishers, including Oyaizu Kaname and Ōhashi Shintarō, and the Home Ministry copyright expert Mizuno Rentarō. The publishers used the meeting to explain their hesitation and requests to Mizuno.[102] It was probably Oyaizu's active involvement and the establishment of a first copyright advisory council that raised the bureaucrats' awareness concerning the required expertise and special knowledge they needed to gain in the field of publishing to make the correct decision for their national industry. However, despite Oyaizu's initiative and an increase in communication between publishers and bureaucrats, the Japanese state decided to accede to the Berne Convention on April 18, 1899, and ratified it on July 15 of the same year. Ultimately, external pressure from Western nations and the imperative to abolish the "unequal treaties" prevailed over the domestic pressure to cater to the needs of their own citizens. Yet, when considering the circumstances surrounding Japan's accession to this multilateral agreement, it remains questionable whether the Meiji leaders ever truly embraced the institution of the Berne Convention. They joined, it seems, solely in the service of their nation and continued to instrumentalize it for Japan's national interests. Japan's entry into the Berne Convention in 1899 marked the beginning of a protracted power struggle between Japan and other members of the international copyright system.

With the turn of the century, the first pipelines facilitating cooperation between state officials and members of society had been established. International copyright law emerged as a new field of law, prompting ministerial bureaucrats to seek advice from members of the industry and scholars of international law, such as Yamada Saburō. This process gave rise to a small circle of copyright experts, comprising bureaucrats, publishers, and academic scholars. Following Japan's accession to the treaty, the demands that were expressed by publishers in connection with positioning Japan within the globalization of international copyright norms moved from the national to the international stage—stirring up the transnational copyright community. It is the beginning of Japan's transnational participation in the international copyright negotiations that will be the subject of the next chapter.

CHAPTER 2

AN UNPREDICTED DEMAND

Japanese Publishers between the Accession to the Berne Convention and World War I

Japan's accession to the Berne Convention in 1899 was part of a comprehensive reform effort undertaken by the Meiji state to adapt to the demands of the new international order imposed by Western imperialism. Responding to this system, Japan introduced various institutions from the great powers, including their legal and banking system, military organization, technologies, and scientific knowledge. Seeking to elevate its status to that of the Western powers, Japan became an active participant in the imperialist system and, following its military victory in the first Sino-Japanese War of 1894-1895, established an empire of its own. Just a decade later, Japan achieved major power status by winning the Russo-Japanese War of 1904-1905 which would lead to the full annexation of Korea in 1910.

During those years, Japan's publishing industry continued to grow fast in conjunction with new technological advancements such as the Linotype machine imported in 1903, a rising mass society, and the country's industrialization and urbanization. A literacy rate of 90% by the end of the Meiji period (1868-1912) and the replacement of primarily opinion-orientated with general-interest magazines led to printed works being read across social lines, and the publication and translations of Western works remained in high demand.[1] Both the Sino-Japanese War and the Russo-Japanese War stimulated an unprecedented request for news among the masses and further contributed to the development of a mass industry throughout the early twentieth century.[2] Questions concerning the specific regulations of the international copyright agreement thus continued to be of great interest to Japan's internationalists, including leading publishers, concerned with bringing Western knowledge into the country.

This chapter centres on the building of transnational networks from the turn of the century until the end of World War I. It follows the lead-up and occurrences around the first official international revision conference joined by Japanese delegates in 1908, including the proposal presented by Japan and the reaction received by the other member states of the Berne Union. The chapter will then examine the developments during World War I, in particular the contribution by Japanese publishers in maintaining flows of international book trade despite the international uncertainty about the validity of the Berne Convention during the time of war. In sum, the chapter seeks to showcase the interplay between domestic developments, including the growing influence of private interest groups and academic experts on the decisions of state leaders, and the broader impact of Japanese state and non-state actors on the international stage within the copyright-related work of the Berne Bureau.

THE COPYRIGHT CONFERENCE OF 1900 AND THE DOUBLE STANDARD OF JAPANESE PUBLISHERS

The private actors involved in the early negotiations around the Berne Convention included not only publishers but also academics, like the above-mentioned private international law scholar, Yamada Saburō. Yamada, who had advised Mizuno Rentarō to study abroad, had himself been on a study stay in Germany, England, France, and the United States since late 1897. Eventually, he decided to continue his studies of international private law in Germany at the University of Göttingen.[3] During his studies, Japan acceded to the Berne Convention which the Meiji leaders ratified in 1899. Yamada, like the publishers, vehemently opposed Japan's accession to the multilateral treaty.[4] He shared the argument of the publishers that copyright protection would hinder the spread of "civilization" in Japan. Yamada's legal thinking was influenced by the work of the Institut de Droit International (Institute of International Law) which had been founded in 1873 in Ghent in Belgium by a group of international lawyers to study and develop questions related to international law. The mission of the Institut de Droit International according to their own statute was to become the organ of the "legal conscience of the civilized world."[5] While in the case of the publishers, the search for profit played a major role in their initiative, for Yamada who was born in 1869, one year after the Meiji Restoration, the greatest emphasis lay on adapting Japan to the "standard of civilization" in line with the aim of the Meiji state.[6]

Towards the end of his stay in Germany, the 1900 World's Fair was held in Paris and displayed everything that made up the early twentieth century, representing new technologies, art, and cultural forms.[7] The universal exhibitions in general promoted a world without war and a peaceful diplomacy through exchange between economies, intellectuals, and culture, and offered an important opportunity for the representatives of different countries to discuss their ideas and reflect on the newest developments in various areas.[8] The first exhibition had been held in London in 1851 around the same time that mainly European authors, inventors, and merchants found a new international awareness that led to their request for a multilateral protection of rights.[9]

During the exhibition, there were as many as 120 conferences on topics of international interest organized alongside the main event, including a one-week conference on the new international copyright agreement which took place between July 16 and July 22, 1900. The conference was organized by the Bureaux Internationaux Réunis pour la Protection de la Propriété Intellectuelle (United International Bureau for the Protection of Intellectual Property; BIRPI), the joint secretariat of the Berne Bureau and the Bureau of the Paris Convention for the Protection of Industrial Property.[10] The reason for the conference was a planned revision of the Berne Convention to achieve a unification of the international agreement and to determine one standard of copyright and translation rights protection. The international conference facilitated the exchange of ideas among those involved in the publishing and copyrights sector. It provided an opportunity for discussions of necessary changes in the protection of intellectual property, influenced public opinion, and catalyzed the revision of the international copyright treaty. This allowed the participants to express their opinions before an official revision conference.[11] The conference was led by Eugène Pouillet, who held the position of president of the Association Littéraire et Artistique Internationale (ALAI) from 1890 to 1905. Among the approximately 200 attendees of the conference were state representatives from the non-member states Romania, Russia and the United States, member states Belgium, France, Italy, Spain, as well as two representatives from the Berne Bureau, and writers' and publishers' representatives from the Unites States and Europe including ALAI. Japan, on the other hand, had not sent an official government representative, most likely because the conference was not an official revision conference and the country had therefore simply not been invited. Instead, Japan was unofficially represented by academic scholar Yamada Saburō and publisher Ōhashi Otowa who were the only representatives from outside Europe and the United States.

Yamada who, because he was in Göttingen, was not far from Paris had decided, privately and at his own expense, to attend the conference based on his academic qualifications and research interests.[12] In Paris, he met with publisher and writer Ōhashi Otowa who had joined publishing house Hakubunkan in 1893.[13] Ōhashi who was working as author and editor for various journals, in 1900 went on a trip through the United States and Europe with the aim of visiting the World's Fair.[14] He decided to join Yamada at the copyright conference as representative of one of Japan's major publishing houses. If it had not been for their private attendance, the voice of the only non-Western member of the Berne Convention would have been excluded from this vital gathering. The notes that Ōhashi kept in a travel diary allow an insight into the week at the congress.[15]

In his travel sketch, Ōhashi Otowa shared his opinion that the international copyright conference was, at its core, very different from other international conferences in that it was a gathering of members' organizations that came together with specific interests in one certain area. According to Ōhashi, if the delegates had no expertise in that area, then it would make no sense for them to attend the event.[16] The first day of the conference was filled with organizational preparations and several greetings by the host country's representatives for cultural affairs. The Minister of Public Instruction, Georges Leygues, closed the day, stating that the complete protection of copyrights would be "essential for attaining universal civilization," clearly conveying the standpoint of his country as one of the main proponents of international copyright law.[17]

The following days of the conference were balanced between discussing a revision draft of the Berne Convention in the mornings and a varied cultural program in and around Paris in the afternoons, followed by daily parties until well into the night with, according to Ōhashi, a constant flow of champagne.[18] Towards the end of the conference, on July 20, the attending countries gave their individual statements regarding the revision of the international agreement. When it was Japan's turn to speak, Yamada raised his voice and for about 20 minutes presented the Japanese case. He emphasized the apparent "differences between Eastern and Western civilization" (*Tōyō bunmei no sa'i-ten*) and the "isolation from the original (European) language of a work" (*gengo bunji no sa'i hanahadashiku kakuzetsu seru o motte*),[19] claiming:

> It is always the better choice to read the original work rather than an imperfect translation. On the other hand, with the help of a translation, the original becomes readable [for a larger audience] and should also increase the sales of the original work. In fact, the readership of many of these works actually increases due to translations, and there is no actual damage to the copyright holders.[20]

The notion of "civilization" that French minister Leygues had just used as an argument for *expanding* the existing copyright laws, was now used by Yamada to be *exempt* from the regulations that were being discussed among the participants of the international—Western—community. When Yamada had finished, Eugène Pouillet commented that despite the divergence of the presented opinion from his own, looking at translation rights from the viewpoint of Japan's "special circumstances," he would try to find an appropriate solution.[21]

Ōhashi reacted with enthusiasm to Pouillet's response and wrote in his travelogue:

> Ah, what a delight! As this conference is actually a private congress, and not a public meeting of the national governments, we cannot see the immediate outcome—however, even though we cannot see it yet, this [occurrence] has unlocked

some potential. (…) All those who listened to Yamada's explanation will be able to understand our situation. Copyright owners and publishers that receive a request for translation from us, should from now simply approve them.[22]

It was thus the private attendance of scholar Yamada Saburō and publisher Ōhashi Otowa and their presentation of Japan's issue with the protection of translation rights that first brought the argumentation of Oyaizu and his publishing colleagues to the international stage, albeit informally. As the ministerial bureaucracy at this point was not internationally involved in the ongoing discussions regarding a possible revision of copyright-related regulations, Yamada's statement was the only indication of where Japan might position itself regarding the protection of international copyright. His talk was a clear foreshadowing to what awaited the international community eight years later when Japan officially boycotted the suggestions by the Berne Bureau and thereby contributed to a stagnation in the globalization process. However, whether the international community understood—or remembered—the weight of the statement by two unofficial representatives of Japan remains questionable, as the requests made by Japan in Berlin in 1908 still came as a shock to the international community.

Following the 1900 conference, Yamada visited the University of Paris where he attended lectures on international private law which put him in touch with Raymond Weiss who, in the 1920s, would become Legal Advisor in the International Institute of Intellectual Cooperation, a sub-committee of the League of Nations that would take over the administration of the Berne Convention following World War I. Weiss was to become one of Yamada's close acquaintances, further adding to his indispensable role for the Japanese state in the copyright negotiations.[23] Hence, for Yamada as a young scholar, the journey to Paris was also an educational exchange, not much different in nature from the educational exchanges of the 1920s that according to Akira Iriye contributed greatly to the prewar cultural internationalism by bringing students and teachers from different countries together.[24] Even though Yamada had close connections to the government and at the time already worked as an advisor in legal matters, his participation in the international copyright conference in Paris remained that of a non-official, private representative of Japan and could be regarded as an annunciation to the transnational movements that increasingly connected the world after World War I.

Tragically, for Ōhashi Otowa the "rushed" trip to Europe overexerted the young publisher.[25] Shortly after his return to Japan, he contracted pleurisy and died in June 1901 at the age of only 32 years.[26] Despite the death of Ōhashi and the associated loss of trail in sources, it can be assumed that Yamada stayed in close contact with the publishing industry—if only for the shared interest in copyright regulations. By the 1920s, these direct connections could be rebuilt.

Yamada's unofficial attendance of the conference resulted in the suggestion by Mizuno Rentarō, the state delegate in charge of international copyrights, to take this opportunity and in upcoming meetings send members of advisory councils (*iin*) instead of government representatives to express the view of the government.[27] The participation of civil experts was one of the main characteristics of the Berne Union that strengthened its juridical system so that, even in the upcoming times of war and political instability, the Union and with it the international copyright treaty continued to exist and promote the further globalization of the publishing industry.[28] Because international organizations like the Berne Union were working on an international alignment of certain "social, juridical, or technical" standards within a specific field of expertise, the national governments needed assistance as regards contents which they received by the civil experts.[29] It was especially the private actors who knew how to make use of the new organizational structures to represent their interests by taking on different roles in correspondence to the different forums in which they were active.[30] For example, publisher Oyaizu Kaname had brought forward the interests of his occupational group by pursuing lobby work inside the ministries and (international) associations like the Tōkyō Chamber of Commerce.[31] Even though the publishers failed in their plea to stop the state delegates from joining the treaty, they remained active "policy entrepreneurs" who continued to highlight the issues at hand and made use of and extended their private and professional networks to influence actively the policymaking process. Advice by private experts was not only shared via the newly established institutions, but also via the emerging expert magazines through which a regular exchange of opinion was taking place. Academic scholars, like Yamada Saburō, often expressed their opinions in magazines directly published by prestigious academic institutions to which they belonged. The state embraced their expert advice and networks, as the mutual goal was to advance the status of the Japanese nation.

From the beginning, Japan's role in the new international copyright system was driven by this pursuit of national power rather than by any universal principles such as the "spread of civilization" through open access to foreign literature. The opportunistic behavior of both state and non-state actors involved in the discussions around international copyright became clear in their stance toward the copyright situation in China. While at the turn of the century European and US-American publishers still showed no interest in the import of Japanese works and were mainly interested in making profit by exporting their works, the same was not the case for China which imported many works from Japan, including many translations of Western works. When it then came to protecting Japan's *own* authors' rights abroad, Oyaizu Kaname took quite a different stance than several years earlier when he had argued that free translations should be possible for the purpose of bringing "civilizational progress" (*bun'un no hattatsu*) to Japan.[32]

In 1901, Oyaizu appealed to Foreign Minister Komura Jutarō with a petition written in the name of the Tōkyō Booksellers' Association to address the current situation regarding the copyright situation in China. Referring to the occurrences surrounding the Boxer Rebellion, he wrote that China's recent "riots and disturbances" demonstrated the "faults in the old regime" and that the country needed reforms that could, however, only be implemented if China invested in the schooling of personnel, established civil and military schools, and sent students abroad to learn about science and technology to understand the means of government.[33] As a member country that used the same written language, China would have the great advantage of being able to import the books from Japan, and with a population of 400 million, Oyaizu noted, they could be a big client for the Japanese publishing industry. China, however, had not entered the international copyright treaty yet and was thus able to freely translate and reprint Japanese publications.[34] Oyaizu claimed that it would have taken Japan substantial capital input and effort to have reached its current state over the past 40 years and to just pass its "civilization" into China for free would mean a great economic loss for the Japanese state, not to mention the impact this would have on the publishers themselves in terms of profit and loss. The Japanese authors would see their rights as defined by the international copyright treaty infringed upon, which is why Oyaizu, in the name of the publishers' association asked the state to take measures to ensure Japanese authors of their rights as regards China.[35]

This petition can be regarded as factually specious, considering the fact that Japan itself had profited greatly from the many free translations of Western works during the previous decades of rapid development, and the Japanese publishers, led by Oyaizu Kaname himself, had only two years prior still fought for staying out of the Convention to continue the free import of copyrights from Western countries. Oyaizu did not mention this in his writing, which reveals the significant role that capital already played in the publishing industry. This is noteworthy, considering that Oyaizu had previously been inclined to emphasize arguments related to the nation's education and cultural development in his petitions regarding free translation and reprint rights from Western countries. However, when it came to China, Oyaizu himself became an important civil actor of the Berne Bureau by bringing the state's attention to China's usage of free translations. The goal of the Berne Bureau was to get as many countries as possible to sign the international copyright treaty. In addition, it can be argued that by acknowledging Japan's "civilization" against a "backward" China and pointing to the ability to pass on this civilization through its literature, Oyaizu had embraced a form of cultural imperialism like what he had observed in Western nations. His comments also indicate that around the turn of the century Japan had already sown the seeds for a "civilizational superiority complex" toward its East Asian neighbors, an idea typically associated more with the later periods of the 1920s, 1930s, and wartime Japan.

Oyaizu's advice seems to have reached the Meiji leaders who in 1903, shortly after his petition was submitted, extended the existing Sino-Japanese Treaty of Commerce and Navigation from 1896 by a "Supplementary Sino-Japanese Treaty of Commerce and Navigation" (Nisshin Tsuika Tsūshō Kōkai Jōyaku). Article 5 of the new treaty included the following:

> The Chinese Government agree [sic] to make and faithfully enforce such regulations as are necessary for preventing Chinese subjects from infringing registered trademarks held by Japanese subjects. The Chinese Government likewise agree [sic] to make such regulations as are necessary for affording protection to registered copyrights held by Japanese subjects in the books, pamphlets, maps and charts written in the Chinese languages and especially prepared for the use of Chinese people. It is further agreed that the Chinese Government shall establish registration offices where foreign trade-marks and copyrights, upon application for the protection of the Chinese Government, shall be registered in accordance with the provisions of the regulations to be hereafter framed by the Chinese Government for the purpose of protecting trade-marks and copyrights.[36]

Whether these measures were the results of Oyaizu's initiative alone is questionable, but he certainly added to the awareness of this problem among the Japanese bureaucrats. From now on the Japanese government closely observed the copyright situation in China as the press of the time reveals: In 1907, the *Tōkyō asahi shinbun* reported on ongoing copyright problems between China and Japan, stating that because of all the free translations of Japanese works that were being made and distributed especially around Shanghai, the bookstores were suffering. As a consequence, the Home Ministry would now be urging the Chinese government to enter the Berne Convention and was currently in the consultation process with the Ministry of Foreign Affairs.[37] Much to the dissatisfaction of the Japanese publishers and the Berne Bureau, the above efforts to convince China to join the international treaty failed. China acceded to the Berne Convention only in 1992.

In addition to his engagement with China, the international appearance and involvement of Oyaizu Kaname in the work of the Berne Bureau was further expanded in 1906 when the International Publishing Bureau of London appointed him as their agent in Tōkyō. The Bureau represented English and American publishers with agencies in the large cities in Europe and America. The *Japan Times* published a short informative note on the appointment of Oyaizu, stating:

> The business carried on by the Bureau consisted in protecting the copyrights as regulated by the Berne Conventions [sic], and in dealing with matters relating to translation and reprint of copyright books. (…) those who wish to reproduce

foreign works in Japan or Japanese works abroad, may obtain very useful information from Mr. Oyaizu.[38]

His official address was added for reference. Henceforth, Oyaizu Kaname took on the role as official promoter of the work of the Berne Bureau.

THE 1908 BERLIN REVISION CONFERENCE AND JAPAN'S PROPOSAL FOR FREE TRANSLATION RIGHTS

In October 1908 the first revision conference of the Berne Convention since Japan's ratification of the treaty was scheduled to take place in Berlin. The Berne Bureau as the main organizer behind the conference envisioned to reach a consensus on translation rights protection—a section of the treaty which continued to divide the transnational copyright community. According to the original 1886 version of the treaty, Berne Union authors held translation rights for a limited period of 10 years from the first date of publication of the original work. Already during the early preparation conferences of the Berne Convention in the 1880s, Sweden had claimed that the Scandinavian countries should receive a special treatment as regards protection of translation rights, as they found themselves in the process of development.[39] Their intervention had failed, but the Scandinavian countries were, like Japan, still interested in keeping the translation rights protection as low a priority as possible.

In contrast, the Berne Bureau planned to raise the general copyright protection to an obligatory 50 years after the author's death and, responding to the long-standing demands by France and the ALAI, henceforth protect translations as original works, in other words, recognize translators' individual rights on a par with authors.[40] Mizuno Rentarō, who had been involved with the Convention for more than a decade since the time of its preparations, represented the Japanese interests abroad. The communication that took place with Japan prior to the conference was mediated via the German Embassy, the Ministry of Foreign Affairs of Japan, and the Home Ministry. Furthermore, any official printed documents related to the conference were sent directly from the Berne Bureau to the Ministry of Foreign Affairs.[41]

Publisher Oyaizu Kaname, who in the meanwhile had been promoted to president of the publisher Maruzen, contacted Mizuno in July 1908 regarding the upcoming trip to Berlin to disclose the opinion of the Booksellers' Association.[42] The content and response to this petition remain unknown, but it is assumed that the Home Ministry had asked Oyaizu directly to submit a written opinion. This assumption is based on the government seeking advice from Oyaizu and his colleague Ōhashi Shintarō the previous year on their "consent and support" regarding the preparations for submitting a revision draft because of several unclear points with respect to copyright protection inside the national 1893 Publication Law which was to be handed to the National Diet by the end of 1907.[43] Ōhashi had taken on the position as vice president of the Tōkyō Chamber of Commerce in 1905 and was strongly supporting Oyaizu in his movement for free translation rights.[44] Subsequently, even though the remaining sources recounting this time are scarce, one can assume that the publishers' written opinion contributed to the proposal that was introduced by the Japanese delegation, namely, by Mizuno Rentarō and Horiguchi Kuma'ichi, the second secretary to the Japanese delegation in Stockholm, at the revision conference in Berlin.

The conference in Berlin lasted a month starting on October 14 and ending on November 14, 1908. Compared to the previous revision conference in 1896, the conference saw an increasingly large number of non-governmental organizations (NGOs) present. While at the last conference and the following negotiation meetings some written opinions of non-governmental actors involved had already been incorporated into the program of the conference and the discussions that followed, in 1908 many NGOs shared their views directly by attending the conference as part of their country's delegation. Among the attending private associations were, for example, the French Societé des Auteurs et Compositeurs Dramatique (Society of Dramatic Authors and Composers) and their Société des Gens des Lettres (Society of Men of Letters), from Italy the Società Italiana degli Autori ed Editori (Italian Society of Authors and Publishers), and from the Netherlands the Vereniging van Letterkundigen (Association of Writers [of Amsterdam]).[45] In addition to the views shared by publishers' and writers' associations, the preparatory documents for the 1908 conference also included a larger range of opinions from other private associations affected by copyright regulations including printers, photographers, theatrical artists, music sellers, and printers.[46] Despite the increasing presence of the private sector in the negotiations of the 1908 conference, Japanese publishers for now remained invisible on the world stage with Japan being represented by the bureaucrats Mizuno Rentarō and Horiguchi Kuma'ichi.

Japan's standing in the international system had changed dramatically since the country had become a member of the Berne Union a decade before. It had achieved major power status by winning the war against Russia in 1905 and was in the process of expanding its own young empire. It had become an obsessive ambition of the Meiji leaders not only to gain equality with the Western nations, but also to surpass them. They needed to show to the rest of the world that Japan was not only able to imitate the Western ways, but that over the period of 2500 years its people, culture and society had developed its own "superior" national qualities.[47] The representation of the two Japanese bureaucrats at the 1908 revision conference fits into this narrative. On the second day of the conference on October 15, they presented Japan's proposal, conveying the arguments provided beforehand by the Japanese publishers. Beginning with Japan's short history in international relations since the country opened up 50 years ago, the proposal emphasized the unique situation of Japan, the different customs and essential difference in language, the importance of free translations for diplomatic purposes, and the need to facilitate the communication of ideas.[48] In wording similar to that used by Oyaizu, the official state proposal explained that the translations would not hinder the sale of the original in Japan— "on the contrary, it favors it"—and that it would lastly not only be Japan that would suffer but the international intellectual relations in general, "arrested by lack of understanding, by the difficulty of getting along."[49] By not granting Japan free translation rights, the peoples of Europe would be "closing a source of inspiration and new ideas."[50] The delegate continued:

> It follows logically that the recognition of the freedom of reciprocal translation between Japan and Europe would be an act of immense importance to open a new way of communication between European and Japanese ideas which are still so distant from each other. If, thanks to this recognition, we aim to understand each other better, all misunderstandings would be dismissed, all ice broken, all suspicions dispelled, in a word, all obstacles would be lifted and smoothed. How pleasant and interesting our international relations, both material and intellectual, would become! Moreover, this mixture, this assimilation of literary and artistic ideas, what flowering of masterpieces would it not give us?[51]

The proposal finished with the comment that, at the time, it was Japan's objection "to put everything in play to introduce and propagate European civilization by importing foreign books" and that "civilization" needed to be unified with the help of freedom of translations between Japan and other countries of the Berne Union.[52]

For the transnational copyright community, the request shook the belief that Japan's entrance to the treaty in 1899 was a success and a possible first-step toward taking on the laws and codes created after Western models.[53] The concept of Japan as a model had already been undermined by the statements made by Yamada and Ōhashi at the copyright conference in 1900. Nevertheless, since they did not represent an official state opinion, this perception persisted. Now the idea of Japan as the "textbook example" of how a non-Western state could merge with the established international system was shattered.[54]

Strangely, the inquiry made by Japan at the 1908 conference has not received the due attention in foreign policy studies on Japan. When it comes to a proposal that, according to historian Naoko Shimazu, stands out in Japan's foreign policy in terms of having demanded the acceptance of a certain international principle at an international conference, historians, including Shimazu herself, tend to point to Japan's "racial equality proposal" at the Paris Peace Conference in Versailles a decade later.[55] Another example given by historian Toyoda Tetsuya was Japan's proposal of the civilizational plurality clause in the statute of the Permanent Court of International Justice, or the "World Court" in July 1920.[56] But already in Berlin in 1908, Japan as a non-Western state confronted the international community with the problem of cultural diversity and boycotted the unidirectional globalization process led by "the West." However, the actual reason for the proposal was not founded in an idealistic aim to improve cross-cultural understanding, but in the drive for profit and prosperity for their own nation.

The German delegate, copyright expert and publicist Albert Osterrieth acknowledged the proposal by asking:

> (…) is Japanese really the only language on the basis of which such an argument can be made? In several Union nations one can find languages or dialects the knowledge of which is limited to a relatively small group of the population: for instance *le breton, le picard, le romanche dans les Grisons, le basque, le welsch dans le pays de Galles*. If we want to accept the Japanese proposal, we will, with certain logic, find ourselves forced to accord the same benefit to these particular languages, and destroy the very system of the Berne Convention.[57]

The portrayal of Japan as a nation in need of "European civilization" feeds into the general understanding of Japan's "opening to the West" during the mid- to late-nineteenth century and the accompanying ideas of the progress of civilization and the modernity of the West. Nevertheless, the Japanese state pursued a strategic interest, intending to leverage the knowledge acquired through translations and direct study of the Western system, including its institutions, with the ultimate goal of gradually eliminating Western dominance. Mizuno shared his impressions about the conference in Berlin via a detailed report that he sent back to the Home Ministry. He wrote less about the content of the conference itself than rather about its participants, the experts of many different countries who seemed to have left a lasting impression on him. He described the representatives as follows:

> Most of them are grey haired men of over 50 and 60 years old, experts in law who know the state of things down to the smallest detail. (…) I admire them. When we look at our department heads or our governors, then they also know their work, but have been handling the same things for the past 10 years.[58]

With his observation Mizuno was in a way foreshadowing the decades ahead and the changes that were about to happen in the Japanese ministerial bureaucracy after

World War I, where a new generation of expert-driven bureaucrats played an increasingly significant role in the decision-making process, pushing for reforms.[59] Kenneth Pyle argued that "in their realism Japanese leaders always sought to read the direction of the flow of events, what they called 'the trend of times' and to act in accordance with it—seeking not to change it but rather to move with it in ways that would work to their own nation's advantage."[60] This was certainly the case for Mizuno.

Besides the realization that the Japanese ministries needed reforms, the conference had another significant influence on Mizuno that he shared in an article around half a year after his return from Germany. The article discussed the obligation to introduce Japanese culture abroad via books and translations. Returning from the conference in Berlin, Mizuno was convinced that, to be on a par with the Western countries, political diplomacy alone would not suffice. One would also have to stimulate international relations through finance, education, trade, and other domestic administrative structures. To do so, however, there would be a need for mutual understanding. Japan had imported culture, namely, art and science— from the West, which would have helped the development of Japanese culture, but, at the same time, it would be necessary that other countries also imported parts of the Japanese cultural system and thereby learned about the current situation in the country. In his article, which was published in the *Shimin* (People), a magazine closely connected to the Home Ministry and to the Ministry of Education, Mizuno complained that the Japanese had been studying Western cultures ever since the Meiji Restauration, but that Western countries would know close to nothing about Japan which would lead to many misunderstandings.[61]

The above realization came to Mizuno during his attendance at the conference in Berlin during which he had been asked several questions by the foreign experts and delegates about the Japanese legal system. He wrote:

> The Japanese understand their [the Westerners'] language, read their books in schools, translate their works and are making an effort to import Western culture. But there are very few foreigners who can understand the Japanese language and there barely exist any books in English language about Japan.[62]

In fact, one of the first Japanese books that was translated into English and published in the United Kingdom had been a translation of politician and educator Ōkuma Shigenobu's *Kaikoku 50nen shi* (official title of translation *Fifty Years of New Japan*) that had originally been published in 1907 with its translation published in 1909, the same year that Mizuno had called for the promotion of Japanese book exporting.[63]

To illustrate his point, Mizuno gave an example of his trip to England during which he had been asked to translate a text on Japanese suffrage for the

Proportional Representatives Society that had been working on a study on suffrage in the different countries of the world. The research on Japan had been demolished due to a lack of information and knowledge.[64] Mizuno was convinced that not only England, but Germany, too, would be interested in translations about the Japanese university system, its administration, regional structure, police administration, education, and law. Thus, according to Mizuno, it would be necessary not only to build up international relations with Europe and the United States, but also to introduce Japanese culture abroad. Since there were few organizations that translated Japanese books into English, one would have to establish translation departments within all the ministries. Furthermore, the state would have to provide financial support to researchers writing books in English. These steps, he wrote, would eventually lead to closer international relations with Europe and the United States.[65]

Mizuno's writings reflect the realization of the Meiji leaders that, to advance to a first-rank nation, Western institutions, material wealth, and an expanding empire alone were not enough. To be considered a great power, other nations needed to respect Japan's civilization and unique cultural achievements.[66] During these years, the pride and self-doubt of the Meiji leaders regarding Japan's place in the international order planted the seeds for the belief that the nation's goals could only be realized through creating its own international order.

By the end of the 1908 conference, the Berne Bureau had failed to introduce an obligatory 50 years of copyright protection, so that member states continued to be divided into those that protected works for 30 years and those that protected works for 50 years after the death of the author. In terms of translation rights, the conference resulted in a major amendment. Henceforth, translation rights were completely integrated into reproduction rights and the translator was recognized as an independent creator on par with the author. Especially for the ALAI, which had long been advocating to change the regulations on translations, this amendment in the Berlin Act meant a great success.[67]

Japan's request for the free usage of translations ended up being rejected by the other members of the Berne Bureau in Berlin. However, as the Japanese delegation had argued with aiming to use the free translations for the purpose of "civilization," and the European imperialist states had made "the spread of civilization" the highest priority of their international activities, Japan's request could also not be ignored. In response, the Act of Berlin introduced the option to indicate reservations on certain paragraphs, including on paragraph 5 on translation rights. Subsequently, Japan together with Estonia, Greece, Italy, and Ireland made use of this option and was able to keep the exclusive right of translation of 10 years as amended by the 1896 revision.[68] In addition, Japan declared a reservation on the public performance of musical works which meant that the country was exempt from remuneration payments to foreign music copyright owners for the public performance of musical works.[69]

The outcome of the conference was met with dissatisfaction by the Japanese publishers who had closely followed the happenings of the conference. They continued their opposition and increased their pressure on the Japanese government regardless of the Western powers' negative response to Japan's proposal for the abolition of translation rights protection. Before the revision was officially ratified in 1910, Ōhashi Shintarō, the owner of the publishing house Hakubunkan, joined Oyaizu Kaname in sharing his expertise and thoughts with the bureaucrats in written petitions and at consultation meetings. While Oyaizu had been actively representing the publishers' interests via the Booksellers' Association, Ōhashi was trying to influence the bureaucrats from a different angle as head of the Temporary Federation of Chambers of Commerce (Rinji Shōgyō Kaigijo Rengōkai). In October 1909, Ōhashi appealed to Foreign Minister Komura Jutarō by repeating Oyaizu's claim that Japan had only reached this "high level of civilization" since opening its borders due to the free import of industrial property and copyrights from foreign countries. Accession to the international copyright agreement would limit this freedom to import and would "stop relationships with other countries."[70] He concluded that the Temporary Federation of Chambers of Commerce joined the Tōkyō Booksellers' Association in its request for free translation rights inside the Berne Convention.[71]

Pressure on Japan's Foreign Minister was also exerted via the ALAI which began to actively interfere in the matter, though—as representatives of publishers and writers from the major publishing nations in Europe—they opposed the Japanese publishers. On November 10, 1909, the editor and author Georges Maillard, who in 1905 had succeeded Eugène Pouillet as president of the ALAI, addressed a five-page letter to Komura Jutarō in which he responded to the reservations on translation rights that Japan had declared for itself in Berlin. Maillard tried to convince the Minister of the importance of protected translation rights from the standpoint of the authors, publishers, and editors of the original work. He also notified Komura of the current discussions and the general consensus among member states to the Berne Convention on introducing an obligatory 50-year copyright protection after the author's death instead of the 30-year protection that existed at the time.[72] But the final point was perhaps most carefully argued by Maillard. He wrote:

> With legitimate satisfaction, Japan, which in a short time has adopted a wide and liberal copyright law, can now bring its country to the same level as the Western nations, thanks to the successful direction it has taken to create a national legal basis. This step was a remarkable one in the great movement

towards unifying international legislation which has enabled the harmonization of peoples. It will therefore be easier for Japan than for other countries full of prejudices, to make further progress and to welcome the declaration of a unified duration of intellectual property applicable in all the countries of the international Berne Union.[73]

By emphasizing Japan's "unique" success of having established the legal grounds for raising the country to the same level as the Western nations and writing that it would now be "easier for Japan than for other countries" to fully accept the international copyright standards, Maillard played on the pride of the Meiji state. This strategy, however, did not show any results, most likely due to the strong opposition of the publishers and Yamada Saburō who were advising the bureaucrats on this matter. Despite the mutual discontent, within Europe about Japan's persistency regarding its 10-year reservations, and within the Japanese publishing industry about not being granted the requested free translation rights, the Japanese government ratified the revised version of the Berne Convention in June 1910.

JAPANESE PUBLISHERS AND THE BERNE CONVENTION DURING WORLD WAR I

With the outbreak of the World War I in 1914 came an uncertainty about the validity of the Berne Convention, as the treaty included no clause regarding the occurrence of war, yet a number of its signatory states were now at war with each other. As this case had no precedent, little information was available for the members of the Berne Convention on how to deal with copyright regulations of other member states in the event of a war.[74] The Berne Convention did stay intact during the course of the war. However, this only became clear over time and would not have been possible without the commitment of the Berne Bureau in cooperation with national and international publishers' and authors' associations.[75] In the case of Japan, which had entered the war as an ally of Britain, it was a collaboration of individual bureaucrats, publishers, and juridical experts that contributed to keeping the international cooperation intact. Previous studies on World War I have neglected these networks that were simultaneously established between publishers involved with foreign publications and the bureaucrats dependent on the work of the publishers and in charge of handling their concerns to gain access to foreign knowledge. These networks challenge the one-sided portrayal of publishers and bureaucrats as being divided by a strict censorship apparatus prior to the 1920s and demonstrate the increasing impact that publishers with access to foreign works, which promised to contribute to the country's development, had on state policies.[76]

Both Yamada Saburō and Mizuno Rentarō brought themselves into the internal discussion about the validity of the contract early on. Yamada had shared his opinion on the believed correct course of action regarding intellectual property rights during war times in a presentation he held at the Legal Philosophy Research Association (Hōri Kenkyūkai)[77] on November 19, 1914. The results of his talk were published in the *Hōgaku Kyōkai zasshi* (Journal of the Jurisprudence Association) in January 1915. Addressing mainly the issues around patent laws, Yamada only briefly touched upon the subject of copyrights, yet clearly positioned himself in the matter. He wrote that "Germans who possess copyrights in other countries besides Germany should also be protected in Japan," and that even in times of war, there should be no need for further conditions or formalities.[78] In Yamada's opinion, the treaty to regulate international copyrights should be compatible with the current situation of war in the same way that in previous wars, such as the Spanish-American War (1898), the First Balkan War (1912-1913) or the Italo-Ottoman War (1911-1912), there had been no doubt about the treaty's validity, indeed nobody had requested its termination.[79] The publication of Yamada's presentation was succeeded by an article by Mizuno Rentarō entitled "War and Copyrights," in which Mizuno referred to Yamada's previous writing and agreed with him that it would not be right to stop the contract all together just because certain member countries had entered war with each other. It would be "barbaric" (*yabanteki*) in these modern times to take a people's private right from them.[80] This example confirms that Tōkyō Imperial University professors in the late nineteenth and early twentieth century were acting as official advisors that oftentimes influenced ministerial policies. Mizuno wrote that he had shared his opinion in a written statement with the director of the Berne Bureau, Ernst Röthlisberger, who had also been arguing for adherence to the contract from the time of the outbreak of the war in 1914.

Besides the juridical discussion around the validity of the Berne Convention, international copyright policies remained on the political agenda during the war due to an addendum that had been added to the revised Berne Convention of 1908 on March 20, 1914. The addendum was a direct response to the anti-foreign cultural policies of the Unites States which had limited the protection for US residents whose home countries did not recognize the rights of American authors.[81] It entitled the contracting states "to limit the protection given to works by authors who do not belong to the Union and do not reside in a country belonging to the Union, when the authors in question belong to a country, that does not give foreigners sufficient mutual protection of rights."[82]

In May 1914, the Swiss Legation contacted Foreign Minister Katō Takaaki with a copy of the additional protocol to inquire whether Japan would also sign the addendum. Following a time of internal consultations, Japan decided to join the addendum, which was authorized during a meeting on February 1, 1915.[83]

Emperor Yoshihito signed the additional protocol a few days later together with Foreign Minister Katō, who clarified that "the ratification was made under the condition that it would in no way affect Japan's stance towards its enemy countries."[84] By making this supplement and distinguishing between the treaty and the war in general, the Japanese government positioned itself clearly as regards the validity of the international copyright treaty at an early time in the war which had the effect that it sparked the discussion in the French Foreign Ministry to think about where France positioned itself in this matter.[85] It can be assumed that the articles by Yamada and Mizuno that had been published a month before had been taken into account by Katō when he added the clarification to the addendum. Even though a direct communication between the different actors cannot be verified, Mizuno Rentarō remained the expert for copyrights in the Home Ministry which meant that he was the person to contact with any uncertainties about copyright matters. Furthermore, Mizuno had served as Vice Home Minister in 1913, a position that he took up again in 1916 which gave him many close contacts inside the ministries and left him an influential position regarding the execution of censorship laws and orders. Besides signing the additional protocol, Katō Takaaki also kept observing and criticizing the copyright situation in China as Oyaizu Kaname had urged the government to do 14 years earlier. The young Republic of China had meanwhile established its own copyright law (1911) and a publication law (1914) that however still included no mention of the rights of foreigners.[86]

Japanese publishers and publishers' organizations were not involved in the process of amending the Berne Convention in the beginning of World War I and were instead occupied with the matter of fixed prices for book and magazine. The decrease in paper imports from Europe was causing a steep increase in paper prices which threatened the livelihood of many publishers. As a first reaction, the 1916 newly selected president of the Booksellers' Association, Ōkura Yasugorō, enacted a price increase for books which laid down the rules of fixed book prices which were to be decided by the association's members.[87] However, the situation around the rising paper prices continued to worsen despite the enactment of fixed book prices, so that in early 1917 a committee was established between Tōkyō's main publishing associations with Ōkura Yasugorō as their head representative. Around the same time, he joined his colleague Ōhashi Shintarō in the managing board of the Tōkyō Chamber of Commerce.[88] In a joint effort of the publishers, a petition was addressed to the House of Representatives to assist in the matter. When this remained unsuccessful, Tōkyō's publishers sought the cooperation of two more associations from Ōsaka and wrote another petition to the House of Representatives. Thereafter, several ministers and ministerial bureaucrat Horikiri Zenjirō as the head of the Home Ministry's Book Division (Toshoka) visited the newly founded Tōkyō Publishers' Association (Tōkyō Shuppan Kyōkai) which had been established in 1914. The need for another association for publishers had arisen due to the recent surge in book trade, changes in selling regulations, and the debate around fixed prices. This culminated in 1914 leading to an increasing desire among booksellers to join the Tōkyō Booksellers and Publishers' Association. The ongoing changes in the Association, initially focused on publishers' needs, prompted the establishment of a new association exclusively for publishers as members.[89] The officials' visit to the publishers convinced them of the gravity of the situation, especially because a similar situation had developed as regards an uncontrolled rise in rice prices. The government reacted by enforcing the Bōri Torishimari Rei (Profiteering Control Ordinance)[90] on September 1, 1917 to limit the uncontrolled increase of profit and keep traders from holding back commodities to make excessive profits.[91]

Despite the negative effects of the paper import shortages and the resulting problems of increasing paper prices, the publishers continued their acquisition of translation rights in accordance with the regulations laid out by the Berne Convention. The number of translations between 1914 and 1918 as recorded in the *Nihon shuppan 100nen shi nenpyō* (100-Year History of Japanese Publishing) shows that there was a decrease from 283 translations a year in 1914 to 116 in 1915 to only 60 in 1916. In 1917, after the usury law had been introduced on the initiative of the publishers, the number of translations rose again to 113 translations a year.[92]

During the war, the cooperation between leading publishers, academic scholars, and ministerial bureaucrats in connection with the publishers' and individual scholars' efforts was further strengthened to maintain the foreign book trade and import of Western works. Universities and other research institutions, as well as bookstores, publishers, and publishing houses with a thematic focus on Western works, were accustomed to placing large import orders of scientific books with foreign publishing houses or literary agents. At the forefront of the Japanese book import industry was the publishing house Maruzen, led by Oyaizu Kaname since 1900. Since its founding in 1869, Maruzen had supplied many state schools, and the ministries, with Western scientific works in new technology, medicine, army, law, politics, and economics, and when the war broke out in Europe, Oyaizu had no intention of stopping his imports from Europe. While the *Maruzen 100nen shi* (100 Years of Maruzen) company history does not include any details about World War I, existing sources reveal that acquisition of book titles continued after the start of the war.[93] For example, on December 8, 1915, Oyaizu ordered 220 copies of William Cunningham's *Modern Civilization in its Economic Aspects* from UK bookseller Allen & Unwin with the stated intention "for class use from the beginning of April."[94] Further orders were placed throughout the war with UK bookseller Asher & Co.[95] In comparison with the import of British or French books, the continuation of the import of German books, which comprised most of the orders from abroad, turned out to be more complicated.

This complication derived from the 1914 "Trading with the Enemy Proclamation" of the UK government that forbade any trade with persons living on enemy territory. At this point, the trade via neutral countries remained unaffected, as did the activities with persons or companies based in Great Britain acting under British law who conducted business with companies on enemy territory.[96] At the beginning of the war, the war between different states, on the one hand, and the people's individual businesses including the publishing business, on the other, were perceived as separate things.[97] Yet, as an ally of Britain, the Japanese publishers decided henceforth to order a large number of German books and periodicals via the Netherlands from the bookseller Martinus Nijhoff so as not to violate British law. By doing so, the publishers avoided any direct negative impact of the "Trading with the Enemy Proclamation".

The situation became increasingly difficult in March 1915 with the UK government's proclamation of an extension to their previous Act as a reaction to Germany's first declaration of unrestricted submarine warfare. The Navy was commanded to henceforth stop all goods imported into and exported from Germany. Prior to World War I, the confiscation of neutral trade goods and neutral ships had only been recognized by international law under the condition that they included dangerous or forbidden goods from a belligerent power as stated in the Treaty of Paris in 1856 and the London Declaration concerning the Laws of Naval War from 1909.[98] The UK government ignored these proclamations by confiscating *all* goods leaving Germany. However, until the end of 1915, the trade of German goods via neutral countries had still been possible. While the French government at this point already forbade any kind of business with enemy subjects in connection with the trade partner's nationality, the UK government still allowed trade depending on where the trade partner lived. In December 1915, the UK government amended the rules under the pressure from the French government and the public and on December 23, 1915 announced "The Trading with the Enemy (Extension of Powers) Act 1915," which prohibited persons in the United Kingdom from trading with any person in foreign countries who either was of enemy nationality or believed to be associated with the enemy in any way.[99] The Act was amended once again in February 1916 with a statutory list which included the names of all companies and persons in different countries that were blacklisted and thereby became illegal trade partners.[100]

As soon as the Japan-based publishers involved realized the impact of the anti-German proclamation from March 1915 in that their ordered books and magazines did not reach them anymore, on September 11, 1915 Oyaizu Kaname petitioned Prime Minister Ōkuma Shigenobu, who at the time was also holding the position as Foreign Minister, to complain that even the import of German goods via neutral countries had become close to impossible and the hitherto easiest way of payment in UK currency much more difficult since the proclamation of the UK government. The curtailment of books from Germany thus impacted not only the Japanese publishers at quite an early stage in the war due to the increasing lack of paper, but with Maruzen having been the main supplier of academic and other non-fiction works from the West, the general public was also impacted in that it had become impossible to import the books ordered for the schools and ministries.

Oyaizu thus found himself under a lot of pressure, not only because of finances, but also because he could not process his clients' orders. In his petition he wrote that books should be treated differently from general goods in that they were the "source of knowledge" from abroad. In these wartimes, as he further elaborated, the exchange of knowledge would be even more important and, therefore, the import of publicly known works that would not pose a danger to the nation should be allowed. The petition would be one of the last of the now 72-year-old Oyaizu Kaname's activities, as president of Maruzen. His successor Nakamura Shigehisa continued his work from 1916 onwards.[101]

The petition's addressee Ōkuma Shigenobu had been engaged in copyright affairs since assuming office as Prime Minister in 1914, specifically concerning the drafting and implementation of the Additional Protocol to the 1908 version of the Berne Convention. Ōkuma reacted to Oyaizu's petition within three days by asking the Japanese ambassador to Britain, Inoue Katsunosuke, to consult with the representatives of the Yokohama Shōkin Ginkō[102] (Yokohama Specie Bank) on the transfer of money in connection with German book imports. The matter was then passed on to the Vice-Minister of Finance within less than a month to start negotiations regarding the financial aspects of the import of German publications. However, the Ministry of Finance also found itself in an unprecedented situation, and the publishers were left in the dark. It took another few months until January 24, 1916 before Inoue Katsunosuke received a reply from the British Foreign Office regarding a possibility of importing German books provided they were of a "philosophical, scientific, technical or educational character only."[103] If certain institutions in Japan wished to make use of this facility, a special permit would be needed for which the British government first requested the submission of a list of books including the number of cases, total value and the port of shipment.[104]

Oyaizu's petition had thus contributed to creating a way for Japanese publishers who wished to import books originating in an enemy territory to get around the "Trading with the Enemy Extension Act" of 1915. Maruzen thereupon made a formal application to the Ministry of Foreign Affairs in which they referred to the licenses that the British Ministry of Trade had issued to British booksellers Asher & Co, Henry Sotheran & Co. and others. The application read that the above publishers were again able to obtain German books, which is why Maruzen hoped that a license would be granted to them "on similar conditions."[105]

However, information travelled slowly, and matters were further impeded by the frequent change of personnel in the different ministries. In October 1916, the publishers received support from the head of the Tōkyō Imperial University and Japan's first professor for physics, Yamakawa Kenjirō. Yamakawa took the initiative to write to the Vice Foreign Minister Shidehara Kijūrō, asking the Ministry of Foreign Affairs to negotiate with the British government in the name of the Tōkyō Imperial University so that in the future, magazines and books addressed to university employees would be delivered without being confiscated.[106] At the beginning of 1917 some changes finally came for the publishers still waiting for their shipments of German books and magazines via the Netherlands. On February 21, 1917, the British Consulate-General in Yokohama was informed by the British Commercial Attaché that, as a result of the 1916 Paris Economic Conference, development of intermediary trade between Great Britain and Japan was to be facilitated. The British government thus decided to compile a list "of the more important firms in Japan which" were "already buying British goods or may wish to buy them, or which" were "exporting goods to the United Kingdom."[107] Maruzen had already been placed, in preparation for the Paris Economic Conference, on a list of non-enemy British and Japanese firms that could function as substitutes for those firms that had been placed on the Statutory List. The Publishing house was listed and thus recommended in the "Booksellers" section.[108] Maruzen's Nakamura Shigehisa wrote several more petitions to the Trade Department of the Japanese Ministry of Foreign Affairs with the appeal to the bureaucrats to mediate until, eventually, in July 1917 a reply came from the British Foreign Office informing the publishers that the desire of Maruzen to obtain a permit to import from the Netherlands a consignment of German periodicals had been granted by the British government under the condition that the books were "sent directly from Holland to Japan and are not brought to the United Kingdom for transshipment."[109] While some of the confiscated parcels were irretrievably lost, a shipment of 1,300 packets of books and magazines ordered in 1916 from Germany via Holland reached Maruzen in 1918.[110]

The mutual wartime effort between politicians and ministerial bureaucrats, Ōkuma Shigenobu, Katō Takaaki, Mizuno Rentarō and others, private publishers like Oyaizu Kaname and his successors, and academics like Yamada Saburō and Yamakawa Kenjirō in maintaining the international copyright treaty and the international cooperation in book trade in general heralded the trend of the following decade during which traditional diplomacy gave way to the makings of an increasingly internationally orientated politics that incorporated the opinion of the citizens. Even though there had already been a few international agreements prior to World War I, one of them being the Berne Convention, the role of non-governmental actors, especially in exercising control over these international agreements, underwent great changes in the aftermath of the war.[111] Despite the fact that the war was already coming to an end by the time that Maruzen received a permit to continue the import of German books, the persistency of individual publishers and success in being able to continue their book import in view of international state policies hindering them from doing so shows their increasing importance and influence in political decision-making.

The first two decades of the twentieth century were shaped both by the conflicts that emerged between Japan and the mainly European copyright community, and by new forces of globalization supported by the publishing industry especially during World War I. With the turn of the century, the Japanese publishing industry and academic Yamada Saburō for the first time made known their resentment toward part of the Berne Convention and especially regarding the plans of the Berne Bureau to unify the applicable duration of copyright protection to the international stage. While, as early as 1900, the above actors had privately attended a copyright conference in Europe to share their voices, at the 1908 revision conference, their standpoint was now *officially* presented as Japan's state position by the respective ministerial bureaucrats who had been consulted by the industry and Yamada Saburō prior to the conference. The first incident of a Japanese boycott of the Berne Bureau's envisioned smooth globalization of international copyright was therefore built upon the initiative of the non-state sector.

While in this case the actors involved hindered the global unification of copyright protection, a few years later during World War I and the accompanying uncertainty regarding the validity of the Berne Convention, it was only with the help of the same publishers and scholar Yamada that the new transnational networks and international cooperation that had developed as part of the globalization efforts of the publishing industry were maintained. The publishers that were involved with foreign publications made their plans to continue book imports known to the ministerial offices and lastly managed to succeed in receiving support not only from the Japanese state but from the international community.

The role of the ministerial bureaucrats in these processes was likewise significant, as the system did not yet provide a direct line between Japanese extra-governmental actors and the Berne Bureau as the institution in charge of handling global copyright administration. The political history of modern Japan academic Shimizu Yu'ichirō has written about late nineteenth and early twentieth century Japanese bureaucrats stating that they combined different structures to cope with their task to change the system of Japanese modernity. According to Shimizu, these structures included "control and participation, competition and cooperation, general and private intentions."[112] As regards the ongoing processes of globalization within the publishing industry like the accession to the Berne Convention and its revision and the continuity of the book trade during World War I, the bureaucrats did exactly that: they were in control, but at the same time began to participate at the level of the publishers or sought the participation of the publishers, as Japan on its way to be internationally recognized as one of the "Five Great Powers" was relying on book imports from abroad. The bureaucrats' need to participate and work in close cooperation with the private sector reached a new urgency with the beginning of the 1920s.

CHAPTER 3

DEFENDING THE EXCEPTION

Copyright Negotiations between the Founding of the League of Nations and the 1928 Rome Revision Conference

Historians of Japan usually interpret the interwar years in opposing ways, focusing either on a progressive civil society that increasingly organized itself in labor unions and business associations, neighborhood groups, and women's federations, or on a powerful bureaucratic state that showed progressive tendencies in some areas but remained conservative in many others.[1] There is still little research that instead looks at the interaction, co-dependency, and the areas of common interest between these two groups. Adding to the opposing interpretations of this period, on the one hand, the 1920s are seen as an important phase in the history of internationalism during which international conferences and newly established international organizations like the League of Nations brought together citizens from different countries in several areas, including the cultural sector. On the other hand, the 1920s are also viewed as the rejection of precisely these new international forces and a "resurgence of nationalism" or the emergence of new far-right movements.[2] Recent scholarship suggests that early Meiji-born Japanese internationalists were not only internationalists but also devoted nationalists, an argument supported by this book.[3] This dual identity became particularly clear over the following decade, especially in the way that Japan positioned itself in the international copyright negotiations.

This chapter explores the establishment and work of new cultural institutions that joined the Berne Bureau in administering copyright regulations in an increasingly globalized world. It examines Japan's response to these emerging multilateral organizations at the domestic level and explores the country's involvement in their activities, particularly in anticipation of the next official international revision conference of the Berne Convention held in Rome in the spring of 1928. Focusing on the difficult preparation process ahead of the conference, this chapter reveals the growing dependency of the ministerial bureaucrats involved on the expertise of private industry actors and the consequent indirect impact that the latter had on the outcome of the international conference.

THE LEAGUE OF NATIONS AND NEW STRUCTURES OF INTERNATIONAL INTELLECTUAL COOPERATION

The outcome of World War I brought with it many changes for Japan both nationally and internationally. Coming out of the war as one of the victor states, Japan's international status had changed to that of one of the "Five Great Powers," but what was happening at the Paris Peace Conference in 1919 showed that there was still an "uncertain nature" of its international status.[4] In January 1919, the victor states of World War I including Britain, France, Italy, Japan, and the United States, came together in Paris to discuss the outcomes of the war. Japan attended the conference not only as one of the major powers, but also as the only non-Western power that had risen to the status of a Great Power—with the important exception that it did not share the same ethnic group.[5] The definition of a great power status was based on Western values and a "shared common heritage of 'Western' civilization" which was the only thing in the pursuit for equality with the Western nations that Japan was unable to attain. Japanese diplomat Makino Nobuaki, the de facto leader of the Japanese delegation to Paris, thus proposed to include a "racial equality" clause into the Treaty of Versailles to be recognized on one level with the Western nations.[6] Thus, like the 1908 revision conference of the Berne Convention, Japan once again challenged the apparent smooth integration into the Western international system. Naoko Shimazu described the demand as "a challenge to 'the club' of Western great powers by the newcomer, attempting to introduce new 'rules of the club' which would make the newcomer's position more comfortable."[7] As has been shown by different historians, most famously by the Tōkyō University law professor Ōnuma Yasuaki in his 1987 essay "Harukanaru jinshu byōdō no risō" (The Unattained Ideal of Racial Equality), the basic principle behind the proposal was, however, not an idealistic claim for universal equality, but the self-interest by Japan in attaining a status equal to that of Western countries. Its own discriminatory behavior towards China and Korea was not addressed.[8] The proposal ended up being turned down by the foreign representatives which led to the Japanese delegation walking out of the conference.

For Japan, the failed demand pushed the country into a paradoxical position that became noticeable in various fields of international relations—including international copyright—that were being discussed at that time and in the following years. For example, at the 1919 International Labor Conference of the International Labor Organization (ILO), Japan aimed to pursue a special exemption for lower working standards, with the argument that, despite having gained the status of a major nation, its still predominantly agricultural economy continued to rely on labor force working long and late hours. While the other Great Powers at the conference were represented by labor unionists that pushed for higher minimums of working standards for their workers, Japan had only sent bureaucrats who asked for special exemptions alongside with China and India. The paradoxical problem was that the demands made to the ILO to be exempt from Western labor standards did not reconcile with the proposal Japan had made for racial equality and its general aspiration of being recognized as one of the Great Powers earlier that same year.[9] The same issue occurred in the negotiations surrounding international copyright which had started but would be taken up again after the end of the war. Japan, being the sole non-Western nation granted a special seat among the "Five Great Powers" at the conference, had essentially met its objective of elevating its "standard of civilization" to Western levels. This aspired goal had been cited as the main reason for Japan's request for unrestricted translation rights of foreign authors' works after joining the Berne Convention in the late 1890s. But, as it became clear during the 1920s and 1930s, the "civilization" argument was quickly dropped in favor of more timely arguments beneficial to Japan in the international copyright debates. In other words, the supposedly idealistic demands for equal treatment and shared knowledge were only made as long as they were beneficial to Japan.

Among the main outcomes of the Paris Peace Conference was the decision to establish the League of Nations, an international organization that would become an integral part of the peace treaties and was to create a system of collective security in which the League would be able to ease conflicts and in the case of hardship could force the aggressors to give in with the help of collective pressure. It was started with the purpose of promoting peace by disarmament, abolish secret diplomacy, and guarantee the free use of the seas to prevent another war like the one the world had just experienced. On January 10, 1920, one year after the Peace Conference, the League of Nations officially came into existence. On its establishment, the League responded to the increasing number of voices of people demanding a new form of diplomacy that represented the will of the people and requested the participation of non-governmental actors on the diplomatic stage.[10] Its committees were made up not only of state representatives, but also of non-governmental actors that contributed to the foreign diplomacy of the League. The concept of an organization that was officially connected to the different states, but primarily relied on societal actors and experts in the field of foreign politics was new in interstate relations, although organizations like the Berne Bureau had already worked under a similar structure.[11] While the League's main focus rested on the maintenance of peace through changes in the military, international economics and social cooperation also played significant roles in its diplomatic approach. Already during the war, a number of civilian groups had been active in Europe and the United States with plans on how to maintain peace in the postwar period and how to prevent future wars from happening. Many saw the answer to this problem in the involvement of international organizations and private actors in the exchange and cooperation between different member states, including their involvement in fields of politics like art and sports that had hitherto been interpreted as "unconventional."[12] The formation of associations, trade unions, groups and federations, as well as the international conferences on topics of mutual interests were characteristics of the renewed internationalism of the 1920s.[13]

In Japan, the decision to found the League of Nations was at first criticized, and especially the Japanese media warned that the establishment of the League could possibly lead to restrictions to the gains that were made during the war.[14] Among Japan's internationalists, the League was widely seen as something positive that not only took on a political role, but also stood for their ideals which espoused gaining peace through cross-national understanding.[15] A debate began that revolved around questions of the function of the League in the realm of culture that was bringing together the different countries and people of the world through mutual cooperation, and of the role of culture as an important part of diplomacy. These discussions were part of a worldwide trend that followed World War I and that Akira Iriye describes as "cultural internationalism."[16] This new international movement expanded the existing structures that had been laid in the nineteenth century to areas beyond the borders of Europe and North America.[17] Out of the original 32 founding members only 10 came from Europe.[18]

Japan joined the League in 1920 as a founding member and even became one of its four permanent council members—the others being France, Great Britain, and Italy, while the United States did not join the organization.[19] Japanese leaders were eager to demonstrate their cooperative engagement as one of the major powers in Woodrow Wilson's new diplomacy, but at the same time they feared that the Western powers would interfere with Japan's expansionist goals in East Asia. Shortly after the founding of the League of Nations in 1920, Japan established its own League of Nations Association of Japan (Kokusai Renmei Kyōkai) mainly to avoid any disadvantage by being left out the circle of nations who had already formed an association and came together in international meetings.[20] The purpose of Japan's Association was to conduct research on the League of Nations, publish material on lectures, cooperate and exchange information with similar organizations on national and international levels, and send representatives abroad to international meetings.[21] Its office was located inside the Tōkyō Chamber of Commerce and Shibusawa Eiichi was appointed president. The by now 80-year-old Shibusawa had at first not agreed to lead the Association until bureaucrat Makino Nobuaki assured him that this society was not to act under the orders of the state but was to cooperate mutually with the state and citizens. Shibusawa thereafter gradually began to acknowledge the importance of having a League of Nations Association, as he was convinced that despite the international negotiations being concluded between governments, the strength of the people was needed to spread internationalism.[22] The Association allowed any Japanese citizen to join as a member, as long as one was introduced by more than two members.[23] Scholar of international law Yamada Saburō was among the founding members of the League of Nations Association of Japan.

The new importance given to the voice of the people in the new multilateral fora was also recognized by Japan's political elite who realized that there was a similar urgency in Japan to connect with the people at a domestic level. This need for a closer cooperation was, however, immediately brought into connection with a need for an increase in control. In 1921, Mizuno Rentarō expressed the opinion that it would be necessary to increase police control, especially in the scientific field (*kagakuteki hōmen*), in connection with the changing and fast developing cultural industry of the current times. Mizuno had meanwhile joined the party Rikken Seiyūkai (Friends of Constitutional Government), had been appointed a member of the House of Peers and, following his first term as Home Minister under Terauchi Masatake between 1916 and 1918, currently served as Parliamentary Commissioner of the Governor-General of Korea. He noted that while at times the study of printed lectures proved important, working at a desk would not always suffice to get a *real* insight into the happenings of the outside world, and that it would therefore be necessary to also build strong ties with society and directly connect with the people.[24] Mizuno's advice was implemented and the bureaucrats increasingly reached out to the private sector for assistance, especially in matters related to publishing and copyright which also ended up on the agenda of the League of Nations shortly after its founding.

One of the central early tasks of the League was to improve the intellectual relations that had come to a halt during the war. In September 1921, a proposal for setting up a committee for the "examination of international questions regarding intellectual cooperation" was accepted by the League's Council and was realized on May 15, 1922.[25] In the beginning, this committee consisted of twelve members, related in some way or another to the cultural scene of their respective home countries of Belgium, Brazil, France, Germany, Great Britain, India, Italy, Japan, the Netherlands, Norway, and the United States.[26] From August 1 to 5, 1922, this newly founded International Committee on Intellectual Cooperation (hereafter ICIC) came together for its first session in Geneva.[27] The Japanese delegate appointed to the committee meetings was Nitobe Inazō, a professor from Tōkyō Imperial University who had been serving as Under-Secretary General in the League's Council since its founding in 1920 and was renowned internationally for his book *Bushido: The Soul of Japan* published in 1900.[28] In a report submitted to the League of Nations on September 19, 1922, the Committee described its own objective as follows: "It has to secure for intellectual work the place which befits it, and it has to assist in the freer and more rapid circulation of the great intellectual currents of the world."[29]

To achieve the above tasks, the Committee aimed to promote cultural cooperation by encouraging research in the areas of education, science, philosophy, and sharing intellectual thoughts and knowledge, amongst others, through the exchange of students and professors, but also through the exchange of publications on a global level. The latter included the planned establishment of a global book register to inform each other of the most recent publications and the kind of research conducted as well as share information on existing libraries in different countries to give intellectual workers the opportunity to cooperate more closely.[30] This task had hitherto been handled by the International Institute of Bibliography[31] in Brussels, an international institution established in 1895 by Belgian author and bibliographer Paul Otlet and lawyer Henri La Fontaine to promote the international exchange of knowledge and bibliographical data, that was meanwhile lacking the funds to continue its work.[32] However, with the plan to systematically exchange publications across the world, the issue or rather absence of global copyright protection re-emerged on the international stage.

THE RE-EMERGENCE OF THE COPYRIGHT PROBLEM

In response to the above developments, from the time of its establishment in 1922 the ICIC placed great importance on the exchange and distribution of publications to achieve mutual understanding across national boundaries and educate and inform the youth of the aims and ideals of the League of Nations.[33]

With these tasks the Committee followed the trend of the times, spearheaded by the book industry itself, in which the value of books as ambassadors between different countries and cultures in the rapid globalization of the post-war period was gaining a whole new recognition. In late 1921, the *Tōkyō asahi shinbun* reported for example on an international book exhibition that was planned to take place in Florence, Italy in the spring of 1922. The aim of the exhibition was to display representative works of literature, and as part of a special exhibition also photographs, films, maps, posters, and even music from countries all over the world. According to the article, the Italian embassy in Tōkyō was "eager" (*hijōna ikigomi*) to introduce "East Asian" culture at the exhibition, and asked for the contribution and support of the Japanese citizens by handing in "magnificent things" (*seidaina mono*) to be displayed at the fair.[34] The article then referenced the afore-mentioned publisher Oyaizu Kaname who said that the International Publishing Bureau which he had been representing as an agent since 1906, had as yet not received any information about the exhibition, but that preparations should be arranged for a participation of the Booksellers' Association in the event. The 78-year-old Oyaizu passed away a few months after expressing this final desire of a participation by Japan's publishing industry. Despite the propaganda efforts of the 1920s and 1930s to spread works on Japanese culture abroad, it took another four decades before Japanese publications fully arrived on the international scene with Japan's first participation in the Frankfurt Book Fair in 1961. However, if it had been up to individual publishers like Oyaizu, this step might have happened much sooner.

Among the ICIC's first initiatives was the plan to reinstate the so-called "Convention for the Immediate Exchange of Official Journals, Public Parliamentary Annals and Documents," concluded in Brussels on March 15, 1886. With the aim of promoting the understanding of different cultures, the ICIC intended to expand the exchange of publications to include also scientific and literary publications. In 1922, countries which had not adhered to the convention of 1886, including Japan, were asked by letter of the council president to share their opinion and adhere to the new convention.[35]

However, things were more complicated than expected with difficulties combining both conventions—the issue was whether to keep the old convention or draft an entirely new one—and finding a consensus among the different member states. Other reasons included the absence of a clear outline of the aims of the ICIC, a lack of funding and little to no detailed knowledge about the administrative dealings of the large number of different nations.[36] But the greatest recognition in the process of institutionalizing global book exchange was that the situation around translation rights was not clear and that the Berne Convention of 1886 in its current state did not protect intellectual property rights sufficiently and thus needed to be revised again if the aim was global exchange of publications.[37]

The issue of how to deal with the international protection of written works was thus gaining momentum once again and was now attributed an even greater importance due to the outcome of the war, as without an overall revision of international copyright regulations, the efforts for exchanging publications could not go far without issues of copyright infringements and unauthorized translations inevitably leading to new international tensions. However, the question remained of who or which institution would take on the responsibility to administer and plan the further globalization process.

With the end of the war, the Berne Bureau found itself in a difficult position regarding its role in the handling of international copyright.[38] From as early as February 1918, the Bureau began making suggestions regarding the postwar continuation and unchanged validity of the Berne Convention. In a report to the Swiss Police and Justice Department, it suggested reinstating and incorporating the Berne Convention—that technically had never been abolished—into the peace treaties. The idea was to thereby get the United States and Austria-Hungary—both involved in World War I but non-member states of the Berne Convention—to join the international copyright union. But regardless of this idea, the Berne Bureau continued also to emphasize vehemently the neutral and unpolitical character of the Berne Union. Much to the displeasure of the Berne Bureau, the latter part was ignored by the drafters of the Treaty of Versailles. Article 306, which officially reinstated the Berne Convention as well as the Paris Convention for the Protection of Industrial Property, stated in an additional reservation that German citizens would be unable to claim fringe benefit remuneration for works that had been reproduced without authorization during the war.[39] Despite imposing an infringement to the regulations of the Berne Convention, which had remained valid throughout the war, these works could continue to be sold for a further year until the summer of 1920 at which point they would have to be destroyed. By the inclusion of intellectual property rights into the Peace Treaty of Versailles, the field of international copyright protection was thus intermingled with war reparations and the political punishment of Germany, taking it out of the neutral framework of the Berne Union. The Berne Bureau thereby lost the political competences that it had built up over the past decades, leaving it merely with its official administrative function.[40]

In addition, the Bureau and the other existing institutions concerned with intellectual cooperation like the Association Littéraire et Artistique Internationale (ALAI) or the International Institute of Bibliography in Brussels were considered too specialized, not completely international and also weakened by the war. The League of Nations explained the following of the previously existing institutions concerned with intellectual cooperation: "(…) not one [of these already existing institutions] was qualified to coordinate the efforts of all the others, and scarcely one could lay international agreements before the Governments with any hope of getting them accepted without lengthy delays."[41]

Subsequently, the political activities connected to regulating authors' copyrights that had hitherto been solely in the hands of the Berne Bureau were now taken on by the ICIC, and while the Bureau continued to exist, its tasks were reduced to administrative handlings.[42] According to Isabella Löhr, this loss of influence on the political stage resulted in the Bureau now relying even more heavily on the help of the national publishers' and booksellers' associations.[43]

As the topic of copyrights was so relevant for intellectual workers and thus for the work of the ICIC, the League's Council authorized the appointment of a so-called Subcommittee on Intellectual Property Rights which came together for the first time in December 1922. The work of this Subcommittee was described by the ICIC as follows:

> (…) keeping itself informed of all the affairs of other Sections, in so far as these affairs may afford material for new laws, regulations or agreements. In agreement with the International Labour Office, it studies problems relating to the legal conditions of intellectual work.[44]

The main themes that the Committee set out to approach at the time of its founding were the protection of scientific property, (which, the commission argued, differed from industrial property and was not yet protected by the existing laws) as well as general copyright protection. Other tasks included the social and legal situation of intellectual workers or problems regarding the international distribution of books.

In tackling these tasks, the ICIC did not act on its own. It was asked to reach out to organizations, associations, and private actors already involved in intellectual property rights and also kept in close contact with the Berne Bureau and ALAI. Close ties were furthermore maintained with the International Chamber of Commerce whose founding idea was born in 1919 at the International Trade Conference in Atlantic City. The International Chamber was to bring together the various national chambers and provide a better exchange in the economic sector. It was officially established in 1920 and was to also be involved in the consultations surrounding the subject of copyrights.[45]

In its early years of existence, however, the Subcommittee did not make much progress, a result of the above-mentioned absence of a clear overview of the state of affairs in the different nations, insufficient funding, and too little personnel with its merely five committee members, who simultaneously also held functions in the ICIC and only met once a year. The initial difficulties of the Subcommittee changed towards the second half of the 1920s with the increase in new organs and associations that facilitated work of the League of Nations and shared a common interest with the Subcommittee in terms of globally protecting intellectual property.[46]

JAPAN'S NATIONAL COMMITTEE ON INTELLECTUAL COOPERATION

The work of the ICIC started with the establishment of National Committees on Intellectual Cooperation in the various member states of the League of Nations. Secretary General James Eric Drummond contacted the Japanese Foreign Minister Matsui Keishirō about this matter in January 1924 informing him of the work conducted by the ICIC so far and of the plan that had been drawn up at the Committee's third Assembly held in Geneva in 1923. It recommended the formation of a National Committee on Intellectual Cooperation in each country which would allow a better organization for cooperation. The letter closed with the request to the Japanese government to consider forming a national committee in Japan to assist the work of the League of Nations. In 1924 other letters with information on the countries that had meanwhile founded their own committee followed.[47] The ICIC was reliant on cooperation with the individual member states, as their funds were very limited and the little available staff made it difficult to put their plans into action. To facilitate the financial struggles of the ICIC, in September 1924 the French government offered to establish an executive organ for the ICIC, the International Institute of Intellectual Cooperation (Paris Institute) in Paris, which took up its work in January 1926 and was to act as a meeting-ground for the national committees and individual experts to exchange ideas and approach mutual problems.[48] By establishing the Paris Institute, France gained a strategic advantage in revising the Berne Convention. This institute, funded by the French government and closely connected to global copyright advocates, played a key role in coordinating international revision conferences. As a result, all drafts and decisions related to the conferences went through this influential government-backed institution.

Japan established its own National Committee on Intellectual Cooperation (Gakugei Kyōryoku Kokunai Iinkai) in April 1926 and thereby joined the 30 nations that had already set up committees. Although these committees all acted as intermediaries between the intellectual life in their respective countries and the League of Nation's ICIC, they were free to determine "their relations with their Governments and their rules of procedure and composition." They were furthermore "free to govern their constitution in accordance with their own views and the conditions and possibilities" in their country.[49]

The first leader of Japan's National Committee was the by now familiar scholar Yamada Saburō, who still held the chair of private international law at Tōkyō Imperial University and, like the other founding members of the Committee, since 1925 was also a member of the Imperial Academy (Teikoku Gakushiin). The Academy was a special organ of the Ministry of Education modeled after the British Royal Society and the Académie Française, whose aim it was to advance the "learning and civilization"[50] through the enhancement of promising scholars.[51] As the previous chapters have shown, Yamada had been actively engaged with foreign politics and international cooperation since his contribution as legal advisor to the drafting of Japan's legal codes in connection with the conclusion of the Anglo-Japanese Treaty for Commerce and Navigation in the mid-1890s. Henceforth, all communication regarding intellectual cooperation, including the work of the Subcommittee on Intellectual Property Rights, had to be read by Yamada, and he quickly became the main mediator between Japan's National Committee and the private industry, on the one hand, and the involved organizations in Europe, including the Berne Bureau, the ALAI, and the Paris Institute, on the other. When for example the Institute was planning an international congress, like the Popular Arts Congress in Prague that took place in 1927, it was Yamada Saburō who was first contacted for further information about the existing research in Japan, and to provide the Institute with information on and names of the specific experts in the field.[52]

While the League's ICIC consisted solely of non-governmental actors, Japan's National Committee also included several state officials affiliated with the Ministry of Foreign Affairs and the Ministry of Education as its board members. Other founding members of the Committee included the professor of Japanese literature and life at Harvard University and professor of the science of religion at Tōkyō Imperial University Anesaki Masaharu, the professor for geophysics at the Tōkyō Imperial University and future representative of Japan at the ICIC, Tanakadate Aikitsu, and secretary to the League of Nations Association of Japan and diplomat Satō Junzō, who would be transferred to represent Japan's National Committee at the Paris Institute in the 1930s.[53]

In June 1926, Yamada published an article in the *Kokusai chishiki* (International Knowledge), the journal of the League of Nations Association of Japan, in which he explained the reason behind the founding of Japan's National Committee with the desire of Japan's academic community to have their own organ to communicate with the ICIC rather than having to communicate via the state.[54] At first, it was planned for the Imperial Academy to be in control of the Committee, but in reality, the task was quickly taken on by the Ministry of Foreign Affairs which adopted a central role in the work of the Committee and secured its position even in the founding manuscript which stated that the Committee acted under the supervision of this ministry.[55] The Japanese government wanted to stay in control of this new diplomacy, but at the same time realized that they were increasingly reliant on the expertise of members of the private industries. This reliance was particularly notable in areas like copyrights, falling under the purview of the newly established National Committee.

With the establishment of the Paris Institute and the various National Committees on Intellectual Cooperation, the initial plan of the ICIC and the Subcommittee on Intellectual Property Rights for global exchange and distribution of publications began to show progress, as the national committees were able to guarantee closer communication and exchange with those engaged in the publishing market of their respective countries. To select suitable works to translate and to publish as part of an *Annual List of Book Recommendations* by the League of Nations, the committees were expected to consult with writers, translators, private organizations involved like literary groups and publishers' associations, and with government services, academies, or intellectual groups.[56]

Japan's National Committee placed the compilation of a catalogue of important Japanese publications to exchange with the Paris Institute on the agenda of the Committee's first session on April 30, 1926, the day of its founding. For this, the Committee sought the help of all the involved ministerial departments and, according to their own report, was greatly influenced by the publishing industry.[57] At the second session in May, it was furthermore decided to use publications to introduce the Japanese culture and economy abroad to promote cultural understanding between East Asia and "the West" and thereby contribute to the fundamental goal of the League of Nations which was to maintain world peace through cultural cooperation.

On June 14, 1926, Yamada Saburō started sending out letters to universities, banks, companies, and government agencies with the request to donate material about Japan in Western languages which would then be passed on to the Paris Institute and to the League's office in Geneva. By late July, many of the original addressees had already replied with their donations, amongst others the Tōkyō Chamber of Commerce, the Imperial Academy, the Institute of Physical and Chemical Research (Rikagaku Kenkyūjo), a number of private companies as well as the Ministry of Finance, and the Ministry of Communications and Transportation.[58] The close correspondence with the Paris Institute furthermore enabled the exchange of book registers with other League of Nations member countries.[59]

Contrary to the portrayal of Japan's National Committee in existing literature, the Committee not only functioned as an exporter of Japanese culture, but also contributed to the diffusion of the ideals of the League of Nations by supplying teachers and children with publications on the League of Nations and International Affairs.[60] Shortly after the establishment of the Committee, Yamada was asked by the Paris Institute to share information on the publishing houses in Japan which until now had undertaken the publication of translations of foreign literature.[61] As importer of books and magazines, Maruzen had already been acting as an agent for the League of Nations since the early 1920s and as a result of the above inquiry, by 1932, the publishing house was also put in charge of publishing the works of the Paris Institute including *The Aims and Organisation of the League of Nations*, *the Bi-annual Education Survey*, and books like *Teachers and World Peace*.[62] Japan's National Committee thus contributed to the creation of a transnational network that linked the organs of the League of Nations, including the ICIC and the Paris Institute, with the Japanese ministries as well as with national experts and other private actors. These structures became increasingly important during the upcoming revision procedures of the Berne Convention.

BUSINESS-STATE COOPERATION IN THE PREPARATIONS OF THE 1928 ROME REVISION CONFERENCE

In 1926 the ICIC's Subcommittee on Intellectual Property Rights was reformed. First, new members were appointed, which enabled a better coordination with the Berne Bureau and the Berne Union member states that were dominant in the book market. One of the new members was the director of the Berne Bureau, Ernst Röthlisberger, who died the same year, but was succeeded by the Swiss lawyer Fritz Ostertag who henceforth functioned as the direct internal mediator between the work of the Berne Bureau and the ICIC.[63] The Subcommittee was furthermore made responsible for coordinating the set-up of a Legal Section inside the newly founded Paris Institute to avoid overlapping work and guarantee an optimal exchange between the various actors involved. In addition, a new and tightened program for the ICIC's engagement with intellectual property rights was formulated which included as one of its three core tasks the "expansion of literary and artistic property rights."[64] However, the distribution of books was removed from the top of the agenda.[65] With this newly restructured Subcommittee on Intellectual Property Rights, in 1926 the plan to bring together the countries of the world for another revision conference of the Berne Convention was finally set in motion by the Paris Institute in cooperation with the Berne Bureau.

Unlike in Europe, where private actors engaged in the publishing sector were engaged directly, in Japan the communication between the above institutions and the respective member states of the Berne Union regarding the planned conference was mediated via the state, more precisely via the Home Ministry and the Ministry of Foreign Affairs. The fact that the inquiry from Europe was not addressed to Yamada Saburō and the ones in charge at Japan's National Committee shows the prevailing confusion regarding the correct communication networks and the complexity of the transnational structures in which the power of the expert community still depended largely on the actions of the state. The lack of direct communication with Japan's National Committee in preparing the revision conference in Rome might also be a reason why the League of Nations' ICIC and the Paris Institute have so far not been the subject of a study in connection with the Japanese publishing industry, even though the publishers greatly supported the preparations of the conference from behind the scenes. Information regarding the newest developments in the Bureau was mainly exchanged via the Swiss Legation in Tōkyō which was in close contact with the Ministry of Foreign Affairs of Japan.[66]

Since a planned revision conference scheduled for 1915 had not been realized due to the war, the last international meeting of members of the Berne Union had been the Berlin conference of 1908. Since then, a number of disagreements between member countries of the Union had developed, including over the issue of having had no unified duration of copyright protection that applied to all members of the Berne Union. This point was especially relevant regarding the international exchange of publications which the ICIC had been working for since its establishment.[67] The handling of copyrights of the growing such new mass media as film or, as a very recent development, radio, which had not been included in the previous version of the Convention, further added to the prevailing uncertainties.

Before another conference could be held, members of the Berne Bureau in cooperation with the Paris Institute first needed to collect and examine related law texts from the different member states. In June 1926, Fritz Ostertag, head of the Berne Bureau, contacted various state leaders, including Home Minister

Hamaguchi Osachi and asked for information about the existing Japanese laws that protected artists in the applied arts.[68] Without having received a reply, on February 17, 1927, Ostertag repeated his inquiry to Hamaguchi, this time informing him of the proposed date for the conference which was scheduled to take place in Rome in October 1927. To facilitate the preparations of the conference, Ostertag attached an explanatory memorandum in support of the propositions made by the Italian government as the conference's host country in cooperation with the Berne Bureau and the Legal Section of the Paris Institute, and a list with revision suggestions that had accumulated during local copyright conferences and meetings in various member states of the Berne Union between 1908 and 1926. Japan was given 10 copies of the propositions and five copies of the request list. The letter closed with an appeal to the minister to advise the Bureau of any observations, propositions or contra-propositions by the Japanese side by June 15, 1927, the day that the members of the Bureau would come together again to discuss the submissions they received in order to incorporate them into an official revision draft.[69]

The Japanese bureaucracy was slow to respond to the above inquiries. In the case of the survey on applied arts from June 1926, the Home Ministry had waited until February 1927, to send a request for an investigation to the Patent Bureau of the Ministry of Commerce and Industry and to the Ministry of Justice. By July 1927, the Berne Bureau was still waiting for a reply from the Japanese government, and that even though the Home Ministry had received several replies from the respective ministries. A similar delay took place regarding the second notification from February 1927 about the planned revision conference. The Home Ministry simply forwarded the request list, compiled during conferences held between 1908 and 1926, to the Ministry of Commerce and Industry and the Ministry of Foreign Affairs for their input.[70]

There are several possible explanations for why the ministries took so long to take any action in response to Ostertag's letter. Most importantly, the new and revised copyright agreement was a precedent in international law and there were simply no experts in the government familiar with this field. Until that time, there existed no designated department for copyrights in the Home Ministry. Kobayashi Hiroji, who was in charge of copyright law in the Police Affairs Bureau of the Home Ministry from 1928 until 1934 explained in a publication on his time in the Ministry that the bureaucrats who were put in charge were no experts and, as in his case, were focusing not only on revising the Copyright Law, but at the same time also on revising the Universal Manhood Suffrage Act (Futsū Senkyo Hō),[71] the Press Law (Shinbunshi Hō),[72] and the Publication Law (Shuppan Hō).[73] Furthermore, a change of cabinet from the first Wakatsuki Reijirō Cabinet to the Tanaka Giichi Cabinet on April 20, 1927 brought with it internal changes of personnel including the succession of Home Minister Hamaguchi by Suzuki Kisaburō, the inauguration of Tsuchiya Shōzō as head of the Book Division, and Yamaoka Mannosuke as head of the Police Affairs Bureau (Keihō-kyoku) within the same ministry. The delay in effectively dealing with and responding to the inquiry by the Berne Bureau was thus most likely a result of internal administrative struggles and demonstrated more clearly than ever the state's growing dependency and need for a closer cooperation with civil experts who were directly engaged in the sector and thus, unlike the majority of the bureaucrats involved, interested in the immediate outcome.

Having received no reaction from Japan, in May 1927 the director of the Paris Institute who was also one of the original five members of the Subcommittee on Intellectual Property Rights, Julien Luchaire, sent out invitations to different publishers' and booksellers' associations and to the large firms importing and exporting books to gather experts on the publication and sale of books together for a meeting to be held in Paris in June. The main topic to be discussed was difficulties which arose in the circulation of books in foreign countries (including tariffs, postal regulations, dimensions of parcels, and censorship). Additionally, questions on the possible publication of an international catalogue on booksellers and publishing houses was on the agenda of the meeting, as well as the difficulties in connection with an international agreement on copyright and translations.[74] The outcome of the meeting was to be submitted in the form of a report to the ICIC and discussed at their next assembly which was to take place in Geneva shortly after. The invited representatives were mostly from Europe, but also Russia and South America sent a representative to participate in the expert meeting. The American Booksellers' Association was invited, but because it did not have the necessary funds available, it asked the Paris Institute if it could send an expert who was already residing in Paris. This could not be arranged on such short notice so the United States was not represented at the meeting but it did provide some information on its stance beforehand to be used for consultation by the other experts.[75]

The existing sources reveal that Japan was not invited and that the Japanese government had neither reacted to the Berne Bureau's February inquiry, nor had it informed the publishers of the meeting of experts. It was already June when the bureaucrats were reminded of the importance of their reaction regarding the upcoming conference by a note that Foreign Minister Tanaka Giichi received from the ambassador to France, Kawai Hiroyuki. Kawai informed Tanaka of a visit he had received on June 16, 1927, by the French writer, lawyer, and representative of several European arts and letters associations, Paul Olagnier. At the meeting, Olagnier had explained to Kawai the main points of the conference and stressed the importance of Japan raising its general copyright protection and giving up its reservations regarding the duration of translation rights protection in accordance with the revised draft that had been passed on by the Paris Institute.[76] At this point, Japan still had 30 years of general copyright protection while the Berne Bureau aimed to raise the protection to a minimum of 50 years. The country furthermore still had its 10-year reservations regarding the protection of translation rights.

Having realized the consequences that their silence regarding the revision proposal might have on its national publishing industry and, more importantly, on the status of Japan, one month after Olagnier's visit to the embassy on July 15, representative bureaucrats of the Home Ministry and the Ministry of Foreign Affairs, the Ministry of Commerce and Industry, and the Ministry of Justice finally came together for an informal meeting at the Ministry of Foreign Affairs to discuss the contents and consequences of Ostertag's letter that had been written six months earlier. The agenda of the meeting demonstrated the early stage that the preparations were in.[77] At the time of the gathering, there still existed no translation of the Italian government and the Berne Bureau's proposal for the bureaucrats to work with. Thus, the translation of the proposal was ordered as one of the first points of action. The Home Ministry was made responsible for distributing the translation and collecting written opinions by the different ministries. The agenda also included discussing the request for a postponement of the conference for which the Ministry of Foreign Affairs was to consult the Italian government. On August 19, the bureaucrats were scheduled to meet again to discuss what they had worked on and produce a detailed Japanese position.[78]

During the one-month period that separated the two meetings, external pressure on the government was increasing. On August 2, 1927, the president of the ALAI, Georges Maillard, contacted the Japanese Ambassador to France, Ishii Kikujirō, to notify him of ALAI's Bulletin in which the reasons for a renunciation of Japan's reservations were listed. The ALAI approached the ambassador with the request to inform Mizuno Rentarō, who was known to be acquainted with the copyright law, of these reasons. Maillard closed by saying: "We [the ALAI] are aware of the fact that the French government has also intervened on this subject with the Japanese government."[79] The ALAI worked alongside French government initiatives, aiming to increase pressure on the Japanese government. As planned, on August 19, bureaucrats from the different ministries involved met again to discuss their stance regarding the contents for debate that they had received from the Italian government. The new head of the Home Ministry's Book Division, Tsuchiya Shōzō, was responsible for dividing the different tasks amongst the ministries because of his experience from meetings he had previously attended. Tsuchiya who had graduated from the Tōkyō Imperial University Law School in 1917, had spent a year abroad, stationed in, amongst other cities, London, before he was made Section Chief of External Affairs at the Home Ministry in 1919. In this position, Tsuchiya had to work on the administration of former enemy property, as well as "control the import of communism and anarchism."[80] Although the administration of property was different from intellectual property and copyright law,

Tsuchiya's background had prepared him well for his work in the Book Division, where besides being responsible for censorship and the prohibition of leftist publications, he had also to deal with revising the international copyright agreement.[81]

According to Tsuchiya's division of the tasks, the Home Ministry was henceforth supposed to oversee the research regarding the extension of the copyright protection, the accession to new areas of protection, and general research regarding the revision of the Berne Convention. The Ministry of Education was given authority over the fields of music and art, while the Ministry of Communications and Transportation was asked to conduct research into the relationship between copyright protection and the radio. The Ministry of Commerce and Industry was put in charge of the relationship between copyright protection of art works and the Design Act. The Ministry of Justice was to regulate the laws for revision, and lastly, the Ministry of Foreign Affairs was to manage the general external affairs.[82] At the same meeting, the head of the Department for Shrine Affairs, Yoshida Shigeru[83], received the unofficial offer to represent Japan at the conference, despite his lack of knowledge in the field of international copyright law. He was scheduled to leave for Rome in late September.[84]

The meeting on August 19 once again and in its full dimension demonstrated how unprepared the bureaucrats were for the upcoming international conference. However, the inactivity of the bureaucrats in cooperating with the committees of the League of Nations was not a phenomenon of the Japanese state alone. The impact of the states' inaction on the expert committees of the League of Nations during the 1920s was already analyzed in 1931 in a study by political scientist Harold Richard Goring Greaves in which he blamed the "national inertia" of the governments and their lack of interest for the failure of the ICIC and the Paris Institute to be more active in their earlier years of existence. According to Greaves, "the Committee has been hampered always and at every step by the parsimony of governments," and "the time for the minister of education to be more important than the minister of war is still beyond the horizon."[85] The slow reaction of the Japanese government to the inquiries from the Berne Bureau regarding their contribution to the revision draft for the Berne Convention supports Greaves' claim. The personal memoirs of the bureaucrats in charge of copyrights inside the Police Affairs Bureau, Kobayashi and Tsuchiya, reveal that their government at the time lacked the competence to handle the request from Europe without consulting those with experience in the industry.[86]

Closer cooperation and the implementation of ICIC's activities only began to improve with the establishment of National Committees because the committees worked in direct collaboration with experts who had the knowledge and a direct personal interest in the matters addressed by the League's committees. In the case of the preparations for the Rome Revision Conference, in late summer of 1927, the government had not much time left to share their opinion with the Berne Bureau and the ICIC and therefore decided to directly reach out to the private sector for assistance in their preparatory work.[87] But despite the, from an international cooperation viewpoint, rather damaging inertia of Japan's bureaucracy, it never was an option and possibly did not even occur to the self-assured ministerial bureaucrats, to allocate from now on officially the preparations for the Berne Convention revision conference to the representatives of the publishing industry. They continued the tasks they had been entrusted even if these responsibilities were beyond their level of expertise.

Before Home Minister Suzuki approached the publishers in late August 1927, the cooperation between the heads of the industry and state bureaucrats had already been intensifying for several months over a different but connected matter. Reason for the increase in cooperation was a petition written in 1926 by the above-mentioned Ōkura Yasugorō, successor of Oyaizu Kaname as head of the Tōkyō Booksellers' Association, regarding the desire of the publishers to revise the national Publication Law and the Copyright Law in favor of the rights of publishers. Since World War I, but increasingly in the 1920s, the publishers became more and more concerned by the fact that while there existed a law that protected the rights of authors (*chosakuken*), there was still no law that explicitly protected their rights as publishers. With the rising importance affiliated with intellectual property, the publishers demanded a revision of the current Copyright Law to include a provision of publishing rights (*shuppanken*),[88] namely, to have a monopoly over the works published by them.

Their request was an outcome of a general uncertainty that was prevailing in the publishing industry in Europe regarding the validity of licensing agreements and the actual meaning of the term "license" as used in the Peace Treaty. Publishers in Germany, in particular, were uncertain of what the term in the Peace Treaty meant and began studying the French and English original texts regarding its usage.[89] The discussions on the true meaning of licensing rights also reached Japan, which, following the war, was not only experiencing a war-triggered economic boom that led to an increase in many publications, but also faced many cases of copyright fraud and doubts about what actually fell under the term of a copyright violation according to the existing licensing agreements.[90] The Ministry of Foreign Affairs began answering many questions concerning this matter, such as an enquiry by the Consulate General Yada Chōnosuke, stationed in New York, who shortly after the end of the war in February 1919 approached the Ministry of Foreign Affairs in Tōkyō with the question of whether it would be legal to import a book to Japan without first consulting the author, in the case that the original work was written by a British author, but had been reproduced in the United States. The Foreign Minister had to consult with the Home Minister before getting back to Yada with the reply that books like that would have to be confiscated by the government according to the revised treaty of the Berne Convention.[91]

As a consequence of the various uncertainties that had been stirred up by the war, the Tōkyō Publishers' Association had already in 1917 taken the step to establish a research initiative for the protection of publishers' rights which was concerned not only with copyrights, but also with the rights of the publishers themselves. The unauthorized publication of works as well as an author's conclusion of a double contract with two different publishers occurred more frequently, primarily as a result of the rise in publications and the ambiguity about the regulations of a common licensing agreement. The Tōkyō Publishers' Association therefore started collecting information and writing reports on the judiciary situation of the different countries, thereby also taking part in the post-war discussions by publishers on the true meaning of copyright licenses. The publishers' efforts to revise the law were temporarily brought to a halt by the Great Kantō Earthquake in 1923 which according to the final official figures left more than 156,000 killed, injured, or missing, and many of the publishing houses, a majority of which was located in Tōkyō, completely destroyed.[92] However, because of the speedy reconstruction efforts, the publishing industry quickly recovered and the foreign book trade even especially prospered as a result of the quake.[93] Following the earthquake and reconstruction of the publishing houses, in the mid-1920s the Tōkyō Publishers' Association took up their plan again to introduce a regulation for publishing rights. On March 25, 1926, head of the Tōkyō Booksellers' Association Ōkura Yasugorō expressed the concern of the publishers in a petition that was submitted to the House of Representatives.[94] The petition was accepted and by the beginning of 1927, a draft for a publishing rights law was placed on the agenda of the next National Diet session.[95] In March, a number of publishers then came together with the instructed parliamentarian in an informal meeting during which the agreement was reached to establish an advisory body between governmental and private actors in order to revise the existing publishing laws.[96] Starting on March 10, 1927 the National Diet officially discussed the matter in several sessions. By the end of the month, the publishers gave a dinner to acknowledge the efforts of a number of parliamentarians in connection with the introduction of such a provision into the existing Copyright Law.[97] This function was attended by nine parliamentarians and the entire managing board of the Tōkyō Publishers' Association. Two parliamentarians, Masuda Giichi and Nagata Shinnojō, had backgrounds in the publishing industry, while others were from law or academia. On March 31, 1927, Association members sought a meeting with Home Minister Hamaguchi to discuss the agreement on establishing a joint consultation platform. On April 4, 1927, their request was granted and committee members from both the government and the Tōkyō Publishers' Association met with Hamaguchi, who assured them that he would investigate the matter. The publishers also held discussions with Matsumura Giichi, the director of the Home Ministry's Police Affairs Bureau, responsible for administering the Copyright Law.[98] The main outcome of the two meetings in March and April was the realization by the state officials that without the cooperation with private industry experts, the state would have been unable to undertake research that adequately covered all relevant areas concerning publication and copyrights.

Subsequently, it was decided that an advisory institution between citizens and the state (*kanmin gōdō no chōsa kikan*) be established to regulate the revision of the Copyright Law and the Publication Law. As a first step, Home Minister Suzuki was to make an informal selection of members from the House of Peers, the House of Representatives, individuals in the publishing industry, and authors as copyright owners. The selected members were then to form a council to propose a plan to conduct research on the law.[99] Despite the government's initial stance against a joint investigation committee involving both state and private actors for the introduction of publishing rights, they eventually approved it "for the benefit of getting a broader range of opinions."[100] On July 18, 1927, they established the council under the name Police Advisory Council (Keiho Iinkai), a committee intended to address public order through the mutual cooperation of both private and governmental actors.[101]

Involved publishers, bureaucrats, and the media of the time considered the Police Advisory Council not to be very effective.[102] In mid-December 1927, it was expected that the Home Ministry would, after prior consultations with the advisory council, present two revision drafts of the Copyright Law and the Publication Law to the National Diet. The representative of the Ministry, however, never mentioned the subject, and when asked by the council how to proceed regarding the drafts, he announced that the Ministry had no intention of consulting this matter before knowing the outcome of the Rome Revision Conference in the spring. The Home Ministry thus took a passive stance for the Japanese government.[103] The Ministry further announced its decision to use the time of the conference to either restructure the core of the Police Advisory Council or, alternatively, to establish an entirely new committee which would place a greater emphasis on having copyright owners, publishers, and other involved actors directly appointed to the committee and carry out research together.[104] That the ministerial bureaucrats brought forward this advance demonstrates that their wish to work together with the private industry not only constituted an empty promise to represent themselves in a more democratic manner, but the success of their work actually heavily depended on collaboration with the above group of actors.

Despite this announcement, the advisory council continued its research on the revision of the Publication Law in a special committee of 10 bureaucrats and legal experts that met between December 1927 and March 1928. But without the direct input of experts from the private industry, they were ultimately unable to present any results.[105]

Publisher Fujita Tomoharu mentioned a few years later in 1933, that despite the establishment of the Police Advisory Council, the government had quickly neglected its involvement with the research regarding publishing rights and had taken no further action besides acquiring some reference works.[106] Head of the Book Division inside the Home Ministry, Tsuchiya Shōzō, gave a little insight into what may have been the problem with this research organization. Up to this point, there had existed no law to settle publishing rights in Japan. Tsuchiya, who as head of the Book Division should have been the person to consult, recalled that he had heard of publishing rights for the first time only around that time. Although he spent his time "studying diligently," there still existed only one reference work on copyrights in the Ministry at the time.[107] Tsuchiya later revealed that he had had a great interest in changing the laws in favor of the publishers, and that he privately studied ways in which the existing laws could be amended, but that by the time he handed in his report, the cabinet had changed and subsequently, his ideas were not implemented.[108] It was not until the spring of 1928, that the newly appointed person responsible for copyrights inside the Police Affairs Bureau of the Home Ministry, Kobayashi Hiroji, took the initiative in response to the events of the conference in Rome and started collecting reference material from abroad.[109]

The main reason the Police Advisory Council is considered unsuccessful was due to its lack of the right expertise and insufficient involvement of outside experts in its work. In addition, old bureaucratic structures and personal changes hindered progress. However, to presume that the committee completely failed would not do it justice. When looking more closely at the actors involved, the organization served as one of the important cardinal points in connecting state and non-state actors around the time of preparations for the next international revision conference. Ahead of the official founding of the advisory council, the networks established between publishers, academic expert and head of the National Committee Yamada Saburō, and state bureaucrats would bear fruit in the months and years of close cooperation to come. In fact, the Police Advisory Council was the precursor to the official copyright councils created in the following decade between bureaucrats, academic experts, and members of the publishing industry.

When, in August 1927, Home Minister Suzuki Kisaburō met with publishers from various publishers' associations to advance the preparations for the Rome Revision Conference, the publishers and ministerial bureaucrats involved were thus already engaged in a close dialogue with each other. In his note regarding the revision conference arranged to take place in Rome and the associated explanatory memorandum of the Italian government, the Berne Bureau, and the Paris Institute, Suzuki wrote that for the ongoing discussions on whether to send representatives of

Japan to the conference as well, it would be vital to collect different private opinions. He expressed his hope that this task would be taken on by the most influential publishers' association of the country and asked the publishers to share their knowledge regarding the explanatory remarks by September 20, 1927.[110]

The message, however, was first to be discussed with the recipients in person which is why the Home Minister invited to his residence a total of 20 representatives from different business associations related to the mass media and in most cases affiliated in one way or another with the publishing industry, namely, from the Tōkyō Booksellers' Association, the Japan Magazine Association (Nihon Zasshi Kyōkai), the Japan Newspaper Association (Nihon Shinbun Kyōkai), the Writers' Association (Bungeika Kyōkai), the Greater Japan Motion Picture Association (Dai Nihon Katsudō Shashin Kyōkai), the Motion Picture Traders' Association (Katsudō Shashin Gyōsha Kumiai), and the Japan Grammophone Trade Association (Nihon Chikuonkishō Kumiai). The publishers were represented by five publishers of different publishing houses with a connection to Western publications, including Ōkura Yasugorō, Hayashi Heijirō (head of the textbook publisher Dai Nihon Tosho), Uehara Seiichirō (head of the textbook publisher Kōfūkan Shoten), Fukunaga Bunnosuke (head of the Christian publisher Keiseisha), and Egusa Shigetada, the director of publishing house Yūhikaku specialized in law publications. Yamaoka Mannosuke, the new head of the Police Affairs Bureau, led the meeting which included a question-and-answer session during which the publishers could address any question they might have had to the bureaucrats.[111]

It is unclear how much the general public was involved in these initial preparations or to what extent they were informed through reports in the media, but judging from an article that appeared in the *Tōkyō asahi shinbun* shortly after the bureaucrats started reaching out to the industry, not much of the negotiations between the heads of the publishers' associations and state bureaucrats leaked through to the press or the general public. The author of the article, copyright scholar Hashimura Sen'ichi, wrote that the contents of the draft had not been studied well enough and that, compared with other countries, not much attention was given to the opinions of writers and publishers. In the end, the article called for a much broader and more public discussion of the revision, and for the draft to be publicly printed and discussed in various forums like local conferences and organizations.[112] The article reinforces the argument that it was a small group of involved actors from the publishing and academic elite that had grown together with the ministerial bureaucracy since the mid-1890s. The issues at hand were still not discussed openly, but the demands for more democratic structures that started to be made by "lower-ranking" members from the industry were a first step in this direction.

At the following supervisory board meeting of the Tōkyō Booksellers' Association on September 5, 1927, Ōkura Yasugorō and his colleagues decided to found a committee alliance with the Tōkyō Publishers' Association and the Japan Magazine Association to discuss each of the associations' points of concern for the revision process to be able to consult the bureaucrats as well as possible.[113] A few days later the publishers were notified that the planned conference had been postponed to spring 1928 and accordingly, the deadline for submitting the respective opinions had been pushed back to the end of October. The communication with the Ministry remained close and the publishers were provided with all the information they needed to form an opinion that would best represent the Japanese publishing industry at large. At the end of September 1927, Suzuki sent them, as additional reference material, the drafts and explanations that had already been submitted by Austria, France, Germany, Switzerland, and the United Kingdom in July.[114]

The joint committee of the three publishers' associations handed in their written opinion on October 12, 1927. The paper stated, amongst other things, that Japan wanted to keep the copyrights on written works at 30 years instead of the proposed 50 years after the author's death. The document argued that an extension of the time of protection would "hinder the development of culture" (*bunka no shinten o sogai suru*) in Japan, which was tantamount to the same argument that had already been given by Oyaizu Kaname 30 years earlier with the exception that "civilization" had been replaced by the more timely term of "culture".[115] The publishers further expressed their clear opposition to the proposed abolition of the reservations held by individual countries on the duration of translation rights. For the purpose of strengthening their argument, the Tōkyō Booksellers' Association had conducted two additional studies that were attached to their submission. The first study entitled "Hōyaku ga genshō ni oyobosu eikyō" (The Impact of Japanese Translations on the Original Work) argued that the sale of the original increased through translations and supported this argument by giving different examples like the increase in sales of the original H.G. Wells *Time Machine* after the work had been translated into Japanese in 1913. It further looked at the connection with works on current affairs and argued that it made a great difference whether these works were immediately translated into Japanese or after a period of 10 years. The supporting examples included for example a translation of Robert Lansing's *The Peace Negotiations* that had been published in the *Tōkyō asahi shinbun* following the end of World War I. It said that "because of the translation, suddenly hundreds of copies of the original were sold."[116] Other related examples of current affairs included the increase in the sales of the original after the translation of the *Erinnerungen des Kronprinzen Wilhem* (official English translation: *Memoirs of the Crown Prince of Germany*) by Wilhelm von Preußen, Frank A. Vanderlip's 1923 *What Happened to Europe* on the European economic development during the war, and *The House Diaries*[117] that had been published as a sequel in the *Tōkyō nichi nichi shinbun*. The same was the case for the translation of writings of Albert Einstein and the Indian poet and Nobel Prize for Literature laureate in 1913 Rabindranath Tagore, which were introduced in magazines and thereby contributed to the sales of the original works. Besides the "current affairs factor," according to the study, also the sale of translated classics contributed to the sale of the originals. Works like *Robinson Crusoe, One Thousand and One Nights*, the *Grimms' Fairy Tales*, or works by Adam Smith or Karl Marx were often read in the original with the help of the translated work or read again in the original after a translation had caught the reader's interest. The study concluded that on average, in Japan a translated work increased sales of the original by 35, in the best-case scenario even by 180.[118]

The other extra study that was handed in was a compilation of different cases of how copyright holders' felt about their work being published in Japan, titled "Nihon ni yakusho no deru koto ga ikani genchosha ni yorokobaru, ka jitsurei no ni, san" (How Content are Authors About Their Work Being Published in Japan: On a Couple of Cases).[119] Here, a number of copyright owners including German playwright Ernst Toller, German author Frank Wedekind and many others were cited about the excitement they felt and their natural consent when being asked about agreeing to a translation of their work into Japanese. The study did not, however, mention whether the authors received a remuneration for their translation rights which should have been the case if the authors were contacted via the official route of their publishers abroad.[120]

The publishing archive of the renowned publisher Mohr Siebeck based in the Berlin State Library holds many letters between its former owner Paul Siebeck, and later his son Oskar Siebeck, and Japanese publishers and translators, and thereby offers an insight into the official procedures at the time. The large early twentieth-century collection of letters exchanged includes many inquiries for translations (written by publishers, university professors, intellectuals, or ministry employees) which in most cases were granted under the prerequisite that a certain remuneration sum was paid for the translation rights. The attempts made by the Japanese side to agree simply to a nominal compensation was found in none of the delivered sources successfully achieved.[121] Thus, the study of the Tōkyō Booksellers' Association rightly acknowledged that the copyright holders were by and large "glad" about their work being published in Japan, but it ignored the fact that the authors should have rightfully also received compensation for the translation of their work.[122]

About one week after the studies and opinions were submitted, the mutual proposal of the three publishers' associations was discussed at a private meeting in the Tōkyō Kaikan in Marunouchi. The attendees on the side of the state included the head of Police Affairs Bureau, Yamaoka Mannosuke, head of Book Division, Tsuchiya Shōzō, secretary to the Home Ministry, Kuji Manabu, and secretary to the Reconstruction Bureau, Takebe Rokuzō, and head of department at the

Court of Appeal (Kōsoin), Kawabe Hisao. The three bureaucrats Kuji, Takebe, and Kawabe would together form the Japanese delegation to Rome.[123] The attending publishers included representatives from the three big publishers' associations: Ōkura Yasugorō, Yamamoto Sanehiko who was the president of Kaizōsha, a publishing house renowned for its academic and educational publications that later became known for the publication of the World Encyclopedia *Sekai Dai-hyakka jiten*, Meguro Jinshichi, and Fujita Tomoharu, who was in charge of the examination process of Publication Law. Even though the exact content of the consultations at the Tōkyō Kaikan cannot be reconstructed, Yamaoka reportedly used the meeting to stress the special efforts that needed to be taken by the committee to represent Japan at the international meeting in Rome.[124]

Over the course of the following weeks, the Police Affairs Bureau collected a number of other private organizations' opinions, for example, from the literature, newspaper, film and broadcasting industry sector, and from organizations connected to trade and industry, including the Federation of the Chambers of Commerce that represented all Japanese chambers as an umbrella organization.[125] The collected opinions were then included in a detailed summary of the respective pro and contra opinions of the different private organizations on selected paragraphs of the proposal by the Italian government. The content of the draft confirms the extent to which the bureaucrats were reliant on the aforementioned opinions of the private sector and to which extent they were willing to comply with its demands.[126]

THE 1928 ROME REVISION CONFERENCE AND JAPAN'S REQUEST FOR AN EXEMPTION FROM THE TRANSLATION RIGHT REGULATIONS

The ministries involved handed their written opinions in to the Home Ministry's Police Affairs Bureau in February and March 1928. These were based on the consultations they had received, also in the form of written opinions, by the publishers and other private organizations beforehand. The final report from the Home Ministry, which was to represent the opinion of the Japanese government, demonstrated a clear influence by the collected opinions of the publishers, and part of their reasoning was even justified directly by the fact that the private organizations held the same opinion. With respect to paragraph 8 on translation rights and the proposal from the Italian government "to abandon the reservations held by the individual countries," the joint committee of different publishers' associations had expressed their clear opposition.[127] The Home Ministry incorporated this opinion in its own statement, writing that there was no reason for abolishing Japan's reservations and "due to the fact that the private organizations agreed with this opinion,

Japan should keep their reservations without any changes."[128] Furthermore, the Ministry of Education had also sought an expert opinion for advice in its written opinion, which was handed in on February 22, 1928, and included a reference report that Yamada Saburō had written and submitted as part of his research activities at the Imperial Academy. The argument for the necessity of free translations to advance "civilization" in the country had vanished from Yamada's argumentation. Given Japan's proposition for racial equality and fair treatment by Western nations, maintaining the argument became challenging, particularly because Yamada himself, along with others, persisted in pursuing this goal through the League of Nations Association after the failed proposal.

Rather than argue with the need to import Western "civilization," Yamada now elaborated on the importance of free translations between members of the Berne Convention in Europe and Japan, emphasizing Japan's role in the "fusion between Eastern and Western culture."[129] A few sentences later, however, Yamada made clear that only translations between Japan and Europe should be excluded from the regulations. Free translations between China and Japan, on the other hand, would negatively affect the sales of the original work.[130] The objective of international cooperation was thus not universally applied but rather tilted in favor of Japanese interests. Yamada's writing illustrates how Japanese internationalists embraced the rhetoric derived from Wilsonian internationalism, emphasizing international cooperation and cultural exchange, to reframe their imperialistic ideas. Basing themselves on this new internationalism, they developed new ways to promote their national interests and legitimize their foreign policies. Looking at Yamada's simultaneous activities inside Japan's League of Nations Association where he was dealing with the issue of international migration with the aim of achieving equal treatment of Japanese people entering countries in Europe or the United States, the general double standard in his foreign policy goals and legal standards becomes obvious.[131] Since his study days and his early career path in the mid-1890s, Yamada had been involved in the removal of barriers to promote internationalism and the free movement of people, goods and items.[132] However, as Terada Kuniyuki has shown, his intention was not to expand these standards universally, and he remained silent about the discrimination that was taking place towards China and Korea in his own country.[133]

Once all the ministries involved had concluded their opinion pieces, the heads of the large publishers' associations gave a dinner for the members of the Japanese delegation to the revision conference in Rome on March 14, 1928. This gave them the opportunity to exchange opinions and any open questions before the plenipotentiary for Japan, Home Ministry bureaucrat Akagi Tomoharu, embarked on his trip to Europe. The attendees included Akagi himself and many other high-ranking bureaucrats, like Yamaoka Mannosuke, Tsuchiya Shozō, and others.[134]

The revision conference in Rome began around seven weeks later on May 7 and lasted three weeks ending June 2, 1928. With the Paris Institute and the League of Nations among the attending institutions, for the first time, two outside organizations, which were not part of any national delegation, were among the participants. Even though in 1908, non-governmental organizations such as the ALAI had already been present, the attending members had all been embedded in their national delegations. In Rome, delegates from the Subcommittee on Intellectual Property Rights, representing their respective governments, enjoyed the advantage of presenting on the international stage what had previously been negotiated at the national level.[135] The entanglement of national and international as well as social and political engagement was characteristic for the revision conference and not only applied to the relationship between the League of Nations and national delegations, but also to professional associations and national politics.[136] In comparison with many of the other attending nations, the international networks of Japan's private associations as well as its National Committee on Intellectual Cooperation were not yet well established and still had to rely solely on the representation of the state officials in charge.

According to Tsuchiya Shōzō, the head of the Book Division, the Home Ministry spared no effort in supporting the Japanese delegates, Akagi Tomoharu and Matsuda Michikazu, who was the Japanese ambassador to Italy and, prior to that, had served as the chief of the Japan Office of the League of Nations in Paris, during the conference, ensuring their best possible representation abroad. The two departments most involved during the conference were the Home Ministry's Police Affairs Bureau and its Book Division. The latter had just doubled its funding and employed new personnel in connection with the heavy upheavals that had surrounded the first national election on February 20, 1928, under the Universal Manhood Suffrage Act of 1925. During this election many proletarian parties were running for seats, supported by the Japanese Communist Party. The candidates ended up winning eight seats, which caused Home Minister Suzuki to order a nationwide mass arrest of about 1600 suspected communists on March 15, 1928. As one consequence of this raid and Suzuki's aim to break up the Communist Party, the Book Division was strengthened.[137]

Every time Tsuchiya Shōzō received a report from Rome, he called together the different ministries for consultation to give further instructions to the delegates. The Police Affairs Bureau had also just employed a new person to take the position of head of copyrights, the aforementioned Kobayashi Hiroji. Kobayashi, who had been transferred to the Bureau at the beginning of the year, as of yet had no detailed experience or knowledge of copyrights, and, according to himself, was struggling with related questions on copyrights and copyright registrations that started to come in on a daily basis. He recalled that Mizuno Rentarō, who at the time held the position of Minister of Education, had offered his assistance to Kobayashi in his copyright-related work.[138] To further improve access to knowledge in this field, Kobayashi appealed to Tsuchiya who instructed him to start gathering foreign books about copyrights. Following Tsuchiya's advice, Kobayashi went to the Tōkyō Imperial University and borrowed several reference works in English, German, and French, as well as expert magazines. The magazine of the Berne Bureau, the *Droit d'auteur*, had already been taken out on subscription by the ministry.[139] The above portrayals reflect the ongoing inexperience of the Ministry and the bureaucrats in charge when dealing with an international expert conference like the revision conference of the Berne Convention.

In the history of international law, the outcome of the 1928 revision conference is generally regarded as not having been very successful. It failed to introduce regulations on the new media of radio, film, and broadcasting. Furthermore, it failed to abolish the reservations on translation rights introduced in 1908, and, finally, it also failed to unite all member states in an obligatory regulation on a 50-year copyright duration which meant that the member states continued to be divided into those that protected works for 30 years after the death of the author and those that protected works for 50 years after the death of the author. One reason for the difficult conference proceedings was the large number of participating states and the new lobby groups of the film, radio, and record industries.[140] Another reason was the boycott by individual countries like Japan.

At the conference Matsuda Michikazu began his statement by pointing out that the conference should avoid a "sudden, and above all radical change" to the status quo.[141] Despite the contradiction to Japan's race equality proposal, Matsuda argued that to harmonize the different systems of the various countries and thereby offer universal copyright protection, the "degree of culture" in the individual countries had to be taken into account.[142] As regards the revision propositions, he stated that Japan would be willing to renounce its reservations concerning the public performance of musical works that it had adopted in 1908 and which had become problematic due to the emergence of the mass medium radio. However, concerning the proposal of the French government to abandon the option of declaring reservations on certain paragraphs, the Japanese government opposed along the lines of the recommendations by the private industry, stating that Japan would have to keep the reservations on the right of translation, and further also disagreed with the introduction of a universal 50 years of copyright protection.[143]

Japan's opposition was the crucial factor to putting the French proposal on hold eventually. According to the conference report, the option to declare a reservation on certain paragraphs had been introduced during the 1908 Berlin revision as a temporary measure. However, at the end of the conference in Rome, the decision of the Commission, which consisted of members from nine different countries, including Akagi Tomoharu for Japan, was not to go through with the planned abandonment and to keep the exemptions in the area of translations. The report stated:

> With regard to new accessions, it is believed that the right of reservation can be maintained by reference to the right of translation. One can understand, indeed, that the states hitherto foreign to the Berne Union, and in particular the countries of a very different language and often of a different (sometimes inferior) form of civilization from that of the Unionist countries, may have a certain mistrust of a system which grants the author the exclusive right of translation throughout for the normal duration of his right. Apparently this right hinders the spread of culture and, for the Eastern nations, the assimilation of Western civilization.[144]

Following the above statement, it was immediately added that "in fact" the contrary was true—as had been demonstrated in a report by M. Louis Renault, professor of law, co-winner of the 1907 Nobel Prize for Peace and member of the Paris Institute, during the previous conference in Berlin. Renault had stressed that the Berne system would "unlikely discourage translators [from translating] and prevent the intellectual relations of the West and the Far East."[145] He asked: "When a Japanese [translator] is willing to undertake the translation of a European work, is it really likely that the requirements of the author or the publisher will prevent him from implementing his project? We sincerely do not believe that."[146] He was convinced that through the regulations of the Berne Convention, Japanese citizens were not cheated and were instead being delivered a correct translation that had been authorized by the author who had trusted in the "knowledge and intelligence" of the person to whom he granted the translation rights.[147] Why then did the Berne Union agree to the continuous granting of this special status to Japan?

It was clear that, in 1928, the opinions regarding the option to be exempt from the regulations of the Berne Convention still differed among the various member states. Nevertheless, the decision was that the conference found it "advisable to maintain the right of reservation for translations."[148] For the members of the Berne Union, the thought of losing Japan as an important non-Western member of the Union was likely worse than having to make concessions in the area of translation rights. The overall outcome of the conference for Japan and the Japanese publishing industry as the driving force behind the statement of the government was, hence, positive in terms of maintaining its special exemptions. But at what cost? The Japanese delegates who in the past had demonstrated their will to be seen as equal to the Western powers, now accepted that the other member states put Japan on the same level as countries with an "inferior civilization". By accepting special conditions on translations in exchange for attaining a status comparable to the Western member states in this multilateral organization, did Japanese state leaders demonstrate their ambition to establish a distinct cultural order in East Asia? As explained by Yamada Saburō in his advice to ministerial bureaucrats, only translations between Japan and Europe were to be excluded from the regulations. Did Japanese officials—on advice of copyright experts—start using the Berne Convention and its international conferences as a tool to advance their own regional hegemony?

The new international order following World War I had affected various international agreements and conventions, including the Berne Convention whose administration was placed under the League of Nation's ICIC. The League and its organs for intellectual cooperation that were established in the individual member states to connect directly with the cultural sector gave an increasing importance and voice to private actors and experts at international meetings. Japanese state officials reacted to these international developments by expanding the cooperation with the people and private industries domestically as well. As to the Berne Convention, this led to the establishment of advisory councils and exchanges of written opinions bringing together the small circle of Japanese internationalists consisting of state officials, publishers, and academic scholars that had been invested in revising the international agreement since the days of Meiji. While the generation of actors involved remained largely the same, they adapted their internationalist rhetoric to fit the changing circumstances and national goals, in particular concerning their expansionist interests in China.

Due to the general unproductive image of the League of Nations regarding its involvement in globalizing copyright regulations, it is not surprising that Japan's non-state involvement in the revision of the Berne Convention during the 1920s and 1930s has also received little scholarly attention. The personal absence of Japan's private sector from the conference adds to the assumption that non-official experts or organizations, including publishers and Japan's National Committee on Intellectual Cooperation, were not involved in the international discussions. However, as this chapter has shown, even though the involvement of the Japanese private sector was not visible on the international stage in the 1920s, its actors were as engaged as their European counterparts in shaping these negotiations. Their voices were represented indirectly by state delegates, for example as part of an official revision draft reflecting Japan's official standpoint, or, from the latter half of the 1920s, by Yamada Saburō as the director of Japan's National Committee on Intellectual Cooperation. The result of these consultations was that Japan once again blocked the efforts of the Berne Union and European publishers' associations to unify copyright protection and to abandon the right to declare a reservation on translator's rights protection.

While the 1928 conference did not bring about significant alterations to the international agreement, recent findings suggest that the previous characterization of the conference as "unsuccessful" regarding its relevance to the interwar development of international copyright protection should be revisited. The conference, along with the broader efforts of the League of Nations during the interwar years, was revealed to be a crucial milestone in the globalization of intellectual property rights.[149] Amidst Japan's opposition to treaty harmonization, the conference witnessed a demand from the French and Brazilian delegations to unite the countries of the Berne Convention with the North and South American states that maintained their own convention, known as the Pan-American Convention. Except for Brazil, none of the countries in the Americas was a member of the Berne Convention. The idea to unite both conventions was developed further during the 1930s and was brought to a conclusion after World War II with the creation of the Universal Copyright Convention in 1952.[150]

Furthermore, the relationships and institutions established during the 1920s would not just vanish as Japan drifted into ultranationalism in the 1930s, but would continue to play a vital role, functioning as a basis for further cooperation. The latter is especially important as prior research on the media and state relationship from the late 1920s through the 1930s tended to focus on the undeniable growing suppression and censorship regulations. However, these works ignore that there were also areas of mutual interest, like international copyright, through which the cooperation between state and private industry actors actually increased and expanded.[151]

Thus, while Japan's internationalists contributed during the 1920s to processes of globalization by their active participation in the League's various globally interconnected initiatives, they also contributed to stirring up new differences, here in the area of international copyright, within the international community. This example shows how nuanced the situation of the interwar years was, and that it may be misleading to portray the 1920s in stark contrast to the 1930s. As the next chapter will demonstrate, the overall political and economic crisis of the 1930s that also affected international copyright negotiations, especially the relationship between Japan and other member states of the Berne Union, can only be understood as a continuation of developments and activities by a group of closely connected actors that had begun to take its course decades earlier.

CHAPTER 4
EXPANDING GLOBAL VISIBILITY
Japanese Copyright Experts and the State During the 1930s Copyright Negotiations

During the 1930s international cooperation initially expanded, resulting from the many national and international committees and institutions being involved in intellectual cooperation that had only been established in the latter half of the 1920s or during the early 1930s, and since then had not sufficiently developed their communication networks. The majority of their respective international activities thus only began to flourish in the new decade. The Paris Institute, for example, which had been struggling with its communication networks since the time of its founding, did not introduce a plan in which it defined its clear outline and aims until 1930, whereupon the communication structures between the institution and other committees greatly improved.[1] As part of the restructuring, in 1930 the ICIC Subcommittee on Intellectual Property Rights was dissolved and the responsibility for copyrights was completely handed over to the Legal Section of the Paris Institute.

The Japanese publishing industry towards and during the 1930s was increasingly state controlled which was the result of the political tensions starting with the "March 15 Incident" in 1928, the "Manchurian Incident" in 1931 which led to Japan's withdrawal from the League of Nations in 1933, the two attempted coups d'état by students of the Imperial Japanese Navy and the Imperial Japanese Army in 1932 and 1936 which became known as the "May 15 Incident," and the "February 26 Incident," as well as the outbreak of the Sino-Japanese War in July 1937. Furthermore, from 1937, the number of books issued decreased due to the outbreak of the war which was causing paper prices to increase and coal supply to the publishing houses to decrease.[2] In 1940, the existing publishers' associations were dissolved and the Japan Publishing Culture Association (Nihon Shuppan Bunka Kyōkai) and the Japan Publishing Distribution Company (Nihon Shuppan Haikyū Kabushiki Kaisha) were established as part of the "New Order" (*shin-taisei*) to centralize and control both publishing and distribution activities under what by then had become a militarist state. Publications that did not conform to the New Order doctrine were censored and prohibited from being published. This situation compelled writers and publishers to either align their work with the state's ideology or withdraw from the cultural scene. From 1940 onwards the suppression of the industry was simultaneously exercised through several governmental organs, including the Home Ministry's Police Affairs Bureau, the military, and the Ministry of Education.[3]

Despite these developments, the 1930s witnessed a general expansion of internationalist activities and global visibility among a small circle of Japanese state and non-state actors dedicated to preserving Japan's special conditions in international copyright law. This phenomenon mirrored the global growth of transnational networks and increased cooperation at a non-state level. This was facilitated by the fact that institutions for cultural cooperation, such as the ICIC or the Paris Institute, had only improved their programs by the late 1920s and early 1930s, developing specific schemes regarding their aims and how to achieve them.[4] Fearing isolation and being left behind in the ongoing debates surrounding international copyright protection, Japanese ministerial bureaucrats responded by intensifying their cooperation with private industry and copyright scholars. This collaboration led to the establishment of new and improved copyright advisory councils, linking political, industrial, media, and academic spheres in an official "intermediate zone" for policymaking in this area.[5]

Expanding on the previous chapters that showed the beginnings and development of personal relationships between publishers, ministerial bureaucrats, and legal scholars, this chapter demonstrates how these networks continued to flourish and that parallel to the growing military suppression of the 1930s, there also existed networks of interdependence between the state and society: strong relationships that shared a common interest and were built on mutual trust but were also still largely closed off from the general public.

These actors, many of whom belonged to the same generation and had experience studying or living abroad, were united in their interest in international cooperation and cultural exchange, as well as their objective of securing advantages for the nation. With alternative avenues like the League of Nations becoming increasingly inaccessible, these actors turned to the international revision conferences of the Berne Convention to assert their demands. Their objectives extended beyond copyright matters; they also sought to justify imperial expansionism under the banner of a redefined internationalism. The activities of this group of "copyright internationalists" continued to exert influence on international copyright negotiations until well into 1939, persisting even after other communication channels connecting the Japanese state to Europe's multilateral organizations had long been severed.

INTENSIFYING CULTURAL COOPERATION VERSUS INTERNATIONAL ISOLATION

The 1928 revision conference of the Berne Convention and its subsequent process of ratification can be seen as a turning point that brought not only the different intellectual workers closer together, but also created new platforms of cooperation for the private cultural organizations and the ministerial bureaucrats. Despite the absence of Japanese private interest organizations from the conference, their standpoint had been made clear to the foreign representatives involved through the delegates Akagi Tomoharu and Matsuda Michikazu. The disagreements that remained between Japan and the other member states at the end of the conference needed to be approached internationally, ideally before the treaty was ratified. Several publishing representatives from Europe therefore decided to follow a strategy of rapprochement with those at the core of Japan's opposition: the publishing industry.

About one year after the 1928 conference, in March 1929, the French ambassador to Japan contacted Foreign Minister Tanaka Giichi, notifying him that the French authors' association, Société des Gens de Lettres, intended to invite Japanese literary societies to participate in their next congress. The congress was scheduled to take place in Paris in May of the same year, aiming to discuss topics like a standard publishing contract, the results of the Berne Convention revision conference, and the potential establishment of an International Federation of Societies of Literature.[6] In 1930, Japan was again contacted in this matter, this time by the Association Littéraire et Artistique Internationale (ALAI) as the representative of various authors't and publishers' associations. Uncertain as to whom to approach regarding the inquiry on whether Japan would be interested in organizing and hosting the next ALAI congress on international copyrights in Tōkyō, the ALAI had first contacted the Paris Institute with the request to provide them with an intermediary. As correspondence letters show, those involved at the Paris Institute were themselves uncertain of the correct procedures and approached the ICIC in Geneva for advice which recommended contacting Aoki Setsu'ichi, one of the chief correspondents at the Tōkyō branch office of the League of Nations.[7] In a letter from October 10, 1930, Raymond Weiss of the Legal Section at the Paris Institute responded to his colleague at the ICIC in Geneva with the information that he had discussed the matter with Aoki. The latter had confirmed his interest in the plan and offered to speak with the Under-Secretary at the League of Nations, Sugimura Yōtarō, during his upcoming visit to Geneva. Weiss further asked the ICIC to let Sugimura know in advance of the importance of the activities of the ALAI, also in collaboration with the work of the Paris Institute.[8]

Meanwhile ALAI's suggestion to have Japan host the next international conference was passed on from the Paris-based assistant director of the Japan Office of the League of Nations, Itō Nobufumi, to the Treaty Department of the Ministry of Foreign Affairs.[9] A few months later, in February 1931, the Ministry of Foreign Affairs received the official request from the director of ALAI, Georges Maillard. In an interview given to the *Tōkyō asahi shinbun*, the head of the Book Division inside the Police Affairs Bureau, then led by Mishima Seiya, shared with the public that the Japanese government agreed with ALAI and would be willing to host the conference in Japan. By hosting the prestigious conference, government officials hoped to increase their international recognition in the publishing sector. However, according to Mishima, state representatives could not make this decision on their own; it would be necessary to sit down with members of the publishing industry and discuss this matter together. For that reason, the Home Ministry contacted the Tōkyō Publishers' Association to arrange a meeting which was organized on February 23, 1931, and brought together representatives from fifteen different cultural organizations, including Fujita Tomoharu for the Publishers' Association, with officials of the Ministry of Foreign Affairs, and—most likely for the logistics involved in hosting an international conference—the Ministry of Railways. The constellation of actors involved was like the one that had come together to prepare the latest revision conference a few years earlier. Together with six other representative authors, composers, filmmakers and artists, Fujita was selected to form a committee that would oversee preparing the ALAI conference and welcoming the foreign guests. The outcome of the meeting was a joint agreement among the attendees to respond to the request made by ALAI with the affirmative decision to hold the conference.[10] Although the publishers, translators, and authors involved were not in direct contact with ALAI, the ICIC, or the Paris Institute, their cooperation with ministerial bureaucrats heavily influenced the planning of the conference and the development of the program over the following months.

From the bureaucrats, Kobayashi Hiroji of the Police Affairs Bureau joined the efforts of his colleagues in coming together with the private organizations and discussing the hosting of the international copyright conference. Since entering the Police Affairs Bureau in 1927, Kobayashi had already established a closer contact with the members of the Tōkyō Publishers' Association in matters related to the publishers' ongoing desire to change the domestic Copyright Law and include a regulation on publishing rights which would bind the author of a work to a publisher by contract, thereby granting the publisher the monopoly on the published work. After the 1928 conference in Rome, preparations for the treaty's ratification and the simultaneous amendment to the Copyright Law began. In the planned revision of the domestic law in connection with incorporating the revised Berne Convention, the Japanese publishers saw the perfect opportunity to work toward advancing their own rights as publishers by introducing a separate provision on publishing rights to include in the existing law.[11] Kobayashi was put in charge of handling the publishers' requests, and, through his participation in the ALAI preparations, strengthened his close cooperation with the publishers even further.[12]

ALAI President Georges Maillard assisted the preparations by sharing information on previously held conferences, ALAI members, and the organization's bulletin with Itō Nobufumi at the Japan Bureau in Paris who then passed the information on to the Japanese Ministry of Foreign Affairs.[13] The Japanese government treated the ALAI conference in connection with the ratification and revision process of the Berne Convention.

Ultimately, the efforts for the preparation of the conference remained unrewarded. Despite the attempted persuasion on the part of the European publishing industry for Japan to give up its reservations on translation rights, the Japanese government ratified the Berne Convention in June 1931 with the same exemptions on translations. Furthermore, Maillard informed Itō at the League of Nations Japan Office on several occasions over the following months that the ALAI conference in Japan had to be postponed for "economic reasons," first from 1931 to 1932 and again from 1932 to 1933 whereupon the correspondence regarding the conference came to a stop.[14] Even though it can be assumed that the lack of funding also played a role in the earlier postponements of the conference, it is likely that the indefinite postponement came as a result of the "Manchurian Incident" and Japan's decision to leave the League of Nations in 1933 which subsequently led to the reaction by European publishers and authors to officially distance themselves from Japan.

The relationship between the League of Nations Association of Japan and the League of Nations had begun to worsen from the end of September 1931 because of the Association's silence regarding Japan's military expansion into Manchuria following the "Manchurian Incident" in 1931. On the night of September 18, 1931, the Japanese Kwantung Army (Kantō-gun) staged a dynamite attack on the Manchurian railroad outside Mukden. Even though the explosion did not cause great damage to the Japanese-controlled South Manchurian Railway, it was used as an excuse to invade Manchuria where the Army felt its position increasingly threatened by the progress of Chinese nationalist leader Chiang Kai-shek in the unification of China. Following this "Incident" and against severe criticism by many of the League's member states, in 1932 the Japanese army established the puppet state Manchukuo (Manshūkoku[15]) as part of the empire of Japan. While some states including Germany, Italy, and the Soviet Union recognized the new state, none of the major powers supported the invasion. The Lytton Report by the League of Nation's Lytton Commission, which was to investigate the causes of the "Incident," concluded in 1932 that Japan had wrongfully invaded Manchuria and that the puppet state should not be recognized by the international community. This recommendation led to Japan's withdrawal from the League of Nations in March 1933.[16]

However, despite the withdrawal and likely out of fear of being internationally isolated, Japanese organizations and committees closely connected with the League of Nations continued and, in some cases, even intensified their activities. The League of Nations Association of Japan also remained active and continued to pursue the same activities as before, only under the different name of Japan International Association (Nihon Kokusai Kyōkai). The change of name was implemented to ensure the continued receipt of financial aid from the Ministry of Foreign Affairs. Although the Association officially shifted its aim to the promotion of international cooperation and contribution to international peace, its activities largely remained the same.[17] The Association also remained inside the International Federation of League of Nations Societies and continued its close relationship with the other member states until the beginning of the Sino-Japanese War in 1937 by which point the members of the Federation demanded an exclusion of Japan from the Federation.[18]

With reference to the effects that the withdrawal from the League of Nations had on Japan's National Committee on Intellectual Cooperation led by Yamada Saburō, international networks and regular correspondence with the ICIC and the Paris Institute were expanded and strengthened rather than diminished. But corresponding to the general upheavals that followed the "Manchurian Incident," such as the decline of party politics, Japan leaving the League of Nations, and the gradual shift towards militarism, the government came increasingly to disregard the autonomy of the National Committee and aimed to increase its own influence in the field of international cultural exchange. The creation of an organization to focus solely on the introduction of Japanese culture abroad was considered especially important now that Japan had left the League of Nations.[19] As a result, on April 11, 1934, a new cultural body under the name of Society for International Cultural Relations (Kokusai Bunka Shinkōkai, henceforth KBS) was created by the Ministry of Foreign Affairs in collaboration with Japan's National Committee on Intellectual Cooperation and the Department of Cultural Affairs in the Ministry of Foreign Affairs.

Inspired by the cultural institutions across Western Europe, preparations for the creation of a larger cultural organ had already been taken up in June 1933, within only three months of Japan having left the League of Nations. The planning team that came together in December 1933 at the Minister of Foreign Affairs' invitation included eleven members from the cultural sector, among them the above-mentioned director of the publishing house Hakubunkan Ōhashi Shintarō, professor of Japanese literature and religion Anesaki Masaharu, who had also been among the founding members of Japan's National Committee, and legal expert Yamada Saburō. The aim of the new institution was to promote and effectively export Japanese culture abroad with the support of and through the cooperation between members of the state and private actors and in line with the activities of the Department of Cultural Exchange and the National Committee on Intellectual Cooperation which acted as its parent body. However, the KBS followed a course different to that of the National Committee, starting with the fact that it did not aim to be primarily private in character and included many high governmental officials and politicians on its board of directors. Furthermore, the KBS was less concerned with global rather than with bilateral cooperation which came because of the Japanese government's opposing attitude toward the multilateral frameworks of the League of Nations following the League's interventions in Japan's China policies.[20] To improve the communication with foreign countries, the KBS also set up several offices abroad starting with a bureau in Paris that was located inside the Paris Institute, as well as bureaus in Berlin, New York, and Buenos Aires, and later expanded to Geneva, Rome, and Melbourne.[21] The composition of members was like the National Committee— for example, Yamada Saburō, chairman of the National Committee, was also a member of the board of directors of the newly established KBS.[22]

The events surrounding the "Manchurian Incident" and the withdrawal from the League of Nations were important factors in the Japanese government's persistence during the 1930s to continue supporting the publishing industry, and in its efforts to strengthen its participation in the League's international copyright negotiations. These actions can only be understood in connection with the government's fear of loss of control following the withdrawal, with its attempt to mend international relations, and the need to justify its military actions on the continent.

Even though the initiative of ALAI in cooperation with the ICIC and the Paris Institute to have Japan host the next international copyright conference had not led to any direct results, it did raise awareness among those engaged in the publishing and media industry of the importance of having their own organ, in a way a Japanese version of the ALAI, that united the will of the publishers, artists, writers, composers, and filmmakers in the area of international copyright protection.[23] The idea of founding an association to serve as a platform for discussion and to represent the Japanese position in questions related to international copyright became even more relevant in light of a sequence of events that occurred simultaneously with the preparations for the ALAI conference and became known as "Whirlwind Plage" (*Purāge senpū*).[24]

The name Plage referred to the German Dr. Heinrich Max Wilhelm Plage, a trained lawyer who in 1931 took up his work as an agent for the Bureau Internationale de l'Edition Mécanique (the international organization representing mechanical rights societies) and for the Cartel des Sociétés d'Auteurs de Perceptions non Théatrales (Cartel of Non-Theatrical Authors' Societies), both of which represented several musical rights' societies in France, the UK, Germany,

Italy, and Austria.²⁵ The European societies' claim for the remuneration of works was directly related to the outcome of the 1928 revision of the Berne Convention which had abolished, for Japan as well, the reservations regarding the right to stage public performances of musical works, and of the introduction of performance and broadcasting rights.²⁶ Under the revised and subsequently ratified (in 1931) Berne Convention, radio broadcasters were now obliged to pay royalties to the foreign copyright holders for public performances and radio broadcasting of musical works. As communication with Europe was still slow at the time, the Japan Broadcasting Society (Nippon Hōsō Kyōkai, NHK) continued their unauthorized broadcasting of European music until in July 1932 the broadcaster received a visit by Plage who had been registering the violations since the enactment of the revised Berne Convention in 1931. Japan's music industry had to pay high sums in remuneration which ultimately led to an amendment of the Copyright Law in May 1934. As a direct reaction to Plage, the first amendment stated that if the foreign author had no legal representative in Japan, remuneration was to be paid "in form of a legal license as specified by cabinet order."²⁷ This regulation disqualified Plage as a legal representative of European music authors and enabled Japanese performers to pay less remuneration. The other amendment gave broadcasters the right to freely play musical works without paying royalties to the copyright holder, which violated parts of the Berne Convention.²⁸ During the same 1934 revision, a new paragraph on publishing rights was added to the Copyright Law to regulate the contractual relationship between publishers and authors. Ōkura Yasugorō, Fujita Tomoharu, and others had been demanding this amendment to the law since the mid-1920s, but although the National Diet had already placed the topic on its agenda in 1927, it was not until it was taken up again in 1933 that the desired provision was decided in parliament.²⁹

Plage's activities, however, not only affected the broadcasting and music industry. He began also to uncover literary copyright violations, especially in the field of translations where until his appearance, still many cases of violation occurred.³⁰ In August 1933, the renowned translator Horiguchi Daigaku, son of ministerial bureaucrat Horiguchi Kuma'ichi who had officially represented Japan during the 1908 Berne Convention revision conference in Berlin, expressed his opinion on the "Whirlwind Affair" in a three-part article that appeared in the *Tōkyō asahi shinbun* between August 15-17. Horiguchi explained in detail the importance of translations of Western European works for the intellectual life of the Japanese and the, allegedly, impossible conditions under which Japanese translators had to work if they followed the conditions of the Berne Convention. He argued that translations were not profitable, but greatly contributed to internationalism by bringing different cultures closer together. He concluded his essay by stating: "Japan has *even* managed to leave the League of Nations. Not even a major power like the United

States has entered the Berne Convention, so Japan should leave the Convention as soon as possible."³¹

In October, Horiguchi received a direct response to his article by the Ministry of Foreign Affairs bureaucrat Satō Junzō, the secretary to Japan's National Committee on Intellectual Cooperation, who also composed a two-part article for the *Tōkyō asahi shinbun*. In his article, which was published on October 17 and 18, 1933, Satō criticized the fact that until then no real effort had been made to improve the cooperation between "the state and the people" to tackle the problem of translation rights together.³² He emphasized that the cooperation between the state and the private sector in this matter should be a priority now. Seeing that publishers and translators in Europe were actively involved in the copyright revision procedures, Satō's motivation can be read as a response to the perceived need to unite Japan for a stronger negotiating position. In addition, the state officials likely wanted to control the formation of transnational non-governmental networks that might have led to a loss of control on the side of the state. Satō informed the readers that while in Europe preparations for the next revision conference had already been taken up, Japan's efforts were still insufficient.

And indeed, until then, the Japanese government had once again not reacted to several recent notifications it had received from Europe regarding another planned revision of the international copyright agreement. On August 31 that year, Foreign Minister Uchida Kōsai received a letter from the Belgian Embassy, informing him of a special commission which had taken up the work to prepare the next diplomatic conference for the revision of the Berne Convention to be held in Brussels in 1935.³³ The reason for the newest revision plans was an envisioned unification of the Berne Convention with the copyright treaties of the Pan-American Convention, last revised in Havana in 1928. The need for a merge of the two conventions had been decided at the previous revision conference in Rome upon the realization that at a time where technical developments and new inventions like radio transmission and the broadcasting of music brought the intellectual output of the world ever closer together, it became increasingly challenging to have two systems existing at the same time. The main difference between the two conventions lay in their procedures: While the Berne Convention automatically protected its members without any formalities, the Pan-American Convention only guaranteed protection after the formal registration of the respective works.³⁴ At the request of the Pan-American Union, two organizations whose task was the study of international law, namely, the American Institute of International Law and the International Institute at Rome for the Unification of Private Law (Rome Institute), undertook a comparative study of the Berne and the Havana Conventions.³⁵ The latter institution had been established in 1926 as an intergovernmental organization by the League of Nations. According to the Belgian ambassador's message to Uchida, the commission also ascribed importance to the stance of the Japanese government and asked for a reply in this regard.[36] However, almost two months later, in October 1933, the Japanese government had still not officially replied to the inquiry.

In his article, Satō also mentioned Horiguchi Daigaku's demand to leave the Convention altogether but advised Japan to think of the future and the possible export as well as translations of Japanese works into foreign languages before taking such a step. According to Satō, the problem was more complex than portrayed by Horiguchi which is why Satō pleaded to study the matter in close detail to find an appropriate solution to the difficult situation of the publishers and translators in Japan.[37]

Two days after the publication of the latter part of the article, the Belgian government repeated its request to the Japanese government in another letter with similar content to the one sent before. This time the letter was addressed to Hirota Kōki, who had been appointed as Foreign Minister after a change of cabinet in September 1933.[38]

THE ESTABLISHMENT OF COPYRIGHT ADVISORY COUNCILS

In early 1934 the Japanese government reacted to the repeated inquiries from Europe by announcing its plan to establish a committee that was to undertake research and clarify any open questions on matters related to copyrights. The events that had led to this reaction included the initiative of the ALAI wanting Japan to host their next copyright conference, the increase in copyright violations followed by the "Whirlwind Plage," an internal debate involving translator Horiguchi Daigaku and Satō Junzō concerning how Japan should position itself at the next revision conference, and lastly, the notifications from Europe inquiring about Japan's opinion on the upcoming conference. The new committee was to serve as a forum for discussions between both private actors from the involved cultural organizations and state bureaucrats. Among the main points of concern was the upcoming Berne Convention revision conference and, as had been the case at previous conferences, the feeling of being discriminated and treated unfairly by the Berne system.[39]

However, before any concrete action was taken, in July 1934 the director of the Berne Bureau, Fritz Ostertag, addressed the member states of the Convention with the remark that the planned conference might have to be postponed until 1936, even though a final decision had not yet been made. At that moment, Ostertag asked the individual states to hand in any observations or propositions they might have by January 1935.[40] In September 1934, the notification by the Belgian embassy that the conference had officially been postponed to the year 1936 reached Foreign Minister Hirota. The reason given for the postponement was that the Rome Act had still not been ratified by several member states. Accordingly, the deadlines for the submission of written opinions were also postponed.[41]

The imperial edict for the establishment of a first mutual research committee was drafted in April 1935. According to the original draft, members were to be selected according to their expertise in the respective arts and were to include from the side of the copyright owners four writers, three musicians, two performing artists, and two scholars, as well as from the consumer-side of copyright two publishers and two industrial promoters of the industries, one record manufacturer, and one expert from the broadcasting industry. Furthermore, the committee was to include five experts in the field of copyright protection and three bureaucrats working in copyrights. Even though translators were among those mainly affected by the international debate, they were not listed individually.[42]

The members of the personnel were announced in mid-July, shortly before the committee was officially established on July 15, 1935, the same day that the revised Copyright Law of 1934 came into force. Besides Home Minister Gotō Fumio who was the selected chairman of the committee, the 28 appointed members included Home Ministry bureaucrats Mizuno Rentarō who had resigned from the political party Rikken Seiyūkai in May and thereafter joined the Cabinet Deliberation Council (Naikaku Shingikai) to advise the Okada Keisuke Cabinet, Akagi Tomoharu who had represented Japan at the previous conference in Rome and now held the position of Vice-Minister for Internal Affairs, Kobayashi Hiroji who had previously been in charge of copyrights in the Home Ministry, publisher Meguro Jinshichi as representative of the Tōkyō Publishers' Association, Masuda Giichi, the leader of the publishing house Jitsugyō no Nihon Sha, as representative of the Japan Magazine Association, as well as Kikuchi Hiroshi, the author and founder of Bungeishunjū publishing company and better known by his pen name Kikuchi Kan.[43] Publisher Masuda Giichi had maintained close ties with the ministries ever since he became a member of the House of Representatives in 1912. Since 1932 he had been holding the office as Vice-Speaker of the House.[44]

The committee's tasks were to provide advice to the Home Minister in questions related to copyright and to study the possible negative effects on Japan of the revision draft for the upcoming international copyright conference. While the latest point was picked up by the country's newspapers, and was openly criticized by several of them, the initial reason for forming the copyright body, which included the consultations and means of exchange with private experts in preparing the international copyright conference, remained largely without comment by the press.[45]

The reaction of the newspapers to the establishment of the advisory council which was referred to as "Copyright Investigation Council" (Chosakuken Shinsakai) turned out everything but positive. The media failed to recognize that one of the main reasons for the establishment of the council was to keep Japan actively engaged, well-informed, and prepared during the multilateral negotiations concerning the Berne Convention. Looking at the political developments of the time, government suppression of left-wing movements had been increasing ever since the 1928 crackdown on Japanese socialists and communists, known as the "March 15 Incident", and continued throughout the 1930s. Censorship and publishing prohibitions for left-wing art and literature were followed up and imposed rigorously, and it was from around the time of the establishment of this Copyright Investigation Council in the mid-1930s that writers, artists, and demands were made of other members engaged in the media industries to place their talents at the service of the state.[46] Home Ministry bureaucrat and House of Peers member Matsumoto Gaku, who was head of the Police Affairs Bureau between 1932 and 1934, for example, was actively engaged in setting up cultural discussion forums and mutual platforms of exchange to unite state and private industry actors with the aim of promoting the interests of the state and unite Japan's industry in the "Japanese spirit" (*Nihon seishin*) to reflect in their works upon the "peculiarity" (*tokuyūsei*) of being Japanese.[47] This was one of the factors contributing to mass conversions away from Marxism and an increase in nationalist art and literature.[48] The tension and anxiety caused by the increasing cultural control was reflected in the headlines surrounding the establishment of the Copyright Investigation Council. The news articles commented on the formation of the council with statements like "this is a first step towards having a state organ for art and literature which includes the authority of the entire industry—from next spring they will sit inside the Home Ministry," or "next it is planned to control art and literature straight from the Home Ministry."[49] The *Tōkyō asahi shinbun* introduced the new committee with the words: "(…) the highest organ for cultural guidance that followed the plan to improve the control of culture [*bunka no tōsei*] which is why the selection of private committee members was attracting a great deal of attention."[50]

In their following coverage the newspaper continued to use expressions like *bungei tōsei* (control of the arts and literature) to describe the nature of the committee.[51] The *Yomiuri shinbun* made similar comments, speculating that this was "the first concrete step towards the control of the arts [geijutsu tōsei]."[52] The *Japan Times* headline read "Home Minister Aims to Foster National Spirit—Committee Composed of Art Leaders to Aid Move in Respective Fields."[53] The *Tōkyō nichi nichi shinbun* was cited with the following words:

> The plan of the Home Office to appoint a copyright committee has been realized. It is true that fine arts and literary accomplishments need Government protection. But to carry such protection to extremes would only result in checking their development.[54]

The *Chūgai shinbun* also had its doubts about the formation:

> The Government has appointed a special committee for protection of copyright so as to facilitate cultural development of the country. This is certainly a worthy project and its success must be heartily desired. Such an attempt on the part of the Government, however, must be warned against degenerating into undue control.[55]

In an article on Mizuno Rentarō's contribution to the advisory council published in the magazine *Kopiraito* in 1973, Itō Nobuo, trained lawyer and professor at the Faculty of Law at Nihon University, addressed the strong concern of the media with the selection of personnel at the time, which, according to Itō, was most probably a result of the recent international tumults of the early 1930s including Japan's and Germany's withdrawal from the League of Nations, the cultural control in National Socialist Germany, and the recent growing control and suppression of the media in Japan.

In addition to the negative newspaper headlines that followed the establishment of the Copyright Investigation Council, a number of reviews, editorials, and opinion pieces also criticized the committee as the beginning of a systematic state-controlled suppression of culture in line with the way it was suppressed in National Socialist Germany.[56] What none of the press articles mentioned, however, was that the close cooperation and consultation between the publishers, academic copyright experts, and the state actors involved had existed for many years before the official establishment of the council. The fact that most of the consultations between publishers and bureaucrats during the previous decades took place behind closed doors and were thus uncommented upon by the media, most probably contributed to the prevailing perception, including the media's, of the mid-1930s as the point in time where the Japanese state started to take stricter controls.

The Japanese media thus failed to recognize the existing ties and the dependency of state actors on the expertise of members of the private industry. Publishers and translators had their own interests in these councils, investing their time and energy for personal benefits or the interests of their private groups. The media also overlooked the continuity of cooperation in connection with the preparations for the Berne Convention revision conference, which, as it turned out, was the main reason behind the establishment of the council.

The Copyright Investigation Council held its first meeting on July 26, 1935, two weeks after its official establishment. The meeting, which took place at the Home Ministry, lasted only 10 minutes and was attended by all of its members. Home Minister Gotō Fumio gave a brief opening remark, in which he explained the importance of the committee in consulting him in any matters related to copyrights, including in the areas of publishing and broadcasting. Gotō furthermore stressed that the committee should not only deal with questions of national interest, but also with matters of international concern especially regarding the upcoming international copyright revision conference in Brussels.[57]

While the media was largely critical of the new Copyright Investigation Council, many of those directly affected by the debate were hoping that the committee would bring a fast solution to the ongoing copyright issues and clearly position Japan in the international negotiations on copyright and translation right protection. The difference in perception of the new organ can be clearly seen in an article by French literary scholar and translator Kusano Teishi who published three articles on the topic of Japan's special reservations on translation rights in the *Tōkyō asahi shinbun* in December 1935. In the articles, he discussed amongst other things the option of leaving the Berne Convention by sharing his personal thoughts on the matter:

> The Home Ministry will introduce the proposal of Japan at the Brussels Conference next year. If the proposal should be rejected, there is a chance that Japan might leave the Convention. (…) If [the translator is] convinced that the translation will not harm the original author and copyright holder, and convinced of its contribution to culture, then there is also the option of boldly [without permission] making the decision to translate.[58]

He, however, added that the Home Ministry had warned about taking these "drastic actions" and had recommended "waiting for the investigation consultations of the Copyright Investigation Council to assess and rationalize the translation-related matters at hand."[59] This, according to Kusano, was "probably the only way to come to a reasonable conclusion concerning the use of the reservations on translation rights."[60] Kusano Teishi's article shows that affected actors did not necessarily share the press views of the time that described the new research board as an "organ of control," but rather put their hope in the research conducted by the committee and its involved private interest members. The latter was most likely a higher priority for them than maintaining art and culture independence, as membership in the council offered the opportunity to avoid the loss of revenues.

In January 1936 Foreign Minister Hirota Kōki was informed by the Belgian embassy of the new date set for the revision conference which was now to take place on September 7, 1936. In November 1935 and February 1936, the Berne Bureau had published two brochures, one being a list of requests that were handed in at a number of congresses and assemblies between 1927 and 1935, and the other one on the propositions, counterpropositions and observations on the Brussels Revision Conference that had been submitted by a number of member states. Japan had so far not handed in a written opinion and was therefore not featured in the booklet.[61] The head of the Police Affairs Bureau informed the Ministry of Foreign Affairs of the receipt of the brochures in early March 1936 and in view of the rapidly approaching conference urgently requested a number of departments from different ministries (including the Ministry of Justice, the Ministry of Education, the Ministry of Commerce and Industry, the Ministry of Communicationst and Transportation and the Ministry of Colonial Affairs) to assist in the translation of the two pamphlets. He stressed the importance of a quick completion of the translations, regardless of whether some mistakes were made or some parts were missing, as these could be fixed at a later point.[62] The translations were done in May which meant that the preparations for the next stage could begin. On May 12 the newspaper *Yomiuri shinbun* reported that the Copyright Investigation Council was beginning its work and starting to prepare for the international conference. According to the article, the Home Ministry was planning to have a week-long conference in the latter half of the month during which the representatives of the different ministries and the members of the Council would together discuss the measures they intended to take. The planned meeting would be the first official convention of the Council at which the core of the entire cultural field would be represented.[63]

As announced, on May 25, 1936, the Home Ministry invited publishers and other representatives of the industries to the Ministry to share and discuss the revision proposal. Due to a change in personnel, the Japan Magazine Association was now led by the founder and director of the publishing company Kōdansha, Noma Seiji. Instead of Meguro Jinshichi, the Tōkyō Publishers' Association was now represented by new leader Egusa Shigetada who had replaced the retired Meguro the same year.[64] Egusa, by then head of the publishing house Yūhikaku, was no stranger to the bureaucrats. Together with Ōkura Yasugorō, he had been among the publishers' representatives invited to consult Home Minister Suzuki Kisaburō prior to the Rome Revision Conference in 1928.[65]

Preserved sources from Egusa Shigetada's life and work are exceedingly scarce which makes it difficult to reconstruct an entire picture of his aspirations as a publisher who, by the late 1930s, led the most important publishing association and was among the main collaborators with the state around the time of the centralization of the publishing industry a few years later.[66] The few surviving pieces of writing suggest that Egusa, just like his forerunners Oyaizu and Ōkura as leaders of the large publishing associations, was both an advocate of internationalism and a devoted nationalist whose initial aim as a publisher and leader of the industry was to contribute to the development of the Japanese nation.

Egusa's publishing house Yūhikaku was specialized in the publication of reference works on law and was renowned for being the main publishing house of the scholars of the Tōkyō Imperial University's influential Faculty of Law. Egusa quickly acquainted himself with the current discussions in the field of law, especially regarding the international copyright agreement, as it affected himself as a publisher. Under his leadership, primarily works on civil law and on commercial law were published.[67] In 1925, he wrote an article for the newspaper *Yomiuri shinbun*, stating his two main wishes as being "to globalize the publishing market" and "to publish the entire Japanese History of Law."[68] He wrote:

> Having a special national language does not help in publishing worldwide, so from now on and with the goal to make the world one's partner, we have to consciously use Esperanto and English. The publishing world as well should embark on the world stage by using the common language.[69]

Egusa's enthusiasm for Esperanto underlines his global state of mind. The Japanese Esperanto movement gained popularity after the Russo-Japanese War (1904-1905) and united its supporters in their belief of a nonhierarchic world order, a "transnational and translocal circulation of ideas and culture," also referred to as "worldism" by historian Sho Konishi.[70] Egusa's liberal attitude also reflected upon his leadership of the Tōkyō Publishers' Association which apparently was a lot more "free" (*jiyū*) than it had been under Meguro.[71] He passed his eagerness to internationalize the Japanese publishing industry on to his son-in-law, Egusa Shirō, who joined Yūhikaku in 1929 for which had given up a promising career as a bureaucrat in the Home Ministry's Department for Social Affairs.[72] Egusa Shirō would become a dominant actor in the postwar copyright negotiations.

When in late May 1936 the publishers received the invitation from the Home Ministry to discuss the revision proposal, they reacted within two days by setting up a special committee between the three large publishers associations to examine the proposal.[73] While drafting an opinion piece, the publishers were informed of a notification that Foreign Minister Arita Hachirō had received from the Belgian ambassador, informing him that the conference had been postponed again, this time indefinitely. A reason for the postponement was not included in the writing.[74] For the Copyright Investigation Council, this information meant that their aim, to prepare Japan's proposal for the revision conference, had become obsolete, and the committee would not gather again for the next two years. Nevertheless, their results were still handed back to the Home Ministry on June 6, 1936.

The fact that the Copyright Investigation Council remained inactive during this time of constant postponement shows how essential a factor the international collaboration was for the committee's actual work. Even though portrayed differently by the media at the time of its establishment, the main task of the committee was not to tighten state control over those engaged in culture. It had been created as a platform for the state to officially receive consultation and advice from the experts from the industries, but also to represent Japan on the international stage with a single united voice which would strengthen its position. Most importantly, this sort of cooperation was not new. In fact, the only difference to the procedures for the consultation of bureaucrats that had taken place prior to that, especially during the preparations of the Rome Revision Conference, was that the platform of exchange had now been given an official name.

Despite being portrayed by the government as a council that was democratizing administration and pluralizing the participation of Japanese citizens in government policymaking, sources reveal how little information on the work of the committee actually trickled through to the general public. The consultations between the Home Ministry and selected elite members of the industry for the most part took place behind closed doors and were therefore not even in the focus of the media. A few writers criticized this limitation of shared information about the Council. Regarding the urgent question of how to deal with translations of foreign literature, in December 1935 French literary scholar Kusano Teishi said he would recommend waiting for the results of the Copyright Investigation Council before taking any individual decisions, but that he could also see why translators continued to translate without permission, if they were convinced that they were not harming the original authors and copyright holders and convinced that by doing so, they would "contribute to Japanese culture."[75] Novelist Serizawa Kōjirō, by contrast, in July 1936 wrote an article for the literary magazine *Shinchō* (New Tide) criticizing the lack of transparency regarding the work of the committee. The intellectuals in his field would hear nothing about the state of affairs or any results of the ongoing investigations for preparing for the Berne Convention revision conference. This claim can be verified by the fact that Serizawa was not yet aware of the fact that the date of the conference had been postponed. According to him, the writers' community did not derive any advantage from the existence of the committee even though some renowned writers (including Kikuchi Kan and Inukai Takeru, of which the latter was simultaneously active as a politician in the Rikken Seiyūkai) had been appointed to the organ. Serizawa was further wondering about the tasks that the committee had been taking on over the past year.[76] His article shows how little informed about the internal procedures and activities of the committee he was as someone directly engaged in the publishing industry, but the public in general was even less informed. Serizawa's short essay reveals that even though there now existed an organ that brought together decision-makers and private individuals from different fields, this privilege remained the reserve of a small group of elites within the industry. However, looking at the numbers of publishers involved in the various associations, it becomes obvious why only a handful of people were included to directly engage in the policymaking process. In the case of the publishers, the Tōkyō Booksellers' Association articles of association read that the association's objective was "to connect the state with the people to promote the development of culture."[77] With membership numbers reaching over 3000 in the Booksellers' Association, and reaching over 350 in the Tōkyō Publishers' Association (and these numbers represented those involved in the industry in and around the city Tōkyō alone), it was no surprise that the elected board members of the big publishers' associations were the same actors that were called into policy-committees of the government.[78] They were the leaders of the industry with the longest experience working as publishers.

The disconnected nature of this small group of "elite publishers" from the masses and the decades of having developed a common grammar with the state actors involved likely played an important role in the following decade during the wartime collaboration with the large publishing houses Maruzen and Kōdansha, or with Egusa Shigetada, the liberal promoter of a more globalized publishing industry, as the first director of the state's central Japan Publishing Distribution Company established in 1941.

The Copyright Investigation Council was not the only new forum of exchange that was established in connection with the planned revision of the Berne Convention and the new awareness regarding foreign copyright protection which was brought to Japan by Wilhelm Plage during those years. Wilhelm Plage's copyright fraud inspections were not only aimed at the broadcasting and music industry, but also focused on unauthorized translations of European works. In many cases, publishers were still not concerned about getting an approval by the foreign copyright holders prior to translating the work.[79]

With an increasing number of accusations in the mid-1930s and the conference in Europe ahead, in July 1935 a group of translators around Horiguchi Daigaku organized the so-called Council for Translation Rights Matters (Hon'yakuken Mondai Kyōgikai). In collaboration with publishers who worked with foreign publications such as Kaizōsha's Yamamoto Sanehiko, the Tōkyō Publishers' Association represented by Meguro Jinshichi and Fujita Tomoharu, newspaper critics of foreign literature, the Japanese Pen Club, the Writers' Association, and the ministerial departments involved, the Ministry of Foreign Affairs and the Home Ministry, a first-time meeting, with over 80 attendees, was held on December 17, 1935 at a restaurant in Tōkyō. After a short introduction of the aims of the assembly, Kobayashi Hiroji as the head of the Police Affairs Bureau gave an explanation about the Brussels Revision Conference and about the revisions to the Berne Convention that had been made to date. The attendees thereafter got the opportunity to exchange their opinions. Also put up for discussion was whether it would be in Japan's interest to stay in the Convention altogether, a debate which was continued by the members of the industry, ministerial bureaucrats, and the Japanese media involved in the following months.[80]

With the notification regarding the new conference date for September in early 1936, the translators in charge of the Council for Translation Rights Matters gathered a number of publishers involved and on April 7, 1936, decided to change the convention's name to International Copyright Convention (Kokusai Chosakuken Kyōgikai) to also include non-translators concerned with the revision of the Berne Convention and international translation rights. A first meeting of the Copyright Convention took place on May 2 in the Marunouchi Tōyōkan and was well attended by renowned translators like Horiguchi Daigaku, Yamanouchi Yoshio, Miki Kiyoshi, and Honda Akira, as well as by around 30 publishers, bureaucrat Kobayashi Hiroji representing the Police Affairs Bureau, and Matsudaira Kōtō representing the Treaty Department in the Ministry of Foreign Affairs. After discussing the current situation of translators and publishers and the inclination of the respective ministerial departments regarding the meeting in Brussels, the attendees agreed on three points of action for the committee, which were, namely,

1) to hold research sessions and mutual consultations between bureaucrats and non-governmental actors including publishers, translators and experts of law
2) to choose a representative Japanese translator to attend the conference in Brussels
3) the production of a pamphlet on the situation of the Japanese translators for the members of the foreign states to consult.[81]

These points of action show that it was the translators *themselves* who chose to intensify cooperation with representatives of the state by holding mutual research sessions and consultations. With Kobayashi's imminent departure for Europe, the last point received priority.[82] While in the process of working on the pamphlet, in late May the committee received a phone call by the Police Affairs Bureau. Like the Copyright Investigation Council, translators and literary critics of the newly formed International Copyright Convention were invited to the Home Ministry on May 28 with the request to give their input on the proposals by the Berne Bureau. A few days later the notification of an indefinite postponement of the Brussels Revision Conference followed and the Convention, like the Council, lost its main raison d'être. Before its subsequent dissolution in October, in July the pamphlet that the organization had been working on was published and distributed.[83]

The pamphlet, composed entirely in French, was entitled "La Situation spéciale des Traducteurs et des Éditeurs au Japon" (The Special Situation of Translators and Publishers in Japan) and consisted of a number of different points of reasoning as to why the other countries should reconsider the application of international copyright norms as regards Japan. In light of the Japanese delegation leaving for Europe to attend the revision conference, members of the new Convention aimed to use this opportunity to explain to the other conference participants the circumstances surrounding the work of a translator and the general situation around foreign literature distribution in Japan. The actions they took reflect their role as "policy entrepreneurs". They leveraged extended private and professional networks to build a team (the International Copyright Convention), defined the problem, using the pamphlet medium for this purpose, and highlighted issues with the current copyright regulations.[84]

The pamphlet began by highlighting the fruitful intellectual exchange between the Soviet Union, China, and Japan. This was attributed to the absence of restrictions on translations from Russian or Chinese, as these two nations were not part of the Berne Convention. Interestingly, as shown in Chapter 2, this very same fact had before led to resentment among Japanese publishers and, in 1901 had caused Oyaizu Kaname to write petitions urging the government to put pressure on China to join the Convention.[85] As concerns the exchange of publications with the Soviet Union, the interaction was also not as "fruitful" as portrayed here, since books entering Japan from the Soviet Union had been among the main targets of harsh censorship regulations since the "March 15 Incident" in 1928. The following sections of the pamphlet pointed out the "conditions in particular" (les conditions tout particulièrement) regarding language, geography, history, and religion that Japanese translators were working under, as well as the high costs for translations. It further emphasized that a translation would give the reader access to the original which would have positive effects on the sales of the original. The last point argued that the "harmonious development of international cultural relations" would be delayed if there were no constant flow of intellectual exchange between Japan and other countries, as without this exchange, the ideas of the foreign nations would be poorly understood in Japan.[86]

At the beginning of 1937, Yamada Saburō forwarded the pamphlet to Raymond Weiss of the Paris Institute in the name of the Japanese National Committee.[87] Yamada and Weiss knew each other well with their first acquaintance dating back almost 40 years during Yamada's unofficial attendance of the 1900 copyright conference in Paris. Weiss thereafter passed the pamphlet on to ALAI's cultural representatives Georges Maillard and Marcel Boutet. He emphasized that it was not his intention to provide propaganda for the argument of the Japanese translators, he merely wanted to pass on new information regarding Japan's already well-known standpoint.[88]

THE PARIS COMMITTEE OF EXPERTS AND THE SECOND GENERAL MEETING OF THE NATIONAL COMMITTEES

The most recent postponement of the Brussels Revision Conference was attributed to two main factors: the delayed ratification of the 1928 Rome revision by some member states and the ongoing disagreements related to the planned unification of the Berne and Havana Conventions. Concerning the unification plans, the Paris Institute decided to seize the opportunity presented by the planned Brussels Revision Conference to bring together members of the continental groups and unite participants from both conventions in a new world convention.[89] To realize this plan, increasing importance was attributed to experts.

In March 1936 the Paris Institute had sent out invitations to several experts and representatives of private organizations concerned with the process of unifying the two copyright treaties and asked them to meet with a Committee of Experts that had been appointed by the League of Nations for this purpose. A first meeting was scheduled to take place at the Paris Institute on April 1.[90] The recommendation to set up a system of expert committees had been part of the restructuring process of the ICIC program introduced at the beginning of the decade. Regarding the role of the committees, the revised program stated:

> It [the ICIC] does not propose that they [the committees of experts] should take the place of national or international intellectual groups or administrations, but that they should establish contact between those bodies which possess the necessary qualifications, prepare the ground for their work, see that their decisions are executed and applied and convert them into practical results.[91]

Members of the new Committee of Experts included the Berne Bureau (represented by Fritz Ostertag), the ALAI (represented by Georges Maillard and Marcel Boutet), the Confédération Internationale des Sociétés d'Auteurs & Compositeurs (The International Confederation of Societies of Authors and Composers),[92] the Secretariat of the League of Nations, both the Rome and the Paris Institute, the Commission Préparatoire à la Conférence Diplomatique de Bruxelles (Preparatory Commission for the Brussels Diplomatic Conference), and the Inter-American Commission of Authors' Rights.[93] The conference concluded with the decision that preparations to combine both treaties were not yet at a stage to be able to meet the recently set revision conference date for September 1936. The Belgian diplomats in charge thus once again found themselves in the position of having to relate the details of a delay to the foreign delegates.

Japanese state leaders reacted with confusion and anger when they heard of the existence of an expert committee that had single-handedly decided to postpone the Brussels Revision Conference. The main motivation for Japanese officials to join the Berne Convention in the first place had been to elevate Japan's national status and in return have the "unequal treaties" abolished. Since then, they had continued to fight for their respect within the international system. With their own interests in mind and out of fear of being isolated from the transnational copyright community, they had continued and strengthened their cooperation even after withdrawing from the League of Nations. The matter of international copyright regulations concerned Japan directly, so it was in the interest of the Japanese leaders to be involved, while also keeping their honor and prestige in the international society. The fact that now Japan had simply been overlooked in the multilateral planning hurt the pride of the Japanese state representatives and strengthened the feeling of resentment against this international system. High-ranking officials demanded an explanation for why Japan had not been consulted and was not represented in the committee. They further demanded a more explicit explanation as to why the revision conference had been postponed again. Foreign Minister Arita Hachirō took up contact with the Belgian ambassador in Tōkyō as well as with Satō Junzō, the representative of the Society for International Cultural Relations (KBS) who was stationed at the Paris Institute. The Japanese embassies in Brussels and Paris exchanged information with the Belgian government and the Paris Institute, and the Japanese Legation in Berne stayed in contact with the Berne Bureau.[94]

The initial reason for the postponement was passed on to the Japanese Ministry of Foreign Affairs on June 3, 1936, via the Belgian Ambassador and the Japanese Legation in Berne which itself had been informed by the Berne Bureau.[95] The following day, bureaucrats of the Home Ministry and the Ministry of Foreign Affairs gathered in a meeting to discuss further steps of action. The *Tōkyō nichi nichi shinbun* reported of the anger of the bureaucrats toward the treatment of Japan and the ignoring of its standpoint by the other member states and the involved private associations. The Ministry of Foreign Affairs made the request to the Belgian government to end "US-European centered rule" and allow the attendance of a Japanese member in the expert committee.[96] If this request was not complied with, Japan would "in the worst case scenario, decide to leave the Convention."[97] Over the previous years, similar accusations of Eurocentrism had dominated the discourse around Japan's withdrawal from the League of Nations which, after Japan's proposal for including a racial equality clause in the League's Charter had been rejected, was seen by many Japanese as acting in the European interests while ignoring those of others, in particular non-white actors. The fact that Japan was now excluded from international meetings concerned with the Berne Convention proved to the Japanese officials that their interests were undervalued compared to those of European members. These accumulating sentiments of resentment, feeling misunderstood, and being underrepresented played a pivotal role in shaping Japan's Pan-Asian policies. As a response, Japan came to envision an Asian League that would represent Asian nations in a manner distinct from the multilateral organizations of the West.

The Belgian government did not take much time to reply and tried to ease the tension. On June 6, Edmond Glesener, Directorate-General for the Arts, Letters and Public Libraries at the Belgian Ministry of Education, wrote to the secretary at the Japanese embassy to provide some more detailed information regarding the function and composition of the expert committee. First and foremost, he wrote that the committee would not be composed of delegates that had been officially nominated by their respective governments, but of representatives of the important international organizations whose mission would be the study of copyrights. The decision to postpone the conference had furthermore not been made by the Belgian government which had simply been complying with the request expressed by the League of Nations and the expert committee. Glesener assured that he would write to the secretariat of the Committee of Experts the same day to inquire about the possibility of inviting to the next session the Japanese delegates who were supposed to attend the conference in September, so that they may still make use of their already planned trip to Europe.[98] Shortly after, Glesener informed the embassy that the participation of a Japanese expert would be granted. However, it would be difficult to organize another conference the same year.[99]

In addition to Glesener's efforts, the legal advisor of the Paris Institute, Raymond Weiss, visited the Japanese embassy in Paris twice where he met with diplomat Mitani Takanobu to find a solution. Mitani had been stationed in Paris as councilor at the Japanese embassy since 1921 and would return to Japan as director of the Treaty Department of the Ministry of Foreign Affairs a year later. Weiss assured Mitani that the Paris Institute would take account of the concerns of the Japanese government in connection with the work of the Committee of Experts, and that it might be possible to arrange another expert meeting in the spring of the following year, 1937.[100] He also gave Mitani a list of names of the experts participating in the committee as well as the protocol of the meeting in April.[101] In July, the Belgian embassy in Tōkyō contacted Foreign Minister Arita again with the newest revision memorandum of the Belgian government and to inform him of a suggestion by the Belgian government to hold a "universal copyright convention" for the unification of the Berne and Havana Conventions just before the revision conference of the Berne Convention. Arita replied that his government would do its best to investigate thoroughly the memorandum and the proposal to hold both conferences around the same time.[102]

While, externally, it was debated whether the ICIC would accept the participation of a Japanese expert in their next meeting of experts, domestically Japan saw to the implementation of some changes in its copyright-related administrative organs. In June 1936 Japan's National Committee on Intellectual Cooperation was transferred and placed under the control of the KBS, established in 1934. The composition of members active in the KBS and in Japan's National Committee had already been overlapping, so that the transfer did not bring about major change which also had to do with the fact that the KBS continued to rely on the large network of contacts that the National Committee had built up. Furthermore, even though the National Committee as of now technically belonged to the KBS and was thereby directly controlled by the Ministry of Foreign Affairs, the members continued to identify themselves with the National Committee.[103] For Yamada Saburō, the transfer brought about his retirement from his position as head of the National Committee, which however did not mean that his expertise was not needed as much. The new chair as director of the KBS was filled by businessman of the steamship industry and House of Peers' member Kabayama Aisuke.

Furthermore, concerning personnel, Kobayashi Hiroji whose task to represent Japan at the planned revision conference had fallen through because of its repeated postponement, was transferred by the Home Ministry to Berlin on another post, leaving the Police Affairs Bureau where he had filled the position in charge of copyrights since 1928. The Tōkyō Publishers' Association invited Kobayashi to discuss details of any ongoing negotiations in this area, followed by a farewell dinner.[104] Kobayashi noted that during his time in Berlin, many questions from different governmental divisions continued to come in, as he had accumulated a lot of knowledge on copyrights—knowledge that his successors were now lacking—during his time at the Police Affairs Bureau.[105] In the end, the year 1936 passed without a decision on a new conference date. There still existed conflicts in opinion among members of the Berne Convention and the member states of the Pan-American Union that hindered the mutual discussions and preparations of a draft.

Japan's National Committee on Intellectual Cooperation, by this point primarily a "nominal organ" to keep up the relationship with the ICIC, was making an effort to update the actors involved in Japan with any new information about the situation in Europe. On March 10, 1937, the committee invited members of the Ministry of Foreign Affairs, the Home Ministry, and the Ministry for Education, as well as representatives of associations, publishers, editors, writers, translators, and other representatives of the industries involved to the bureau of the KBS.[106] The event had been organized to give Satō Junzō, who was currently on a visit to Japan while normally based in Paris as mediator between the KBS and the Paris Institute, the chance to inform the attendees of the newest developments as regards the Institute's recent efforts regarding the globalization of copyright law. The Tōkyō Publishers' Association was also invited to the meeting as a special member.[107]

Satō shared the results of the meeting with Henri Bonnet who had succeeded Julien Luchaire as the director of the Paris Institute in 1930, and Raymond Weiss at the Paris Institute, and added that Japan was almost ready to nominate an expert candidate to take part in the consultations of uniting the Berne and Havana Conventions. He further wrote that it was most likely that Yamada Saburō was going to attend the Second General Meeting of the National Committees which was scheduled to take place in the summer. The KBS had decided that Yamada should attend the conference as representative of both Japan's National Committee on Intellectual

Cooperation as well as the KBS which, as mentioned before, still relied on the National Committee in their communication with the ICIC and the Paris Institute.[108]

Also to inform the public about events in Europe, Satō furthermore wrote a three-part essay about Japan's position on the Berne Convention that was published by the *Tōkyō asahi shinbun* between March 21 and 23, 1937.[109] Especially the last section entitled "The Wish for a Combined Effort of Bureaucrats and Citizens" offers an insight into the way the relationship between the state and the private industry was perceived at the time. While in the first two articles, Satō illustrated the content and history of the Berne Convention including the points for revision and the draft proposals, the last article focused on the importance of Japan sending an expert to Paris to contribute to the draft by the Committee of Experts which would be used as important reference material during the planned revision conference. He wrote: "Japan's special situation as regards translation rights has not been considered at previous conferences because the European countries simply did not know enough about the Japanese publishing and music industry."[110]

Playing into the narrative of being misunderstood, Satō continued, stating that the upcoming conference presented an ideal opportunity to rectify past mistakes of inadequately explaining the situation of the Japanese publishing industry to other countries. The goal was to share these details with the countries of the world through their respective representatives. By providing concrete numbers about income and royalties in the publishing and music industry, Japan hoped to garner understanding from the transnational copyright community. Lastly, he added:

> In today's world where international relations are constantly growing closer together, the activities of private actors also influence—either directly or indirectly—any kind of diplomatic negotiations. The author therefore believes that at the upcoming revision conference of the Berne Convention past mistakes should not be repeated and that one should try to give one's best to attain a closer cooperation with the private industry.[111]

As this example illustrates, the issue of state and private industry cooperation in diplomatic decision-making was now more openly discussed but had been taking place for many decades prior to the 1930s.

As Satō had announced to his colleagues at the Paris Institute in March, Yamada Saburō, joined by Sugiyama Naojirō who, was a professor of French law at Tōkyō Imperial University, attended the Second General Meeting of the National Committees which was held from July 5-9, 1937 in Paris. To increase the number of participants, the dates had been selected to take place during the time of the Paris World Fair which was held from May 25 until November 25, 1937. According to Yamada, he did not have any plans to attend the conference after leaving his official position as director of the National Committee but was asked to do so by the Foreign Minister and the KBS. This fact alone shows how essential he and his networks had become.

About 450 participants from 37 different countries attended the meeting. The agenda was divided into four different themes covering (1) the work of the ICIC between 1931 and 1937, (2) the organization and activities of the National Committees, (3) the structure of the ICIC, and lastly, (4) the function of intellectual cooperation in the organization of the contemporary world. The second theme included reports given by representatives of National Committees on their respective activities. Yamada's contribution was entitled "Intellectual Co-operation and Mutual Knowledge of National Cultures."[112] Although it is likely that the KBS expected Yamada to use this opportunity to propagate the "peculiarity of Japanese culture" to add to three pamphlets that they had distributed prior to the conference to the other member states, Yamada decided not to go into detail on this topic but instead talked about the activities of the Japanese National Committee over the past eight years, about the institutional changes since the committee was transferred to the KBS and the initiative of the latter organization to "harmonize the cultures of the East and the West," and about its goal to introduce the East Asian culture to the West.[113]

However, what really occupied Yamada was not the task for which he had been sent to the conference, namely, to represent the National Committee and the KBS. As his writings reveal, he was well aware of the fact that a few days later the ICIC would hold its next general conference with one of the points on the agenda entitled "Universal Regulations for Copyright."[114] He also knew that he would not be given the right to speak at that conference, and that currently not only the Paris Institute was progressing with their preparations for the Brussels Revision Conference, but the Paris Committee of Experts was also entering their final round of discussions for their revision draft. Thus, the General Meeting of the National Committees offered a last chance to emphasize Japan's standpoint with the aim of influencing the ongoing negotiations.[115] After several representatives handed in their proposals on the activities of the organization of the ICIC, Yamada took the opportunity to, what he would later describe as "firmly" (*danzen*), present the proposal on "Intellectual Cooperation and Translation Rights" (Gakugei kyōryoku to honyakuken) in the name of the Japanese National Committee.[116] In the proposal, Yamada shared the main content of the translators' pamphlet that had been published by the International Copyright Convention because of the different consultative meetings the previous year as well as of previous written opinions on translation rights by the publishers' associations involved. He stated:

> The chief functions of the International Committee on Intellectual Cooperation are to develop mutual understanding between the nations and to bring the

various national cultures into closer contact with each other. Among the various methods adopted to these ends—exchange of publications, art exhibitions, exchange of professors and students—there can be no doubt that the problem of translation is of outstanding importance.[117]

Although he did not follow Satō's advice to share concrete details on the translators' and publishers' income or royalty situation, information that was included in the pamphlet, Yamada did share the main points of the translators and publishers in Japan, namely, that a translation into Japanese would, unlike was the case with more widely known languages, "not seriously effect [sic] the circulation of the original work."[118] His argument was based on the report "The impact of Japanese translations on the original work" that had been submitted to the Home Ministry by the Tōkyō Booksellers' Association in late 1927 as part of the preparations for the 1928 Rome Revision Conference:

> The facts prove on the contrary that the publication of a Japanese translation increases the sales of the (…) original. (…) the same rules should not govern translation rights in all cases alike; they must be varied according to the country and the circumstances. Unless due allowance is made for differences of conditions the only result will be to discourage translators, and to hamper that contact between dissimilar cultures which it is particularly necessary to promote.[119]

According to Yamada, free translations into Eastern languages would be "to the benefit of the authors, who would gain both in reputation and financially, and also of the peoples, who would thus be able to gain a better insight into each other's ways."[120] He also compared the means of communication, which between Tōkyō and Europe or America were "slow," and it would be "rare and frequently difficult" to maintain contact between these parts of the world. He added that "it would often happen that even the most conscientious translator would be held up or discouraged by the formalities with which he has to comply."[121] Yamada concluded the report with the following request to the Paris Institute:

> I am aware that the League of Nations and the International Institute of Intellectual Co-operation [Paris Institute] contemplate the amendment of the Berne Convention in such a manner as to bring the American and European systems into closer harmony. I hope that by making due allowance for the facts of the situation those two bodies will further the removal of all restrictions on translations as between Eastern and Western countries. In that way they could make a decisive contribution to the inter-penetration of Eastern and Western civilizations, and in so doing promote the development of pacific relations

between peoples whom distance and tradition are liable to keep asunder and whom it is on the contrary essential to bring closer together.[122]

Yamada's words carried all the more weight considering that on the third day of the conference, July 7, the Second Sino-Japanese War started with the so-called "Marco Polo Bridge Incident" near Beijing after which Japan's escalating military aggression that was justified with the claim to "free" Asia from European colonial powers further distanced Japan from the member states of the League of Nations.[123] In other words, the claim for free translations rights between Eastern and Western countries was used and portrayed as an option to avoid an escalation of tensions.

After Yamada had finished presenting his report, ICIC chairman and Oxford scholar of Greek literature Gilbert Murray named representatives from America, France, Greece, Italy, Japan, Poland, Switzerland, and the United Kingdom to form a special committee that should investigate the issue raised by Yamada for Japan. The discussion of this problem with the Deputy Secretary-General of the League of Nations Massimo Pilotti revealed that most of the committee members expressed the opinion that Japan's plea was justified, even though there were still some differences in opinion on how to approach the problem. Some members suggested the compromise of limiting translation rights to 23 years after the author's death (as opposed to 30 or 50 years for general reproduction rights) while others suggested reducing the licensing fee to be paid to the author as low as possible. Overall, the members of the National Committees agreed that this was a matter that should be passed onto and dealt with by the ICIC.[124]

The Paris Institute, as host of the Second General Meeting, included the issue in their report that was handed to the ICIC as reference for the upcoming General Conference of the ICIC. It stated:

> A special regime regarding translations is demanded in a brochure published by the Society of Japanese Translators and transmitted to the International Institute by the Japanese National Committee on Intellectual Co-operation. This work stresses the danger of discouraging, by the excessive demands of authors, the efforts being made to develop in the Far East the knowledge of representative works of European civilization. The International Institute has brought these considerations to the groups concerned. The latter, indeed, have been the first to recognize that there is a certain basis for such preoccupations. Thus, the International Congress of Publishers, in its London session in June 1936, expressed the desire that, in the establishment of rights of translation for literary works, due weight should always be given to the advantages derived by the original work from its translation into foreign languages. It further asked that consideration be given, in drawing up the terms of contracts, to

the difficulties of translation and adaption, and of the circumstances peculiar to each country.¹²⁵

The report was later included as an annex to the General Report of the 19ᵗʰ General Conference of the ICIC which began only three days after the meeting of the National Committees. Even though Yamada was among the attendees, he was not an official member of the board of the ICIC and thus not allowed to comment. In his stead, ICIC member and professor of the Science of Religion at Tōkyō Imperial University Anesaki Masaharu explained Japan's proposal as part of the session on "Universal Regulations for Copyright."¹²⁶ When he had finished, the American history professor and diplomat James Thompson Shotwell spoke up in support of the Japanese request. Shotwell, who had been one of the attendees of the Paris Peace Conference and was among the initiators of the establishment of the International Labour Organisation in 1919, had been actively promoting the entrance of the United States into the League of Nations ever since its establishment. As president of the League of Nations Association of the United States he was further striving to change the US copyright regulations to conform with international agreements.¹²⁷ According to Shotwell, the question of translation rights and the ability to declare reservations on certain paragraphs of the treaty needed to be sufficiently considered from the viewpoint of intellectual cooperation and cultural harmony, which is why he was supporting Japan's proposal.¹²⁸ Examining the historical perspective of the US relationship with copyright protection, the support extended by the United States to Japan's demand for free translation rights is not surprising. In fact, as a nation that had and still was relying heavily on the import of literature from Great Britain, the United States had previously emphasized the significance of free access to knowledge. Yamada later explicitly thanked Shotwell and Raymond Weiss of the Paris Institute for their help in diffusing Japan's point of view.¹²⁹

Yamada's persistence had indeed achieved the desired awareness for this issue among the organizations involved. The ICIC stated in their official session report that it aimed to arrange another expert meeting to formulate definite proposals regarding the World Conference. It continued: "The committee also expressed the desire that account should be taken in these proposals of the views expressed by the Japanese National Committee on Intellectual Co-operation and by Professor Shotwell regarding the need for increasing the reciprocal influence of civilizations by appropriate measures governing translation rights."¹³⁰

The report was addressed once again at the 18ᵗʰ General Assembly of the League of Nations in September 1937, showing the wide reach of Yamada's initiative. As part of the general resolutions of the Assembly and in reflection of the League's stance toward the work of the Paris Institute and the ICIC, the resolution stated the following: "The Assembly (…) now considers it desirable that in these proposals [the unification of the copyright treaties of Berne and Havana] account should be taken of the need to foster the mutual integration of civilizations, particularly by appropriate regulation of translation rights."[131] The Tōkyō Publishers' Association interpreted this statement as a sign that their argumentation and efforts had been successful.[132]

Although the Paris Institute did not give the hoped-for concession to Yamada's report, it did raise awareness of the situation of a primarily import-oriented publishing industry and stimulated further dialogue. Japanese internationalists, including ministerial bureaucrats and diplomats, publishers, translators, and academic scholar Yamada Saburō, may have exploited their position within the Berne Convention to pursue nationalistic ambitions. Nevertheless, the initiatives by Japan's non-state actors to raise awareness of the diverse circumstances in the world regarding translations can be considered an important milestone in the globalization of intellectual property rights. Even more so than during the 1908 Berlin Revision Conference where Mizuno Rentarō had brought forward the argument of Japan being a "country in development" that was dependent on translations from the West to develop further, now the translators and publishers, with the help of Yamada Saburō, were given an almost *direct* voice in the negotiations. This increased the overall awareness to the problem that the institutions in Europe including the ALAI, the Berne Bureau, or the ICIC unilaterally represented the liberal-individualistic concept of copyright which was depicted as that of the entire "civilized" world. The activities by the Japanese internationalist copyright community were an important step towards the 1952 established Universal Copyright Convention which loosened the barriers of translation rights to encompass all nations, including developing and literature import-oriented ones, into a global treaty.[133]

PREPARATIONS OF THE BRUSSELS REVISION CONFERENCE AND THE SECOND EXPERT MEETING

After a two-year pause, the Copyright Investigation Council (Chosakuken Shinsakai), which had been established in 1935, came together again on November 18, 1937. Originally, the committee had planned to meet again just before the scheduled departure of Japan's representative Kobayashi for Brussels in 1936, but because the conference had been postponed, the consultations of the Council had also been delayed, demonstrating the importance of the international negotiations for the justification of the committee's existence.[134]

Since the last meeting, several new faces had joined the Council. Among the new attendees was the above-mentioned Mitani Takanobu, bureaucrat from the Ministry of Foreign Affairs who was serving as delegate to the Paris Institute, publisher Egusa

Shigetada, who had been invited onto the board in July, and the president of the publishing house Kōdansha, Noma Seiji. Discussion topics included selecting a Japanese expert to join the Committee of Experts, at that point both Berlin-stationed Kobayashi Hiroji and Paris-stationed Satō Junzō had been suggested by the Japanese Home Ministry and the ambassador to France, the issue of translation rights, and the general issue of whether it was even in Japan's interest to remain a member of the Berne Convention. When discussing the problem of translation rights, Yamada Saburō's report for the Imperial Academy that had been used in the written opinion of the Ministry of Education prior to the 1928 Rome Revision Conference was cited again in detail. Mizuno Rentarō, who was still active in the Copyright Investigation Council despite having resigned from public office, proposed to invite his close acquaintance Yamada Saburō to the next meeting as Yamada had been exchanging information at the General Meeting of the National Committees and was more informed about recent developments in Europe.[135] Mizuno's suggestion was resolved a week later as the KBS organized an information session about Yamada's attendance of the General Meeting in Paris. For this meeting not only Yamada, but also many members of the Copyright Investigation Council were invited, including the leaders of the major private interest associations, like publisher Egusa Shigetada[136] or writer Anesaki Masaharu, and bureaucrats involved like the new head of the Book Division of the Police Affairs Bureau Kunishio Kōichirō, and members of the Ministry of Foreign Affairs' Department of Cultural Affairs.[137]

At the beginning of 1938, Japan's state officials finally decided who should represent Japan at the next Meeting of Experts regarding the unification of the Berne and Havana conventions. The selected name was communicated to Henri Bonnet, the head of the Paris Institute. As expected, the two chosen candidates were Kobayashi Hiroji and Satō Junzō. Around this time, the draft proposals for a unified treaty to introduce at the world conference were being finalized and were passed on by the Belgian government as the host country of the next conference in collaboration with the Paris Institute. While prior to the last revision conference in Rome in 1928 the communication regarding the upcoming conference had still been mediated via the ministries, now Yamada Saburō was the first to be contacted with the new draft as well as with changes and requests from Europe, which is a reflection of his central role and active engagement with the Paris Institute and other European organizations involved with copyrights.

On May 27, 1938, head of the Legal Section at the Paris Institute Raymond Weiss contacted Yamada with the most recent draft for the Brussels Revision Conference. The letter reveals the close personal relationship that existed between the two men and their families. In the letter, Weiss thanked Yamada for the study reports and the respective translations he had received with information on Japan's intellectual cooperation and on the legal status of foreigners in Japan. Regarding his office work, Weiss reported on his productive cooperation with Satō Junzō and also on a visit he had received by Kobayashi Hiroji who came to see him to again stress Japan's special situation as regards translation rights, which according to Weiss had made him resume the report that Yamada had presented at the Second General Meeting of the National Committees. Besides the private notes included, the main reason for Weiss' letter was an attached personal copy of the revision memoir. Weiss wrote that the draft would soon be officially sent by the Belgian government to the Japanese government. For now, he was hoping that Yamada would share his opinion in advance when he found the time.[138] This is a clear example of the rising value of consultations involving members of international organizations, experts, and societal advisors.

Knowing that the revision of the draft would soon be in the hands of the government, on July 22, 1938, Yamada did share his opinion with foreign minister Ugaki Kazushige, an army general who had been appointed in the first Konoe Cabinet just two months earlier. He explained that if the government were to remain silent while it observed the ongoing discussions on unifying the treaties of Berne and Havana without taking action, then Japan would not only lose its free translation rights in accordance with the existing US-Japan Copyright Treaty from 1906, but would also permanently lose the opportunity to secure free translation rights with the nations of the Berne Union.[139] This would be a great failure in the Japanese cultural development.[140]

When Ugaki received Yamada's note, the Home Ministry had already received two drafts from the Belgian government. The first was the Paris draft, a revision proposal aimed at aligning the Berne Convention more closely with the Pan-American Convention. The second was the Montevideo draft, which suggested revisions to bring the Havana treaty of the Pan-American Convention closer to the Berne Convention. In addition, the convocation of the Committee of Experts for October 1938 was announced, and it was to build on the draft version prepared at the experts' first meeting in April 1936, taking into consideration the suggestions they had received since then, any recent developments, and the preparations for the planned international conference.[141]

As had become custom, the two drafts were immediately passed on to the publishers for their input. The Tōkyō Publishers' Association discussed the proposals with the Japan Magazine Association and submitted their opinion on August 19, 1938, adding that if their request for free translation rights did not go through, then at least the licensing fees for translation rights should be kept as cheap as possible.[142] In an attached comment, the publishers argued again that translations would stimulate cultural exchange, internationalization, and the general promotion of intellectual cooperation. On August 21, the submission was discussed at the Home Ministry with head of the Tōkyō Publishers' Association, Egusa Shigetada.[143]

Before Japan's observations were officially handed back to the Paris Institute, the Copyright Investigation Council was convened again on September 8 to discuss the written opinion that had been submitted by the publishers on merging the two copyright treaties. Besides the general members of the committee, including Noma Seiji,[144] Egusa Shigetada, and Mizuno Rentarō, the meeting was again attended by Yamada Saburō, even though he was not an official member of the committee.[145] At the meeting, it was decided that Takayanagi Kenzō, a leading professor in Anglo-American law at Tōkyō Imperial University, would be sent to present Japan's case despite the initial appointment of Kobayashi Hiroji earlier that year.[146] The reason behind this decision was that the expert conference was unexpectedly moved forward from mid-November to mid-October, and Takayanagi was the only possible candidate already in Europe for different reasons. The travel time from Japan to Paris was almost two months which was a great disadvantage to Japan in the diplomatic negotiations. However, since Japan required a representative on site, it was necessary to overlook that Takayanagi was not an expert and had no background in the field of copyrights.[147] The statement ultimately submitted by Japan once again adopted precisely the opinion prepared by the publishing industry.[148]

From October 19-21, 1938, the Committee of Experts gathered for the second time at the Palace of the Academies in Brussels, bringing together a mix of individual experts, government representatives, and representatives of non-governmental organizations to discuss the drafts and recent developments for the establishment of a universal copyright convention. The official international revision conference of the Berne Convention was meanwhile scheduled to take place in the fall of 1939. The expert attendees included representatives from Argentina, Belgium, Brazil, France, Germany, Japan, the United States, the directors of the Berne Bureau and the ALAI, members of the Paris Institute and the Rome Institute, the Secretary of the League of Nations, and in the case of the United States, of the National Committee on Intellectual Cooperation. Japan was represented by Satō Junzō and Takayanagi Kenzō, who was assisted by Suzuki Takeo, another Tōkyō Imperial University professor for commercial law who like Yamada was also a member of the Imperial Academy. As the conference had been rescheduled one month earlier than its originally planned date, the three representatives of Japan had limited time to prepare. They ultimately formulated their official statement based on a telegram text, the few materials available on site at the Paris Institute, and the text presented by Yamada Saburō at the General Meeting of the National Committees in 1937, which itself drew upon the texts prepared by Japan's translators.[149]

After some opening words by the representative for Belgium, the first challenge of the meeting was addressed: So far, the committee had received only seven government opinions. In particular, the important opinion of the United States was still missing. Japan's submission from October 7, 1938, had also not yet reached the Belgian government, nor had Germany's submission, both of which had been handed in within just two weeks before the start of the conference.[150] In addition, the comments that did reach the Belgian government were largely confined to the Paris draft with suggestions on how to revise the Berne Convention while leaving the Montevideo draft without comment. This further added to the challenging situation on day one of the conference.

Considering the world situation in late 1938, it remains questionable whether these chaotic conditions at the start of the Meeting of Experts, including the missing or late submissions of opinions, surprised the attending experts and bureaucrats in any way. Just three weeks earlier, on September 30, 1938, the Munich Agreement between National Socialist Germany, the United Kingdom, Italy, and France had prevented a war between Germany and Czechoslovakia by granting Germany the annexation of the Sudetenland, an act of appeasement which allowed Hitler to expand German territory. The Agreement was broken only six months later in March 1939. At the same time Spain was still fighting a civil war which had begun in 1936, and US President Franklin D. Roosevelt had in 1937, in his so-called "Quarantine Speech," already called for an international "quarantine" of aggressor nations, by which he meant Germany, Italy, and Japan. Even though the Meeting of Experts was still held and brought together the different nations' representatives to find an agreement on copyright, the attendees likely already faced each other with a certain resentment and were aware that their nations found themselves on the path to a global war.

The fact that Japan's opinion had not reached the committee in time did not hinder the discussion of Japan's opinion which was brought forward "forcefully and with repeated emphasis" during the first day of the meeting by Takayanagi Kenzō.[151] After the introductory greetings, Takayanagi stood up and spent one hour presenting Japan's case before the other committee members. He began by referencing the presentation made by Yamada at the General Meeting of the National Committees on Intellectual Cooperation the previous year and listed the very same reasons for the need to introduce a free translation system.[152] The only variation he made was as regards the languages in question, he did not refer to "Eastern and Western languages" as Yamada had done, but instead separated the languages into "languages that primarily used Chinese characters", that is, Japanese and Chinese, and countries that used different characters.[153]

He further made use of the statistics introduced in the 1936 pamphlet of the translators to speak about the difficult situation of translators and publishers in Japan. While repeating many facts about Japan's stance regarding translation rights, by then well-known, Takayanagi went one step further by stating that his country's diplomatic relationships, which Japan had an interest in continuing, depended on the adaptation of the paragraph on translation rights in the planned universal convention on copyrights.[154]

This threat can be interpreted as a last resort against the sanction resolution that the Council of the League of Nations had adopted against Japan on September 30 that year because of the aggravation of the Sino-Japanese War in July 1938. In this resolution, individual nations were asked to apply sanctions against Japan and to fully support China.[155] By threatening to make Japan's international cooperation generally dependent on the outcome of these negotiations, Takayanagi disrupted the superordinate unity of the Berne Union, which, until then, had continued to follow peacefully a mutual interest despite the growing nationalistic sentiments and military conflicts.

REACTIONS BY THE TRANSNATIONAL COPYRIGHT COMMUNITY

The reactions to Japan's proposal differed greatly but certainly led the discussions of the transnational copyright community at the time. Two developments deserve special attention when looking at Takayanagi's demands and the criticism and consent that the proposal received: At the time of the Meeting of Experts, Japanese troops had invaded China in July 1937, resulting in the, undeclared, Second Sino-Japanese War which was quickly escalating with ultimately nearly a million Japanese soldiers deployed in China and the world press covering the brutality of the fighting, often involving blatant war crimes. Furthermore, almost simultaneously with the conference, on November 3, 1938, Prime Minister Konoe Fumimaro announced his so-called "New Order for East Asia" (Tōa Shin-Chitsujo) which was portrayed as a mutual aid chain, a joint defense and economic union between Japan, Manchuria, and China against Western imperialism. The announcement reflected Japan's intention to dominate East Asia and was the founding concept of the Greater East Asia Co-Prosperity Sphere (Dai Tōa Kyōeiken) announced two years later in 1940. As regards this final step of withdrawal from the community of nations, the consent that Japan's proposal for free translations received from various international scholars can be understood as a form of appeasement strategy. Similarly, the 1940 Olympics that were supposed to be given to Rome to host were instead given to Japan because the British government and the International Olympic Committee under no circumstances wanted to further complicate the situation with Japan.[156]

For example, following the Meeting of Experts, the delegate of the American National Committee on International Intellectual Cooperation, Francis Deak, published a report on the happenings and results of the conference. Referring to the statements made by Takayanagi and Satō on behalf of Japan, Deak acknowledged the different conceptions of copyright between the, as he put it, "occidental and oriental schools of thought" which he explained as follows:

> The traditional conception of copyright seeks to protect the rights of the creator—a conception underlying most of the national treaties in force as well as the draft conventions prepared both by the Paris Committee and the Montevideo Committee: this may be called the individualistic conception. On the other hand, modern technological developments, especially in the Western hemisphere, and the consequent increase in the use of literary and artistic creations and the assertion by Japan of a position of equality of Asiatic civilization with that of the West, brought to the fore another conception which seeks to limit, to a greater or lesser extent, the creator's right in the interest of the public; this may be called the social conception of copyright.[157]

Deak wrote that the above question needed to be studied and resolved or balanced before a consensus on a unified convention could be reached. He went as far as to suggest that the American domestic copyright law should *also* take into consideration the following two conflicting interests:

> (…) [on the one hand] the individual who writes or composes and [on the other hand] the scholarly and industrial interests which desire to make use of literary and artistic creations, not merely on account of the profit which accrues to them, but also for the benefit of the public at large who wish to enjoy them.[158]

In contrast to the support received by Shotwell or Deak, Japan's demand was at the same time heavily criticized, even in Japan itself. The renowned law journal *Nihon hōgaku* (Japanese Law) published a three-part article on the theory of free translations following Takayanagi's presentation. The article criticized not the demand for free translation rights per se, but the attempt to establish a free translation right system limited to the translations between East Asia and Europe which was justified as a "cultural demand for Asia," especially since Japan was currently the only representative of East Asia in the Berne Union.[159] The author of the articles, the copyright scholar Itō Nobuo, wrote that, from a global point of view, the demand for free translation rights as part of the new universal copyright agreement would be an appropriate request, and a change in copyright law that considered society as a whole, and not just the capitalistic publishing organizations and the author's individual profit which had been expanding since the eighteenth century was worth discussing. However, Itō argued that the right to translate freely should not be limited to Europe and East Asia, but should also be applied among East Asian countries, in particular, between China and Japan. This was not part of the request though, and so Itō claimed that Japan was not interested in the initial idea to overcome international crises and bring the world together through free translations but used its demand to justify its "New Culture in East Asia" (Shin-Tōa Bunka) that was to liberate Asia from the imperialist powers and return sovereignty to Asian countries. The ultimate goal of the "New Cultural Order" was to construct a new East Asia under Japanese leadership that was independent of "the West," but at the same time was built upon mutual understanding for which the common possession of ideas and the exchange of culture, including the free translation of works, was vital.[160] Thus, if China joined the revised and unified universal copyright treaty, it would also profit from the regulations to freely translate works from Europe and the United States which would bring great prosperity to the country. This argumentation directly connected Japan's imperialist ambitions with the idea of being internationally engaged.

The demand expressed by Takayanagi was not new but had been adapted to changing external circumstances and national goals over several decades. As has been demonstrated in the past four chapters, the request for free translations had already originated in the late 1890s and was initiated not by the state, but by its advisors: publishers, translators, and legal scholars. The request to limit the free translations to Europe and East Asia was also not new. Yamada Saburō had proposed it ahead of the 1928 Rome Revision Conference, arguing that the vast linguistic differences between regions would significantly impact the time, costs, and efforts required for translating a work. Hence, it was actually a small group of elite non-governmental actors upon whose advice part of the 1930s cultural policies of the "New Order" were created. As was discussed in Chapter 1, in 1901, Oyaizu Kaname had already appealed to his government to take measures regarding the Chinese publishing market. It had the potential of becoming a significant client for the Japanese industry if the free translation of Japanese works could be halted. Furthermore, from his earliest petitions on free translation rights, Oyaizu had emphasized that "in the case of Japan, the translated work would, unlike in Europe where the right to freely translate was harming the authors' rights and the sales of the original publication, not result in a decrease of the sales of the original, because the language is so different from the European languages."[161] In terms of the complexity of their writing systems and grammar, Japanese and Chinese, with Japanese using the Chinese character with two more syllable writing systems added, however, was quite similar when compared with the significant simpler writing systems of European languages. The argument that a translation would not decrease the sale of the original could, according to Oyaizu, thus not be applied to Chinese translations of Japanese works.[162] In other words, the Japanese publishers had de facto no interest in granting to China the same exceptions they demanded of Western countries.

The reason Japan's long-existing demand for free translation rights received such an unprecedented international echo during the 1930s was probably connected to the fact that publishers and translators were now able to more or less *directly* share their voice through the improved networks and communication routes established by the League of Nations, especially strengthened in the 1930s. In the decades before, Japan's situation had only been discussed at the copyright conferences, which had given the international community little time to discuss Japan's special request. At the same time, the increasing networks and international contacts made it increasingly difficult to disregard the law unnoticed, as had been demonstrated by the "Whirlwind Plage".

All these factors contributed to creating the impression that the situation had shifted in connection with Japan's growing militarism. In reality, the actors involved simply continued along a path laid decades earlier. They adapted their rhetoric slightly but maintained their "international mindset" and nationalistic devotion throughout, laying the groundwork for a postwar revival of international cooperation.

OUTBREAK OF WORLD WAR II

Japan's cooperation with the transnational copyright community continued until well into 1939. On January 27, 1939, Japan's National Committee on Intellectual Cooperation came together once again at its 13th meeting and discussed the reports of the three Japanese participants of the Meeting of Experts, Takayanagi Kenzō, Satō Junzō, and Suzuki Takeo, with its members and Yamada Saburō. It was decided that after some modifications, their joint report would be published in the name of the KBS and passed on to the representatives of private organizations and to the bureaucrats involved.[163] Suzuki Takeo reported on the conference in an article that was published in the magazine *Hōgaku Kyōkai zasshi* (Journal of the Jurisprudence Association) in February 1939. By that time, the copyright experts were waiting for the results of the Pan-American expert conference to be held in Lima in December 1938. Suzuki wrote that he hoped that the next Meeting of Experts, which was set to be held in the fall of 1939, would decide whether to include the right to freely translate as a main principle of the new treaty, allowing Japan to continue its cultural cooperation with other countries.[164]

Meanwhile, the Japanese government had decided to react to the League of Nation's sanction resolution by discontinuing all diplomatic relations with the subsidiary organizations of the League of Nations which included cutting off any form of formal or informal contact with the ICIC and the Paris Institute.[165] At the meeting in January, it was further decided to dissolve Japan's National Committee on Intellectual Cooperation by March 31, 1939.[166] Regarding the future promotion of the Japanese culture abroad, it was planned that the KBS, which unlike the National Committee was to continue to exist, should strengthen its cooperation with the publishing industry. Anesaki Masaharu and Yamada Saburō were expected to lend their support in this matter.[167]

While contact with the various organs of the League including the Advisory Committee on Opium, the Permanent Central Opium Board, the Advisory Committee on Social Questions, the International Committee on Intellectual Co-operation, the Economic Committee, the Health Organization and its Eastern Bureau came to a stop after the decision of the Japanese government, the ongoing revision of the Berne Convention represented an exemption in the breaking-off of diplomatic relations with the organs of the League of Nations. In the case of the committee's work towards the revision of the Berne Convention, the Japanese government under no circumstances wanted to give up its ability to participate in the negotiations that were still ongoing, and the Berne Bureau continued to incorporate Japan in its actions as did the Legal Section of the Paris Institute, reflecting the profoundness of the created networks. This continued cooperation included the planned attendance of representatives of Japan in the third Meeting of Experts which was scheduled for May 1939. Subsequently, one of the main agenda items for the meeting of Japan's National Committee on Intellectual Cooperation in January was the sharing of information at the scheduled Meeting of Experts with the attendees.[168]

This time Anesaki Masaharu was selected to represent Japan, but in the end the conference was never realized. Anesaki, who had embarked on his travels to the United States and Europe in March 1939 was informed in May that, because of unfinished preparations on the South American side, the Meeting of Experts had been postponed until November. However, with the toutbreak of the war in Europe on September 1, paving the way to converge with the Sino-Japanese War and the rising tensions between the United States and Japan to become World War II, this meeting never took place. Japan remained part of the discussions around how to deal with the topic of translation rights in the planned world convention up until the end of 1939. In October, the magazine of the Berne Bureau *Droit d'auteur* ran a last special on "Le problème du droit de traduction" (The Problem with Translation Rights).[169] The article expressed the Berne Bureau's understanding attitude with the "disadvantageous situation" of Japan's translators and publishers who were cited from their mutual pamphlet. The Berne Convention would have made an effort to consider all points of view at the 1908 and 1928 revision conferences, but ever since the professional occupation as a writer had developed from the eighteenth century, an author deserved and should be paid for his work and lastly the Bureau was thus of the opinion that all arguments brought forward by Japan "cannot undermine the soundness of the principle on which this right rests."[170] The article concluded:

> We [the Berne Bureau] do not see that the situation has changed in recent years in a way that makes the abolishment of the right of translation necessary. (…) if we are willing on both sides to see things as they are, it is only reasonable to maintain the status quo. Even in a country like National Socialist Germany,

where the individual is clearly subordinate to the community, the right of translation prevails, because the interest of the community is to protect those who create literary and artistic works. On this point, the liberal and authoritarian conceptions meet, and we feel a peculiar satisfaction in sending a signal for such an agreement in a time where the world hears the sound of weapons and where among the belligerent it is the inevitable and natural norm to distance oneself philosophically from the adversary.[171]

The Bureau had thus decided not to yield to the Japanese demand for "free translation rights". However, at the same time, it did not perceive an urgency to change the status quo, under which Japan, by then one of the major powers, still enjoyed privileged conditions compared to the other member states of the Berne Convention. The Paris Institute continued its work under complicated circumstances until Germany invaded Paris in 1940, when preparations came to a complete stop.[172] Maruzen, which had been an agent to the publications of the League of Nations and the Paris Institute since 1932, paid its last unpaid invoices to the Paris Institute in the summer of 1939.[173] Thereafter, Maruzen along with 14 other publishing houses became involved in the plans of Prime Minister Konoe Fumimaro to turn Japan into an "advanced state of National Defense" (*kōdō kokubō kokka*) under the "New Order" of 1940 which aimed at the centralization of the entire state modelled after the "Gleichschaltung" in National Socialist Germany. These reforms also had an impact on the publishing industry and the many publishing associations which were regarded as not being able to fulfill a unified and central representation of Japan's publishing market. Consequently, in 1940 the government began dissolving many publishers' associations, while at the same time preparations to establish a central publishing organ under the New Order and its all-encompassing supra-organization, the "Imperial Rule Assistance Association" (Taisei Yokusankai) were started. In the case of the Tōkyō Publishers' Association, which had maintained a close relationship with the bureaucrats in the past, it was decided to involve members of the organization immediately in the New Order upon the dissolution of the association.[174] The Publishers' Association was merged with the Magazine Association to form the centralized Japan Publishing Culture Association (Nihon Shuppan Bunka Kyōkai), which had the task to indoctrinate the "new culture" (*shin-bunka*) among the people and abroad. The final composition of the association included several bureaucrats, amongst others from the Cabinet Information Division (Naikaku Jōhōbu), the Ministry of Education, the Navy and Army, the Ministry of Trade, and representatives from the publishing houses Maruzen, Kōdansha, Heibonsha, Kaizōsha, and Jitsugyō no Nihon Sha.[175]

Why did Japan, as a member state, persistently oppose the adoption of an international standard within the Berne Convention? Several factors likely played into Japan's continued blockage of an envisioned unification of translation rights in international copyright law. First, the fact that Japanese officials opposed to changing their standpoint was a matter of national pride. After their proposal to include a clause on racial equality into the Charter of the League of Nations had been rejected, Japan was left insecure of its international standing. The copyright negotiations were utilized to showcase Japan's power in international negotiations to the global copyright community. Japan sought to break free from subordination to Western powers and assert its independence. Second, 1930s copyright diplomacy gave an increasing voice to private actors. Various international and cultural institutions that had been rather unsuccessfully active during the 1920s, improved their programs and networks and by the early 1930s displayed a much greater success than during the previous decade. Particularly Japan's publishers and translaters had a genuine interest in Japan's translation rights exemptions which were directly linked to their financial gain. Benefiting from the activities and strengthened transnational structures of the above institutions, these actors increased their involvement in the international copyright negotiations. Out of fear of isolation, also domestically, the Japanese leaders increased their own cooperation with the private sector by establishing various advisory councils through which they were schooled by members of the private industry. The arguments presented by the non-state experts were embraced by state representatives, who then incorporated them into the national standpoint. The close cooperation and common rhetoric that had developed among the involved group of elitist state and non-state actors within Japan over the course of several decades offers a possible explanation for the continued collaboration of the heads of the publishing industry with the state even after the media was suppressed and centralized under the Japanese military at the end of the decade.

Finally, the question arises as to why Japan's leaders, who throughout the 1930s conveyed their growing resentment and sense of unfair treatment by the Berne Convention, did not withdraw from this multilateral agreement. While the matter of copyright protection was of interest to Japan, did it justify Takayanagi's threat to leave diplomatic relations altogether should Japan's demands not be granted? Or was the Japanese government's continued participation in this international agreement not a means to maintaining connection with the great powers at precisely the moment that other avenues were closed off to imperial Japan and its people? The Japanese state, in its pursuit to avoid complete isolation from the international community, strategically utilized the realm of intellectual cooperation and international copyright to justify its higher political objectives. Throughout the latter half of the 1930s, this translated into establishing a new regional order under Japanese leadership. By framing their imperialist ambitions to achieve international cooperation and harmony, Japan continued its international activities and maintained communication with European international organizations as late as 1939. The international revision negotiations around the Berne Convention thus constituted one example of global interconnections that survived until the late 1930s.

CHAPTER 5
TOWARDS INDEPENDENCE
Publishers, Translators, and UNESCO in the Postwar Period

On November 21, 2007, Ichihara Tokurō, the former secretary of Noma Shōichi, son of Noma Seiji and postwar president of the publishing house Kōdansha, gave a speech on the occasion of the 30th anniversary of the first meeting of the International Publishers' Association in Kyōto in 1977. He opened his speech with the statement: "The movement for the internationalization of the Japanese publishing market began in the mid-1950s."[1] Ichihara's perception of the beginning of Japan's internationalization in the publishing industry constitutes no exception in publishing research. The globalization of the market is oftentimes brought into connection with the occurrences of the late 1950s and early 1960s. While still in the process of recovering from the effects of World War II, it was during these later postwar years that the newly founded Japan Book Publishers' Association (Nihon Shoseki Shuppan Kyōkai) joined the International Publishers' Association. In addition, "Kōdansha International," a book export campaign by publisher Noma Shōichi to improve the visibility of Japanese publications abroad was launched. The country also for the first time participated in the Frankfurt Book Fair and opened the doors to its own International Book Fair in Tōkyō a decade later.[2] The growth of the Japanese publishing industry from the second half of the 1950s onwards reflected the period of rapid economic growth in general business. Publishers were keen on expanding to new markets and started exporting Japanese works not only to other Asian countries, Europe and to North and South America, but from 1956 onwards also increasingly to Soviet Russia, China, and North Korea.[3] At the same time, during the onset of the Cold War, publishers from the United States and Communist countries were competing to have their works translated in Japan. Often, they would present special deals to Japanese publishers, including the waiver of any remuneration costs.[4]

During an interview with Ichihara Tokurō regarding his time as secretary of Kōdansha as the leading postwar publisher in Japan, he also remarked that the cooperation that took place between Noma Shōichi and ministerial bureaucrats had no connection to the prewar personnel and that the bureaucrats involved were all new members without an existing link to the occurrences of the prewar period.[5] In contrast to these common perceptions about the beginning of the globalization of the Japanese publishing industry, Chapters 1 to 4 above have shown that the contribution by the publishing industry to the globalization of its publishing market had already begun in the late nineteenth century and continued to do so throughout the first half of the twentieth century with the active participation of publishers, translators, and copyright scholars in the international copyright negotiations. While the end of World War II marked the commencement of a new era for the Japanese publishing industry, in terms of internationalization, it simply indicated the continuation of existing structures that had been established over the course of half a century. This included the networks of the copyright advisory bodies between leaders of the publishing industry and involved state representatives. After the war, these platforms were simply reactivated, and Japan rejoined the international copyright negotiations to continue their prewar negotiations concerning Japan's position in the transnational copyright community. Some of the involved actors were still from the generation of internationalists born around the time of the Meiji Restoration. As previous chapters showed, Japan's internationalist elite was flexible enough to adapt their activities and rhetoric according to the changing external circumstances. The same was true in the early postwar years, where imperialist propaganda was replaced by a focus on Japan's role as a leader in regional publishing cooperation. Likewise, the argumentation for the need to maintain special exemptions on translation rights shifted from a former focus on "cultural harmony between East and West" to "the people" and what a change in law would mean for the reading culture of Japan's citizens.

This fifth and last chapter examines the postwar years up to Japan's abolishment of its old copyright law in 1970. It traces continuities and discontinuities in Japan's transnational activities surrounding the globalization of international copyright protection to explore the relevance of previous activities and relationships on the final and complete integration into the international system. The first section of the chapter focuses on the domestic administrative transformations and the early revival of the copyright movement under the US Occupation with its Supreme Commander of the Allied Powers (SCAP). It argues that despite the creation of new advisory bodies and the restructuring of administrative procedures, the Occupation followed by Japan regaining its sovereignty in 1952 did not bring major changes to the existing structures in copyright negotiations between the state and the publishing industry. On the contrary, SCAP and with it the Japanese government depended on the cooperation with and the input and initiatives of the prewar Japanese experts. Some of those involved were still from the first generation of early Meiji-born elitists who had advised the state officials for decades. It would take a different generation to loosen this bond. The second part of the chapter explores the impact of Japan's domestic changes on its involvement in the postwar transnational copyright community, its admission to the Universal Copyright Convention (UCC) concluded by UNESCO in 1952, and the challenges and final opposition of the publishers surrounding Japan's eventual decision to abolish its special exemptions and bring its Berne Convention up to international standards. Following the trend of the times, Japan's internationalists wanted to transform Japan's image and thereby raise its international status towards that of a peace-loving, first world nation that placed great value on international cultural exchange and cultural diplomacy. Within the period of postwar decolonization that led to many newly independent nations looking to join the international copyright treaty, the special reservations that Japan had originally been granted for being a "nation in development" stood in direct opposition to its newfound pride and its desire to take a new place in the international community and in close cooperation with UNESCO become a regional leader in publishing.

THE CONTINUATION OF INTERNATIONAL COPYRIGHT NEGOTIATIONS UNDER SCAP AND UNESCO

World War II de facto ended on September 2, 1945, when Japanese delegates signed a declaration of unconditional surrender aboard the battleship USS Missouri in the bay of Tōkyō—less than a month after the dropping of two atomic bombs on Hiroshima and Nagasaki and a massive Soviet campaign in Manchuria, ending the Japanese-Soviet Non-Aggression Treaty of 1941. On August 30, two weeks after the emperor had announced in his famous public radio broadcast that Japan would accept the Potsdam Declaration and three days before the declaration of surrender was formally signed, US Army General Douglas MacArthur arrived in Japan and announced the general occupation policy for Japan, including the abandonment of suppression of freedom of speech and publishing. During the war, numbers of productions had fallen due to the lack in supplies and the only books that did get produced were propaganda works and Japanese classics to strengthen the war spirit. By the end of the war in 1945, many publishing houses and printers had been bombed and burned down. With MacArthur's announcement, publishers were from then on theoretically free of any government control, but in reality, the Civil Information and Educational Section (CIE) of SCAP strictly controlled and censored the market, with an immediate prohibition on translations and imports of foreign works. These regulations were only loosened in 1948 after a long process of petitioning from the publishers.[6]

For the Berne Union and the Pan-American Union, the end of the war allowed a continuation of the negotiations to unify their copyright treaties that for the most part had been interrupted by the war.⁷ The copyright community was, however, in need of a new international organization that would continue the work of the Paris Institute and the ICIC, like the coordination of activities and taking the lead in bringing the different member states together. With the establishment of UNESCO in November 1945, such an organization was founded as the direct successor to the ICIC. UNESCO not only absorbed the ideals of the former organization, but also took on most of its personnel.⁸

From the time of its founding, UNESCO placed intellectual property rights on its agenda and continued the procedure of the Berne Bureau and the ICIC to centralize the global regulations of intellectual property rights.⁹ The Subcommittee for Information and Mass Media[10] was assigned the field of intellectual property and took up its work in 1946. It first decided to separate the revision plans for the Berne Convention from the plans to establish a Universal Copyright Convention and allocated the responsibility for holding the revision conference of the Berne Convention back to the Berne Bureau. UNESCO then started preparations for the Universal Copyright Convention that was concluded in Geneva in 1952.[11]

While the Berne Bureau and UNESCO quickly resumed the prewar efforts to move forward with intellectual property right protection, Japan's publishing industry in the immediate postwar found itself in an internal conflict revolving around the control of paper, the publishers war guilt, and the ban on trade which effected foreign imports and translations. The people were eager to read, but many publishers were struggling with the immediate effects of the war which included not only the loss of machinery, but also the little to no available printing paper which led to an enormous rise in paper prices. Furthermore, with the dissolution of the previously existing publishers' associations in connection with the centralization of the media in the late 1930s, at the end of the war, the industry found itself completely disorganized. Nevertheless, also in Japan, the copyright movement soon revived again.

After Japan signed the Japanese Instrument of Surrender on September 2, 1945, the country with all its laws including copyright regulations was placed under the supervision of SCAP for the next seven years. This Occupation period, like the Meiji Restoration, is oftentimes characterized by discontinuity, although an increase in studies on these two points in Japanese history emphasizes the elements of continuity, demonstrating that the break was not as abrupt as past historians have claimed it to be.[12] Unlike common perceptions, SCAP's reforms did not affect the character of the national bureaucracy as much as often thought, and old structures, personnel, or existing relations to other political units were kept in place, while SCAP's primary goal was to make Japan's administration more efficient.[13]

When SCAP assumed control, it dissolved the centralized wartime publishing organ that had been administering the publishing industry since 1943. The dissolution on September 30, 1945 was followed immediately by the founding of a new publishers' association, the Japan Publishers' Association (Nihon Shuppan Kyōkai) which was to serve as "an instrument of service and guidance to Japanese publishers."[14] The new organization, which cooperated closely with SCAP, was expected to resume its work quickly which was made possible primarily through the decision of the Joints Chief of Staff to use existing bureaucratic structures and keep the old trade structures in place.[15] The president of the publisher Yūhikaku, Egusa Shirō, and *Asahi shinbun* Journalist Suzuki Bunshirō were appointed as the leaders of the association. With the help of its own magazine under the association's name *Nihon Shuppan Kyōkai*, monthly updates of the latest news related to publishing and copyright regulations were provided to those in the industry.

Regarding the prewar administration and handling of the international copyright agreement, the main discontinuity brought about by the SCAP administration was the abolition of the Home Ministry, including its Police Affairs Bureau and the Book Division, which had previously assumed responsibility for all copyright-related affairs. The functions of the Ministry were dispersed over several different ministries and agencies with the Ministry of Education in charge of copyright.[16] In addition to continuing to handle the daily affairs of government, the ministerial bureaucrats now also took on a new role of consulting members of SCAP on their reform programs.

At the end of the war, the Berne Convention as well as a bilateral copyright treaty concluded between Japan and the United States in 1906 were in theory still valid, but SCAP's occupation policy during the early postwar years forbade any foreign trade including the import and translations of foreign works.[17] Nevertheless, the copyright movement began to reemerge quickly. This resurgence was partly due to the continuity of individuals and entities involved in the prewar copyright landscape who remained active after the war. The Copyright Investigation Council that had been founded in 1935 as a mutual organ of exchange between bureaucrats and private actors from the industry had remained active during the war, mostly even in its original composition. Akagi Tomoharu, Kikuchi Kan, Mizuno Rentarō, and the film producer and later president of the film production company Shōchiku, Kido Shirō, remained part of the committee of 23 members with backgrounds in the private industry, the ministerial bureaucracy, academia, or the National Diet. Yamada Saburō, the above-mentioned scholar for private international law, who had already closely worked with the council throughout the 1930s, by 1943 was listed as an official member. In the same year he was appointed as a member of the House of Peers by the emperor.[18]

While World War II is generally described as a period with no valid copyright protection, for instance, the US-Japan Treaty was considered to have become invalid with the outbreak of the Pacific War, there were also many publishers who continued to protect foreign copyrights during the war.[19] In Japan, the members of the Copyright Investigation Council were among those who continued to follow the regulations of the Berne Convention. Because there are so few sources, little is known about their work during the war, but at what was possibly their last meeting before the end of the war on November 15, 1944, the committee discussed the issue of reimbursing German authors for the reproduction and translations of their works and the intellectual property rights of the original author. When Kido Shirō suggested reproducing only parts of the original, in this case, of textbooks, Akagi Tomoharu referred to the fact that even the reproduction of only certain parts of a textbook was regulated by the Berne Convention and that any unauthorized reproductions would violate the author's individual property rights.[20] The presence of the above individuals contributed to the reformation and re-establishment of copyright-related activities and discussions in the post-war period. As had been the case in the past, the ideas and initiatives regarding Japan's stance in the international copyright negotiations continued to be brought forward not by the state, but by those engaged in the publishing business, a method which SCAP supported as part of its attempt to strengthen public participation in the democratization process.

A major change that took place in the postwar period is that for the first time Japanese authors and other copyright *owners* including translators raised their voice in favor of extending the rights of the author. In November 1946, a group of literary scholars and translators, artists, film and theatre makers, and musicians gathered and founded the Japan Authors' Association (Nihon Chosakka Kumiai). Its leader was the translator and literary critic Nakajima Kenzō (1903-1979), who as a former member of the prewar International Copyright Convention had been one of the authors of the Pamphlet "La Situation Spéciale des Traducteurs et des Éditeurs au Japon" that Yamada Saburō had distributed at the Paris Institute and the ICIC at the beginning of 1937 to strengthen Japan's claim for free translation rights. Many translators that had previously fought for free translation rights, now supported the protection of literary works and translations.

In a first petition from August 1947, the newly formed Authors' Association shared the opinion that while its members agreed that literary and artistic works had a cultural value to them and, whenever possible, should be available to the general public, the original ideas of the author should nevertheless also be protected which is why they pleaded to keep the general copyright protection on written works at a minimum of 30 years in upcoming revisions.[21] This demand in favor of copyright *owners* rather than copyright *holders* announced a growing changing interest between translators or authors and publishers who had used the same path and argumentation ever since translation rights had been incorporated into the Berne Convention in 1908.

A hint of why the translators turned away from their prewar standpoint was given in an article written by translator Nakajima Kenzō that was published in

December 1947 in the *Ningen* (Human Being), an influential journal of the postwar literary world. Nakajima started his article which was addressed to his fellow colleagues by explaining that Japan's "late-coming" (*kōshinsei*) at the time of the Meiji Restauration had caused the country to be opportunistic in terms of translations of foreign works. However, after Japan's rapid modernization following the Meiji Restauration, this "late-coming" of the country would still be noticeable, as would be the absence of one unified culture within Japan. For that reason, he argued that translations would always be needed and at the same time criticized the limitations that translators experienced under the occupiers, especially in consideration of the envisioned UNESCO mission for world peace that required a deep understanding of each others' cultures. Nakajima then, however, appealed to his fellow translators to accept the situation of not being able to translate newer works and instead turn to older works from before the nineteenth century that so far had not received much attention. He finished his article stating that it would be a "disgrace" (*chijoku*) to still call Japan a country of translations, the country would be far enough in its development to recognize a new beginning. Those who would not see that could in Nakajima's words only be referred to as "half-civilized beings" (*han bunmeijin*).[22]

The copyright situation continued to be discussed in different fora. In March 1948, various authors and writers came together and established the Japan Copyright Union (Nihon Chosakuken Renmei) to represent the interest of Japanese copyright owners. The members shared the opinion that for the unresolved issues regarding the duration of copyrights, an organization made up exclusively of private actors should exist and that the postwar copyright movement should place importance on establishing the field of copyright as an independent field, free from bureaucratic influence and decision-making. Immediately after its founding, it set up a small committee and addressed its first petition, signed by translator Nakajima Kenzō to the National Diet.[23] A dissolution bill to dissolve the Home Ministry which hitherto had handled the petitions by members of the publishing industry had been passed just three months prior, so that the communication routes and responsibilities for copyright-related matters needed to be clarified which likely was the reason for a prolongation of a quick processing of the petition.

The petition included five points of concern regarding the current Copyright Law and its ongoing revision. Under point three, the copyright owners requested the dissolution of the 1935 established Copyright Investigation Council. According to their reasoning, they were in need of their own organization, a mediating organ to solve the increasing disagreements in connection with copyrights. Instead of being dependent on a state committee, the translators and writers envisioned a similar organization as the Labour Relations Commissions (Rōdō Iinkai) that acted as an independent mediator and protector of legal rights of workers in Japan and was codified inside the Labour Union Law (Rōdō Kumiai Hō)[24] which had been created in 1945 and was replaced by a new Labour Union Law in 1949.[25] Furthermore, point five stated that the existing Copyright Law had been established 50 years prior and would not be suitable for the current state of things anymore, despite having been minorly revised several times. In the name of Nakajima Kenzō, the translators and other copyright owners therefore urged the parliament to establish a new research committee (*chōsa iinkai*) to conduct extensive research on the complications surrounding the Copyright Law and its revision.[26]

It took until December 1948 that the Minister of Education Shimojō Yasumaro passed the petition and his personal comments on to Prime Minister Yoshida Shigeru. With regard to point three and the requested establishment of a new intermediary organ in place of the existing Council, Shimojō wrote that while he did not approve of dissolving the Council altogether, he did consent to the idea of establishing a new mediating organ. Concerning point five, he wrote that regarding the present situation under the Allied Occupation, he believed it to be rather difficult to undertake an overall study on the revision of the Copyright Law. However, Shimojō agreed that one could begin by investigating certain parts of the treaty.[27]

This petition and the government's internal response to it show once again the initial inertia of the state in the matter of single-handedly taking up the prewar negotiations on copyright regulations. The same idleness applied to SCAP which in theory was the main actor in charge of copyright regulations during the time of occupation, but until 1949 failed to conduct any updated research on the international copyright agreement and Japan's position in the international debate surrounding its revision process. It is likewise important to note that the initial idea to reform the prewar Copyright Investigation Council was not suggested by SCAP or by governmental representatives, but by the translators wanting to strengthen their independent voices.

After the founding and dissolution of several new copyright associations to realize the translators' ambitions for creating an independent organ, in December 1949, the postwar upheaval finally calmed down with the establishment of the Japan Copyright Council (Nihon Chosakuken Kyōgikai). The association emerged from its predecessor, the Japan Copyright *Advisory Council* (Nihon Chosakuken *Shingikai*) that had been founded in June that year, but was dissolved and founded again as the Japan Copyright Council only six months later in order to clearly distinguish itself from a ministerial *shingikai*.[28] As the previous chapters have shown, the system of advisory councils (*shingikai*) had already existed since the 1890s, but during the Occupation, the old system was reformed by occupation authorities with the initial goal to eliminate bureaucrats from the councils and enshrine the consultation system in legislation. Upon realizing that the bureaucrats were instrumental in the formation process of these councils and in policy-formulation in general, the overall aim of SCAP changed to henceforth still include bureaucrats, but limit their influence, work towards pluralizing participation in state policymaking, and seek the advice from people outside the government.[29]

The members of the Japan Copyright Council, however, wanted *complete* independence from any governmental participation. The Council received no state support and was entirely made up of private members with translator Nakajima Kenzō as its leader. The main goal at the time of its founding was to regulate the relationship between copyright owners and copyright users through mutual consultations. The involved organizations at the time of its founding included seven copyright owner associations consisting mainly of authors, eleven copyright user associations consisting of publishers, as well as a board of 32 individual members including publisher Egusa Shirō of Yūhikaku, and the director of the publishing house Kōdansha, Noma Shōichi. Despite the above early efforts of the copyright owners and especially of Nakajima Kenzō to return to the negotiations around the revision of the Copyright Law, their abilities were still limited by the Allied Forces, and it was to take another couple of years until Japan's return to sovereignty in 1952 when the copyright movement was able to unfold its whole potential.

JAPAN'S REENTRY INTO THE TRANSNATIONAL COPYRIGHT COMMUNITY

While Japan's participation in the international copyright discussions was temporarily put on hold, in June 1948, 35 other nations participated in the long-awaited Brussels Revision Conference, which had originally been scheduled to take place in the mid-1930s, during which the Berne Convention was once again revised. The main change to the treaty was the introduction of an obligatory 50 years of copyright protection for all member states which the ALAI as the main representative of Europe's publishers and authors had tried to achieve since the beginning of the century. Japan had not been invited to the conference and was excluded from attending even as an observer. Yet, despite the absence from this important international gathering, no efforts were made by members of the Japanese state to pick up their internal studies and continue the negotiations that had come to a halt during the war. Once again, the initiative to participate in the international law-making came solely from the private sector.

While now the Berne Convention had once again been revised, the prewar plans to establish a universal copyright convention to also target other nations that were not yet a member of any international copyright treaty and at the same time bring together those nations that were members of separate conventions in one universal treaty, were still standing. Following the Brussels Revision Conference, a UNESCO Committee of Copyright Experts continued the prewar procedure of the Berne Bureau, the Paris Institute, and the ICIC to collect opinions from governments, national commissions, governmental and non-governmental organizations, as well as from individual authorities to study the current situation as regards copyright matters with the goal of getting a general overview of the copyright conditions around the world.[30] The experts were hoping to find answers to the most urgent question which had not changed since the prewar gatherings: "What are the best means for taking a first step toward [the] establishment of international rules for protection of literary, artistic and scientific works which would be, in so far as possible, in harmony with the various national legislations now in force."[31] The three options could be summed up as (1) joining an existing multilateral treaty which seemed increasingly difficult to administer, (2) concluding bi-partite or multi-partite treaties which however, on a world-wide scale was feared to cause an "inextricable labyrinth of provisions," or (3): "[the establishment of] a convention open to adherence by all and adopted by the greatest number of countries possible which would have the advantage of obtaining the simultaneous assent of all the signatory countries and of establishing a uniform stand on the subject."[32]

The task entrusted by UNESCO to the experts was to address the difficulties, find solutions, and draft an outline for a new convention. For that, the copyright laws of all countries needed to be analyzed, the subjects then systematically grouped in categories and classified in special indexes to facilitate the work of the experts. To approach this enormous task, reports were conducted that drew upon different source material, including personal files from copyright experts or the replies to the questionnaires sent out by UNESCO that had been submitted not only by governments, but also by non-governmental organizations and individual authorities.[33]

While prior to the Brussels Revision Conference but after 1945, Japan had been excluded from all international copyright communication now administered by UNESCO in cooperation with the Berne Bureau, from the late 1940s, this changed in direct connection with the development of the UNESCO movement in Japan. The early movement for the admission of Japan to UNESCO had been initiated by private individuals and began as early as 1946 with the establishment of a UNESCO association in Sendai. In the following year, further associations were formed across the country and by May 1948, the National Federation of UNESCO Cooperative Associations in Japan (Nihon Yunesuko Kyōkai Renmei) was founded with the main purpose of achieving Japan's admission to UNESCO.[34] In the late 1940s, the private initiators were joined by US SCAP officials who began strongly to support Japan's integration into the international community by urging UNESCO to invite individuals from Japan to participate in the international meetings.[35] The SCAP authorities stood in direct contact with UNESCO and began to act as mediators, increasing the involvement of the Japanese government in the activities of UNESCO. This included bringing Japan (back) into the ongoing discussions on copyrights.

The Japanese government received a first general questionnaire from the UNESCO Committee of Copyright Experts via the Diplomatic Section of General Headquarters (GHQ) in February 1949, but did not respond.[36] UNESCO received replies from 40 different countries which were discussed at a conference of the Committee of Copyright Experts at UNESCO from July 4-9, 1949, the same month that the Japanese government set up a Liaison and UNESCO Section in the Ministry of Education to coordinate its activities.[37] The final recommendation of the experts by the end of the conference read as follows: "The Committee of Experts (…) recommends that, taking into account the detailed directives hereafter described, UNESCO shall establish, after consultation with the United Nations, procedure suitable to lead the adoption of a Universal Copyright Convention."[38] The recommendation was followed by several points that the new convention should adhere to. It further decided to address a questionnaire to member and non-member states of UNESCO which included six questions on the planned convention, including the question: "(d): whether the State wishes to include any reservation, especially one concerning translation of works from another language into the national language or language of the States."[39] This questionnaire titled "Request for Views of Governments on a Universal Copyright Convention" addressed by UNESCO to governments around the world was sent out from December 1949. In Japan, however, due to the administrative hinderance of having to be transmitted via the Diplomatic Section of GHQ, the Ministry of Foreign Affairs in charge of handling the request did not receive its copy until June 6, 1950. In the letter attached, Deputy Chief of Staff at SCAP, Cloyce K. Huston, requested the government give its "prompt consideration," as the Head of the Copyright Division of UNESCO had expressed his wish to receive a quick update on this matter.[40]

In the same month, translator Nakajima Kenzō once again shared his opinion, this time in the renowned law expert magazine *Hōritsu jihō* (Law Reporter) with which he likely reached the involved bureaucrats inside the Ministry of Foreign Affairs and the Ministry of Education. Nakajima explained the copyright situation and wrote that Japan should at the earliest possible opportunity join the 50 years of copyright protection as defined by the recent Brussels Act. According to him, the public information regarding copyrights would have to be improved and more opinions of legal experts were needed to investigate the matter. He closed his article with the words: "I wish for a quick establishment of an 'academic copyright society' [*chosakuken gakkai*]. The existing plans need to be implemented. For this, we not only need legal experts, but [we must] also to include members from all different sectors."[41] By sharing his opinion in expert magazines, Nakajima further stimulated a debate in the wider circle of stakeholders and increased the pressure on the government to take action.

Whether or not the government was directly influenced by Nakajima's latest appeal, or by a combination of the preceding requests from members of the industry and SCAP, one month later in July 1950, the Ministry of Education ordered restructuring the statute of the Copyright Investigation Council established in 1935 which had remained active during the war. The revision had the Minister of Education (as a replacement of the former Home Minister) select eligible members, mainly from the private sector, for the advisory council. The change came into effect on July 31.[42] Following the change of legal basis, from August 3, the Ministry of Education did what had been advised by the Japanese copyright owners already in 1948 and started contacting 22 organizations involved with copyright to recommend candidates for a new council which was to consist of 60 members, including 25 scholars and experts, 25 individuals recommended by civilian bodies, and 10 state representatives from government agencies involved.[43] On August 17, 1950, the Minister of Education announced the council's official regulations.[44] It was named Advisory Council for Drafting a Revised Bill of the Copyright Law (Chosakuken Hō Kaiseian Kisō Shingikai) and was given the task of revising Japan's 30-year copyright protection regulation, its reservations on the protection of translations, and research measures regarding music, broadcasting, and film rights which were not protected under the current law, and also to look into the matter of copyright regulations concerning the use of school textbooks. Among the selected experts were the publishers Egusa Shirō, Noma Shōichi, translator and French literary scholar Kusano Teishi, legal expert Yamada Saburō, film producer Kido Shirō, and former Home Ministry bureaucrat Akagi Tomoharu who had represented Japan at the Rome Revision Conference. They were all long acquainted with each other through the prewar negotiations and their participation in different councils.[45]

As time was limited, the Ministry of Foreign Affairs sent the official answer of the Japanese government to the UNESCO questionnaire on August 25, 1950, *before* the new council was able to discuss with its members in detail the propositions that had been suggested by UNESCO. In their reply, the government added the following request to the GHQ: "It is requested that the Diplomatic Section, General Headquaters, Supreme Commander for the Allied Powers, be good enough to take necessary actions so that the head of the Copyright Division of UNESCO may be appropriately advised of the views of the Japanese Government on this matter."[46] The reply from the government did, however, bring with it a misunderstanding that resulted from an unclear phrasing in the draft: Under paragraph 2(2), it stated: "The Convention should not abridge any legal right of protection derived from any existing multilateral or bilateral treaty and it should be construed to encourage continued adherence and further adhesion to such treaties."[47]

The Japanese government interpreted the above phrase as not affecting the existing regulations on Japanese translation rights as defined in the Berne Convention. Thus, in their reply to the question on translation rights and whether the Convention should include a right of reservation concerning protection of the right of translation of works, the Japanese government replied that "it is not necessary to provide for the reservation of the protection of the right of translation," believing that the new contract would not pose a juxtaposition to Japan's current regulations.[48] Even though the government had handed in its reply to the GHQ within a short time frame of only two months since the receipt of the questionnaire, it did not reach UNESCO in time for the next Committee of Copyright Experts conference held in Washington from October 23 to November 4, 1950, which resulted in Japan being allowed to attend merely as an observer, not as an active participant in the conference.[49] The representative onsite was Kubota Fujimaro, head of the Administration Bureau (Kanrikyoku) in the Ministry of Education.[50] Japan's inactivity at the meeting was a problem insofar as, during the first two meetings of the newly established Advisory Council for Drafting a Revised Bill of the Copyright Law on November 17 and 20, it became clear that the appointed experts including publisher Egusa Shirō and legal scholar Yamada Saburō wanted to keep the reservations on translation rights under all circumstances, a standpoint which the Japanese government had failed to make clear in its reply to UNESCO.[51]

The first expert meeting of the Advisory Council had been attended by 15 council members, but no one from the copyright owners' side was present to represent the opinion of the authors and translators. At the second meeting, the number of attendees rose to 18. In addition to the usual mix of experts from the publishing industry and involved ministerial bureaucrats, another important attendee was Katsumoto Masaakira, a professor of law at the University of Tōkyō who would represent Japan at the Universal Copyright Conference of UNESCO two years later. During the second meeting, Yamada Saburō together with Egusa Shirō urged the governmental representatives to keep the 10-year reservations on translation rights which, according to the publishers, would have a "historic meaning" in Japan.[52] The discussion rounds of the council meeting followed up on the style of the meetings of earlier decades with representatives from different interest groups concerned with copyrights sharing the standpoint of their respective sector. Over the following months, more discussion rounds were held at the Ministry of Education. In addition to the translation rights issue, another major topic was the question of whether Japan should join the Brussels Act from 1948 which had regulated the copyright protection to 50 years after the death of the author. Japan technically still held on to the 30-year regulation of the Rome revision to which the country would return after regaining its sovereignty with the end of the Occupation in 1952.[53]

While the Advisory Council for Drafting a Revised Bill of the Copyright Law continued its discussions, the UNESCO Committee of Copyright Experts was following up on its last conference and compiled a "Supplementary Request for

Views Concerning a Universal Copyright Convention" which as regards the reservations stated that "a state may not make its adherence subject to reservations."[54] Unlike the first draft, the second draft did not conform with the regulations of the Berne Convention that Japan adhered to and ignored the Japanese regulations of a 10-year limit to the rights of translations.[55] The UNESCO representative to Japan, S. M. Lee forwarded the letter to Nishimura Iwao, head of the Liaison and UNESCO Section inside the Ministry of Education, on April 25, 1951, with the request to return the questionnaire by June 15 that year.[56]

Upon receipt of the supplementary request, on May 16, the Ministry called in a consultation meeting with the Advisory Council, followed by four additional consultations over the next three weeks with the last meeting held on June 4, 1951. By June 12, the official statement of the Japanese government, this time a direct reflection of the expert opinions, was released. While in reply to the previous questionnaire, the Japanese government had stated their consent to the abolition of any reservation of the protection of the right of translation, their official answer now stated the opposite, namely, that the Japanese government "cannot agree to the regulations on translation rights."[57] The opinion was handed in just in time to be consulted at the 6th General Assembly of UNESCO from June 18 until July 13, 1951, in Paris.[58] During the time of the conference, Japan was officially admitted to UNESCO on July 2.

Despite the timely submission of Japan's opposition to the proposal of UNESCO, shortly after, the wish of the private interest groups to participate in the international discussions was once again hampered by the ministerial bureaucrats who disregarded an invitation by UNESCO that had asked copyright experts, including those from Japan, to attend the assembly. However, it cannot be ignored that this invitation reached Japan at a time of great change with the return of the country's sovereignty only a few months away. The amount of administrative work facing the ministerial bureaucrats at the time was most likely a significant contributor to their inactivity regarding the international copyright negotiations. It can also be assumed that during this time, the bureaucrats involved tried to avoid any conflict with UNESCO and were willing to sacrifice the interests of the experts and private publishing industry in favor of the reason of the state. The private experts expressed their "deep regret" (*senzai no konji*) over the government's failure to respond to UNESCO's invitation which led to the absence of a Japanese representative at this important conference.[59]

Whether it was because of the contradiction in the two statements of the Japanese government regarding the reservations on translation rights, or because there was no representative onsite to convey Japan's standpoint in person, reservations on translation rights were not envisaged in the preliminary draft of the Universal Copyright Convention distributed to the governments on August 14 with the request to reply by December 1951. Again, publishers' and translators' associations were contacted for two consultation meetings in November during which the members came to the same conclusion as at their previous meetings concerning translation rights. Building on these expert opinions, the Japanese government handed in their official opinion to UNESCO on December 14, 1951. This time, it clearly stated that the Japanese government wished to hold on to their reservations on translation rights, but it is questionable whether the ministerial bureaucrats at this point were still willing to fight for this cause and saw it as an advantage for their national standing.[60]

The Advisory Council for Drafting a Revised Bill of the Copyright Law continued its investigations until the end of 1951 when its activities were discontinued. In relation to the revision of the Japanese Copyright Law, the council's existence is deemed to have achieved little success, primarily because it was unable to present a revision outline.[61] It did, however, fulfill an important role in providing a first postwar forum of exchange between the state, the private industry, and legal scholars concerned in the copyright revision process that enabled a direct continuity from the prewar to the postwar cooperation. Many of the involved actors were long acquainted with each other and familiar with the process of international negotiations in the field of copyright. For the publishers, translators, writers, legal practitioners, broadcasters, and filmmakers involved, the forum offered an opportunity to influence the official standpoint of the government that was shared with UNESCO and then with the world.

Nonetheless, the continuity of cooperation and common grammar between a solid group of private industry actors, scholars, and bureaucrats surrounding Yamada Saburō, Akagi Tomoharu, Egusa Shirō, Kido Shirō, and Kusano Teishi was a main contributor to the difficult and lengthy process of adapting Japan's standpoint regarding translation right protection to international standards over the following years. The above actors had worked together for decades, sat on councils together and defended their mutual cause in the media and abroad. For them, Japan's exemption on translation rights had reached a "historic meaning" and was not questioned even in light of the new postwar circumstances.[62] It would take a new generation for this viewpoint to change.

POST-OCCUPATION CHANGES AND THE UNIVERSAL COPYRIGHT CONVENTION

On April 28, 1952, the Peace Treaty came into effect, returning to Japan its state sovereignty with the exception of its foreign and security policy that was bound to the Security Treaty between the United States and Japan signed on September 8, 1951. With respect to copyright protection, the return to sovereignty meant that Japan's copyright regulations no longer fell under the control of the CIE at SCAP and that the country officially returned to its latest ratified revision of the Berne

Convention, the Rome revision of 1928. To prepare for the change in administration, two weeks before, the House of Councillors,[63] the reformed upper house of the National Diet of Japan, had held a meeting for which also three external expert witnesses (*sankōjin*) had been invited, namely translator Nakajima Kenzō, professor of law at Chūō University Katsumoto Masaakira, and copyright lawyer Kido Yoshihiko. The meeting was primarily led by Nakajima who gave a detailed outline over the importance of clarifying the administration of copyright once the Peace Treaty came into effect. Much to the resentment of the publishing industry, the Peace Treaty stated that the war period would be added to the existing duration of copyright protection which was also among the points of discussion. The meeting with the external copyright experts shows how few preparations and research had been undertaken over the past seven years to confront the upcoming changes.[64] In the days that followed, further meetings of both houses of the National Diet were held to discuss the topic of the plan to introduce a UNESCO Universal Copyright Convention and of Japan's position on international copyright law and its existing membership in the Berne Convention. However, after the first inclusion of participants from outside the government on April 15, the meetings between state representatives continued without external input. While the state officials emphasized the fact that the Japan Copyright Council was kept up to date, the Council was rather *told* of the plans of the government instead of being directly involved in the negotiation process.[65] On April 24, Okazaki Katsuo, minister without portfolio who from October that year would take on the position as Foreign Minister, attended one of the meetings stressing the fact that the Ministry of Foreign Affairs would be unable to handle all the individual copyright-related consultations with different countries on its own and was therefore relying also on the opinions of experts, although he primarily referred to experts inside the National Diet, meaning those few members of both chambers with a background in the publishing or broadcasting industry.[66] Discussions were also taken up regarding the future tasks of the still existing prewar Copyright Investigation Council as a council to exchange opinions between ministries involved, the National Diet, and the private industry.[67] It was decided that the Copyright Investigation Council should continue its work, but that its name was to be changed from *shinsakai* to *shingikai* to distance itself from the prewar organization, if in name only. But for Nakajima Kenzō and his Japan Copyright Council who had requested the complete dissolution of the Copyright Investigation Council, established in 1935, and who now with the newly gained independence raised concern over the private industry potentially falling back under the control and dependence on the ministerial bureaucrats in international negotiations, these steps were not sufficient. Three days before the Peace Treaty was ratified, Nakajima, who had already petitioned a similar request in 1948, issued a statement at the annual general meeting of the Japan Copyright Council. In this statement, he highlighted the Council's opposition to the bureaucratic control of copyrights and copyright administration by the Ministry of Education with its plan to establish a new copyright council (*chosakuken shingikai*). He emphasized the need to establish a copyright industry that was controlled privately and not by the state.[68] Although Nakajima's statement was discussed in a House of Councillors' session in May, it did not receive the anticipated sympathy of the National Diet members who argued that the envisioned copyright council established by the ministry would be democratic in nature and would incorporate extra-governmental opinions.[69] Despite Nakajima's efforts, in June that year, a new council thus was in fact established with the simultaneous dissolution of the prewar Copyright Investigation Council.[70]

The translators around Nakajima Kenzō reacted by making use of the newly established sovereignty and power to the people that came with it and decided to take matters into their own hands. Their program included the collection of private expert opinions on the Copyright Law which were shared with the general public through lectures and scientific events. At a session of the House of Councillors' Educational Committee in early June, Uraguchi Tetsuo, a publisher of the postwar magazine *Manga taimusu* (Manga Times) and member of the right-wing Rikken Yōseikai (Constitutional Health Party), had emphasized the same need to work together with experts and make discussions public. He asked his fellow colleagues to invite members of the Ministry of Foreign Affairs in addition to external experts, like Nakajima Kenzō who had been invited in April, to ask for their assistance in handling copyright-related questions. But the private industry was one step ahead in implementing these ideas.[71]

The activities of the translators and authors included collecting expert opinions and communicating the results to the public. Their Japan Copyright Council also established its own Department of Foreign Affairs to improve external communication on international copyright negotiations. The perhaps greatest change compared to the prewar private interest groups was that from 1952 when the Japan Copyright Council started sending their own representatives to UNESCO to enable the committee to directly get involved, exchange opinions, study recent copyright developments abroad and, most importantly, further break loose from their previous dependency on the state authorities as regards attending international conferences.[72] The first member of the copyright committee that was sent to Europe was the editor of the *Rīdāzu daijesuto* (Readers Digest) magazine, Mitsui Takanobu, and other private individuals followed in the upcoming years.[73] With the exception of publisher Ōhashi Otowa's private attendance of the Copyright Conference of 1900, the above actors were the first to attend official international copyright meetings as members of the Japanese publishing industry. At these meetings, they sat around a discussion table with governmental representatives, intergovernmental and international non-governmental organizations. Despite the translators' efforts and increasing global visibility, it remained the state that was the primary driver when it came to making the ultimate decisions influencing changes to international copyright law.

The first major copyright-related conference, which Japan was able to attend as a sovereign state, was the Universal Copyright Conference that was held in Geneva from August 18 until September 6, 1952. It had been 24 years since the idea to unify the two main copyright systems had first been raised in Rome. After having analyzed the copyright situation in each country and evaluated the replies to the questionnaires from around the world, the aim of this conference was to conclude a treaty that would enable all states of the world to join under one unified law by reducing copyright regulations to a basic standard so that the protection of rights was internationally aligned. The suggested duration for both general copyright protection and translation right protection was set at 25 years and was thereby lower than the regulations of the Berne Convention except for the terms of those countries—including Japan—who still held their 10-year translation right reservations at the 1896 level of the Berne Convention. This time, Japan, which had regained its sovereignty only four months earlier, officially sent seven representatives led by the ambassador to Switzerland and the expert for civil law and copyright law Katsumoto Masaakira. Katsumoto had been one of the members of the early postwar governmental Advisory Council for Drafting a Revised Bill of the Copyright Law and had thus been in direct consultations with the publishing industry prior to the conference.

At the international meeting, it was a Japanese delegate (although not clearly stipulated in the extant documents, most likely Katsumoto Masaakira himself)[74] who first steered the topic of the conference to the issue of translation rights:

> (...) [e]very endeavor must be made to facilitate the translation of works from the more advanced countries, with a view to attaining UNESCO's aim of spreading culture and educating mankind for justice and freedom. Another reason for facilitating translations is to bring cultural assistance to the underdeveloped countries—a programme to which the Specialized Agencies are directing their efforts.[75]

Even though the Japanese request received consent from a number of different countries including Argentina, Belgium, Chile, Greece, India, Ireland, Jugoslavia, Mexico, Thailand, and Turkey, it also received strong opposition from Brazil, Canada, Cuba, Denmark, Finland, the Netherlands, Norway, Sweden, the United Kingdom, and the United States. The latter even said that Japan's claim was a "definite handicap for the ratification of the United States," likely because the

United States did not want to in any way be disadvantaged by the treaty they had chosen to join.[76] Japan, together with Greece and Turkey, which also held reservations on translation rights, ultimately failed to convince UNESCO to incorporate a right to a reservation into the UCC treaty.

According to the UCC, instead of 10 years, the right to translate was henceforth effectively protected for the period of 25 years. But the UCC added one compromise for countries that by UCC definition could be defined as "developing countries". These were entitled to issue a so-called compulsory licensing on translations, granting a free translation of protected works without prior permission of the author after the period of seven years. Additionally, the UCC decided to introduce a "safeguard clause" which, on the one hand, guaranteed that the new treaty would not affect the existing regulations among member countries of the Berne Convention, while on the other hand, allowed copyright owners to make use of the more extensive UCC protection if a work was published simultaneously in a Berne and a UCC country. For Japan, this meant that in many cases the reservations on the duration of copyright and translation right protection, favoring Japanese publishers, were not valid.[77] At the end of the conference on September 6, 33 countries signed the Convention, including the United States which thereby for the first time entered a multilateral copyright treaty with the countries outside of the Americas. Japan together with eight additional countries including Belgium, Greece, Turkey, and Thailand decided to make use of the 220 extra days they had been granted before needing to sign the treaty, which the country eventually did on January 3, 1953. The dissatisfaction over the clause on translation rights, however, continued and even though the treaty was signed now, it still had to be ratified.

To further discuss Japan's situation, in April 1953 the Ministry of Education established another advisory council, the Copyright System Investigation Committee (Chosakuken Seido Chōsakai) which took up its research activities in October 1953. The council's chairmanship was given to Yamada Saburō in what was certainly the most obvious case of prewar-postwar personal continuities. The fact that Yamada, as a close acquaintance to the ministerial bureaucrats, was chosen as chair was not a rare case. As studies have shown, the chairmanships and memberships of advisory councils were primarily filled with persons who had long been tied to the bureaucrats and who therefore could be trusted to represent the opinion and policies of the latter.[78] The close relationship of the ministerial bureaucrats with the chairs of the postwar advisory councils has led researchers to question the effectiveness of the postwar reforms of the consultation system under SCAP and the desired changes to the predominance of the bureaucracy in policy-making. In the field of copyright, the consultation system did not result in major changes when comparing pre- with postwar Japan. Japan's state officials remained the most influential actors in Japan's international relations in this field. However, alongside them, individuals like Yamada Saburō and the heads of the publishing industry had played a significant role in advising the state actors ever since research about the international agreement was first taken up in the mid-1890s. Yamada was joined in the council by his close and longtime acquaintances, former Home Ministry bureaucrat Akagi Tomoharu and publisher Egusa Shirō. Other members included the law professor Katsumoto Masaakira and the publisher Nunokawa Kakuzaemon.[79] With Yamada as chairman there existed little room for a change in opinion regarding the question of translation right protection. He still emphasized the importance of reading French, German, and English literature for the competence of the Japanese population, and once again pointed out how few translations existed of Japanese works abroad.[80] Subsequently, the discussions surrounding the ratification of the UCC or a further revision of the Berne Convention stagnated.

When Japan had still not ratified the universal treaty by March 1955, the US embassy contacted the Ministry of Foreign Affairs regarding the stance of the Japanese government in this regard. For the United States this was an urgent matter, because the 1906 bilateral copyright treaty between Japan and the United States had been made subject to either abrogate or continue in effect like the Berne Convention under Article 7 of the Peace Treaty for Japan. The bilateral copyright treaty was to abrogate within the month of April the following year.[81] As a reaction, a special subcommittee was appointed inside the ministry to discuss options regarding a future copyright agreement between the United States and Japan. The special committee was led by Akagi Tomoharu, thus by another dominant member of the small group of actors involved from prewar copyright negotiations, who at a session in April 1955 collected member opinions to include in a preliminary report that was to be submitted to the parliament later that year. There were both votes that supported a bilateral treaty with the United States, and those who preferred seeing Japan ratify the UCC and thereby settle questions regarding the applicable regulations with the United States. Furthermore, the majority of the members advocated establishing a treaty between the two countries rather than having no treaty at all.[82]

The Japan Copyright Council followed the above events closely and, so as not to be passed over as copyright owners, reacted by submitting their own opinion to the government at the beginning of June. In their petition, the translators and authors demanded a fast normalization of US-Japan copyright relations through Japan's ratification of the UCC. Nakajima Kenzō had been sharing his opinion of the need for Japan to revise its laws in line with international standards for years, and now, once again, published an article in the newspaper *Tōkyō shinbun* in which he criticized those who still held on to the belief that Japan was a one-sided import country and would remain as such. According to Nakajima, the concerned opponents should reflect on their image of Japan especially in light of the recent efforts to translate actively Japanese novels into foreign languages.[83]

The discussion continued during the summer of 1955 no sign of harmonization between the two opposing groups that had formed: on the one hand, the publishers as copyright *holders* and the bureaucrats who continued to defend their prewar standpoint, and, on the other hand, the translators and other copyright *owners* who were seeking to find a way for Japan to move on from old structures and from, in their opinion, outpaced world perceptions. While the Copyright Department within the Ministry of Education at this point remained silent and waited for the instructed subcommittee to present their results, the media reported on both viewpoints.[84]

In September, shortly before the UCC was to go into effect, the newspaper *Asahi shinbun* gave an overview of the situation that was troubling both state and private interest groups involved alike. The article featured an interview with the publisher and copyright law scholar Azuma Suehiko who, in June, had been the third member of the private Japan Copyright Council to be sent to UNESCO in Paris to conduct research for the Council. Most likely influenced directly by his stay in Europe, in September the *Asahi shinbun* published Azuma's opinion that it would not make sense to continue to hold on to the 10-year reservations on translation rights, as cultural exchange had greatly increased and a work would not be of such great value after a period of 10 years had passed. He wrote: "If Japan started exporting works abroad, it would be of great advantage, if these works were protected. Thus, we should change our point of view that sees Japan as a country that merely imports culture to one that sees it as the culture export country that it has in the meanwhile become."[85]

More importantly, according to Azuma, Japan, with its current attitude towards international copyright, was conveying to other countries the message that it only thought of its own interests while ignoring the rights of other countries. Azuma was thus convinced that "also for the reason of international trust, Japan should ratify the UNESCO Treaty [UCC]."[86] He then added an astonishing side comment, claiming that the general bureau of UNESCO had assured Japan that upon ratifying the treaty, UNESCO would immediately push for the country to become a permanent member-nation of the UN Security Council, which in turn, would allow Japan in a later process to work on revising certain points of disadvantage to the country.[87] If his claim is accurate, then UNESCO tied Japan's participation in the UCC to broader geopolitical considerations, using Japan's desire to be included in the Security Council to achieve UNESCO's goals. The special veto power that comes with a permanent seat on the Council would have enhanced Japan's authority and legitimacy in the international system, which is what the state representatives had long wished to achieve.

This condition likely tilted the conflict that the bureaucrats found themselves in, favoring ratification. This conflict that the bureaucrats were facing resembled the one that ministerial bureaucrats, like Mizuno Rentarō and others, had encountered at the end of the last century when deciding whether Japan should join the Berne Convention. The earlier decision centered on whether to align Japan's legal system with Western nations by joining an international agreement, seen as a step toward "modernization" in Western terms, or to persist in the free import and translation of Western knowledge, thereby contributing to the country's development. The latter argument had been especially pushed by the publishing industry which had aimed to continue the free translations of works. Almost 60 years later, the focus was placed on a reinvention of Japan as a First World country that was defined by pacifism and an "American-style capitalism with democracy as its political mode."[88] Problematic for the consultation process was that the opinions of copyright owners and users on how to achieve the envisioned reinvention in general greatly differed. The translators as copyright owners argued that Japan should let go of its status as a "culture import country" and join the other First World nations by accepting the same protection of copyrights. They expressed the fear that Japan would again isolate itself from the international community.[89] However, the publishers and other copyright users were focused on the loss of income that came with the abandonment of the 10-year reservations. As the publishers and copyright experts involved like Yamada Saburō continued to maintain a close relationship with the ministerial bureaucrats involved, their demands could not easily be ignored by the state.

When the preliminary report of the subcommittee on US-Japan relations was submitted to the parliament, the Japan Copyright Council likewise presented their addendum document in favor of Japan's ratification of the UCC.[90] However, the addendum of the private copyright council was only reluctantly included in the negotiations. According to historian Miyata Noboru, the Ministry of Education deliberately delayed the inclusion of the addendum as they did not agree with its content.[91]

The final decision of the Japanese government to approve the ratification of the UCC in December 1955 was likely the result of an interplay between the pressure exerted by the Japan Copyright Council, the Japanese National Commission for UNESCO, the US government, and the provisional copyright agreement between the United States and Japan which was nearing expiration. In addition, if Azuma's assertion regarding UNESCO's assurance to support Japan's quest for a permanent seat on the UN Security Council upon joining the UCC were true, it would have played a significant role in the decision of the state officials.

Japan ratified UNESCO's new copyright treaty on April 28, 1956, and was now an official member of two international copyright agreements that, however, guaranteed different copyright protections. While the 1948 Brussels Act (that Japan had still not joined) had introduced the obligatory 50 years of copyright protection, translation rights were still not unified and the option to claim reservations against the duration remained an issue for UNESCO as well as for the Berne Convention and the UCC member states involved.

After Japan's ratification to the UCC had been settled, from June 11-15, 1956, UNESCO held its first session of an Intergovernmental Copyright Committee that had already in 1952 been established by Article 9 of the UCC. Topics that were up for discussion at the first session included the regulations of news and other press information, the placement of the symbol ©, protection of performing artists, recorders and broadcasters, and many other issues. Among the participants were not only official state delegates, which included, from Japan, a bureaucrat from the Ministry of Foreign Affairs, one from the Ministry of Education and a minister plenipotentiary and permanent delegate of Japan to UNESCO, but also so-called "observer" participants which included the United Nations and Specialized Agencies, and intergovernmental and non-governmental organizations. Japan was, for the first time at an intergovernmental copyright meeting, represented not only by its government, but also by the private interest association Japan Copyright Council that sent its managing director, the sound engineer for radio and film, Taguchi Ryūzaburō, to the meeting in Paris.[92] The participation of private individuals of the Copyright Council that acted as official advisors to the Japanese delegation continued in the years to come.

However, the members' hope that at last they would be given more room to act independently and participate in the negotiations was soon thwarted again. At the 1958 UNESCO Intergovernmental Copyright Committee meeting, the film critic and member of the Copyright Council, Sasaki Norio, who had travelled to Geneva to report on the conference, interviewed Abe Isao, one of Japan's state representatives and Councillor at the Embassy to Japan in Berne. In connection with the resolution that was made regarding the administration of future co-operation between the Berne Bureau and the Secretariat of UNESCO, Abe replied that if the choice was his to make, the Berne Bureau and UCC should not have a mutual board, but members of the Berne Union should continue to have their own bureau. He further stressed that Japan should not get pulled into the whirlwind surrounding the unification of Berne and UCC, but instead work on establishing and revising its domestic copyright policies.[93]

The state's disinterest to participate in the international negotiations became even more obvious two years later, in 1960, when the government received UNESCO's invitation to the 5th Intergovernmental Copyright Committee meeting. The invitation was not communicated to any of the private associations involved, which consequently led to the Japan Copyright Council not having had enough time to prepare and ultimately having been unable to attend. In the association's written history, members of the Council expressed their regret of having had to depend on the explanations and imported studies from abroad and emphasized their wish to take part in the modernization process of a global copyright agreement. It would require some time to prepare to be able to join international discussions on issues related to copyright and meet with members of UNESCO and copyright experts with the competency required.[94] Once again, Japan's bureaucrats themselves were the cause for Japan being left out of an international meeting that its private industry would have wanted to join.

With the new decade, the pressure on the government to rethink Japan's copyright position increased both by the media and by the Japan Copyright Council. The members of the copyright owners' association went against their own self-declared postwar ethos to stay clear of politics and not to interfere or engage in political movements, and in 1961 asked for a general reform of Japan's copyright administration.[95] They backed this request with the argument that those affected by the administration were actually for the most part civilians. In their annual report, the copyright owners stated that despite the recent difficulties, they wished to continue cooperating with the state, and that therefore, it would be necessary to investigate what had caused the rift between the two groups. They were certain that one main reason for the disagreement was the difference in opinion about the handling of international copyright regulations.[96] Lastly, the members of private interest groups were still hampered by the dominant bureaucrats in their aim to contribute to finding ways for a harmonic co-existence of the two copyright bodies.

THE RETURN OF THE PUBLISHERS

Compared to the postwar efforts of translators and authors as copyright owners who were eager to contribute to the globalization of international copyright regulations, the publishers as copyright users took longer to recover. They faced challenges like the wartime suppression of the media, ongoing postwar control of paper and capital, and restrictions on freedom of speech imposed by the Allied occupiers until 1952. By the time that Japan regained its sovereignty, the publishing industry was decentralized and despite the founding of many smaller publishers' organizations and the direct input of a number of directly engaged publishers like Egusa Shirō, it still lacked a main publishers' association like the prewar Tōkyō Publishers' Association or the Tōkyō Booksellers' Association that had represented the demands and aims of the publishers on a national and international level. In 1957, such an association came to the scene with the founding of the Japan Book Publishers' Association (Nihon Shoseki Shuppan Kyōkai) that to this day is closely associated with one of its founding members, Noma Shōichi.

Noma Shōichi was born as Takagi Shōichi in 1911 in Okayama Prefecture and studied law at the Tōkyō Imperial University from where he graduated in 1934. He entered the Home Ministry but decided to leave it shortly after to work at the semi-privatized South Manchurian Railway Company. There he was put in charge of the Correspondence Department for General Affairs (Sōmubu Bunshoka) a year later. In 1938 he was transferred to the Correspondence Department of the Train Division of Harbin (Harupin Tetsudōkyoku Sōmubu Bunshoka). His private secretary Ichihara Tokurō wrote that it was his time in Harbin that gave Takagi Shōichi his "international mindset" that would influence him later in life.[97] Here, he met the widow of Noma Seiji, the founder of the Kōdansha publishing company, who introduced Shōichi to his future wife, the widow of Noma Seiji's eldest son. The couple married in 1941 which made him a part of the renowned Noma family, hence his name Noma Shōichi.[98] Noma Shōichi joined the publisher Dai-Nihon Yūbenkai Kōdansha (from 1958 Kōdansha Corporation) in July 1941 and was appointed managing director on July 19, but with the outbreak of the Pacific War in December, military rule and extreme suppression of the press increased, leading to the complete centralization of the publishing industry under state guidance. Kōdansha followed the national polity (*kokutai*). In 1943, Noma was appointed as vice leader of a small planning department inside the state-run Japan Publishing Association (Nihon Shuppankai) that monopolized the publishing agency during the war. Noma Shōichi's career in the publishing industry thus began in a state-controlled wartime institution, working in close cooperation with the ministerial bureaucrats. The relations with state representatives would remain important for his activities long after the end of the war. In 1945, Noma was appointed president of his late father-in-law's publishing house, but due to Kōdansha's war responsibility problem, he resigned just a year later. In May 1949, he was rehabilitated by the GHQ and once again took up his position as president of Kōdansha in June of that year.[99]

From the mid-1950s, an economic upturn began that was also noticeable in the publishing industry which by the late 1950s had changed from a period of reconstruction to a period of recovery and upswing. In the aftermath of the postwar decentralization of the industry, a group of publishers, led by Noma and the president of Heibonsha, Shimonaka Yasaburō, collectively advocated for the establishment of a new representative association for publishers. This initiative materialized in March 1957 with the founding of the Japan Book Publishers' Association which saw the participation of 181 publishing houses as founding members. At the founding ceremony, Shimonaka said: "Publishing houses are small- to medium-sized enterprises. But our work contributes to the development of culture in our country. Therefore, our responsibility is actually very broad. It is vital that we stand together as small- to medium-sized companies. For that reason, it was important to establish this organization."[100]

In the ongoing international copyright discussions, the ability to stand together and represent the publishers as one group was especially important. At the time of the establishment of the Association in 1957, the UNESCO Intergovernmental Copyright Committee was already meeting in its second year and while copyright owners were present in Europe via the initiative of the Japan Copyright Council, Japanese publishers still did not appear as a single entity to have their rights represented. However, since Noma and several other publishers involved were already familiar with the existing unresolved copyright issues through their direct engagement in the Copyright Council, soon after its founding, in June 1957, the publishers established their own Committee for Copyright and Publishing Rights Issues (Chosaku-Shuppanken Mondai Iinkai). In addition, and with the goal of improving the international exchange of Japan's publishing industry, in 1958 the Japan Book Publishers' Association joined the International Publishers' Association (IPA) which is considered a major milestone in the internationalization of the Japanese publishing industry. Until then, Japanese publishers had only received fragments of information about the work of the IPA. In 1962, Japan, represented by both Noma, who had meanwhile replaced Shimonaka as representative of the publishers, and Shimonaka, first participated in an IPA meeting in Barcelona. During the same meeting, for the first time a representative of UNESCO was present. In his speech to the attendees of the IPA, Noma recommended the following: "We should not only import foreign culture, but we should also overcome the hindrance of language translations and introduce to other countries the outstanding culture of Japan."[101] Shimonaka and Noma added that Japan would be interested in hosting an IPA meeting in the near future and distributed an English pamphlet to introduce their new association to the attendees.[102]

The shift of the Japanese publishing industry towards prioritizing the export of Japanese works was among several factors that coalesced in the early 1960s, prompting Japan's state representatives to reconsider their longstanding stance on translation rights. Japan's complete integration into the Berne Convention was a gradual process that began around that time. One of the most significant factors contributing to this shift was the observed generational change during this period. Ministerial bureaucrat Akagi Tomoharu who had attended the Rome Revision Conference and had been a member of many pre- and postwar advisory councils on copyright, died in 1963. Yamada Saburō whose life mission had been to bring the "Western standard of civilization" to Japan, amongst other missions, by fighting for the right freely to translate Western works, died in 1965 at the age of 96. Until the last years of his life, he had been active in the copyright revision process. Scholar Takayanagi Kenzō, who had made the controversial request for Japan at the Meeting of Experts in the late 1930s, died in 1967. By the mid to late 1960s, the main defenders of Japan's special exemptions had thus either died or had come of age which cleared the path for a new generation that aimed to move forward and align Japan with international copyright standards.[103] Another factor that played into the developments of the 1960s was the growing internationalization of the Japanese publishing industry reflected in the joining of the International

Publishers' Association, the annual attendance of the Frankfurt Book Fair from 1963, or the petitions of translators and authors urging the state officials to align Japan's copyright laws fully with international standards. Finally, the increasing public discourse on decolonization and the rights of the newly formed nation states concerning intellectual property protection influenced how Japan aimed to present itself globally, not as part of the developing nations, but as a powerful nation with a rich history within the international legal system. Thus, for Japan the eventual abolition of its special exemptions, which were associated with developing nations and young nation states navigating their path in the international system, became a matter of national pride.

The first signs of a general shift could be seen in April 1962 when the Ministry of Education established the Copyright System Council (Chosakuken Seido Shingikai) which consisted of six copyright owners (from writers' and musical associations), five copyright users (including Noma Shōichi as president of the newly founded Japan Book Publishers' Association, and members of broadcasting, record, and film producers' associations), 16 intellectuals (e.g. academics, lawyers, museum employees, and members of independent research associations), and three bureaucrats from the Ministry of Foreign Affairs, the Cabinet Legislation Bureau, and the Ministry of Justice.[104] Publishing houses and organizations concerned with copyright protections were asked to share their opinions and wishes for the revision.[105] In addition, the copyright protection for general works, initially set at 30 years after the author's death, was extended by three years. While this was a modest progression toward the 50 years of protection adopted by the majority of member states, it signaled a period of change in a system that had remained unchanged since the end of the previous century.

In May 1965, a first statement of the Ministry's Copyright System Council was released that advised Japan to give up the reservations on the protection of translation rights, as the only other countries besides Japan that still held on to the same reservations were Turkey, Thailand, Yugoslavia, and Iceland, in other words "small countries" (*shōkoku*).[106] While the report was openly received by the government, it still encountered strong resistance from the publishers who were for the first time since the end of the war represented in their entirety. Whenever the Ministry's Council held a meeting, the publishers' internal committee on copyright questions came together immediately after to discuss the views of the publishers and decide on possible requests to submit to the government. It also collected many opinions from intellectuals and legal scholars and from 1964 directly consulted with the bureaucrats regarding the topic of copyright duration and translation rights.[107]

When in April 1966, after 278 consultation meetings, the Copyright System Council submitted its final suggestion to abolish Japan's reservations on translation rights, the publishers reacted with an opposing report of their own entitled "Kokumin bunka to 'hon'yakuken'" (The People's Culture and Translation Rights).[108] The title of the publication already hinted that the publishers were once again flexibly adapting their rationale for retaining special reservations to align with the prevailing trends of the times. While in the 1930s, the original argument of wanting to bring "modernization and civilization" to Japan had largely given way to the argument of developing better relations among "the people" (*kokumin*) of the East and the West, now in postwar and democratic Japan, it was the people that were used as an argument. Building on the rhetoric of being defenders of "the people," the report was openly published and "the readers" were directly addressed as such. Regarding the argument of the Copyright System Council that Japan was now a "major nation" (*taikoku*), the publishers responded that it would be "childish" (*kodomo-jimita*) to argue that Japan's international rank would rise by abandoning the reservation rights which currently were only retained by "small nations" like Turkey, Yugoslavia, and Thailand.[109] The publishers claimed that Japan would have an "inferiority complex" (*rettōkan*) of being a "culture import country," a fact which, according to them, had not changed in postwar Japan, despite the recent efforts to introduce more Japanese publications abroad.[110] Finally, they claimed that in the end, it would be the readers, or the people, who would suffer from abandoning the reservations on translation rights. The extra expenses that were needed to cover the royalty payments would either have to be subtracted from the payment of the translators (and thereby lead to a reduction in the quality of the translation) or added to the sale price of the book.[111] Addressing themselves directly to the readers, the publishers wrote: "This [the discussions around a possible abandonment of the reservations on translation rights protection] is no longer just the problem of a small number of publishers and translators, but causes damage to everyone, including especially the state economy which presents a large problem for the international balance of payments."[112] To ensure that their demands reached those responsible for actual political decision-making, at the end of their publication, the publishers asserted that they had no choice but to emphatically address their demands to the politicians and the government.[113]

Despite the publishers' final initiative to maintain the status quo, the Ministry of Education adopted the opinion presented by their Copyright System Council, primarily composed of experts and industry members. In October 1966, the Ministry ordered the elimination of the paragraph on translation rights, thereby ultimately aligning with the standards of the Berne Union.[114] It was, however, a few years more, precisely until 1970, before a final cabinet decision was handed to the National Diet.[115] A main reason for the delay was that the results of the 1967 Berne Convention revision conference in Stockholm once again required further examinations as it posed unprecedented questions and challenges to the copyright landscape.

THE 1967 STOCKHOLM REVISION CONFERENCE AND THE PROMOTION OF THE PUBLISHING SECTOR IN DEVELOPING COUNTRIES

The 1967 Stockholm Revision Conference followed the period of postwar decolonization and one of its main objectives was to address the challenges associated with integrating newly independent states into the Berne Convention. In October 1966, the Cultural Affairs Bureau of Japan's Ministry of Education contacted the postwar Japan Book Publishers' Association with the draft for the Berne Convention revision conference that was planned for June 1967. As a direct response to the decolonization and the connected problems in the international copyright landscape, the draft included a "Protocol Regarding Developing Countries" and suggested that developing countries should have the right to declare reservations amongst others in the areas of translation and duration of protection. Basing itself also on the prewar example and comments by Japan, UNESCO had, at the 1948 Brussels Revision Conference, already criticized copyright as a "barrier" to the "free flow of culture among all the peoples of the world."[116] As one result, the 1952 UCC had introduced lower levels of protection, a crucial criteria for the United States joining the treaty, but the level of protection for member states of the Berne Convention remained high. This became an issue when the decolonization began in many parts of the world, as it confronted the transnational copyright community with a new world order, and started a conflict between industrial and developing nations, once again, and with a greater intensity, stirring up questions about the access to knowledge and information as resources in a global world. At the centre of the controversies stood the so-called "colonial clause" or "territorial clause" which was part of the Berne Convention and had been used by the colonial powers to apply the treaty to its respective territories. The clause had been in place since the founding of the Convention in 1886, first declared by the United Kingdom, France, and Spain, and later by other nations including, in 1928, by Japan.[117] With the new postwar world order from the 1950s onwards, many developing countries raised the very same questions that Japanese publishers, translators, and legal scholars had asked decades prior: How should the copyright community accommodate the needs of newly independent and developing states and how could these states be integrated into the existing international copyright treaties?[118] Cultural historian Eva Hemmungs Wirtén, who specialized in book history and the history of information and patents, sees the content of the protocol as the conference's host country Sweden's attempt to transfer its identity as originally itself a "small nation" into a maker of politics that was now speaking up for developing nations.[119] Sweden, like Japan, had joined the Berne Convention as a nation in development in 1904, and now stood at the other end of the spectrum as a "paragon of development and social welfare."[120]

In preparation for the Stockholm Revision Conference, the Ministry of Education also invited individual publishers to various discussion rounds (*zadankai*) held by the Ministry of Education such as a roundtable in early 1967 on "publishing rights and translation rights". It was a small roundtable which brought the publisher Nunokawa Kakuzaemon together with three scholars of law including Suzuki Takeo, who had already joined Yamada Saburō and Takayanagi Kenzō at the Meeting of Experts in Paris in 1938. Ahead of the scheduled conference, the attendees discussed the pros and cons of Japan's reservations. The legal scholars concordantly shared the opinion that the state of the world would have changed with Japan having advanced to a major nation and that even if there *were* fewer literary works translated from Japanese into European languages than the other way around, Japan should learn to accept this.[121] Suzuki also emphasized that it was Japan's task now to think globally and not only be concerned with its own culture. While agreeing with the argument given by the legal scholars, especially concerning the fact that Japan had indeed become a major nation, Nunokawa Kakuzaemon tried to convince his fellow discussants of the clear contra-opinion of the publishers. He stated that the long-term efforts of the late Yamada Saburō and others for the perpetuation of the special exemption could not have been for nothing, that an abolition of the reservations would become an economic problem and books would become more expensive. By the end of the discussion round, however, it became clear that the repeated arguments of the publishers no longer achieved the intended goals.[122] The publishers continued their plea to the state officials to hold on to the 10-year reservations on translation rights, complaining of "unfair treatment" (*futō na futan*) that would make the postwar era continue for Japanese publishers.[123] As the leader of the main publishers' association, Noma Shōichi continued to lead the publishers in their demand, but at the same time also appeared to have let go of the publishers' fight already and, in close cooperation with UNESCO, turned to the international market for new opportunities.

UNESCO had already begun emphasizing the importance of promoting the publishing sector in developing countries from the early 1960s. To approach this task, the organization reached out to existing networks of the publishing industry for assistance. As an initial step, a UNESCO representative attended the above-mentioned International Publishers' Association (IPA) meeting in Barcelona in 1962 where first contacts with individuals and private interest groups engaged in the industry were established including the first contact with Noma Shōichi.

With the aim of preparing the Stockholm Revision Conference that was to put special emphasis on the changes in the copyright landscape, at the 13th UNESCO General Meeting in 1964, the Ministry of Education and the Japanese National Commission for UNESCO (Nihon Yunesuko Kokunai Iinkai), which had been established in 1952 to keep in close contact with UNESCO and promote international exchange and activities, were asked to hold a regional publishing expert conference for Asia.[124] The objective of the regional conference was to address problems regarding the development of the publishing industry in Asia and to develop a concrete plan to address these problems. It also contributed to the research and preparations for the Stockholm Revision Conference that was to focus on developing countries and their access to knowledge. The ultimate aim of UNESCO was to bring as many new states to join the Berne Convention and to create a more universal form of copyrights within the Berne Convention.

Japanese state officials immediately embraced the idea of an Asian regional publishing conference. After the events of World War II, Japan was in the process of rebuilding its international image and demonstrating to the rest of the world that it was a democratic and peaceful nation. Becoming a regional leader in publishing was expected to elevate the country's global standing and enhance Western perceptions of Japan and its culture. Among the Japanese populace, it furthermore aimed to foster the "international mindset" that Japanese internationalists had proudly possessed since the early Meiji days. In this way, internationalist activities continued to serve national goals, also in the area of publishing and international copyright. The Ministry immediately turned to the Japan Publishers' Association and its president Noma for his cooperation in the planning process.[125] In addition, in 1965 during Noma's attendance at the IPA meeting in Washington, he was approached by Julian Behrstock, then head of the Division of Free Flow of Information at UNESCO, to discuss the possibility of opening a centre for the development of the Asian book market in Tōkyō. At the UNESCO General Conference, the plan was officially drawn up and from 1967, classes on "Publishing in Asia" were offered at the newly established centre which, from 1969, became officially known as the UNESCO Tōkyō Book Development Centre (Tōkyō Shuppan Sentā).[126]

The plans for holding a regional publishing expert conference began to take shape in January 1966 with the establishment of a committee comprising members of individual publishers' organizations, the Ministry of Foreign Affairs, the Ministry of Education, and the Japanese National Commission for UNESCO. Noma Shōichi was appointed chairman of the committee. The conference was held from May 25-31, 1966, and was attended by 20 member states of UNESCO in Asia and 85 participants engaged in the publishing industry. Besides the usual governmental representatives, which included, from Japan, representatives of the Ministry of Education, the Ministry of Foreign Affairs, and the Ministry of International Trade and Industry, the conference welcomed observers of international governmental organizations like the United Nations, observers of non-governmental organizations including the International Copyright Society, the IPA, the International Pen Club, many representatives of UNESCO including its National Commission to Japan, and a large number of private associations including the Japan Book

Publishers' Association.¹²⁷ Considering that it was only as from the Stockholm Revision Conference in 1967 that non-governmental organizations were allowed to send delegates to official international copyright conferences, the variety of participants at the 1966 conference in Tōkyō was quite remarkable. With publisher and head of Japan's Book Publishers' Association Noma Shōichi as its chair and organizer, the expert conference announced the changing role of private associations and non-governmental international institutions that were officially given their own voice at international revision conferences for the first time in 1967.

During one of the sessions, the three main obstacles to the "expansion of international book exchange across borders" were discussed which were, namely, trade, translations, and copyrights. The conference report stated that research about joining the Berne Convention had already been taken up and that the participants were exchanging advantages and disadvantages of Asian developing countries joining the treaty. In addition to the financial burden, it was noted that the procedure would be very time consuming. One proposition was to exempt members of developing countries for the time being from remuneration payments. Another suggestion was to have UNESCO act as an intermediary and to hold copyright prices down.[128] According to Noma's former secretary, Ishihara Tokurō, the meeting concluded successfully and had a great impact on the model of the UNESCO book development and distribution.[129] Julian Behrstock later congratulated Japan on its "'very important' role in furthering Asian regional cooperation among news agencies and in promoting book production and distribution."[130] To a certain extent, the former imperialist ambitions of Japan's internationalists had been replaced by an aspiration to take the lead in regional cooperation.

At the opening of the Stockholm Revision Conference, the membership of the Berne Union comprised 57 countries, including several developing countries and, with the exception of the United States and the Soviet Union, most of the developed nations. Japan's delegation was made up of 14 participants including diplomats based in the host country Sweden, bureaucrats of the Patent Office, the Cultural Affairs Bureau of the Ministry of Education, the Treaties Bureau of the Ministry of Foreign Affairs, and a representative of the Copyright System Council. But for the first time, Japan was also represented by several non-governmental organizations, in this case from the broadcasting media.[131] The conference itself revolved around the topic of translations and brought out the existing tensions between import and export nations and between users and producers of intellectual works.[132] Following decolonization, the newly independent states had to sign a so-called "continued adherence" with which they either affirmed or denounced the law of the Berne Convention.[133] Japan found itself in the middle between developing countries like India and Tunesia, and the old copyright export nations Britain, France, and Italy. Despite the intention of the government to let go of their own reservations, Japan's delegation stated in their official comments: "The countries of the Union which accept or accede to the Stockholm Act should have the free choice of whether they abandon the benefit of the reservations they have previously formulated."[134]

After all, the final Act and Protocol did not abolish the translation right reservations and focused instead on the needs of developing nations. To respond to criticism of unfair treatment, which was expressed at several conferences during the 1960s, most notably at the African Study Meeting on Copyright held in Brazzaville in 1962, the Stockholm Act introduced a "Protocol Regarding developing Countries" which granted developing nations the option to make certain reservations regarding translations and duration of protection. However, the protocol was later described as "nearly a complete failure" as its provisions turned out to be useless for the developing countries that could not afford to wait the required 25 years after the death of the author for the free use of contemporaneous material for their educational system, or the 10 years for a translation of a textbook which would lose its value after a few years.[135] The Japanese delegation observed the discussions closely, and while its members returned with no changes to the regulation regarding their own reservations, the decision to align Japan's laws with international standards was made. This move was not only a statement regarding Japan's role in the world but also a step to distance itself from developing countries.

Various publishers' and magazine associations nevertheless tried convincing the government until the spring of 1970 with the help of petitions including a survey that had inquired 270 intellectuals and translators about the 10-year translation right regulation with the result that 225 spoke out for a continuation of the special rule. The survey had most likely deliberatelyt included many translators of children's books, a genre which, in the postwar decades, was in great demand so that their translators wanted to continue having access to free works after a 10-year period. But this time, the publishers' efforts remained in vain.

In May 1970, a new Copyright Law for Japan was announced. It was the first major revision since joining the Berne Convention in 1899. Major changes included the extension of the term of copyright protection, including protection of motion pictures and photographs, to 50 years after the author's death, the extension of copyright protection for recorded music broadcast, and the abolition of "the patently unfair provision" of special reservations on translation right protection.[136] It was planned that publishers and translators would be given a 10-year transition period before the reservations were completely abolished. The media supported Japan's decision to bring its Copyright Law up to international standards. The *Japan Times* for example concluded an article which introduced the new law with the phrase: "[…] we hope Japan's new Copyright Law will not be allowed to fall behind the times as in the case of the old."[137] The new Copyright Law entered into force on January 1, 1971. The treaty maintained an option to express a revision for keeping the 10-year regulation until December 31, 1980, by which point this option would be completely abolished, and translations of foreign works would benefit from protection of 50 years after the death of the author.

Another major change that the 1967 revision conference in Stockholm had brought about was the replacement of BIRPI, the joint administrative bureau comprising the Berne Bureau and the Paris Bureau that had been promoting the global protection of copyright and ensuring the communication among members of the intellectual property treaties since 1893, with its direct successor, the World Intellectual Property Organization (WIPO). Its constituent instrument, the WIPO Convention, was signed on the last day of the Stockholm Conference on July 14, 1967, and entered into force in 1970. The Berne Union was simultaneously integrated into WIPO. As a member-state led, intergovernmental organization, the latter joined the United Nations in 1974. Finally, the global copyright protection was further expanded under the TRIPS Agreement (Agreement on Trade-Related Aspects of Intellectual Property Rights), an international legal agreement which was concluded in 1994 between all member states of the World Trade Organization (WTO). Because TRIPS came as a compulsory prerequisite to joining the WTO which in turn granted important access to the markets of the world, the treatment aimed to entice nations that had not yet shown interest in joining the Berne Convention. Both Russia and China were among the latecomers to joining international copyright agreements, but, pressured by global market developments and the ongoing TRIPS negotiations, they eventually acceded to the Berne Convention in the early 1990s.[138]

The end of World War II had brought about many changes, but, simultaneously, the postwar decades, extending into the early 1970s, were characterized by elements of both continuity and change. In this chapter we illustrated how this dynamic interplay manifested within the sphere of international copyright. Both nationally and internationally, there were institutional changes, with the establishment of new organizations and associations to oversee the administration and communication related to the global protection of intellectual property rights. However, in many instances, these new bodies retained much of the old personnel and functioned in ways similar to their predecessors.

Japan's internal conflicts and uncertainties on how to proceed internationally affected the global expansion of intellectual property rights until Japan's final abolition of its old Copyright Law in 1970. In the immediate postwar period, US occupation authorities undertook little to no changes in the bureaucratic structures around the handling of the international copyright agreement. The first postwar initiative to move forward with the copyright negotiations that had come to a halt during the war came not from SCAP or the Japanese government, but from the publishing industry, precisely from the translators who were the first ones to question Japan's old stance toward copyright regulations with the goal to raise Japan's law to international standards. In close cooperation with authors, translators, as copyright owners, arranged themselves as independent interest groups, most notably the Japan Copyright Council, with which they began to conduct private research, gather information, and for the first time actively participate in international meetings of UNESCO. In their ambitions, however, they were hampered by the dominant group of elite state officials and publishers who continued to act in synchrony and held on to their prewar views, causing a conflict within the wider publishing industry, now divided into copyright holders and owners. The bureaucrats continued to rely on the expertise of the private experts without whose input they were struggling to keep up with the international conversation. However, with the postwar publishing industry increasingly divided over the question of how to position itself internationally, and the miscommunication and lack of interest from the state, Japan continued to hinder the globalization and revision efforts of the transnational copyright community.

The stagnation in Japan's copyright revision only changed from the late 1950s and 1960s and was influenced by a combination of different factors. During this period, a generational change occurred with the intensely involved prewar defenders of Japan's special copyright exemptions either coming of age or dying. Economic and sociopolitical developments like the era of High-Growth with its increase also in Japanese book exports brought about new opportunities for publishers to expand to foreign markets and take on a leading role in developing the publishing market in Asia. In addition, the decolonization in many parts of the world pressured the Japanese government to choose a stance between being viewed as a nation dependent on foreign publications for its development or aligning its laws with those of the industrialized nations. The final decision made by Japanese state officials to ratify the UCC and align its Copyright Law with the revised Berne Convention stemmed from both a changed international postwar order as well as an internal generational shift. In this context, state representatives perceived it as their task to highlight Japan's new position in the world and distinguish it from the newly developing nations, a realization that was prompted by private individuals.

CONCLUSION

The creation of the Berne Convention as the world's first multilateral copyright agreement in 1886 and the following initiative by the Berne Bureau to expand the protection of copyright came as a response to an increasingly globalized world in which new inventions and technologies made it possible for written works to reach distant places with much greater ease than before. This development of new communication and travel routes led to the duplication and copying of written material with the original authors and publishers losing sight and control of their works. Intellectual property rights, consequently, became a tool of cultural imperialism initiated and dominated at first by France, later by Germany and the Anglo-American world. The movement for expanding and harmonizing intellectual property protection was championed by international organizations, like the Berne Bureau, the League of Nations' International Committee on Intellectual Cooperation, and later UNESCO, organizations which themselves were created and operated by those powerful states with an interest in copyright protection. These organizations worked in close collaboration with informal networks of experts, scholars, and advisors that shared their ideas, concerns and opinions and nevertheless continued to rely on the authority and legitimacy of their respective states.

Politics in Publishing highlights Japan as a significant example of a state within entire regions often overlooked by previous scholarship, yet crucial in shaping our globalized world. By examining Japan and incorporating perspectives that were often underrepresented, like those of publishers, translators, and legal experts, alongside the typically studied state officials involved in the formulation of international copyright law, this study extends the scope of international copyright history and the history of international organizations beyond the European context. It broadens the general transnational approach in this field and offers a more nuanced understanding of Japan's role in the emerging international system.

The book follows Japan as an actor in the "old" Berne universe along two central avenues, combining an "outside-in" with an "inside-out" perspective. It analyzes how the changing international order led to administrative changes on the domestic level, specifically influencing the dynamic between Japanese state and non-state actors involved in copyright. It simultaneously traces the engagement of this group of actors in international organizations and fora contributing to the development of international law. Western states looked closely to Japan as their showcase example of how a non-Western nation could integrate into the system of international law. They witnessed state representatives participating in the revision conferences and had access to the official statements made by Japan. What has remained hidden from the international community and, until now, from the historiography of international copyright law is the considerable influence wielded by non-state actors at the domestic level, which played a pivotal role in shaping Japan's stance during international copyright negotiations. Shielded from the eyes of the transnational copyright community, in Japan a triangular relationship developed between ministerial bureaucrats and other state representatives, academic experts from the Faculty of Law of Tōkyō Imperial University, and leading members of the publishing industry. In the copyright negotiations these actors became interdependent and developed a common rhetoric that was adapted to the changing international landscape, always mindful of Japan's position in the international system.

Historians of copyright have started to explore the role of international organizations and non-governmental organizations in the history of international copyright law. This book adds the missing history of Japan as a non-Western nation within the globalization of intellectual property rights, focusing on copyright of literature. It reveals why it took Japan over 70 years to align its laws fully with the international standard, gives insights into domestic power struggles and the evolving relationship between state and non-state actors pursuing various interests, and into the ways these actors used the concept of "internationalism" to pursue their nationalistic, capitalistic, and, at times, ultranationalistic goals. This book shows that the international activities of state officials in promoting free access to translations were never based on a single ideological principle. Instead, they were influenced by several factors, including a growing dependency on advice from leading members of the capitalist-driven private industry and academic copyright experts who often shared a common background with the state leaders. Additionally, their activities stemmed from a continuous uncertainty regarding Japan's place in the international community, a sense of mistrust toward Western nations. This sense of mistrust was particularly acute after the rejection of the racial equality proposal for the draft of the Covenant of the League of Nations at the Paris Peace Conference in 1919 and the perceived need to assert Japan's status as a major power within the international system. These elements collectively contributed to the changing justifications for Japan's special treatment.

Politics in Publishing suggests that Japan's missing history within the larger history of the Berne Convention was shaped not only by "the Japanese state" but also significantly by members of the private and profit-driven publishing industry, as well as academic scholars of copyright law. These actors responded to changes in the international order by setting up new institutions to make themselves heard and by adapting their argumentation according to external movements. In this book the author reveals how, during the preparation phases ahead of the international revision conferences of the Berne Convention, it was often the non-state actors who took the initiative to respond to foreign requests and exerted influence on the state officials involved. For this they made use of different channels including petitions and written opinions shared directly or via intermediate associations such as private interest groups or the Tōkyō Chamber of Commerce, private consultations and advice given during mutual advisory council meetings, or recommendations shared via newspapers, legal expert magazines, and pamphlets.

Due to the close cooperation with Japan's state leaders and their increasing mutual dependency, this group of state and non-state actors developed shared arguments that were used in the copyright negotiations to hinder an expansion of Japan's copyright regulations and thereby a unification of international copyright protection, especially as regards translation rights. This common rhetoric with the arguments for Japan's special treatment was adapted in response to external circumstances and shifting goals. On numerous occasions, the small group of Japanese internationalists criticized the dominance of the Western powers in the system of the Berne Convention, but conveniently used arguments like the need for Western civilization as an allegedly developing nation or the need to work towards cultural harmony to their own advantage. While criticizing the Western hegemony in international copyright law, Japanese state leaders came to value the same laws as a source of power in the East Asian region.

When the negotiations regarding membership of Japan in the Berne Convention were first taken up in the mid-1890s, the Meiji leaders were convinced that Japan needed to implement Western norms and institutions to gain recognition in the international system. While many of the leading publishers at the time were themselves internationalists who agreed with this narrative, they also exploited it with their own profit in mind, petitioning the government to exempt Japan from international copyright standards for the sake of bringing "civilization" to the country. State and non-state actors alike started engaging with the newly emerging international organizations and the transnational copyright community, convinced that the future international order would lie in liberal internationalism. At the same time, they were concerned with the status and rank of Japan among the other great powers and with Japan's interests, for the publishers these were economic interests, for the state actors they were interests related to the import of knowledge and thus power, that might be ignored by an international order dominated by Western nations.

After World War I the engagement with international organizations was further increased in line with a new postwar order of international cooperation and attempted collective security. During the 1920s, Japanese internationalists actively participated in the newly established international organizations around the League of Nations. At the same time, the events surrounding the rejection of Japan's racial equality proposal in 1919 led to a growing distrust of the Anglo-Saxon powers and an uncertainty regarding Japan's place in the international system. Making use of the rhetoric of the times, during those years the arguments in favor of Japan's exemptions from the international copyright standard were changed to wanting to improve "cultural harmony" among the East and the West through mutual understanding.

In the 1930s, after Japan's withdrawal from the League of Nations, Japanese experts and government officials kept this argumentation while at the same time using the fora of the international copyright conferences to advance their imperialist agenda at precisely the moment that other avenues were closed off. They continued to request special conditions on translation rights, insisting, however, that free translations should occur only between the East and the West and should exclude certain intra-Asian translations like those between Japan and China. Japan as the only Asian member of the Berne Convention at that time used its demand to promote its new cultural order in East Asia, positioning Japan as a leader. This order aimed to liberate Asia from imperialist powers, asserting independence from the West. Notably, the proposed cultural order was said to be based on common knowledge exchanged through translations.

After World War II, the arguments justifying Japan's special status within international copyright law was again adapted to a new international order. In general, the postwar international copyright revision discussions were a continuation of the prewar efforts rather than a new start with many of the same personnel still involved. However, with the beginning of the decolonization in many parts of the world from the late 1940s and questions on how to integrate developing countries in the intended global expansion of copyright protection, it became increasingly difficult for Japanese publishers to keep up their arguments on why Japan as a first world nation should still be exempt from the laws that applied to the other industrialized member states. Their argumentation shifted to include and directly address the "people" who would suffer if Japan gave up its special reservations on translation rights. Old acquaintances of the state representatives, including the leaders of the publishing industry or the private international law professor at Tōkyō Imperial University, Yamada Saburō, continued to advise the state officials inside several newly established advisory councils to hold on to the prewar regulations. While the publishers were eager to maintain the status quo, interests of translators and authors as copyright owners shifted toward an extension of copyright protection.

State officials were advised by both groups, but the trust and reliance of the state officials on the advice of their older acquaintances can be interpreted as one of the main reasons why both the ratification of the Universal Copyright Convention in 1956 and the final revision of the Berne Convention in 1971 took another two decades after the end of World War II before ultimately being brought to a conclusion.

What persisted throughout the decades described is the manner in which actors involved operated under the guise of "internationalism," using and, at times, manipulating this concept in various ways to advance Japan's contemporary national goals alongside private capitalist interests. Consequently, the close circle of involved state and non-state actors managed to consistently delay the Western-envisioned harmonization of international copyright law for over 70 years.

The eventual change in opinion among both publishers and state representatives in the 1960s came as a result of three main factors: first, a generational change occurred of those engaged in the copyright negotiations; second, the decolonization that took place in many parts of the world set in motion discussions on the application of copyright regulations in developing nations and thereby presented an opportunity for the Japanese state to rebuild its international image as a leader in publishing that could lend support to developing nations looking to join the system of international copyright law; and third, economic growth and new transnational contacts between Japan's publishing industry and UNESCO opened up new capitalist opportunities for the hitherto heavily import-oriented Japanese publishing industry. Japan eventually aligned its Copyright Law with the principles of the Berne Convention, becoming effectively a proponent of copyright principles, because it now recognized a greater advantage for Japan's power status in harmonizing its laws with the international standard. As illustrated in this book, over the span of 70 years from the late nineteenth century to the 1960s, the group of non-state actors acted in alignment with the evolving international system. During this time, politics displayed high levels of responsiveness to the needs and wishes of these actors and of dependence on its expertise.

By exerting influence on state actors domestically, publishers, academic experts, and translators likewise made major contributions to how Japan positioned itself on an international stage, especially at the international conferences. Their opinions were integrated in the official government statements or distributed in written form by international organizations ahead of the conferences. However, as was demonstrated throughout the book, this integration occurred only when these opinions were in line with the interests of the state officials. As was shown in Chapter 2, ever since the 1908 revision conference in Berlin, when Japan officially announced that it would not accept the translation rights regulations of the Berne Convention, the transnational copyright community paid close attention to the requests of its first non-Western member as they did not want to see their system fail. This becomes especially clear when Japanese representatives, after having withdrawn from the League of Nations in 1933, threatened also to leave the Berne Convention. Members of the League reacted by granting the requested concessions to Japan, despite its status as a non-member at the time. This allowed Japan to maintain its reservations and provided the country with a platform for sharing its imperial visions. This step can be viewed as a form of appeasement by the other League members during a period of escalating military aggression. Simultaneously, it can be seen as an effort to uphold the successful example of the integration of a non-Western nation into a system built on Western legal norms. The international copyright meetings were among the last official connections the international community had to Japan when many other avenues were already long closed off after Japan had officially left the League of Nations.

While the official exchange and cooperation with international organizations was vital to the globalization of intellectual property rights, *Politics in Publishing* also shows that at times the non-state expert communities took on an overarching role to a level above the formal international organizations through which they were expected to interact. As shown in Chapter 4, when Japan withdrew from the League of Nations during the early 1930s, even after the "Manchurian Incident" experts involved in international copyright law continued to cooperate across borders and organized conferences despite having left the organization officially in charge of administering the Berne Convention. The examples that appear in this book on existing networks in copyright history, networks that stretch over decades and beyond the realm of the official organizations responsible for handling communications around international agreements, support the arguments of scholars advocating for a "Third UN," in addition to member states and UN secretariats. They also highlight the necessity of describing interactions with and among global organizations using terms other than state, market, and civil society.[1] As this book demonstrates through the case of Japan, the involvement of expert panels and advice from professionals located outside the system was not unique to the UN era. With the aim of further uncovering non-Western agency in the history of international organizations, future research should focus on networks of a "Third League of Nations" and a "Third Berne Bureau," incorporating cases beyond that of Japan analyzed here.

In 1971, with the most recent and still valid significant revision of the Berne Convention and the integration of the Berne Union into the World Intellectual Property Organization (WIPO), a new era in copyright history began. This period, more so than the end of World War II, brought forth major challenges, particularly in addressing the rapid development of computer technology and software. Nevertheless, the conflicts between nations that rely on the import of cultural goods and those that primarily export these goods continue to this day with constant new challenges facing the international community like how to deal with copyright in the digital age.²

On December 30, 2018, Japan quietly and without much media attention once again extended its copyright protection from 50 to 70 years after the death of the author. The revision had first been discussed during the negotiations of the original Transpacific Partnership Agreement (TPP), from which the United States withdrew under Donald Trump in 2017. During the original discussions, in 2006, a group of Japanese interest groups including the Japan Writers' Association (Nihon Bungeika Kyōkai) made a request to the Agency for Cultural Affairs (Bunka-chō) inside Japan's Ministry of Education to extend copyright protection according to the American Copyright Act of 1976 which first protected works for the life of the author plus 50 years and in 1998 was revised and extended to 70 years. The issue was henceforth discussed inside the so-called Culture Advisory Council (Bunka Shingikai) which, in 2007, established its own subcommittee for conducting research on a possible extension of the 50 years of copyright protection. Private interest organizations contributed to the research with the help of a Forum on the Issue of Extending Copyright Protection, abbreviated as "thinkC" (Chosakuken Hogo Kikan no Enchō Mondai o Kangaeru Fōramu). The forum organized public symposia on the topic and prepared a collection of pro and contra opinions from different viewpoints, which is available on their website and in its structure resembles the report prepared by the Home Ministry's Police Affairs Bureau prior to the 1928 Rome Revision Conference discussed in Chapter 3.³ In December 2018 it was announced that from the end of the month Japan would extend its protection to 70 years after the author's death. According to different newspapers, no clear rationale was given for this final decision besides the fact that the 70-year copyright protection was already a global norm.⁴ This most recent example clearly demonstrates that the development of certain mechanisms of longer than 70 years, which were explained in this book, has generated deeply-rooted path dependencies and that to date, the collaboration between ministerial bureaucrats and the private sector in questions related to intellectual property rights plays a vital role in the field's decision-making process.

In conclusion, *Politics in Publishing* offers a history of Japanese agency within the globalization of intellectual property rights from the late 1890s to 1971. It considers the dynamics of change nationally, as well as the impact actions taken by Japanese state and non-state actors had on Berne Union members, ultimately shaping the development of international copyright law. This influence was examined in the context of key international organizations, including the Berne Bureau, the League of Nations with its ICIC, the Paris Institute, and UNESCO. While it was the aim of this book to make the history of international organizations more global and, likewise, to contribute to a global history of publishing and thereby overcome

Eurocentric historical narratives, it was not the purpose to deny the strong position of especially Europe in the global standardization of copyright norms. In 1970, Japan also brought its Copyright Law in line with international regulations and integrated into the system of intellectual property protection that was clearly based on late nineteenth century Europe. As Isabella Löhr suggested, the history of international copyright could thus indeed be read as a "history of cooperation" or as the history of a global standardization of copyright norms.[5] In the conclusion to her study on the globalization of intellectual property rights, Löhr, however, likewise emphasized what Sebastian Conrad and Andreas Eckert pointed out about current approaches to global history, namely, that "the history of Globalization is not a linear narrative about ever greater interconnectedness of the world" and that "cross-border exchanges [...] not only contribute to the homogenization of the world and the creation of uniformity, but have also always produced fragmentation and new differences."[6]

Japan's participation in the international negotiations was one such example. Its integration into the international copyright system was not a smooth and linear process rather it brought with it many disagreements and moments of friction, which at times caused all the efforts for global copyright unification to stagnate. At other times, the country functioned as a promotor and catalyst for sharing the ideas behind the Berne Convention. Ian Clark has argued that for the powerful nation states during the twentieth century, globalization was a "realm of choice," that is, it was up to the states to either support globalization processes for which the burden might have had to be shifted to domestic sectors or boycott them by giving priority to domestic interests which could result in international fragmentation. The choices could either be made between states or within states, but globalization could, according to Clark, nonetheless often be described as "an effect of state policies, even if not their direct or proximate goal."[7] As this book has shown, for most of the twentieth century, Japan supported globalization processes in copyright only then when it saw a clear advantage for advancing its national status. The decisions to support or boycott certain international regulations were not made by the state alone but were shaped by the interests of specific occupational groups and by a complex interaction between business, academia, and the state, with the actors involved closely interwoven. In Japan's transnational copyright history, the successes in standardizing international copyright as well as the conflicts that arose and oftentimes led to a stagnation of negotiations or to the smallest of compromises thus began with the individual actors within the state.

NOTES

INTRODUCTION. POLITICS IN PUBLISHING

1. Sara Bannerman, *International Copyright and Access to Knowledge* (Cambridge: Cambridge University Press, 2016), pp. 3-4; Eva Hemmungs Wirtén, *No Trespassing: Authorship, Intellectual Property Rights, and the Boundaries of Globalization* (London: University of Toronto Press, 2004), p. 10.
2. The treaties of the Pan-American Union included the Mexico City Convention of 1902, the Convention of Rio de Janeiro of 1906, the Buenos Aires Convention of 1910, and the Convention of Havana in 1928. For more information on the multilateral copyright treaties of the American states see J.M. Yepes and Pareira da Silva, *Commentaire théorique et pratique du pacte de la Societé des Nations et des statuts de l'Union Panaméricaine* (Theoretical and Practical Commentary on the Pact of the League of Nations and the Statutes of the Panamerican Union) (Paris: Pedone, 1934).
3. The secretariat was founded as the "Bureau de l'Union Internationale pour la protection des oeuvres littéraires et artistiques" (Office of the International Union for the Protection of Literary and Artistic Works) and was financed by the member states of the Berne Union. In 1893 the Berne Bureau was merged with the secretariat of the Paris Convention for the Protection of Industrial Property, established in 1883. The new bureau was named "Bureaux Internationaux Réunis pour la Protection de la Propriété Intellectuelle", in short BIRPI. The Berne Bureau was only given the nickname BIRPI from the 1960s, which was also when it moved from Berne to Geneva. World Intellectual Property Organization, ed., *Guide to the Berne Convention for the Protection of Literary and Artistic Works* (Paris Act, 1971) (Geneva: WIPO, 1978), pp. 112-113.
4. Natasha Wheatley, *The Life and Death of States: Central Europe and the Transformation of Modern Sovereignty* (Princeton: Princeton University Press, 2023), p. 2.
5. Eva Hemmungs Wirtén, *Cosmopolitan Copyright: Law and Language in the Translation Zone* (Uppsala: Uppsala Universitet, Institutionen för ABM, 2011); Bannerman, *International Copyright and Access to Knowledge*.

6. Yoshimura Tamotsu, "Kyū-chosakuken hō o meguru hitobito – tokushū chosakuken hō 100nen" (The People of the Old Copyright Law: Special Edition 100 Years of Copyright Law), *Copyright: Chosakuken hō 100nen kinengo* vol. 39, no. 459 (June 1999): pp. 44-53; Ōie Shigeo, *Chosakuken o kakuritsu shita hitobito* (The People Behind the Creation of the Copyright Law), 2nd ed. (Tōkyō: Seibundō, 2004); Hemmungs Wirtén, *Cosmopolitan Copyright*, pp. 39-58.
7. Martin Kretschmer, Lionel A. F. Bently, Ronan Deazley, "Introduction: The History of Copyright History," in *Privilege and Property: Essays on the History of Copyright*, eds. R. Deazley, M. Kretschmer, L. Bently (Cambridge: Open Book Publishers, 2010); Kathy Bowry, "Who's Writing Copyright's History?" *European Intellectual Property Review* vol. 18, no. 6 (1996): pp. 322-329; Martti Koskenniemi, "Histories of International Law: Dealing with Eurocentrism," *Rechtsgeschichte* vol. 19 (2011): pp. 152-176; Arnulf Becker Lorca, "Eurocentrism in the History of International Law," in *The Oxford Handbook of the History of International Law*, Bardo Fassbender and Anne Peters, eds., pp. 1034-1057 (2012).
8. Bannerman, *International Copyright and Access to Knowledge*, pp. 4-5; Peter Drahos, *A Philosophy of Intellectual Property* (Aldershot: Dartmouth, 1996); Isabella Löhr, *Die Globalisierung geistiger Eigentumsrechte – Neue Strukturen internationaler Zusammenarbeit 1886-1952* (The Globalization of Intellectual Property Rights: New Structures of International Cooperation) (Göttingen: Vandenhoeck & Ruprecht, 2010), pp. 273-274; Martti Koskenniemi, *The Gentle Civilizer of Nations: The Rise and Fall of International Law, 1870-1960* (Cambridge: Cambridge University Press, 2002); Susan Sell and Christopher May, "Moments in Law: Contestation and Settlement in the History of Intellectual Propertyt," *Review of International Political Economy* vol. 8, no. 3 (2001): pp. 467-500.
9. Hemmungs Wirtén, *Cosmopolitan Copyright*, p. 15; Hemmungs Wirtén, *No Trespassing*, pp. 3-13; Bannerman, *International Copyright and Access to Knowledge*, pp. 1-12; Sydney J. Shep, "Books without Borders: The Transnational Turn in Book History," in *Books without Borders Vol. 1 – The Cross-National Dimension in Print Culture*, eds. Robert Fraser, Mary Hammond (New York: Palgrave Macmillan, 2008): pp. 13-37.
10. Akira Iriye, *Global Community: The Role of International Organizations in the Making of the Contemporary World* (Berkeley: University of California Press, 2002); Patrick Manning, *Navigating World History* (New York: Palgrave Macmillan, 2003); Christer Jönsson and Jonas Tallberg, eds., *Transnational Actors in Global Governance: Patterns, Explanations, and Implications* (New York: Palgrave Macmillan, 2010); A. LeRoy Bennett, *International Organizations: Principles and Issues*, 5th edition (New Jersey: Prentice Hall, 1991); Madeleine Herren, "Governmental Internationalism and the Beginning of a New World Order in the Late Nineteenth Century," in *The Mechanics of Internationalism*, Martin H. Geyer and Johannes Paulmann, eds. (London: Oxford University Press, 2001).

11. Patricia Clavin, "Defining Transnationalism," *Contemporary European History* vol. 14, no. 4 (2005): pp. 438-439; Steven Vertovec, *Transnationalism* (London/New York: Routledge, 2009); Akira Iriye, *Cultural Internationalism and World Order* (London: The Johns Hopkins University Press, 1997), p. 181; Manning, *Navigating World History*, p. 15.
12. Kenneth Pyle, *Japan Rising: The Resurgence of Japanese Power and Purpose* (New York: Public Affairs, 2007), p. 399.
13. Hemmungs Wirtén, *Cosmopolitan Copyright*, p. 14.
14. Jessamyn Abel, *The International Minimum: Creativity and Contradiction in Japan's Global Engagement, 1933-1964* (Honolulu: University of Hawaii Press, 2015), p. 8.
15. Löhr, *Die Globalisierung geistiger Eigentumsrechte*, p. 15.
16. Martin Kohlrausch, Kathrin Steffen, Stefan Wiederkehr, "Introduction," in *Expert Cultures in Central Eastern Europe: The Internationalization of Knowledge and the Transformation of Nation States since World War I*, Martin Kohlrausch, Kathrin Steffen, Stefan Wiederkehr, eds. (Osnabrück: fibre Verlag, 2010), p. 10.
17. Kohlrausch, Steffen, Wiederkehr, *Expert Cultures*, p. 10.
18. Herren, "Governmental Internationalism," pp. 121-144.
19. Herren, pp. 122-127.
20. Herren, p. 122; Löhr, *Die Globalisierung geistiger Eigentumsrechte*, p. 52.
21. Löhr, p. 15.
22. To avoid confusion, in this book "Paris Institute" is used.
23. Löhr, *Die Globalisierung geistiger Eigentumsrechte*, p. 16.
24. Löhr, p. 159.
25. Sluga and Clavin, *Internationalisms*.
26. Herren, *Networking the International System*.
27. Tatiana Carayannis, Thomas G. Weiss, *The "Third" United Nations: How a Knowledge Ecology Helps the UN Think* (Oxford: Oxford University Press, 2021); Daniel Laqua, ed., *Internationalism Reconfigured: Transnational Ideas and Movements Between the World Wars* (London: I.B. Tauris & Co Ltd, 2011); Jean-Jacques Renoliet, *L'Unesco oubliée: La societé des nations et la coopération intellectuelle (1919-1945)* (Paris: Publications de la Sorbonne, 1999); Thomas W. Burkman, *Japan and the League of Nations: Empire and World Order, 1914-1938* (Honolulu: University of Hawai'i Press, 2008); *Nitobe Inazo: From Bushido to the League of Nations,* Nagao Teruhiko, ed. (Sapporo: Hokkaido University Press, 2006); Poul Duedahl, ed., *A History of UNESCO: Global Actions and Impacts* (New York: Palgrave Macmillan, 2016); Tomoko Akami, "A Quest to be Global: The League of Nations Health Organization and Inter-Colonial Regional Governing Agendas of the Far Eastern Association of Tropical Medicine 1910-25," in *The International History Review* vol. 38, no. 1 (2016): pp. 1-23.
28. Thomas G. Weiss, Tatiana Carayannis and Richard Jolly, "The 'Third' United Nations," *Global Governance* vol. 15 (2009): pp. 123-142.

29. Löhr, *Die Globalisierung geistiger Eigentumsrechte*, pp. 273-274.
30. Madeleine Herren, "Towards a Global History of International Organization," in *Networking the International System: Global Histories of International Organizations*, Madeleine Herren, ed. (Heidelberg: Springer, 2014), pp. 1-12; Christopher Hughes and Shinohara Hatsue, *East Asians in the League of Nations: Actors, Empires and Regions in Early Global Politics* (Singapore: Palgrave Macmillan, 2023); Goto-Shibata Harumi, *The League of Nations and the East Asian Imperial Order, 1920-1946* (Singapore: Palgrave Macmillan, 2020); Steffen Rimner, *Opium's Long Shadow: From Asian Revolt to Global Drug Control* (Harvard University Press, 2018).
31. Hirobe, "Kokusai Renmei Chiteki Kyōryoku Kokusai Iinkai no sōsetsu to Nitobe Inazō" (Establishment of the International Committee on Intellectual Cooperation and Nitobe Inazō), *Bungaku kenkyūka kiyō* vol. 121 (February 2007): p. 1.
32. Saikawa Takashi, "Kokusai bunka kōryū no nashonarizumu – senzenki Nihon ni okeru 'gakugei kyōryoku' jigyō o chūshin ni" (Nationalism of International Cultural Exchange: The Case of Japan's Intellectual Cooperation with the League of Nations), *Jisedai Ajia ronshū* vol. 1 (March 2008): pp. 11-30; Saikawa Takashi, "Kokusai bunka kōryū ni okeru kokka to chishikijin" (The State and Intellectuals in International Cultural Exchange), in *Kokusai bunka kankeishi kenkyū* (International Cultural History Research), Ken'ichirō Hirano, Kazuko Furuta and Akio Tsuchida et al., eds. (Tōkyō: University of Tōkyō Press, 2013): pp. 431-453; Saikawa Takashi, "Returning to the International Community: UNESCO and Post-war Japan, 1945-1951," in *A History of UNESCO: Global Actions and Impacts*, Poul Duedahl, ed. (New York: Palgrave Macmillan, 2016); Terada Kuniyuki, *Actors of International Cooperation in Prewar Japan: The Discourse on International Migration and the League of Nations Association of Japan* (Baden-Baden: Nomos, 2018).
33. Garon, *Molding Japanese Minds*, p. 17; examples include Richard Mitchell, *Censorship in Imperial Japan* (Princeton: Princeton University Press, 1983); Gregory J. Kasza, *The State and the Mass Media in Japan, 1918-1945* (London: University of California Press, 1988); Chalmers Johnson, *Japan: Who Governs? The Rise of the Developmental State* (New York: Norton, 1995).
34. Garon, *Molding Japanese Minds*, p. 17.
35. Carol Gluck, *Japan's Modern Myths: Ideology in the Late Meiji Period* (Princeton: Princeton University Press, 1985); Carol Gluck, "The End of Elsewhere: Writing Modernity Now," *The American Historical Review* vol. 116, no. 3 (June 2011): 676-687; William Miles Fletcher, *The Search for a New Order: Intellectuals and Fascism in Prewar Japan* (Chapel Hill: University of North Carolina Press, 1982).
36. Sheldon Garon, "From Meiji to Heisei: The State and Civil Society in Japan," in *The State of Civil Society in Japan*, Frank J. Schwartz, Susan J. Pharr, eds., pp. 42-62 (Cambridge: Cambridge University Press, 2003), p. 44; Garon, *Molding Japanese Minds*; Sheldon Garon and Mike Mochizuki, "Negotiating Social Contracts," in *Postwar Japan as History*, Andrew Gordon, ed. (Oxford: University of California Press, 1993), pp. 145-166.

37. For an exception that focuses on state-society cooperation in the area of cultural policymaking, see Maj Hartmann, "Matsumoto Gaku: A Bureaucrat between Culture and Politics in the Beginning of the 1930s," *New Ideas in East Asian Studies* vol. 1 (2017): pp. 1-10; For an example in the field of film policy, see Peter B. High, *The Imperial Screen: Japanese Film Culture in The Fifteen Years War, 1931-1945* (Madison: The University of Wisconsin Press, 2003). An important work in the field of the New Bureaucrats' social policy is Roger H. Brown, "(The Other) Yoshida Shigeru and the Expansion of Bureaucratic Power in Prewar Japan," *Monumenta Nipponica* vol. 67, no. 2 (2012): pp. 283-327.

38. Anthony Giddens, *Capitalism and Modern Social Theory: An Analysis of the Writings of Marx, Durkheim and Max Weber* (Cambridge University Press, 1971), p. 159.

39. Richard C. Snyder, H.W. Bruck and Burton Sapin. "Decision-Making as an Approach to the Study of International Politics," in *Foreign Policy Decision-Making*, Richard C. Snyder, H.W. Bruck, Burton Sapin, eds., pp. 14-185 (The Free Press of Glencoe, 1962), p. 66; see also: Snyder, Bruck, and Sapin, *Foreign Policy Decision-Making* (Revisited) (New York: Palgrave Macmillan, 2002).

40. Snyder, Bruck and Sapin, "Decision-Making as an Approach to the Study of International Politics," p. 67; Valerie M. Hudson, "Foreign Policy Analysis: Actor-Specific Theory and the Ground of International Relations," *Foreign Policy Analysis* vol. 1, no. 1 (March 2005), pp. 1-30.

41. Herbert Passin, "Intellectuals in the Decision-Making Process," in *Modern Japanese Organization and Decision-Making*, Ezra F. Vogel, ed. (Tōkyō: Tuttle, 1980 Second Edition), p. 264; Peter M. Haas, "Introduction: Epistemic Communities and International Policy Coordination," *International Organization* vol. 46, no. 1 (Winter 1992): pp. 1-35.

42. John W. Kingdon, *Agendas, Alternatives, and Public Policies*, 2nd edition (Boston: Little, Brown & Company, 1985), p. 122.

43. Von Staden, *Business-Government Relations in Prewar Japan*, p. 42.

44. Von Staden, p. 40.

45. Schwartz, *Advice and Consent*, p. 58.

46. An exception in English-language scholarship is the 2005 edited volume *Japanese Copyright Law: Writings in Honour of Gerhard Schricker* in which copyright scholar Peter Ganea is featured with a short essay on "Japan's Copyright History," which, however, only serves as a brief overview of the more detailed descriptive histories that have been published in this field in Japan. Peter Ganea, "Copyright History," in *Japanese Copyright Law: Writings in Honour of Gerhard Schricker*, Peter Ganea, Christopher Heath, Hiroshi Saitō, eds. (The Hague: Kluwer Law International, 2005), pp. 1-10.

47. Tōkyō Shosekishō Kumiai, ed., *Tōkyō Shosekishō Kumiai 50nen shi* (50-Year History of the Tōkyō Booksellers and Publishers' Association) (Tōkyō: Tōkyō Shosekishō Kumiai, 1937); Ōkubo Hisao, ed., *Senzen Tōkyō-Ōsaka shuppan gyōshi dai-1kan* (Prewar History of the Tōkyō-Ōsaka Publishing Industry vol. 1) (Kanazawa: Kanazawa Bunpokaku, 2008; Reprint of Tōkyō Shuppan Kyōkai, *Tōkyō Shuppan Kyōkai 15nen shi* (15-Year History of the Tōkyō Publishers' Association), Tōkyō: Shuppan Kyōkai Jimusho, 1929).

CHAPTER 1. BEFORE BERNE

1. Iriye, *Global Community*, p. 11; Löhr, *Die Globalisierung geistiger Eigentumsrechte*, p. 49.
2. Edward Mack, *Manufacturing Modern Japanese Literature: Publishing, Prizes, and the Ascription of Literary Value* (Durham: Duke University Press, 2010), p. 18; Amy J. Lloyd, "Education, Literacy and the Reading Public," *British Library Newspapers* (Detroit: Gale, 2007).
3. Victor Foucher, *Le Congrès de la propriété littéraire et artistique tenu à Bruxelles en 1858* (Paris: Librairie de Michel Lévy Frères, 1858).
4. On the early work of the association, see *Association Littéraire et Artistique Internationale, son histoire, ses travaux, 1878-1889* (Paris: Bibliothèque Chacornac, 1889).
5. Bannerman, *International Copyright and Access to Knowledge*, pp. 3-4; Löhr, *Die Globalisierung geistiger Eigentumsrechte*, p. 67.
6. Löhr, *Die Globalisierung geistiger Eigentumsrechte*, pp. 67-70.
7. Orii Yoshimi, "The Dispersion of Jesuit Books Printed in Japan: Trends in Bibliographical Research and in Intellectual History," *Journal of Jesuit Studies* vol. 2, no. 2 (April 2015): pp. 189-207.
8. Mack, *Manufacturing Modern Japanese Literature*, pp. 20-22.
9. Mack, p. 35.
10. Giles Richter, "Marketing the Word: Publishing Entrepreneurs in Meiji Japan, 1870-1912" (Ph.D. diss., Colombia University, 1999), p. 37; on Japan's early modern publishing history see also Yokota Fuyuhiko, *Nihon kinsei shomotsu bunka-shi no kenkyū* (Research on the History of Japan's Early Modern Book Culture) (Tōkyō: Iwanami Shoten, 2018); Yokota Fuyuhiko, ed., *Shuppan to ryūtsū* (Publishing and Distribution), *Hon no bunka-shi* vol.v 4 (Cultural History of Books, vol. 4) (Tōkyō: Heibonsha, 2016).
11. Mack, *Manufacturing Modern Japanese Literature*, p. 19; Peter Kornicki, *The Book in Japan: A Cultural History from the Beginnings to the Nineteenth Century* (Leiden: E. J. Brill, 1998), pp. 5-7.
12. Richter, "Marketing the Word," p. 67; Mack, *Manufacturing Modern Japanese Literature*, p. 32.
13. Edo is the former name of Tōkyō which was renamed in 1868.
14. James L. Huffman, *Creating a Public: People and Press in Meiji Japan* (Honolulu: University of Hawai'i Press, 1997), p. 27.
15. Huffman, pp. 51 and 60; Mack, *Manufacturing Modern Japanese Literature*, p. 27; Richter, "Marketing the Word," p. 58; see also Yamamoto Taketoshi, *Kindai Nihon no shinbun dokusha-sō* (The Readership of Modern Japan) (Tōkyō: Hōsei Daigaku Shuppankyoku, 1981), pp. 401-433.
16. Alan J. Lee, *The Origins of the Popular Press in England, 1855-1914* (London: Croom Helm, 1976), pp. 21-72; Simon Potter, *News and the British World: The Emergence of an Imperial Press System, 1876-1922*, (Oxford: Clarendon Press, 2003), pp. 12-35.

17. Richter, "Marketing the Word," p. 58.
18. Richter, pp. 55-56.
19. Richter, p. 219.
20. Tsuruoka Satoshi, "Inoue-ki jōyaku kaisei kōshō to chiteki zaisanken – Mondai teiki to gōi keisei" (The Treaty Revision Negotiations During the Inoue Term and Intellectual Property Rights (1): Problem Statement and Consensus Building), *Hōgaku kenkyū* vol. 89, no. 5 (May 2016): pp. 80, 87.
21. Kornicki, *The Book in Japan*, p. 245.
22. Kornicki, pp. 179-184; Mack, *Manufacturing Modern Japanese Literature*, p. 35.
23. Kornicki, p. 244.
24. Kornicki, p. 245.
25. Kornicki, pp. 249-250.
26. Earl H. Kinmoth, "Fukuzawa Reconsidered: Gakumon no Susume and its Audience," *The Journal of Asian Studies* vol. 37, no. 4 (August 1978): pp. 677-696.
27. Ganea, "Copyright History," p. 2.
28. Richter, "Marketing the Word," pp. 131-165.
29. Shuppan Jōrei, Ordinance No. 444/1869. Full text in *Hōrei zensho* (Collection of Laws and Regulations), (Tōkyō: Naikaku Kanpōkyoku, 1869), pp. 174-177.
30. Ganea, "Copyright History," pp. 3-5.
31. Shuppan Jōrei, Ordinance No. 135/1875. Full text in *Hōrei zensho* (Collection of Laws and Regulations) (Tōkyō: Naikaku Kanpōkyoku, 1875), pp. 162-170.
32. Kornicki, *The Book in Japan*, p. 250; Tsuruoka, "Inoue-ki jōyaku kaisei kōshō to chiteki zaisanken (jō)," pp. 79-115.
33. Ganea, "Copyright History," p. 5.
34. Shuppan Hō, Law No. 15/1893. Full text in *Hōrei zensho* (Collection of Laws and Regulations) (Tōkyō: Naikaku Kanpōkyoku, 1893), pp. 84-89.
35. Clive Parry, ed., *The Consolidated Treaty Series* vol. 180 (New York: Oceana, 1979), pp. 258-272.
36. Kerim Yasar, *Electrified Voices: How the Telephone, Phonograph, and Radio shaped Modern Japan*, 1868-1945 (New York: Columbia University Press, 2018), p. 95.
37. Terada, *Actors of International Cooperation in Prewar Japan*, p. 41.
38. Yoshimura, "Kyū-chosakuken hō o meguru hitobito," p. 45; Ōie, *Chosakuken o kakuritsu shita hitobito*, p. 99.
39. Nishio Rintarō, ed., *Mizuno Rentarō kaisōroku – kankei bunsho* (Memoirs of Mizuno Rentarō: Related Documents) (Tōkyō: Yamagawa Shuppansha, 1999), p. 18; Yoshimura, "*Kyū-chosakuken hō o meguru hitobito – Mizuno Rentarō*," pp. 44-47.
40. Chosakuken Hō, Law No. 39/1899, amended as Chosakuken Hō, Law No. 48/1970. Full text of the original law in *Hōrei zensho* (Collection of Laws and Regulations) (Tōkyō: Naikaku Kanpōkyoku, 1899), pp. 105-115.

41. Yoshimura, "Kyū-chosakuken hō o meguru hitobito," pp. 45-46.
42. Yamada Saburō, "Bankoku hanken hogo dōmei ni oite" (Regarding the Union for the Protection of International Copyright) *Hōgaku Kyōkai zasshi* vol. 15, (1 May 1897): pp. 496-506.
43. Yamada Saburō, *Kaikoroku* (Memoirs) (Tōkyō: Yamada Saburō Sensei Beiju Shukugakai, 1957), pp. 1-4; Terada, *Actors of International Cooperation in Prewar Japan*, pp. 38-39.
44. Terada, p. 44.
45. Terada, pp. 39-40.
46. Fukui Yūsuke, "Shuppan kanren giin to seiron media no hensen – zasshi no senmonka to shōgyōka" (National Diet Members Engaged in Publishing and the Changes in the Political Debate Media: The Specialization and Commercialization of Magazines), in *Kindai Nihon no media giin: 'seiji no mediaka' no rekishi shakaigaku* (The Media-Diet-Member of Modern Japan: A Historical Sociology of the 'Mediatization of Politics'), Satō Takumi and Kawasaki Yoshinori, eds. (Ōsaka: Sōgensha, 2018), p. 192.
47. Marshall, "Professors and Politics," p. 75.
48. Kohlrausch, Steffen, Wiederkehr, "Introduction," p. 10.
49. Marshall, pp. 81-82; Kingdon, *Agendas, Alternatives, and Public Policies*.
50. Passin, "Intellectuals in the Decision Making Process," p. 282.
51. Ōie, *Chosakuken o kakuritsu shita hitobito*, p. 106.
52. The association was originally founded in 1887 under the name of Tōkyō Book Publishing Businessmen's Association (Tōkyō Shoseki Shuppan Eigyōsha Kumiai). In 1902 its was changed to Tōkyō Booksellers and Publishers' Association (Tōkyō Shosekishō Kumiai).
53. In the few works that mention Oyaizu Kaname, there is an inconsistency in the reading of his unusual name. Giles Richter transcribes the name as Koizu Yaname. Miyata Naboru transcribes his name as Oyaizu Kanando. In newspaper articles of the time one can also find the transcription Oyaizu Iname. In a letter to British publisher Allen and Unwin from 1915, Oyaizu signs his name as "K. Oyaidzu" [Oyaizu]. The *Japan Times* in the contemporary reports likewise refers to Oyaizu as Oyaizu Kaname, the transcription that has been adopted in this book and that is also used by Tomizawa Yoshiko, who has published on Oyaizu, as well as by the National Diet Library of Japan. Letter from Maruzen Company to Allen & Unwin, December 8, 1915, Collection of George Allen & Unwin Ltd.: Correspondence files AU FSC 20/129 (accession number MS 3282), University of Reading, The Archive of British Publishing and Printing Reading Sources; "The Tōkyō Chamber of Commerce," *Japan Times* (October 11, 1897), p. 3.
54. Tomizawa Yoshiko, ed., *Oyaizu Kaname tsuien* (Following the Life of Oyaizu Kaname) (Tōkyō: Tomizawa Yoshiko, 1978); Tōkyō Shoseki Kabushikigaisha, ed., *Bukkō*

yakuin nami kōrōsha tsuitō kinen (Commemoration of Deceased Officers and Distinguished Persons) (Tōkyō: Tōkyō Shoseki, 1931).
55. Nara Katsuji, *Meiji Ishin to sekai ninshiki taikei: Bakumatsu no Tokugawa seiken shingi to seii no aida* (The Meiji Restoration and Worldview Systems: Between Loyalty to the Tokugawa Administration in the Bakumatsu Era and Conquest of the Barbarians) (Tōkyō: Yūshisha, 2010).
56. Tōkyō Shoseki Kabushikigaisha, *Bukkō yakuin nami kōrōsha tsuitō kinen*, p. 13; Shōtō Fujii, "Oyaizu Kaname-shi" (Oyaizu Kaname), *Shin Nihon* vol. 6, no. 11 (November 1913): p. 39; "Bunmeiteki shōjin ippyakunin (sono 14) Maruzen Shoten shachō: Oyaizu Kaname kun" (100 Civilized Merchants: Maruzen's President Oyaizu Kaname), *Jitsugyō no sekai* vol. 12, no. 7 (April 1915): p. 15.
57. Tōkyō Shoseki Kabushikigaisha, *Bukkō yakuin nami kōrōsha tsuitō kinen*, p. 14.
58. Richter, "Marketing the Word," p. 149.
59. Tomizawa, *Oyaizu Kaname tsuien*, p. 6.
60. Fujii, "Oyaizu Kaname-shi," p. 39.
61. Garon, "From Meiji to Heisei: The State and Civil Society in Japan," pp. 49-51.
62. Tōkyō Shosekishō Kumiai, *Tōkyō Shosekishō Kumiai 50nen shi*, p. 1.
63. Tōkyō Shosekishō Kumiai, *Tōkyō Shosekishō Kumiai 50nen shi*, pp. 15-18.
64. Until 1890, the Chambers were active via their two predecessors, the Chambers of Commercial Law (Shōhō Kaigisho) and the Tōkyō Association of Commerce and Industry (Tōkyō Shōkōkai).
65. Matsumoto Takanori, ed., *Senzenki Nihon no bōeki to soshiki-kan kankei – jōhō, chōsei, kyōchō* (Pre-war Japan's Trade and Inter-Organizational Relations: Information, Regulation, and Cooperation) (Tōkyō: Shinhyōron, 1996), pp. 276-278.
66. Tōkyō Shosekishō Kumiai, *Tōkyō Shosekishō Kumiai 50nen shi*, p. 46.
67. Tōkyō Shosekishō Kumiai, pp. 46-48, 61; Matsumoto, *Senzenki Nihon no bōeki to soshiki-kan kankei*, p. 278.
68. Tōkyō Shosekishō Kumiai, p. 15.
69. Tōkyō Shosekishō Kumiai, pp. 84-89.
70. Tōkyō Shosekishō Kumiai, p. 86.
71. Tōkyō Shosekishō Kumiai, p. 85.
72. Tōkyō Shosekishō Kumiai, p. 87.
73. Tōkyō Shosekishō Kumiai, p. 87.
74. Tōkyō Shosekishō Kumiai, p. 87.
75. Adrian Johns, *Piracy: The Intellectual Property Wars from Gutenberg to Gates* (Chicago: University of Chicago Press, 2011), p. 309.
76. Johns, p. 324.
77. Johns, pp. 312-317.
78. Hemmungs Wirtén, *Cosmopolitan Copyright*, p. 22.

79. Richter, "Marketing the Word," p. 3.
80. Richter, p. 219.
81. Fukui, "Shuppan kanren giin to seiron media no hensen," pp. 169-201.
82. The Tōkyō City Council was a local assembly that existed from 1889 until 1943.
83. Von Staden, *Business-Government Relations in Prewar Japan*, p. 32.
84. Ehud Harari, "The Institutionalisation of Policy Consultation in Japan: Public Advisory Bodies," in *Japan and the World: Essays on Japanese History and Politics in Honour of Ishida Takeshi*, Gail Lee Bernstein and Haruhiro Fukui, eds., pp. 144-157 (London: Macmillan, 1988), p. 147.
85. Kudō Eiichi, "Jitsugyōka toshite no Sakuma Teiichi – Meiji-ki jitsugyōka-zō no ichi ruikei" (Sakuma Teiichi as a Businessman: A Type of Meiji Era Businessman), *Meiji Gakuin ronsō* vol. 127 (June 1967): pp. 15-40.
86. "Tōkyō shikai" (Tōkyō City Council), *Tōkyō asahi shinbun* (October 10, 1897 morning issue), p. 3.
87. Ōie, *Chosakuken o kakuritsu shita hitobito*, p. 106.
88. "Kaisei jōyaku jisshi ni kan suru yūryo" (Concerns Regarding the Implementation of the Treaty Revision), *Tōkyō asahi shinbun* (July 6, 1898, morning issue), p. 2.
89. "Bill relating to Copyright Law," *Japan Times* (January 20, 1899), p. 3.
90. Henry Wheaton, *Elements of International Law* (London: Sampson Low, Son, and Company 1866; Reprint Oxford: At the Clarendon Press, 1936), p. 20.
91. Mizuno Rentarō, "Bankoku hanken hogo dōmei ni oite" (Regarding the Union for the Protection of International Copyright), *Kokka Gakkai zasshi* vol. 12, no. 142 (December 15, 1898): p. 2118.
92. Schwartz, *Advice and Consent*, p. 53.
93. Shimizu Yu'ichirō, "Lessons Learned: Japanese Bureaucrats and the First World War," trans. Angelika Koch, in *The East Asian Dimension of the First World War: Global Entanglements and Japan, China, and Korea 1914-1919*, Jan Schmidt and Katja Schmidtpott, eds. (Frankfurt/New York: Campus, 2020), p. 274.
94. Shimizu, p. 274.
95. Itagaki Taisuke, "Yukoku" (Warning), *Kanpō* (August 9, 1898), p. 77.
96. Itagaki, "Yukoku" (Warning), p. 77.
97. Kurata Yoshihiro, *Chosakuken shiwa (rekishi sensho 11)* (The True History of Copyright (History Anthology 11)) (Tōkyō: Senjinsha, 1980), p. 175.
98. Nishio, *Mizuno Rentarō kaisōroku*, p. 419.
99. "Honkaigijo rokuji," *Tōkyō Shōgyō Kaigijo geppō dai-80gō* (The Monthly Report of the Tōkyō Chamber of Commerce, no. 80) (April 1899), Tōkyō Shōkō Kaigijo (keizai shiryō sentā), Zenkoku Shōkō Kaigijo kankei shiryō, dai-1ki – Tōkyō Shōkō Kaigijo kankei shiryō 1877-1907, 01/27, 08391, pp. 24-32, here p. 27.
100. Tōkyō Shosekishō Kumiai, ed., *Tōkyō shosekishō denki shūran* (Biographical Collection of the Tōkyō Book Commerce) (1912; repr., Tōkyō: Seishōdō Shoten, 1978), p. 78.

101. Tōkyō Shosekishō Kumiai, *Tōkyō Shosekishō Kumiai 50nen shi*, pp. 89-90.
102. Tōkyō Shosekishō Kumiai, p. 90.

CHAPTER 2. AN UNPREDICTED DEMAND

1. Regine Mathias, "Reading for Culture," *Senri Ethnological Studies* vol. 28 (1990): p. 114; Mack, *Manufacturing Modern Japanese Literature*, p. 18.
2. Giles Richter, "Entrepreneurship and Culture: The Hakubunkan Publishing Empire in Meiji Japan," in *New Directions in the Study of Meiji Japan*, Helen Hardacre, ed. (Leiden: E. J. Brill, 1997), p. 591.
3. Kawakami Tarō, "Nihon ni okeru kokusai shihō 70nen – toku ni Yamada Saburō oyobi Egawa Eibun o chūshin toshite" (70 Years of International Private Law in Japan: with a Special Focus on Yamada Saburō and Egawa Eibun), *Kokusaihō gaibun zasshi* vol. 65, no. 4 (October 1966): p. 9; Yamada Saburō, "Bankoku hanken hogo dōmei ni oite" (Regarding the Union for the Protection of International Copyright) *Hōgaku Kyōkai zasshi* vol. 15 (1 May 1897): pp. 496-506.
4. Yamada, *Kaikoroku*, p. 41.
5. Terada, *Actors of International Cooperation in Prewar Japan*, p. 37.
6. Terada, p. 42.
7. Sharon A. Minichiello, "Introduction," in *Japan's Competing Modernities: Issues in Culture and Democracy 1900-1930*, Sharon A. Michiello, ed. (Honolulu: University of Hawai'i Press, 1998), p. 2.
8. Jean-Christophe Mabire, *L'Exposition Universelle de 1900* (Paris: L'Harmattan, 2000), p. 123; "The Paris Universal Exhibition," *The Lancet* vol. 155, no. 3998 (1900): pp. 1086-1087.
9. Sam Ricketson, "The Public International Law of Copyright and Related Rights," in *Research Handbook on the History of Copyright Law*, Isabella Alexander and H. Tomás Gómez-Arostegui, eds. (Cheltenham: Edward Elgar Publishing, 2016), p. 290.
10. Terada, *Actors of International Cooperation in Prewar Japan*, p. 46.
11. Mizuno Rentarō, "Nihon to chosakuken no hogo" (Japan and Copyright Protection), *Kokka Gakkai Zasshi* vol. 15, no. 167 (January 1901): pp. 43-44.
12. "Le Japon et la protection des droits des auteurs," *Droit d'auteur* vol. 3, no. 10 (1900): pp. 126-131; Itō Nobuo, "Hon'yaku jiyū no riron to jissai (1)" (The Theory and Practice of Translation Freedom), *Nihon hōgaku* vol. 5, no. 5 (May 1939): p. 55.
13. Richter, "Entrepreneurship and Culture," pp. 590-602.
14. Tsubouchi Yūzō, "Henshūsha Ōhashi Otowa" (The Editor Ōhashi Otowa), in *Zasshi 'Taiyō' to kokumin bunka no keisei* (The Magazine 'Taiyō' and the Formation of National Culture), Suzuki Sadami, ed. (Kyōto: Shibunkaku, 2001), p. 159.
15. Ōhashi Otowa, *Ōbei shōkan* (A Travel Sketch of Europe and the United States) (Tōkyō: Hakubunkan, 1901).

16. Ōhashi, p. 121.
17. Ōhashi, p. 127.
18. Ōhashi, pp. 130-136.
19. Ōhashi, p. 139.
20. Ōhashi, p. 163.
21. Ōhashi, p. 141.
22. Ōhashi, pp. 141-142.
23. Kawakami, "Nihon ni okeru kokusai shihō 70nen," p. 9.
24. Iriye, *Global Community: The Role of International Organizations in the Making of the Contemporary World*, p. 45.
25. Tsubouchi, "Henshūsha Ōhashi Otowa," p. 165.
26. Tsubouchi, p. 165.
27. Mizuno, "Nihon to chosakuken no hogo," pp. 43-44.
28. Löhr, *Die Globalisierung geistiger Eigentumsrechte*, p. 53.
29. Löhr, p. 53.
30. Löhr, p. 53.
31. Löhr, p. 56.
32. Tōkyō Shosekishō Kumiai, pp. 84-89.
33. "Shinkoku ni tai suru hanken hogo no gi ni tsuki seigan" (Petition in the Matter of Copyright Protection for China), in *Tsuika Nisshin tsūshō kōkai jōyaku teiketsu ikken* (A Matter Concerning the Supplementary Sino-Japanese Treaty of Commerce and Navigation), December 1901, Gaimushō Gaikō Shiryōkan (Diplomatic Archives of the Ministry of Foreign Affairs, henceforth DA MoFA), Ajia Rekishi Shiryō Sentā (Japan Center for Asian Historical Records, henceforth: JACAR), Ref. B06151056600, pp. 0221-0223 (for the page numbers of JACAR documents, the numbers provided on the scanned microfilms are given. If no numbers are provided, the listed page number refers to the number of the corresponding PDF slide. Where it is a quote from a report or other document that includes page numbers, the page numbers given are those of the original document).
34. The People's Republic of China did not become a member of the Berne Convention until October 15, 1992.
35. "Shinkoku ni tai suru hanken hogo no gi ni tsuki seigan" (Petition in the Matter of Copyright Protection for China), DA MoFA, Ref. B06151056600, pp. 0221-0223; Kurata, *Chosakuken shiwa*, p. 181.
36. "The New Commercial Treaty with China," *Japan Times* (January 20, 1904), pp. 2, 6.
37. "Nisshin-kan no chosakuken mondai" (The Sino-Japanese Copyright Problem), *Tōkyō asahi shinbun* (July 5, 1907, morning issue), p. 4.
38. "The International Publishing Bureau," *Japan Times* (July 4, 1906), p. 2.
39. Hemmungs Wirtén, *Cosmopolitan Copyright*, p. 22.
40. Hemmungs Wirtén, p. 43.

41. "Bungakuteki oyobi bijutsuteki chosakuken hogo bankoku dōmei ikken" (A Matter Concerning the Berne Convention for the Protection of Literary and Artistic Works), in *Bungakuteki, bijutsuteki, chosakuken hogo bankoku kaigi ikken* (Matters Concerning the International Conference of the Berne Convention), 1905-1908, DA MoFA, JACAR, Ref. B07080266800; Letter from the German Embassy to Hayashi Tadasu, in *Bungakuteki, bijutsuteki, chosakuken hogo bankoku kaigi ikken* (idem), April 1, 1908, DA MoFA, JACAR, Ref. B07080266900, p. 0033.
42. Nihon Shoseki Shuppan Kyōkai, ed., *Nihon shuppan 100nen shi nenpyō* (A 100-Year History Chronology of Japan's Publishing) (Tōkyō: Nihon Shoseki Shuppan Kyōkai, 1968), p. 258.
43. "Kōgyō to chosaku ni tsuite" (On Performances and Literary Works), *Tōkyō asahi shinbun* (July 30, 1907, morning issue), p. 3.
44. "Kōgyō to chosaku ni tsuite," *Tōkyō asahi shinbun* (July 30, 1907, morning issue), p. 3.
45. Bannerman, *International Copyright and Access to Knowledge*, p. 170.
46. Bannerman, p. 170.
47. Pyle, *Rising Japan*, pp. 106 and 111.
48. *Actes de la conférence réunie à Berlin du 14 octobre au 14 novembre 1908* (Berne: Bureau de l'Union Internationale Littéraire et Artistique, 1909), p. 201.
49. *Actes de la conférence réunie à Berlin*, p. 201.
50. *Actes de la conférence réunie à Berlin*, p. 201.
51. *Actes de la conférence réunie à Berlin*, pp. 202-203.
52. *Actes de la conférence réunie à Berlin*, pp. 201-203.
53. "Le Japon et la protection des droits des auteurs," *Droit d'auteur* vol. 3, no. 10 (1900): pp. 126-131, quoted from Wirtén, *Cosmopolitan Copyright*, p. 40.
54. Naoko Shimazu, *Japan, Race and Equality: The Racial Equality Proposal of 1919* (London/New York: Routledge, 1998), p. 185.
55. Shimazu, *Japan, Race and Equality*, p. 3.
56. Toyoda Tetsuya, "Japan's Early Challenge to Eurocentrism and the World Court," in *Modern Japanese Thought and International Relations*, Felix Rösch and Atsuko Watanabe, eds. (London: Rowman & Littlefield, 2018), p. 45.
57. Albert Osterrieth, "Mémoire concernant la protection du droit de traduction," *Droit d'auteur* vol. 22, no. 2 (1909): p. 26 quoted from Hemmungs Wirtén, *Cosmopolitan Copyright*, p. 41.
58. Mizunō Rentarō, "Berurin tayori" (News from Berlin), *Keisatsu Kyōkai zasshi* vol. 104 (1909), p. 39.
59. Shimizu Yu'ichirō, *Kindai Nihon no kanryō* (The Bureaucrats of Modern Japan) (Tōkyō: Chūō Kōron Shinsha, 2013). An English translation was published in 2019: Shimizu Yu'ichirō, *The Origins of the Modern Japanese Bureaucracy*, trans. Amin Ghadimi (London: Bloomsbury Academic, 2019).

60. Pyle, *Rising Japan*, p. 51.
61. Mizuno Rentarō, "Hon'yaku kikan no setchi ni oite" (On Establishing the Duration for Translations), *Shimin* vol. 4, no. 5 (June 1909), p. 16.
62. Mizuno, "Hon'yaku kikan no setchi ni oite," pp. 16-17. Mizuno's perception here is incorrect. There already existed many English language publications on Japan at the time, written by Japan enthusiasts, foreign exchange students, diplomats, and bureaucrats.
63. Ōkuma Shigenobu, *Fifty Years of New Japan*, trans. Marcus B. Huish (London: Smith, Elder & Co, 1909).
64. Mizuno, "Hon'yaku kikan no setchi ni oite," p. 17.
65. Mizuno, pp. 18-19.
66. Pyle, *Rising Japan*, p. 136.
67. Hemmungs Wirtén, *Cosmopolitan Copyright*, p. 43.
68. Ganea, "Copyright History," p. 6.
69. Ganea, p. 7.
70. "Kōgyō shoyūken oyobi chosakuken dōmei ni kan suru iken" (An Opinion About Industrial Property Rights and the Copyright Alliance), in *Kanzei ni kan suru kengi seigan zassan* vol. 2 (Collection of Tax Related Petition Propositions), October 1909, DA MoFA, JACAR, Ref. B12083075500, pp. 0481-0483.
71. "Kōgyō joyūken oyobi chosakuken dōmei ni kan suru iken," JACAR, Ref. B12083075500, pp. 0481-0483.
72. Letter from the Association Littéraire et Artistique Internationale to Unknown Japanese Recipient, in *Bungakuteki, bijutsuteki, chosakuken hogo bankoku kaigi ikken* (Matters Concerning the International Conference of the Berne Convention), November 10, 1909, DA MoFA, JACAR, Ref. B07080267000, pp. 0174–0176.
73. Letter from the Association Littéraire et Artistique Internationale to Unknown Japanese Recipient, JACAR, Ref. B07080267000, p. 0176.
74. Löhr, *Die Globalisierung geistiger Eigentumsrechte*, p. 88.
75. Löhr, pp. 86-87.
76. On Japan and World War I, see, for example, Jan Schmidt, *Nach dem Krieg ist vor dem Krieg – Medialisierte Erfahrungen des Ersten Weltkriegs und Nachkriegsdiskurse in Japan (1914-1919)* (Frankfurt: Campus, 2020); Jan Schmidt and Katja Schmidtpott, eds., *The East Asian Dimension of the First World War: Global Entanglements and Japan, China, and Korea 1914-1919* (Frankfurt/New York: Campus, 2020); Naraoka Sōchi, *Taika 21 kajō yōkyu to wa nan datta no ka. Daiichiji Sekai Taisen to Nitchū tairitsu no genten* (What were the Twenty-One Demands? The First World War and the Origin of the Japanese-Chinese Antagonism) (Nagoya: Nagoya Daigaku Shuppankai, 2015); For more on censorship during World War I, see Mitchell, *Censorship in Imperial Japan*, pp. 172-179; Okuda Shirō, "Genron no jōkei – 1918nen" (The Prospects of Speech in 1918), *20c.21c. Masukomi jānarizumu ronshū*, 1994, pp. 46-67.

77. The Legal Philosophy Research Association was established in 1897 as a research society on legal matters affiliated with the Tōkyō Imperial University Faculty of Law.
78. Yamada Saburō, "Tekikoku shinmin no mutaizaisanken (kotoni tokkyoken oyobi chosakuken)" (The Intangible Property Rights of the Subjects of Enemy Countries (Especially Patent Rights and Copyrights)), *Hōgaku Kyōkai ztasshi* vol. 33, no. 1 (January 1915): p. 133.
79. Yamada, p. 133.
80. Mizunō Rentarō, "Sensō to chosakuken" (War and Copyrights), *Hōgaku Kyōkai zasshi* vol. 33, no. 1 (January 1915): pp. 135-143.
81. Löhr, *Die Globalisierung geistiger Eigentumsrechte*, pp. 141-142.
82. Memorandum of the Legation of Denmark in Tōkyō, in *Bungakuteki, bijutsuteki, chosakuken hogo bankoku kaigi ikken 3* (Matters Concerning the International Conference of the Berne Convention, vol. 3), October 29, 1914, DA MoFA, JACAR, Ref. B07080267800, p. 0135.
83. "Bungakuteki oyobi bijutsuteki chosakuken hogo shūsei 'Berunu' jōyaku tsuika giteisho gohijun no kengai ikken" (A Case Concerning the Ratification of the Additional Protocol of the Berne Convention for the Protection of Literary and Artistic Works), in *Sūmitsuin, jōsō hei naikaku tsūhō 3 (1912-1920)* (Privy Council: Report to the Throne and the Cabinet), February 1, 1915, Kokuritsu Kōbunshokan (National Archives of Japan, NAJ), JACAR, Ref. A03034340700, p. 1.
84. Document of Emperor Yoshihito approving and ratifying the Additional Protocol of the Berne Convention, in *Bungakuteki, bijutsuteki, chosakuken hogo bankoku kaigi ikken 3* (Matters Concerning the International Conference of the Berne Convention, vol. 3), February 2, 1915, DA MoFA, JACAR, Ref: B07080267900, pp. 0210-0211; Letter from Foreign Minister Katō Takaaki to the Federal Chancellor of the Swiss Delegation Arthur Hoffmann, in *Bungakuteki, bijutsuteki, chosakuken hogo bankoku kaigi ikken 3* (idem), February 2, 1915, DA MoFA, JACAR, Ref: B07080267900, p. 0210.
85. Löhr, *Die Globalisierung geistiger Eigentumsrechte*, p. 90.
86. "Shina shuppanhō ni kan suru ken (tsuketari chosakukenritsu ni kan suru ken)" (Regarding China's Publication Law (appendix regarding the copyright law)), in *Shuppan oyobi hanken kankei zakken – shuppan no bu 2* (Various Matters Regarding Publishing and Copyright), March 1915, DA MoFA, JACAR, Ref: B13080841900.
87. Ōkubo Hisao, *Shuppan – Shosekishō jinbutsu jōhō taikan: Shōwa shoki* (Information Overview of People Engaged in Publishing and Bookselling) (Kanazawa: Kanazawa Bunpokaku, 2008; Reprint of *Nihon shuppan taikan* (Overview of Japanese Publishing), Tōkyō: Shuppan Taimususha, 1930), pp. 33-34; Tōkyō Shosekishō Kumiai, *Tōkyō Shosekishō Kumiai 50nen shi*, pp. 149-150.
88. "Tōkyō Shōgyō Kaigijo rokuji" (Recordings of the Tōkyō Chamber of Commerce), *Tōkyō Shōgyō Kaigijo geppō dai-10kan dai-3gō* (The Monthly Report of the Tōkyō Chamber of Commerce, vol. 10, no. 3) (March 1917), Tōkyō Shōkō Kaigijo (keizai

shiryō sentā), Zenkoku Shōkō Kaigijo kankei shiryō, dai-1ki – Tōkyō Shōkō Kaigijo kankei shiryō 1877-1907, 01/27, 08526, pp. 44-46, here p. 45.
89. Ōkubo, *Senzen Tōkyō-Ōsaka shuppan gyōshi*, p. 22.
90. Bōri Torishimari Rei, Ordinance No. 20/1917, issued by the Teraguchi government. On the anti-profiteering legislation, see also Morohashi Eiichi, "Daiichiji Sekai Taisen to zeizaisei seisaku: sōryokusen ni okeru senji ritokusei no dōnyū to sono igi" (The First World War and Fiscal Policy: The Introduction and Significance of the Wartime Capital Gains Tax in Total War), *Shigaku zasshi* vol. 125, no. 8 (2016), pp. 1395-1419.
91. Hisao, *Senzen Tōkyō-Ōsaka shuppan gyōshi*, pp. 49-50, 77.
92. Nihon Shoseki Shuppan Kyōkai, *Nihon shuppan 100nen shi nenpyō*, pp. 302, 308, 316.
93. Maruzen kabushiki-gaisha, ed., *Maruzen 100nen shi: Nihon kindaika no ayumi to tomo ni* vol. 1-3 (The 100-Year History of Maruzen: Along with the Steps of Japan's Modernization) (Tōkyō: Maruzen, 1980/1981).
94. Letter from Maruzen Company to Allen & Unwin, December 8, 1915, Collection of George Allen & Unwin Ltd.: Correspondence files AU FSC 20/129 (accession number MS 3282), University of Reading, The Archive of British Publishing and Printing Reading Sources.
95. Letter from Asher & Co to Maruzen, in *Ōshū Sensō no keizai bōeki ni oyobosu eikyō hōkoku zakken – Eikoku seifu ni oite yūbinbutsu ōshū ikken* (Report on the Impact of the Great War on Economic and Trade Matters: A Case of Postal Seizure by the British Government), April 20, 1916, DA MoFA, JACAR, Ref. B11100547500, p. 0058.
96. John McDermot, "Trading with the Enemy: British Business and the Law During the First World War," *Canadian Journal of History* vol. 32, no. 2 (August 1997): pp. 204-205.
97. Morohashi Eiichi, "Daiichiji Sekai Taisen ki no taiteki torihiki kinshi seisaku to Nihon" (Japan and the Trading with the Enemy Policy During the First World War), *Kokusai buki iten shi* vol. 4 (History of Global Arms Transfer, vol. 4) (July 2017): p. 118.
98. Morohashi, "Daiichiji Sekai Taisen ki no taiteki torihiki kinshi seisaku," p. 119, quoted from Kazuhito Kentarō, "Dentōteki kokusaihō ni okeru tekisen – Tekika hōkaku no seitōka konkyo (2 kan)" (The Justification Grounds in Traditional International Law for Seizing Enemy Ships and Goods), *Ōsaka hōgaku* vol. 64, no. 5 (2015): pp. 1119-1160.
99. Lassa Oppenheim, *International Law: A Treatise, vol. 1 – Peace* (New York: Longmans, Green and Co., 1920), p. 122; Morohashi, "Daiichiji Sekai Taisen ki no taiteki torihiki kinshi seisaku," p. 119.
100. Frauke Lachenmann and Rüdiger Wolfrum, eds., *The Law of Armed Conflict and the Use of Force – The Max Planck Encyclopedia of Public International Law* (Oxford: Oxford University Press, 2017), p. 1221.

101. "Chinjōsho: Doitsu koku no shuppanbutsu (shoseki oyobi zasshi rui) yu'nyū ni kan suru ken" (Petition: Matters Concerning the Import of German Publications (Books and Magazines)), in *Ōshū Sensō no keizai bōeki ni oyobosu eikyō hōkoku zakken – Eikoku seifu ni oite yūbinbutsu ōshū ikken* (Report on the Impact of the Great War on Economic and Trade Matters: A Case of Postal Seizure by the British Government), September 11, 1915, DA MoFA, JACAR, Ref. B11100547500, pp. 0016-0017.
102. The Yokohama Shōkin Ginkō was a semi-state owned Japanese foreign trade bank that existed from 1880 until 1947 when it was reorganized under SCAP into the Tōkyō Ginkō.
103. Letter from British Foreign Office to Japanese Ambassador Inoue Katsunosuke, in *Ōshū Sensō no keizai bōeki ni oyobosu eikyō hōkoku zakken – Eikoku seifu ni oite yūbinbutsu ōshū ikken* (Report on the Impact of the Great War on Economic and Trade Matters: A Case of Postal Seizure by the British Government), January 24, 1916, DA MoFA, JACAR, Ref. B11100547600, p. 0151.
104. Letter from British Foreign Office to Japanese Ambassador Inoue Katsunosuke.
105. Letter from the British Embassy Tōkyō to Foreign Trade Office, in *Foreign Office and Foreign and Commonwealth Office: Embassy and Consulates, Japan: General Correspondence*, June 7, 1916, FO 262/1236, The National Archives (TNA) – Foreign Office.
106. Letter from Yamakawa Kenjirō to Shidehara Kijurō, in *Ōshū Sensō no keizai bōeki ni oyobosu eikyō hōkoku zakken – Eikoku seifu ni oite yūbinbutsu ōshū ikken* (Report on the Impact of the Great War on Economic and Trade Matters: A Case of Postal Seizure by the British Government), October 12, 1916, DA MoFA, JACAR, Ref. B11100547600, p. 0185.
107. Letter from the Office of Commercial Attaché to UK Embassy, c/o British Consulate-General Yokohama, in *Ōshū Sensō no keizai bōeki ni oyobosu eikyō hōkoku zakken – Eikoku seifu ni oite yūbinbutsu ōshū ikken* (idem), February 21, 1917, DA MoFA, JACAR, Ref. B11100547800, p. 0357.
108. Letter from the British Embassy Tōkyō to Foreign Trade Office, in *Foreign Office and Foreign and Commonwealth Office: Embassy and Consulates, Japan: General Correspondence*, June 9, 1916, FO 262/1236, TNA – Foreign Office.
109. Letter from the Foreign Office to Viscount Sutemi Chanda, in *Ōshū Sensō no keizai bōeki ni oyobosu eikyō hōkoku zakken – Eikoku seifu ni oite yūbinbutsu ōshū ikken* (Report on the Impact of the Great War on Economic and Trade Matters: A Case of Postal Seizure by the British Government), July 24, 1917, DA MoFA, JACAR, Ref. B11100547900, p. 0460.
110. Letter from Maruzen to British Consulate General, in *Foreign Office and Foreign and Commonwealth Office: Embassy and Consulates, Japan: General Correspondence*, October 4, 1918, FO 262/1342, TNA – Foreign Office.
111. Morishima Morito, "Kokumin gaikō no kichō" (The Basic Idea Behind National Diplomacy), *Kokusai chishiki* vol. 6, no. 6 (June 1926): pp. 16-17.
112. Shimizu, *Kindai Nihon no kanryō*, p. 335.

CHAPTER 3. DEFENDING THE EXCEPTION

1. Iriye, *Cultural Internationalism and World Order*, pp. 49-57; Mitchell, *Censorship in Imperial Japan*, p. 173; Garon, *Molding Japanese Minds*, p. 17.
2. Iriye, *Cultural Internationalism and World Order*, p. 89; Saikawa, "Kokusai bunka kōryū no nashonarizum," pp. 11-30.
3. Hughes and tShinohara, *East Asians in the League of Nations*; Liang Pan, "National Internationalism in Japan and China", in *Internationalisms: A Twentieth Century History*, Glenda Sluga and Patricia Clavin, eds. (Cambridge: Cambridge University Press, 2016), pp. 170-190.
4. Shimazu, *Japan, Race and Equality*, p. 2.
5. Shimazu, p. 1.
6. Shimazu, p. 91.
7. Shimazu, p. 186.
8. Ōnuma Yasuaki, "Harukanaru jinshu byōdō no risō – Kokusai Renmei jōyaku e no jinshu byōdō jōkō teian to Nihon no kokusaihō kan" (The Unattained Ideal of Racial Equality: The Proposal of a Racial Equality Clause to the Covenant of the League of Nations and the Japanese View of International Law), in *Kokusaihō, kokusai rengō to Nihon: Takano Yūichi sensei koki kinen bunshū* (International Law, the United Nations and Japan: The Collection of Commemorative Essays for Professor Yūichi Takano's 70th Birthday), Ōnuma Yasuaki, ed. (Tōkyō: Kōbundō, 1987), pp. 131-132; on this issue, see also Shimazu, *Japan, Race and Equality*, 166; Terada, *Actors of International Cooperation*, pp. 88-90.
9. Dorothy Sue Cobble, "Who Speaks for Workers? Japan and the 1919 ILO Debates over Rights and Global Labor Standards," *International Labor and Working-Class History* vol. 87 (2015): pp. 213-234.
10. Morishima, "Kokumin gaikō no kichō," pp. 16-17.
11. Iriye, *Cultural Internationalism and World Order*, p. 57; Burkman, *Japan and the League of Nations*, p. 2; Morishima, "Kokumin gaikō no kichō," pp. 16-17.
12. Shibasaki Atsushi, *Kindai Nihon to kokusai bunka kōryū – Kokusai Bunka Shinkōkai no setsuritsu to tenkai* (Modern Japan and International Cultural Exchange: Establishment and Evolution of the 'Association for the Advancement of International Culture') (Tōkyō: Yūshindōkōbunsha, 1999), p. 36.
13. Iriye, *Cultural Internationalism and World Order*, pp. 57-58.
14. Saikawa, "Kokusai bunka kōryū no nashonarizumu," p. 14.
15. Saikawa, "Kokusai bunka kōryū no nashonarizumu," p. 14.
16. Iriye, *Cultural Internationalism and World Order*, pp. 3, 49.
17. Iriye, pp. 57-58.
18. Iriye, pp. 51-58.
19. Burkman, *Japan and the League of Nations*, p. ix.

20. On the League of Nations Association of Japan, see Terada, *Actors of International Cooperation in Prewar Japan*; Ikei Masaru, "Nihon Kokusai Renmei Kyōkai – sono seiritsu to henshitsu" (The League of Nations Association of Japan: Its Formation and Transformation), *Hōgaku kenkyū* vol. 68, no. 2 (February 1995), pp. 23-48; Ogata Sadako, "The Role of Liberal Nongovernmental Organizations in Japan," in *Pearl Harbor as History: Japanese-American Relations 1931-1941*, Dorothy Borg and Shunpei Okamoto, eds. (New York: Columbia University Press, 1973), pp. 459-486.
21. Shibasaki, *Kindai Nihon to kokusai bunka kōryū*, pp. 40-41.
22. Ikei, "Nihon Kokusai Renmei Kyōkai," p. 28.
23. "Japanese Form League Society: Baron Shibusawa Will Head New Organization in Tokyo," *Japan Times* (May 20, 1920), p. 8.
24. Mizuno Rentarō, "Jūdai naru keisatsukan no ninmu" (The Important Duties of a Police Bureaucrat), *Keisatsu Kyōkai zasshi* vol. 265, no. 44 (1921): p. 2.
25. League of Nations, "The International Institute of Intellectual Cooperation" (Paris 1927), in *Kokusai Renmei Gakugei Kyōryoku Kokusai Iinkai oyobi Kokusai Gakuin kankei ikken – Gakugei Kyōryoku Kokunai Iinkai kankei* (The International Committee on Intellectual Cooperation and the International Institute of Intellectual Cooperation: Regarding Japan's National Committee on Intellectual Cooperation), September 1927, DA MoFA, JACAR, Ref. B04122162900, p. 6.
26. "Committee on Intellectual Cooperation: Note by the Secretary-General," in *Kokusai Renmei Gakugei Kyōryoku Kokusai Iinkai oyobi Kokusai Gakuin kankei ikken – Gakugei Kyōryoku Kokunai Iinkai kankei dai 1kan* (The International Committee on Intellectual Cooperation and the International Institute of Intellectual Cooperation: Regarding Japan's National Committee on Intellectual Cooperation, vol. 1), June 19, 1922: JACAR, Ref. B04122191600, p. 0025.
27. Yamada Saburō, "Kokusai renmei to gakugei kyōryoku – Nihon gakugei kyōryoku iinkai no sōsetsu" (The League of Nations and Cultural Cooperation: The Establishment of Japan's National Committee on Intellectual Cooperation), *Kokusai chishiki* vol. 6, no. 6 (June 1926): pp. 2-3.
28. Nitobe Inazō, *Bushido: The Soul of Japan* (Philadelphia: Leeds and Biddle, 1900; Reprint Tōkyō: Kodansha International, 2002).
29. "Report by M. de Jouvenel submitted to the Second Committee on September 19th, 1922," in *Kankōbutsu no kokusaiteki kōkan ni kan suru 1886nen jōyaku kankei ikken (kokusai renmei kankei kankōbutsu kōkan jōyakuan o fukumu)* (Matters Regarding the 1886 Treaty for the International Exchange of Publications (Including a Treaty Proposal on the Exchange of Publications Regarding the League of Nations), 1922, DA MoFA, JACAR, Ref. B04122477900, p. 1.
30. Yamada, "Kokusai renmei to gakugei kyōryoku," p. 5.

31. In 1910, Otlet and La Fontaine established the Union of International Associations, which held the first international discussions on intellectual cooperation and is considered to have played a pivotal role in the founding of the League of Nations.
32. Daniel Laqua, Wouter Van Acker and Christophe Verbruggen, eds., *International Organizations and Global Civil Society. Histories of the Union of International Associations* (London: Bloomsbury Academic, 2019), p. 3.
33. Iriye, *Cultural Internationalism and World Order*, pp. 69-72.
34. "Zensekai no shoseki o atsume" (Collect Books from All Over the World), *Tōkyō asahi shinbun* (December 29, 1921, evening issue), p. 2.
35. Letter from the Council of the League of Nations to Japanese Minister of Foreign Affairs, in *Kankōbutsu no kokusaiteki kōkan ni kan suru 1886nen jōyaku kankei ikken (Kokusai Renmei kankei kankōbutsu kōkan jōyakuan o fukumu)* (Matters Regarding the 1886 Treaty for the International Exchange of Publications (Including a Treaty Proposal on the Exchange of Publications Regarding the League of Nations)), November 20, 1922, DA MoFA, JACAR, Ref. B04122477900, p. 0096.
36. Satō Junzō, "Kokusai Renmei to gakugei kyōryoku" (The League of Nations and Cultural Cooperation), *Gakugei Kōen Tsūshinsha panfuretto* 48 (Pamphlet of the Academic Lectures News Agency) (1927): pp. 1-15; "Report by M. de Jouvenel," JACAR, Ref. B04122477900, p. 4.
37. Satō, "Kokusai Renmei to gakugei kyōryoku," pp. 1-15; "Report by M. de Jouvenel," JACAR, Ref. B04122477900, p. 4.
38. Löhr, *Die Globalisierung geistiger Eigentumsrechte*, p. 102.
39. Löhr, p. 97, quoted from Marcel Plaisant, *La création artistique et littéraire et le droit* (Paris, 1920), p. 104.
40. Löhr, *Die Globalisierung geistiger Eigentumsrechte*, p. 102.
41. League of Nations, "The International Institute of Intellectual Cooperation," JACAR, Ref. B04122162900, p. 5.
42. Löhr, *Die Globalisierung geistiger Eigentumsrechte*, p. 102.
43. Löhr, p. 102.
44. League of Nations, "International Committee on Intellectual Cooperation: Eighth Plenary Session," in *Chiteki Rōdō Iinkai* (Scientific Labor-Relations Board), August 16, 1926, DA MoFA, JACAR, Ref. B06150868600, p. 20.
45. "International Committee on Intellectual Cooperation: Eighth Plenary Session," JACAR, Ref. B06150868600, p. 20; Frederick P. Keppel, "The International Chamber of Commerce," in *Documents of the American Association for International Conciliation* (New York: American Association for International Conciliation, 1922), pp. 187-210; Löhr, *Die Globalisierung geistiger Eigentumsrechte*, pp. 192-194.
46. Harold Greaves, *The League Committees and World Order: A Study of the Permanent Expert Committees of the League of Nations as an Instrument of International Government* (London:

Oxford University Press, 1931), p. 120; Löhr, *Die Globalisierung geistiger Eigentumsrechte*, p. 195.

47. Letter from Acting Secretary General of the League of Nations to Foreign Minister Matsui Keishirō, in *Kokusai Renmei Gakugei Kyōryoku Kokusai Iinkai oyobi Kokusai Gakuin kankei ikken – Gakugei Kyōryoku Kokunai Iinkai kankei* (The International Committee on Intellectual Cooperation and the International Institute of Intellectual Cooperation: Regarding Japan's National Committee on Intellectual Cooperation), November 19, 1924, DA MoFA, JACAR, Ref. B04122163000, 0023; Letter from Acting Secretary General of the League of Nations to Foreign Minister Matsui Keishirō, in *Kokusai Renmei Gakugei Kyōryoku Kokusai Iinkai oyobi Kokusai Gakuin kankei ikken – Gakugei Kyōryoku Kokunai Iinkai kankei* (idem), January 29, 1924, DA MoFA, JACAR, Ref. B04122163000, 0008.

48. Greaves, *The League Committees and World Order*, p. 122.

49. "Suggestions Relative to the Organisation of National Committees on International Cooperation," in *Kokusai Renmei Gakugei Kyōryoku Kokusai Iinkai oyobi Kokusai Gakuin kankei ikken – Gakugei Kyōryoku Kokunai Iinkai kankei* (The International Committee on Intellectual Cooperation and the International Institute of Intellectual Cooperation: Regarding Japan's National Committee on Intellectual Cooperation), December 5, 1923, DA MoFA, JACAR, Ref. B04122163100, pp. 0162-0163.

50. "The Teikoku Gakushiin" (The Imperial Academy), *Japan Times* (June 14, 1906), p. 3.

51. The Imperial Academy was founded in 1879 by Fukuzawa Yūkichi as the Tōkyō Academy (Tōkyō Gakushiin). In 1906 it changed its name to Imperial Academy.

52. Letter from the Director of the International Institute (Henri Bonnet) to Yamada Saburō, in *Kokusai Renmei Gakugei Kyōryoku Kokusai Iinkai oyobi Kokusai Gakuin kankei ikken – Gakugei Kyōryoku Kokunai Iinkai kankei dai-3ken* (The International Committee on Intellectual Cooperation and the International Institute of Intellectual Cooperation: Regarding Japan's National Committee on Intellectual Cooperation, vol. 3), December 17, 1926, DA MoFA, JACAR, Ref. B04122192800, p. 0106.

53. Gakugei Kyōryoku Iinkai, ed., *Gakugei no kokusai kyōryoku* (International Cooperation of the Arts and Sciences) (Tōkyō: Kokusai Renmei Kyōkai, 1927), in *Kokusai Renmei Gakugei Kyōryoku Kokusai Iinkai oyobi Kokusai Gakuin kankei ikken – Gakugei Kyōryoku Kokunai Iinkai kankei* (The International Committee on Intellectual Cooperation and the International Institute of Intellectual Cooperation: Regarding Japan's National Committee on Intellectual Cooperation), 1927, DA MoFA, JACAR, Ref. B04122163400, pp. 0079-0101, here pp.17-18 (report pages).

54. Yamada, "Kokusai Renmei to gakugei kyōryoku," p. 11.

55. Saikawa, "Kokusai bunka kōryū no nashonarizumu," p. 23; Shibasaki, *Kindai Nihon to kokusai bunka kōryū*, p. 43.

56. "International Institute of Intellectual Cooperation: Compilation of Lists of Works for Translation," in *Kokusai Renmei Gakugei Kyōryoku Kokusai Iinkai oyobi Kokusai Gakuin kankei ikken – Gakugei Kyōryoku Kokunai Iinkai kankei dai-3ken* (The International Committee on Intellectual Cooperation and the International Institute of Intellectual Cooperation: Regarding Japan's National Committee on Intellectual Cooperation, vol. 3), n.d., DA MoFA, JACAR, Ref. B04122192800, pp. 0133-0134.
57. Report from Japan's National Committee for Intellectual Cooperation to Kuriyama Shigeru, in *Kokusai Renmei Gakugei Kyōryoku Kokusai Iinkai oyobi Kokusai Gakuin kankei ikken – Gakugei Kyōryoku Kokunai Iinkai kankei* (The International Committee on Intellectual Cooperation and the International Institute of Intellectual Cooperation: Regarding Japan's National Committee on Intellectual Cooperation), July 10, 1926, DA MoFA, JACAR, Ref. B04122163200, pp. 0272-0273.
58. Report by Japan's National Committee for Intellectual Cooperation, in *Kokusai Renmei Gakugei Kyōryoku Kokusai Iinkai oyobi Kokusai Gakuin kankei ikken – Gakugei Kyōryoku Kokunai Iinkai kankei* (idem), July 21, 1926, DA MoFA, JACAR, Ref. B04122163200, pp. 0261-0262.
59. Report from Japan's National Committee for Intellectual Cooperation to Kuriyama Shigeru, JACAR, Ref. B04122163200, pp. 0272-0273.
60. Saikawa, "Kokusai bunka kōryū no nashonarizumu," p. 28.
61. International Institute of Intellectual Cooperation: Compilation of Lists of Works for Translation, JACAR, Ref. B04122192800, pp. 0133-0134.
62. International Federation of League of Nations Societies, "XVth Plenary Congress, Budapest 24-28 May, 1931 – Resolutions," in *Kokusai Renmei Kyōkai kankei dai-9kan* (Matters related to the League of Nations Association, vol. 9), May 1931, DA MoFA, JACAR, Ref. B05014052300, pp. 0206-0224, here pp. 9-10 (report pages); "Dépositaires des publications de lʾIICI – Maruzen Co. Ltd., Tōkyō" (Depositories for IICI Publications), in Dépositaires des publications de l'IICI – Envois d'office aux dépositaires (Shipments to Custodians), FR PUNES AG 1-IICI-H-X-11.40. IIIC 1925-1946, UNESCO Archives.
63. Löhr, *Die Globalisierung geistiger Eigentumsrechte*, p. 195.
64. Löhr, p. 197.
65. Löhr, p. 197.
66. Regarding Germany's ratification, see Letter from the Swiss Legation in Tōkyō to Foreign Minister Uchida Yasuya, in Kakkoku seifu kamei oyobi keihi buntan (Each Nation's Government Membership and Cost Sharing), February 1, 1920, DA MoFA, JACAR, Ref. B07080268900, p. 0067; Regarding Belgium's ratification, see Letter from the Swiss Legation in Tōkyō to Foreign Minister Uchida Yasuya, in *Kakkoku seifu kamei oyobi keihi buntan* (idem), November 16/December 23, 1920, DA MoFA, JACAR, Ref. B07080270500, p. 0325.
67. Löhr, *Die Globalisierung geistiger Eigentumsrechte*, p. 100.

CHAPTER 3. DEFENDING THE EXCEPTION   211

68. Letter from Fritz Ostertag to Hamaguchi Osachi, in *Bungakuteki oyobi bijutsuteki hogo bankoku dōmei kaigi kankei ikken – Rōma kaigi kankei (1928nen) dai-1kan* (Matters Concerning the International Conference of the Berne Convention: Regarding the Rome Conference (1928), vol. 1), June 14, 1926, DA MoFA, JACAR, Ref: B04122545000, p. 0038.
69. Letter from Fritz Ostertag to Hamaguchi Osachi, in *Bungakuteki oyobi bijutsuteki hogo bankoku dōmei kaigi kankei ikken – Rōma kaigi kankei (1928nen) dai-1kan* (Matters Concerning the International Conference of the Berne Convention: Regarding the Rome Conference (1928), vol. 1), February 17, 1927, DA MoFA, JACAR, Ref: B04122545000, p. 0011.
70. "Chosakuken kaigi hikōshiki dai-1ji uchiawasekai" (First Unofficial Meeting on the Copyright Conference), in *Bungakuteki oyobi bijutsuteki hogo bankoku dōmei kaigi kankei ikken – Rōma kaigi kankei (1928nen) dai-1kan* (Matters Concerning the International Conference of the Berne Convention: Regarding the Rome Conference (1928), vol. 1), July 15, 1927, DA MoFA, JACAR, Ref: B04122545000, pp. 0017-0018.
71. Futsū Senkyo Hō was an unofficial term used for the new Electoral Law Shūgiin Gi'in Senkyo Hō (Law No. 37/1889) as amended by Law No. 47/1924 and passed by the National Diet in 1925. Full text of the original law in *Hōrei zensho* (Collection of Laws and Regulations) (Tōkyō: Naikaku Kanpōkyoku, 1889), pp. 21-49.
72. Shinbunsho Hō, Law No. 41/1909. Full text in *Hōrei zensho* (Collection of Laws and Regulations) (Tōkyō: Naikaku Kanpōkyoku, 1909), pp. 130-137.
73. Kobayashi Hiroji, *Genkō chosakuken hō no rippō riyū to kaishaku – Chosakuken hō senbun kaisei no shiryō toshite* (Legal Reasoning and Interpretation of the Current Copyright Law: As Material for the Full Revision of the Copyright Act) (1958; repr., Tōkyō: Daiichi Shobō, 2012), p. 2.
74. Letter from the Information Section of the Paris Institute to the Deutsche Verlagsanstalt, January 20, 1927, in file Diffusion internationale du livre – Correspondance communiquée par l'Institut international de coopération intellectuelle (International Distribution of Books – Correspondence Communicated by the IIIC), in series Registry files (1919-1927) Intellectual Cooperation, in League of Nations Secretariat Fonds, 1927, R1084/13C//56211/57650, League of Nations Archives.
75. Letter from the Information Section of the Paris Institute to US publisher R.R. Bowker & Co, April 29, 1927, in file Diffusion internationale du livre – Correspondance communiquée par l'Institut international de coopération intellectuelle, in series Registry files (1919-1927) Intellectual Cooperation, in League of Nations Secretariat Fonds, 1927, R1084/13C/57650x/56211, League of Nations Archives.
76. Letter from Kawai Hiroyuki to Tanaka Giichi, in *Bungakuteki oyobi bijutsuteki hogo bankoku dōmei kaigi kankei ikken – Rōma kaigi kankei (1928nen) dai-1kan* (Matters Concerning the International Conference of the Berne Convention: Regarding the Rome

Conference (1928), vol. 1),June 17, 1927, DA MoFA,JACAR, Ref. B04122545000, pp. 0007-0009.
77. "Chosakuken kaigi hikōshiki dai-1ji uchiawasekai" (First Unofficial Meeting on the Copyright Conference),JACAR, Ref. B04122545000, pp. 0017-0021.
78. "Chosakuken kaigi hikōshiki dai-1ji uchiawasekai," pp. 0017-0021.
79. Letter from Georges Maillard to the Japanese Ambassador to France Ishii Kikujirō, in *Bungakuteki oyobi bijutsuteki hogo bankoku dōmei kaigi kankei ikken – Rōma kaigi kankei (1928nen) dai-1kan* (Matters Concerning the International Conference of the Berne Convention: Regarding the Rome Conference (1928), vol. 1), August 11, 1927, DA MoFA,JACAR, Ref: B04122545100, pp. 0108-0109.
80. Naiseishi Kenkyūkai, ed. *Tsuchiya Shōzō shi danwa sokkiroku. Naiseishi kenkyū shiryō* (Tōkyō: Naiseishi Kenkyūkai, 1967), pp. 59-60.
81. Naiseishi Kenkyūkai, *Tsuchiya Shōzō shi danwa sokkiroku.*
82. "Chōsakuken kaigi junbi chōsa – kinō kakushō uchiawasekai" (Preparatory Survey for the Copyright Conference: Yesterday's Meeting with all Ministries), *Tōkyō asahi shinbun* (August 20, 1927, evening issue), p. 2.
83. The bureaucrat Yoshida Shigeru referred to here is not to be confused with the diplomat Yoshida Shigeru (1878-1967) who was a member of the Japanese legation at the Paris Peace Conference and served five times as Japan's prime minister in the immediate postwar period.
84. "Chōsakuken kaigi junbi chōsa – kinō kakushō uchiawasekai," *Tōkyō asahi shinbun* (August 20, 1927, evening issue), p. 2.
85. Greaves, *The League Committees and World Order*, pp. 130-131.
86. Kobayashi, *Genkō chosakuken hō no rippō riyū to kaishaku*, pp. 1-6; Naiseishi Kenkyūkai, *Tsuchiya Shōzō shi danwa sokkiroku*, pp. 55-60.
87. Ōkubo, *Senzen Tōkyō-Ōsaka shuppangyō-shi*, p. 190.
88. The provision for Publishing Rights was first proclaimed on May 1, 1934, and was slightly amentded in the 1970 Copyright Law. Shuppanken, provision of the Chosakuken Hō, Law No. 48/1970, Art. 3 paras 79-88; "Go-shomei genpon, Shōwa 9nen, hōritsu dai-48gō, chosakuken hō-chū kaisei" (Signature Original, 1934, Law No. 48, Copyright Law Amendment), in idem, May 1, 1934, NAJ,JACAR, Ref. A03021927100.
89. Löhr, *Die Globalisierung geistiger Eigentumsrechte*, pp. 99 and 103; Ōkubo, *Senzen Tōkyō-Ōsaka shuppangyō shi*, p. 117; Fujita Tomoharu, "Shuppanken hō seitei no hitsuyō to kono seitei undō no keika" (On the Necessity of Enacting the Publication Law and the Progress of its Enactment Movement), *Hōritsu jihō* vol. 5, no. 9 (1933): p. 23.
90. Fujita, "Shuppanken hō seitei no hitsuyō to kono seitei undō no keika," p. 23.
91. "Eikoku chosakusha no shōnin nakushite Beikoku ni oite fukusei seru shoseki o Nihon e yūnyū shi eru ya ina ya kan shi gigimon toiawase no ken – ji Taishō 8nen 2gatsu" (Regarding the Question Whether it is Possible to Import a Book that Was

Reproduced in the United States into Japan Without the Consent of the British Author – from February 1919), in *Shuppan oyobi hanken kankei zakken – shuppan no bu dai-3ken* (Various Matters Regarding Publishing and Copyright: Publishing Section, vol. 3), January 1919, DA MoFA, JACAR, Ref. B13080844500.

92. Janet Hunter, "'Extreme Confusion and Disorder'? The Japanese Economy in the Great Kantō Earthquake of 1923," *The Journal of Asian Studies* vol. 73, no. 3 (August 2014), p. 756, quoted from Bureau of Social Affairs, Home Office, Japan, *Outline of the Reconstruction Work in Tokyo and Yokohama* (Tōkyō: Bureau of Reconstruction, 1929); for a detailed analysis of the Great Kantō Earthquake and its impact on the Japanese publishing industry, see: Mack, *Manufacturing Modern Japanese Literature*, pp. 51-89.
93. Letter from Maruzen Company to Stanley Unwin, September 1923, Collection of George Allen & Unwin Ltd.: Correspondence files AUC 1-10, University of Reading, The Archive of British Publishing and Printing Reading Sources.
94. "Chosakuken hō-chū kaisei no seigan" (Petition for a Copyright Law Revision), in *Giin kaifu seigan shorui gengi* vol. 12 (Original Opinions on Petitions Handed to the Parliament), 25 March, 1926, Kokuritsu Kobunshokan, JACAR, Ref: A14081020200, p. 0781.
95. Ōkubo, *Senzen Tōkyō-Ōsaka shuppangyō shi*, p. 181.
96. As this was an informal meeting, no official records exist besides the reference to the meeting by the Tōkyō Shuppan Kyōkai. Ōkubo, *Senzen Tōkyō-Ōsaka shuppangyō shi*, p. 183.
97. For the sessions' proceedings, see Kokkai Kaigiroku, *Shūgiin Shuppanbutsu Hōan Iinkai* (House of Representatives' Committee for Drafting a Publication Bill), sessions 8-10, March 14-18, 1927, NDL.
98. Ōkubo, *Senzen Tōkyō-Ōsaka shuppangyō shi*, pp. 182-184.
99. Ōkubo, 184; Fujita, "Shuppanken hō seitei no hitsuyō to kono seitei undō no keika," p. 24; "Keisatsu seido kaizen no tame 'Keiho Shingikai' setchi ni kettei su" (On the Decision to Establish a 'Police Advisory Council' to Improve the Police System), *Tōkyō asahi shinbun* (June 10, 1927, morning issue), p. 2.
100. Ōkubo, *Senzen Tōkyō-Ōsaka shuppangyō shi*, p. 44.
101. Ōkubo, p. 44.
102. Fujita, "Shuppanken hō seitei no hitsuyō to kono seitei undō no keika," p. 24; Naiseishi Kenkyūkai, *Tsuchiya Shōzō shi danwa sokkiroku*, p. 58.
103. "Chosakuken to shuppanken: Kaiseihō wa fu-teishutsu" (Copyright and Publishing Rights: Revised Law Not Submitted), *Yomiuri shinbun* (December 12, 1927, morning issue), p. 4.
104. "Chosakuken to shuppanken: Kaiseihō wa fu-teishutsu," *Yomiuri shinbun* (December 12, 1927, morning issue), p. 4.

105. "Keiho Iinkai Tokubetsu Iinkai hōkoku yōshi" (Summary Report of the Police Advisory Council's Special Committee Meeting), in *Private Papers of Yamaoka Mannosuke*, December 5, 1927, A-IV-4-29, Kensei shiryōshitsu, NDL; "Keiho Iinkai tokubetsu iinkai gijiroku," pp. 1-7 (Record of Proceedings of the Police Advisory Council's Special Committee Meeting), in *Private Papers of Yamaoka Mannosuke*, December 14, 1927 – March 17, 1928, A-IV-4-38, Kensei shiryōshitsu, NDL.
106. Fujita, "Shuppanken hō seitei no hitsuyō to kono seitei undō no keika," p. 24.
107. Naiseishi Kenkyūkai, *Tsuchiya Shōzō shi danwa sokkiroku*, p. 58.
108. Naiseishi Kenkyūkai, pp. 58-59.
109. Kobayashi, *Genkō chosakuken hō no rippō riyū to kaishaku*, p. 5; Naiseishi Kenkyūkai, *Tsuchiya Shōzō shi danwa sokkiroku*, p. 60.
110. Tōkyō Shosekishō Kumiai, *Tōkyō Shosekishō Kumiai 50nen shi*, p. 202; Ōkubo, *Senzen Tōkyō-Ōsaka shuppangyō shi*, p. 190.
111. Nihon Zasshi Kyōkai, *Nihon Zasshi Kyōkai shi*, p. 146.
112. Hashimura Sen'ichi, "Chosakuken kaigi (jō)" (Copyright Conference (part 1)), *Tōkyō asahi shinbun* (September 2, 1927, morning issue), p. 5.
113. Tōkyō Shosekishō Kumiai, *Tōkyō Shosekishō Kumiai 50nen shi*, p. 205.
114. Tōkyō Shosekishō Kumiai, pp. 205-206.
115. Tōkyō Shosekishō Kumiai, p. 207.
116. Naimushō Keiho-kyoku, "Bungakuteki oyobi bijutsuteki hogo bankoku dōmei rōma kaigi no teian oyobi riyū narabi ni teikoku seifu kunrei, teian ni tai suru teikoku iken yōshi, kankei sho-kanchō minkan sho-dantai tōshin iken" (Proposal and Explanations for the Rome Conference of the Berne Convention with Instructions from the Imperial Government, an Overview of the Imperial Viewpoint and the Opinions of Government Authorities and Private Sector Organizations involved), in *Bungakuteki oyobi bijutsuteki chosakubutsu hogo dōmei kaigi kankei ikken – 'Burasseru' kaigi (1935nen)* (Matters Concerning the Conference of the Berne Convention: "Brussels" conference (1935), n.d., DA MoFA, JACAR, Ref: B04122522200, p. 149.
117. The House Diaries or "The Intimate Papers of Colonel House" refer to the papers of Edward Mandell House, an American diplomat and advisor to President Woodrow Wilson, whose papers were published by Yale University Professor Charles Seymour and shed a light on the American participation in World War I and the Paris Peace Conference; see: *The Intimate Papers of Colonel House*, arranged as a narrative by Charles Seymour, Sterling Professor of History, Yale University, vols. 1 and 2 (Boston: Houghton Mifflin Company, 1926).
118. Naimushō Keiho-kyoku, "Bungakuteki oyobi bijutsuteki hogo bankoku dōmei," JACAR, Ref: B04122522200, p. 150.
119. Naimushō Keiho-kyoku, pp. 149-155.
120. Naimushō Keiho-kyoku, pp. 149-155.

121. Letter from J.C.B. Mohr (Paul Siebeck) to Professor Makoto Hori Keiō University, January 11, 1927, Collection 488, A 0429, 2, pp. 135-136, Mohr Siebeck Publishing Archive, Berlin; Letter from Imperial University Tōkyō Student Itahashi Isutomu to J.C.B Mohr (and reply), May 16, 1930, and reply from June 25, 1930, Collection 488, A 0451, 1, pp. 64-67; Letter from Honorary Professor at Chuō University G. Konno to J.C.b. Mohr/Paul Siebeck (and reply), July 6, 1937 and reply from August 6, 1937, Collection 488, A 0489, pp. 1, 188-189.
122. Naimushō Keiho-kyoku, "Bungakuteki oyobi bijutsuteki hogo bankoku dōmei," JACAR, Ref: B04122522200, p. 152.
123. *Actes de la conférence de Rome 7 mai – 2 juin 1928* (Berne: Bureau de l'Union Internationale Littéraire et Artistique, 1929), p. 135.
124. Ōkubo, *Senzen Tōkyō-Ōsaka shuppangyō-shi*, p. 199.
125. Naimushō Keiho-kyoku, "Bungakuteki oyobi bijutsuteki hogo bankoku dōmei," JACAR, Ref: B04122522200, pp. 135-168.
126. Naimushō Keiho-kyoku, "Bungakuteki oyobi bijutsuteki hogo bankoku dōmei," JACAR, Ref: B04122522200, pp. 125-134.
127. Tōkyō Shosekishō Kumiai, *Tōkyō Shosekishō Kumiai 50nen shi*, pp. 206-209.
128. Naimushō Keiho-kyoku, "Bungakuteki oyobi bijutsuteki hogo bankoku dōmei," JACAR, Ref: B04122522200, pp. 64, 128.
129. Naimushō Keiho-kyoku, p. 116.
130. Naimushō Keiho-kyoku, p. 116.
131. Terada, *Actors of International Cooperation in Prewar Japan*, pp. 37-83.
132. Terada, p. 264.
133. Terada, p. 264.
134. Tōkyō Shosekishō Kumiai, *Tōkyō shosekishō kumiai 50nen shi*, p. 213.
135. Bannerman, *International Copyright and Access to Knowledge*, p. 171; Löhr, *Die Globalisierung geistiger Eigentumsrechte*, p. 207.
136. Löhr, *Die Globalisierung geistiger Eigentumsrechte*, p. 207.
137. Mitchell, *Censorship in Imperial Japan*, pp. 200-201; Naiseishi Kenkyūkai, *Tsuchiya Shōzō shi danwa sokkiroku*, p. 61.
138. Kobayashi, *Genkō chosakuken hō no rippō riyū to kaishaku*, p. 5.
139. Kobayashi, p. 5.
140. Sam Ricketson, *The Berne Convention for the Protection of Literary and Artistic Works: 1886-1986* (Deventer: Kluwer law and taxation, 1987), p. 103; Löhr, *Die Globalisierung geistiger Eigentumsrechte*, pp. 121, 157.
141. *Actes de la conférence de Rome*, p. 163.
142. *Actes de la conférence de Rome*, p. 163.
143. *Actes de la conférence de Rome*, p. 163.
144. *Actes de la conférence de Rome*, p. 214.
145. *Actes de la conférence réunie à Berlin*, p. 248.

146. *Actes de la conférence réunie à Berlin*, p. 248.
147. *Actes de la conférence réunie à Berlin*, p. 248.
148. *Actes de la conférence réunie à Berlin*, p. 214.
149. Löhr, *Die Globalisierung geistiger Eigentumsrechte*, pp. 126, 158.
150. Löhr, pp. 126, 158.
151. Mitchell, *Censorship in Imperial Japan*; Jonathan E. Abel, *Redacted: The Archives of Censorship in Transwar Japan* (Berkeley: University of California Press, 2012).

CHAPTER 4. EXPANDING GLOBAL VISIBILITY

1. Greaves, *The League Committees and World Order*, p. 132.
2. Okano Takeo, *Nihon shuppan bunka-shi* (A Cultural History of Japanese Publishing) (Tōkyō: Shunpodō, 1962); Furuya Natsuko, "Postwar Publishing Trends in Japan," *The Library Quarterly: Information, Community, Policy* vol. 32, no. 3 (July 1962): pp. 208-222 and 209.
3. Kurozawa Fumitaka, "Das System von 1940 und das Problem der politischen Führung in Japan," *Zeitschrift für Geschichtswissenschaft* vol. 47, no 2. (1999), pp. 130-152; Furuya, "Postwar Publishing Trends in Japan," p. 209.
4. Greaves, *The League Committees and World Order*, p. 132.
5. Schwartz, *Advice and Consent*, p. 43.
6. Letter from French Ambassador to Japan to Foreign Minister Tanaka Giichi, in *Kokusai Bungaku Geijutsuka taikai kankei ikken* (Matters Concerning the General Conference of the Association Littéraire et Artistique Internationale), March 14, 1929, DA MoFA, JACAR, Ref. B04122478300, pp. 0006-0007.
7. The League of Nations Tōkyō Office was established in September 1925.
8. Letter from Raymond Weiss of the IIIC Legal Section to the Secretariat of the League of Nations, Section des Bureaux Internationaux et de la Cooperation Intellectuelle, October 10, 1930, in the file Correspondance concernant l'Association littéraire et artistique international (Correspondance Regarding the Association Littéraire et Artistique Internationale), in series Registry files (1928-1932) Intellectual Cooperation, in League of Nations Secretariat Fonds, 1919-1946, R-2215-5B-788-23134, League of Nations Archives.
9. Letter from Itō Nobufumi to the head of the Ministry of Foreign Affairs Treaty Department Matsunaga Naokichi, in *Kokusai Bungaku Geijutsuka taikai kankei ikken* (Matters Concerning the General Conference of the Association Littéraire et Artistique Internationale), October 13, 1930, DA MoFA, JACAR, Ref. B04122478300, pp. 0030-0031.
10. "'Kokusai Bungei Geijutsu' bankoku taikai – konshū ku gatsu Nihon de kaisai," (International Conference of the '[Association] Littéraire et Artistique Internationale' – Hosted by Japan in September This Autumn), *Yomiuri shinbun* (February 24, 1931,

morning issue), p. 11; Tōkyō Shuppan Kyōkai, *Tōkyō Shuppan Kyōkai 25nen shi*, p. 79; "(Statement Release) Tōkyō to have World Literary Conference: Decision Reached to Respond to Request Sent From French Capital," in *Kokusai Bungaku Geijutsuka taikai kankei ikken* (Matters Concerning the General Conference of the Association Littéraire et Artistique Internationale), February 1931, DA MoFA, JACAR, Ref. B04122478300, p. 0095; "Kokusai bungaku geijutsu kyōkai no honbu ni okeru taikai kaisai o enjo suru koto ni kan suru no ken" (Matters Concerning the Support of Hosting the Convention at the ALAI Headquarters), in *Kokusai Bungaku Geijutsuka taikai kankei ikken*, February 23, 1931, DA MoFA, JACAR, Ref. B04122478300, pp. 0045-0052.

11. Kobayashi, *Genkō chosakuken hō no rippō riyū to kaishaku*, p. 6.
12. Tōkyō Shuppan Kyōkai, *Tōkyō Shuppan Kyōkai 25nen shi*, p. 74.
13. Various Correspondence Concerning the General Conference of the Association Littéraire et Artistique Internationale, in *Kokusai Bungaku Geijutsuka taikai kankei ikken* (Matters Concerning the General Conference of the Association Littéraire et Artistique Internationale), 1931, DA MoFA, JACAR, Ref. B04122478300, pp. 0060, 0090, 0114, 0117; "Kokusai bungei kyōkai sōkai: Nihon de kaisai o judaku ni kettei" (Japan Agrees to Hold the General Conference of the International Literary and Artistic Association), *Tōkyō asahi shinbun* (September 19, 1931, morning issue), p. 3; Tōkyō Shuppan Kyōkai, *Tōkyō Shuppan Kyōkai 25nen shi*, p. 80.
14. Various Correspondence Concerning the General Conference of the Association Littéraire et Artistique Internationale, JACAR, Ref. B04122478300, pp. 0060, 0117, 0127.
15. Increasingly also transcribed with the Pinyin transcription Manzhouguo.
16. Gordon M. Berger, "Politics and Mobilization in Japan, 1931-45," in *The Twentieth Century*, vol. 6 of *The Cambridge History of Japan*, Peter Duus, ed., pp. 99-153 (Cambridge: Cambridge University Press, 1988); Louise Young, *Japan's Total Empire: Manchuria and the Culture of Wartime Imperialism* (London: University of California Press, 1998); Kari Shepherdson-Scott, "Conflicting Politics and Contesting Borders: Exhibiting (Japanese) Manchuria at the Chicago World's Fair, 1933–34," *The Journal of Asian Studies* vol. 74, no. 3 (August 2015): p. 543.
17. Ikei, "Nihon kokusai renmei kyōkai," pp. 43-44; Shibasaki, *Kindai Nihon to kokusai bunka kōryū*, p. 42; Burkman, *Japan and the League of Nations*, pp. 139-141; Ogata Sadako, "The Role of Liberal Nongovernmental Organizations in Japan," in *Pearl Harbor as History: Japanese-American Relations 1931-1941*, Dorothy Borg and Shunpei Okamoto, eds. (New York: Columbia University Press, 1973), pp. 459-486.
18. Ikei, "Nihon kokusai renmei kyōkai," pp. 39-44.
19. Saikawa Takashi, "From Intellectual Co-operation to International Cultural Exchange: Japan and China in the International Committee on Intellectual Cooperation of the League of Nations, 1922-1939" (Ph.D. diss., Universität Heidelberg, 2014), p. 128.

20. Saikawa, "From Intellectual Co-operation to International Cultural Exchange," pp. 125-126.
21. Shibasaki, *Kindai Nihon to kokusai bunka kōryū*, p. 32; Kokusai Bunka Shinkōkai, *KBS 30nen no ayumi* (The Steps of 30 Years of KBS) (Tōkyō: Kokusai Bunka Shinkōkai, 1964), pp. 12-15.
22. Saikawa, "From Intellectual Co-operation to International Cultural Exchange," p. 95.
23. "Kokusai Bungei Kyōkai sōkai: Nihon de kaisai o judaku ni kettei" (Japan Agrees to Hold the General Conference of the International Literary and Artistic Association), *Tōkyō asahi shinbun* (September 19, 1931, morning issue), p. 3.
24. *International Convention for the Protection of Literary and Artistic Works* – Rome, June 2, 1928, Treaty Series no. 12 (London: H.M. Stationary Office, 1932), p. 35.
25. Katō Atsushi, "Nihon – Berunu jōyaku to chosakuken hō no keisei," in *Gurōbaruka no naka no kindai Nihon – kijuku to tenkai*, Hidemasa Kokaze and Yoshiya Suetake, eds. (Tōkyō: Yūshisha, 2015), pp. 220-221.
26. Ganea, "Copyright History," p. 7.
27. Ganea, p. 8.
28. Ōie Shigeo, *Nippon chosakuken monogatari – Purāge hakase no tekihatsu roku* (Japan Copyright Story: A Record of the Revelations by Dr. Plage) (1981; repr., Sagamihara: Seizansha, 1999), pp. 16-17, 28-32 and 99; Peter Ganea and Sadao Nagaoka, "Japan," in *Intellectual Property in Asia: Law, Economics, History and Politics*, Paul Goldstein and Joseph Straus, eds. (Munich: Springer, 2009), p. 135.
29. For the minutes of the relevant parliamentary sessions, see Kokkai Kaigiroku, Shūgiin Shōnen Kyōgo Hōan Iinkai (House of Representatives' Committee for Drafting a Juvenile Education Bill), sessions 3-15, February 17 – March 11, 1933, NDL; as well as Kokkai Kaigiroku, Shūgiin Shōnen Kyōgo Hōan Iin Shuppanken Hōan Shō Iinkai (House of Representatives' Subcommittee on Publishing Rights of the Committee for Drafting a Juvenile Education Bill), sessions 1-3, March 6-10, 1933, NDL.
30. Ōie, *Nippon chosakuken monogatari*, p. 82.
31. Horiguchi Daigaku, "Hon'yakuken no mondai (1) – futō na kenrikin yōkyū" (The Translation Right Problem – Unfair Premium Demands), *Tōkyō asahi shinbun* (August 15, 1933), p. 5; Horiguchi Daigaku, "Hon'yakuken no mondai (2) – gaikoku tōjisha wa kodai mōsō" (The Translation Right Problem – The Foreigners Concerned are Megalomaniac), *Tōkyō asahi shinbun* (August 16, 1933), p. 9; Horiguchi Daigaku, "Hon'yakuken no mondai (3) – jōyaku kara dattai seyo" (The Translation Right Problem – Let's Withdraw From the Treaty), *Tōkyō asahi shinbun* (August 17, 1933), p. 9.
32. Satō Junzō, "Berunu jōyaku kaisei ni sonau (jō) Hon'yakuken mondai ni tsuite" (Preparing the Revision of the Berne Convention (Part 1) On the Translation Rights

Issue), *Tōkyō asahi shinbun* (October 17, 1933), p. 9; Satō Junzō, "Berunu jōyaku kaisei ni sonau (ge) Hon'yakuken mondai ni tsuite" (Preparing the Revision of the Berne Convention (Part 2) On the Translation Rights Issue), *Tōkyō asahi shinbun* (October 18, 1933), p. 9.

33. Letter from the Belgian Ambassador to Uchida Kōsai, in *Bungakuteki bijutsuteki chosakubutsu hogo dōmei kaigi kankei ikken – 'Burasseru' kaigi (1935) dai-1kan* (Regarding the Conference for Copyright Protection of Literary and Artistic Works: 'Brussels' Conference (1935), Vol. 1), August 31, 1933, DA MoFA, JACAR, Ref. B04122521500, p. 0015.
34. "Report on the Status of International Copyright Protection Submitted to the Committee for the Study of Copyright of the American National Committee on International Intellectual Cooperation," in *Bungakuteki bijutsuteki chosakubutsu hogo dōmei kaigi kankei ikken – 'Burasseru' kaigi (1935) – Chosakuken Tōitsu Senmon Iinkai kankei* (Regarding the Conference for Copyright Protection of Literary and Artistic Works: 'Brussels' Conference (1935) – Regarding the Committee of Experts for the Unification of Copyright), 1938, DA MoFA, JACAR, Ref. B04122522600, pp. 1-27, here pp. 2-3.
35. "Report on the Status of International Copyright Protection submitted to the Committee for the Study of Copyright of the American National Committee on International Intellectual Cooperation," JACAR, Ref. B04122522600, pp. 1-27.
36. Letter from the Belgian Ambassador to Uchida Kōsai, in *Bungakuteki bijutsuteki chosakubutsu hogo dōmei kaigi kankei ikken – 'Burasseru' kaigi (1935) dai-1kan* (Regarding the Conference for Copyright Protection of Literary and Artistic Works: 'Brussels' Conference (1935), Vol. 1), August 31, 1933, DA MoFA, JACAR, Ref. B04122521500, p. 0015.
37. Satō Junzō, "Berunu jōyaku kaisei ni sonau – Hon'yakuken mondai ni tsuite (1)" (Preparing for the Revision of the Berne Convention – On the Problem of Translation Rights), *Tōkyō asahi shinbun* (October 17, 1933), 9; Satō Junzō, "Berunu jōyaku kaisei ni sonau – Hon'yakuken mondai ni tsuite (2)," *Tōkyō asahi shinbun* (October 18, 1933), p. 9.
38. Letter from the Belgian Ambassador to Hirota Kōki, in *Bungakuteki bijutsuteki chosakubutsu hogo dōmei kaigi kankei ikken – 'Burasseru' kaigi (1935) dai-1kan* (Regarding the Conference for Copyright Protection of Literary and Artistic Works: 'Brussels' Conference (1935), Vol. 1), October 20, 1933, DA MoFA, JACAR, Ref. B04122521500, p. 0018.
39. "Chosha no jinkakuken hogo e: chosakuken hō kaisei seian" (Protecting Authors' Personal Rights: Revision Proposal for the Copyright Law), *Yomiuri shinbun* (February 2, 1934 morning issue), 2; "Chokurei: Chosakuken Shinsakai kansei" (Imperial Edict: Government-regulated Copyright Investigation Council), in *Kōbun ruiju dai-59hen – Shōwa 10nen/dai-4kan/kanshoku 2/kansei 2* (Official Document 59th Edition –

1935/Vol. 4 Government Service 2/Government-regulated Organization 2), July 18, 1935: JACAR, Ref. A14100445700.
40. Letter from the Berne Bureau to the member states of the Berne Convention, in *Bungakuteki bijutsuteki chosakubutsu hogo dōmei kaigi kankei ikken – 'Burasseru' kaigi (1935) dai-1kan* (Regarding the Conference for Copyright Protection of Literary and Artistic Works: 'Brussels' Conference (1935), Vol. 1), July 20, 1934, DA MoFA, JACAR, Ref. B04122521500, p. 0048.
41. Letter from the Belgian Ambassador to Hirota Kōki, in idem, September 20, 1934, DA MoFA, JACAR, Ref. B04122521500, p. 0046.
42. "Chokurei: Chosakuken Shinsakai kansei" (Imperial Edict: Government-regulated Copyright Investigation Council), in *Kōbun ruiju dai-59hen – Shōwa 10nen/dai-4kan/kanshoku 2/kansei 2* (Offical Document 59th Edition -- 1935/Vol. 4 Government Service 2/Government-regulated Organization 2), July 18, 1935: JACAR, Ref. A14100445700, p. 8.
43. "Bunka Nihon shidō no saikō kikan naru" (It Will Become the Highest Organ for Japan's Cultural Instructions), *Tōkyō asahi shinbun* (July 16, 1935, evening issue), p. 2.
44. For more detailed information on National Diet members with a background in the media industries, see: Satō and Kawasaki, *Kindai Nihon no media giin: 'seiji no mediaka' no rekishi shakaigaku*.
45. Critical articles, which are introduced in the following paragraphs, were to be found, for example, in the *Tōkyō asahi shinbun*, the *Tōkyō nichi nichi shinbun*, the *Chūgai shinbun*, the *Yomiuri shinbun*, and in the *Japan Times*.
46. Simone Müller, "The 'Debate on the Literature of Action' and Its Legacy: Ideological Struggles in 1930s Japan and the 'Rebirth' of the Intellectual," *The Journal of Japanese Studies* vol. 41, no. 1 (Winter 2015): pp. 9-44.
47. Unnō Fukuju, "1930 nendai no bungei tōsei – Matsumoto Gaku to bungei konwakai," (Literary Control in the 1930s: Matsumoto Gaku and the Literary Social Gathering), *Sundai shigakkai* vol. 52 (March 1981): pp. 1-38; Hartmann, "Matsumoto Gaku," pp. 1-10.
48. Tsurumi Shunsuke, *An Intellectual History of Wartime Japan: 1931-1945* (London: Routledge, 2010).
49. Itō Nobuo, "Mizuno Rentarō to Chosakuken Shinsakai" (Mizuno Rentarō and the Chosakuken Shinsakai), *Kopiraito* vol. 13, no. 2/146 (May 1973): p. 9.
50. "Bunka no saikō shidō ni Nihon bunkain sōsetsu" (Establishment of Japanese Cultural Body for the Best Guidance of Culture), *Tōkyō asahi shinbun* (March 18, 1935, evening issue), p. 2.
51. "Chosakuken Shinsakai sōsetsu" (Establishment of the Chosakuken Shinsakai), *Tōkyō asahi shinbun* (July 6, 1935, evening issue), p. 1.

52. "Shinsakai gō-sutoppu" (Committee Stoplight), *Yomiuri shinbun* (July 23, 1935, morning issue), p. 5.
53. "Home Ministry Aims to Foster National Spirit," *Japan Times* (July 14, 1935), p. 2.
54. "Japanese Press Opinion: N'nichi [*Tōkyō nichi nichi*] – Copyright Committee," *Japan Times* (July 16, 1935), p. 2.
55. Translation quoted from the *Japan Times* and not after the original article: "Japanese Press Opinion: Chugai – Copyright Committee," *Japan Times* (July 18, 1935), p. 2.
56. Itō, "Mizuno Rentarō to Chosakuken Shinsakai," p. 9.
57. "Dai-ikkai Chosakuken Shinsakai gijiroku" (Protocol of the First Session of the Chosakuken Shinsakai), in *Bungakuteki oyobi bijutsuteki chosakubutsu hogo dōmei kaigi kankei ikken – jōyaku hijun jisshi kankei dai-2kan* (Regarding the Conference for Copyright Protection of Literary and Artistic Works: Regarding the Enactment of Ratifying the Treaty, Vol. 2), July 26, 1935, DA MoFA, JACAR, Ref. B04122548300, pp. 0-6, here pp. 1-3.
58. Kusano Teishi, "Hon'yakuken no ryūho (3) – saiginmi ni motozuku gōriteki un'yō" (Reservations on the Right to Translate: Their Rational Application Based on Re-evaluation), *Tōkyō asahi shinbun* (December 8, 1935, morning issue), p. 13.
59. Kusano, "Hon'yakuken no ryūho (3)," p. 13.
60. Kusano, p. 13.
61. *Conférence de Bruxelles – tableau des voeux émis par divers congrès et assembles* (Berne: Bureau de l'Union Internationale Littéraire et Artistique, 1935); *Conférence de Bruxelles – propositions, contre-propositions et observations présentées par les administrations des pays de l'Union* (Berne: Bureau de l'Union Internationale Littéraire et Artistique, 1936).
62. "Bungakuteki oyobi bijutsuteki chosakubutsu hogo ni kan suru kokusai jōyaku kaisei ni kan suru ken," in *Bungakuteki oyobi bijutsuteki chosakubutsu hogo dōmei kaigi kankei ikken – 'Burasseru' kaigi (1935) dai-1kan*, March 20-26, 1935, DA MoFA, JACAR, Ref. B04122521500, pp. 0070-0073.
63. "Chosakuken Shinsakai futaake: mumei jidai no tsuikyūken tōtō de bankoku kaigi ni sonafu" (The Opening of the Chosakuken Shinsakai: Preparing for a Universal Conference with the Droit de Suite etc. in the Era of Unrecognized Artists), *Yomiuri shinbun* (May 12, 1936, morning issue), p. 7.
64. Tōkyō Shuppan Kyōkai, *Tōkyō Shuppan Kyōkai 25nen shi*, pp. 43, 137.
65. Nihon Zasshi Kyōkai, *Nihon Zasshi Kyōkai shi* vol. 1, p. 146.
66. "100nen kanpani no chie: Yūhikaku (Tōkyō-bu) – hōritsusho o chūshin ni" (100 Years of Company Wisdom: Yūhikaku (Tōkyō Branch) – Focusing on Law Publications), *Mainichi shinbun* (July 31, 2017 morning issue), p. 9.
67. Ōkubo, *Shuppan – shosekishō jinbutsu jōhō taikan*, pp. 139-140.

68. Egusa Shigetada, "Watashi no futatsu no onegahi: sekaitekina shuppan to hōritsu-sho" (My Two Main Requests: International Publishing and Law Books), *Yomiuri shinbun* (May 10, 1925, morning issue), p. 4.
69. Egusa Shigetada, "Watashi no futatsu no onegahi: sekaitekina shuppan to hōritsu-sho," *Yomiuri shinbun* (May 10, 1925, morning issue), p. 4.
70. Sho Konishi, "Translingual World Order: Language without Culture in Post-Russo-Japanese War Japan," *The Journal of Asian Studies* vol. 72, no. 1 (February 2013): p. 92.
71. Natsukawa Kiyomaru, *Shuppanjin no yokogao* (Profile of the Publisher) (Tōkyō: Shuppan Dōmei Shinbunsha, 1942), p. 7.
72. Suekawa Hiroshi, "Egusa Shirō," in *Gendai no shuppanjin 50nin shū (50 Contemporary Publishers)* (Tōkyō: Shuppan Nyūsusha, 1956), p. 30.
73. "Dai-2kai Chosakuken Shinsakai gijiroku" (Protocol of the Second Session of the Chosakuken Shinsakai), in *Bungakuteki oyobi bijutsuteki chosakubutsu hogo dōmei kaigi kankei ikken – jōyaku hijun jisshi kankei dai-2kan* (Regarding the Conference for Copyright Protection of Literary and Artistic Works: Regarding the Enactment of Ratifying the Treaty, vol. 2), November 18, 1937, DA MoFA, JACAR, Ref. B04122548300, pp. 6-45, here pp. 8-9; Tōkyō Shuppan Kyōkai, *Tōkyō Shuppan Kyōkai 25nen shi*, pp. 91, 137.
74. Letter from the Belgian Ambassador to Arita Hachirō, in *Bungakuteki bijutsuteki chosakubutsu hogo dōmei kaigi kankei ikken – 'Burasseru' kaigi (1935) dai 1kan* (Regarding the Conference for Copyright Protection of Literary and Artistic Works: 'Brussels' Conference (1935), vol. 1), May 30, 1936, DA MoFA, JACAR, Ref. B04122521500, p. 0074; Letter from the Belgian Ambassador to Arita Hachirō, in *Bungakuteki bijutsuteki chosakubutsu hogo dōmei kaigi kankei ikken – 'Burasseru' kaigi (1935) dai 1kan* (idem), June 3, 1936, DA MoFA, JACAR, Ref. B04122521500, p. 0084.
75. Kusano, "Hon'yakuken no ryūho (3)," p. 3.
76. Serizawa Kōjirō, "Chosakuken Shinsakai ni taishite" (Regarding the Chosakuken Shinsakai), *Shinchō* vol. 33, no. 7 (July 1, 1936): pp. 178-180.
77. Tōkyō Shosekishō Kumiai, *Tōkyō Shosekishō Kumiai 50nen shi*, p. 1.
78. Tōkyō Shosekishō Kumiai, p. 1; Tōkyō Shuppan Kyōkai, *Tōkyō Shuppan Kyōkai 25nen shi*, p. 144.
79. Ōie, *Nippon chosakuken monogatari*, pp. 82-83.
80. Yamanouchi, "Kokusai chosakuken kyōgikai hōkoku," p. 1; Ōie, *Nippon chosakuken monogatari*, pp. 84-85.
81. "Burasseru kaigi e hon'yakuka daihyō mo – Purāge arashi, bōei no kyōgi" (Send Also Translator Representatives to the Brussel Conference: Whirlwind Plage, Protection Consultations), *Yomiuri shinbun* (May 3, 1936, morning issue), p. 7.
82. "Burasseru kaigi e hon'yakuka daihyō mo," *Yomiuri shinbun* (May 3, 1936, morning issue), p. 7; Yamanouchi Yoshio, ed., "Kokusai Chosakuken Kyōgikai hōkoku"

(Report of the Kokusai Chosakuken Kyōgikai), *Nihon Hon'yaku Kyōkai* (October 1936), in *Bungakuteki bijutsuteki chosakubutsu hogo dōmei kaigi kankei ikken – 'Burasseru' kaigi (1935) dai-1kan* (Regarding the Conference for Copyright Protection of Literary and Artistic Works: 'Brussels' Conference (1935), Vol. 1), 1936, DA MoFA, JACAR, Ref. B04122521400, p. 5.

83. Chosakuken Chōsakai, ed., "Société des Traducteurs Japonais – La situation spéciale des traducteurs et des éditeurs au Japon," in *Bungakuteki bijutsuteki chosakubutsu hogo dōmei kaigi kankei ikken – 'Burasseru' kaigi (1935) dai-1kan* (idem), 1936, DA MoFA, JACAR, Ref. B04122521400, pp. 1-7.
84. Mintrom, Norman, "Policy entrepreneurship and policy change," pp. 649-667.
85. "Shinkoku ni tai suru hanken hogo no gi ni tsuki seigan," JACAR, Ref. B06151056600, pp. 0221-0223.
86. Chosakuken Chōsakai, "Société des Traducteurs Japonais," JACAR, Ref. B04122521400, pp. 1-7.
87. League of Nations International Committee on Intellectual Co-operation, "Report of the Committee on the Work of its Nineteenth Plenary Session," Geneva, August 1937, pp. 1-104, here pp. 71-74, in *Kokusai Renmei Gakugei Kyōryoku Kokusai Iinkai oyobi Kokusai Gakuin kankei ikken dai-5kan* (Matters Concerning the International Committee on Intellectual Cooperation and the International Institute, Vol. 5), DA MoFA, JACAR, Ref. B06050094600, pp. 0256-0308.
88. Letter from Raymond Weiss to Georges Maillard, January 9, 1937, in Association Littéraire et Artistique Internationale, FR PUNES AG 1-IICI-E-IV-6. IIIC 1925-1946, UNESCO Archives; Letter from Raymond Weiss to Marcel Boutet, January 9, 1937, in Association Littéraire et Artistique Internationale, FR PUNES AG 1-IICI-E-IV-6. IIIC 1925-1946.
89. "Report on the Status of International Copyright Protection Submitted to the Committee for the Study of Copyright of the American National Committee on International Intellectual Cooperation," JACAR, Ref. B04122522600, pp. 3-4.
90. Conference Invitation Letters Sent Out by Regular Study Committee, in *Droit d'auteur.* Conférence de Bruxelles, March 30, 1936, FR PUNES AG 1-IICI-E-IV-45. IIIC 1925-1946, Paris, UNESCO Archives.
91. "Editorial: Instruction in the Aims of the League of Nations," *Educational Survey* vol. 2, no. 1 (January 1931), p. 8.
92. This confederation, which is often abbreviated as CISAC, was established in 1926 in France by 18 authors' societies from 18 European countries with the aim to promote their rights globally.
93. "Société des Nations: Comite d'experts pour l'étude d'un statut universel du droit d'auteur" (League of Nations: Committee of Experts for the Study of a Universal Copyright Statute), in *Bungakuteki bijutsuteki chosakubutsu hogo dōmei kaigi kankei ikken – 'Burasseru' kaigi (1935) dai-1kan* (Regarding the Conference for Copyright Protec-

tion of Literary and Artistic Works: 'Brussels' Conference (1935), Vol. 1), April 1936, DA MoFA, JACAR, Ref. B04122521600, p. 0143.
94. Correspondence Regarding the Participation of Japan in the Committee of Experts, in *Droit d'auteur*. Conférence de Bruxelles, March-June 1937, FR PUNES AG 1-IICI-E-IV-45. International Institute of Intellectual Co-operation (IICI) 1925-1946, Paris, UNESCO Archives; Various Correspondence Regarding the Conference for Copyright Protection of Literary and Artistic Works: 'Brussels' Conference, 1935: JACAR, Ref. B04122521500; Various correspondence regarding the conference for copyright protection of literary and artistic works: 'Brussels' conference, 1935, JACAR, Ref. B04122521600.
95. Letter from the Belgian Ambassador to Foreign Minister Arita Hachirō, JACAR, Ref. B04122521500, p. 0084; Letter from the Berne Bureau to the Japanese Legation in Switzerland, in *Bungakuteki bijutsuteki chosakubutsu hogo dōmei kaigi kankei ikken – 'Burasseru' kaigi (1935) dai-1kan* (Regarding the Conference for Copyright Protection of Literary and Artistic Works: 'Brussels' Conference (1935), Vol. 1), June 3, 1936, DA MoFA, JACAR, Ref. B04122521500, p. 0104.
96. "'Mō kanben naranu' Nihon ooi ni okoru – Chosakuken kaigi no onagare ni kanshi" ('Enough Is Enough' Japan is Greatly Angered: Regarding the Course of Events at the Copyright Conference), *Tōkyō nichi nichi shinbun* (June 5, 1936), reprinted without page number in *Bungakuteki bijutsuteki chosakubutsu hogo dōmei kaigi kankei ikken – 'Burasseru' kaigi (1935) dai-1kan* (idem), 1936, DA MoFA, JACAR, Ref. B04122521400, p. 0414.
97. "'Mō kanben naranu' Nihon ooi ni okoru," p. 0414.
98. Letter from Edmond Glesener to Yoshitomi, Secretary of the Japanese Embassy, in *Bungakuteki bijutsuteki chosakubutsu hogo dōmei kaigi kankei ikken – 'Burasseru' kaigi (1935) dai-1kan* (idem), June 6, 1936, DA MoFA, JACAR, Ref. B04122521500, p. 0115.
99. Letter from Edmond Glesener to Yoshitomi, Secretary of the Japanese Embassy, in *Bungakuteki bijutsuteki chosakubutsu hogo dōmei kaigi kankei ikken – 'Burasseru' kaigi (1935) dai-1kan* (idem), June 16, 1936, DA MoFA, JACAR, Ref. B04122521600, pp. 0130-0131.
100. Letter from Raymond Weiss to Folie, in *Droit d'auteur*. Conférence de Bruxelles, June 19, 1936, FR PUNES AG 1-IICI-E-IV-45, IICI 1925-1946, Paris, UNESCO Archives.
101. Letter from Satō Naotake to Foreign Minister Arita Hachirō, in *Bungakuteki bijutsuteki chosakubutsu hogo dōmei kaigi kankei ikken – 'Burasseru' kaigi (1935) dai-1kan* (Regarding the Conference for Copyright Protection of Literary and Artistic Works: 'Brussels' Conference (1935), Vol. 1), June 18, 1936, DA MoFA, JACAR, Ref. B04122521600, p. 0129.

102. Letter from the Belgian Embassy to Foreign Minister Arita Hachirō, in *Bungakuteki bijutsuteki chosakubutsu hogo dōmei kaigi kankei ikken – 'Burasseru' kaigi (1935) dai-1kan* (idem), July 6, 1936, DA MoFA, JACAR, Ref. B04122521600, pp. 0165-0166; (Response) Letter from Arita Hachirō to the Belgian Ambassador, in *Bungakuteki bijutsuteki chosakubutsu hogo dōmei kaigi kankei ikken – 'Burasseru' kaigi (1935) dai-1kan* (idem), July 14, 1936, DA MoFA, JACAR, Ref. B04122521600, p. 0174.
103. Saikawa, "From Intellectual Co-operation to International Cultural Exchange," p. 128.
104. Tōkyō Shuppan Kyōkai, *Tōkyō Shuppan Kyōkai 25nen shi*, p. 91.
105. Kobayashi, *Genkō chosakuken hō no rippō riyū to kaishaku*, p. 6.
106. Saikawa, "From Intellectual Co-operation to International Cultural Exchange," p. 131.
107. Tōkyō Shuppan Kyōkai, *Tōkyō Shuppan Kyōkai 25nen shi*, p. 94.
108. Letter from Satō Junzō to Henri Bonnet, in *Droit d'auteur*. Conférence de Bruxelles, 15 March 1937, FR PUNES AG 1-IICI-E-IV-45, IICI 1925-1946, Paris, UNESCO Archives; Saikawa, "From Intellectual Co-operation to International Cultural Exchange," pp. 131-132.
109. Satō Junzō, "Berunu jōyaku to Nihon no tachiba – kokusai kaigi enki no riyū" (The Berne Convention and the Standpoint of Japan: The Reason for the Postponement of the International Conference), *Tōkyō asahi shinbun* (March 21, 1937 morning issue), p. 7; Satō Junzō "Berunu jōyaku to Nihon no tachiba (2) – Yottsu no shin kokusai jōyaku an (- Four New Proposals on the International Treaty)," *Tōkyō asahi shinbun* (March 22, 1937 morning issue), p. 7; Satō Junzō, "Berunu jōyaku to Nihon no tachiba (3) – kanmin itchi no kyōryoku o nozomu" (– Wishing a Combined Effort of Bureaucrats and Citizens), *Tōkyō asahi shinbun* (March 23, 1937, morning issue), p. 7.
110. Satō, "Berunu jōyaku to Nihon no tachiba (3)," p. 7.
111. Satō, p. 7.
112. Report from the Committee on the Work of its Nineteenth Plenary Session, League of Nations, p. 7.
113. Yamada Saburō, "Gakugei kyōryoku to hon'yakuken mondai" (Intellectual Cooperation and the Translation Right Problem), *Kokka Gakkai zasshi* vol. 52, no. 2 (February 1938): pp. 163-194.
114. Yamada, p. 179.
115. Yamada, pp. 179-180.
116. Yamada, p. 180.
117. "International Institute of Intellectual Cooperation: Second General Conference of National Committees on Intellectual Cooperation: Proposals of the Japanese National Committee on Intellectual Cooperation," in *Bungakuteki bijutsuteki chosakubutsu hogo dōmei kaigi kankei ikken – 'Burasseru' kaigi (1935) dai-1kan* (Regarding

the Conference for Copyright Protection of Literary and Artistic Works: 'Brussels' Conference (1935), Vol. 1), July 1937, DA MoFA, JACAR, Ref. B04122521400, pp. 0-5.
118. "International Institute of Intellectual Cooperation," p. 3.
119. "International Institute of Intellectual Cooperation," pp. 3-4.
120. "International Institute of Intellectual Cooperation," pp. 1-5.
121. "International Institute of Intellectual Cooperation," p. 4.
122. "International Institute of Intellectual Cooperation," p. 5.
123. Alvin D. Coox, "The Pacific War," in *The Cambridge History of Japan*, Peter Duus, ed. (Cambridge: Cambridge University Press), pp. 315-382; see also Burkman, *Japan and the League of Nations*.
124. Yamada, "Gakugei kyōryoku to honyakuken mondai," p. 186.
125. League of Nations International Committee on Intellectual Co-operation, "Report of the Committee on the Work of its Nineteenth Plenary Session," p. 56.
126. Yamada, "Gakugei kyōryoku to honyakuken mondai," p. 186.
127. Harold Josephson, *James T. Shotwell and the Rise of Internationalism in America* (London: Associated University Presses, 1975), pp. 230-231.
128. "8gatsu futsuka tsuki Pari yori Yamada hakase no chūkan hōkoku (Kabayama iinchō ate)" (Regarding Yamada Saburō's Interim Report from Paris on August 2 (Addressed to Committee Leader Kabayama (Aisuke), August 2, 1937, in *Kokusai Renmei Gakugei Kyōryoku Kokusai Iinkai oyobi Kokusai Gakuin kankei ikken dai-5kan* (Matters Concerning the International Committee on Intellectual Cooperation and the International Institute, vol. 5), DA MoFA, JACAR, Ref. B06050094600, pp. 0237-0238.
129. Yamada, "Gakugei kyōryoku to honyakuken mondai," p. 188.
130. League of Nations International Committee on Intellectual Co-operation, "Report of the Committee on the Work of Its Nineteenth Plenary Session," p. 16.
131. Actes de la Dix-Huitième Session Ordinaire de l'Assemblée, Annex 2 (Travaux de l'organisation de coopération intellectuelle), *Société des Nations – Journal Officiel*, Supplement Special No. 175 (Geneva, 1937), 87, in *Kokusai Renmei Sōkai kankei ikken – dai-18kai sōkai kankei* (Matters Concerning the General Assembly of the League of Nations: 18th General Assembly), DA MoFA, JACAR, Ref. B04014031500, p. 87.
132. Tōkyō Shuppan Kyōkai, *Tōkyō Shuppan Kyōkai 25nen shi*, p. 146.
133. Bannerman, *International Copyright and Access to Knowledge*, pp. 105-106.
134. "Dai 2kai Chosakuken Shinsakai gijiroku" (Minutes of the Second Meeting of the Copyright Investigation Council), in *Bungakuteki oyobi bijutsuteki chosakubutsu hogo dōmei kaigi kankei ikken – jōyaku hijun oyobi jisshi kankei dai-2maki* (Matters Concerning the Conference for Copyright Protection of Literary and Artistic Works – Ratification and Implementation of the Convention, Vol. 2), DA MoFA, JACAR, Ref. B04122548300, p. 9.
135. "Dai 2kai Chosakuken Shinsakai gijiroku," pp. 7-45.

136. The Tōkyō Shuppan Kyōkai states that their vice president Ōhashi Shin'ichi (1885-1959), who was director of Hakubunkan publishing company, participated, but according to the attendance list of the Home Ministry, Egusa Shigetada participated. Tōkyō Shuppan Kyōkai, *Tōkyō Shuppan Kyōkai 25nen shi*, pp. 97-98; "Go-shussekisha shimei (kaku i-ro-ha jun)" (Name List of Attendants (All in I-Ro-Ha-Order), in *Bungakuteki bijutsuteki chosakubutsu hogo dōmei kaigi kankei ikken – 'Burasseru' kaigi (1935) dai-1kan* (Regarding the Conference for Copyright Protection of Literary and Artistic Works: 'Brussels' Conference (1935), Vol. 1), DA MoFA, JACAR, Ref. B04122521400, p. 0415.
137. "Go-shussekisha shimei (kaku i-ro-ha jun)," JACAR, Ref. B04122521400, p. 0415.
138. Letter from Raymond Weiss to Yamada Saburō, in *Droit d'auteur – Traduction*, May 27, 1938, FR PUNES AG 1-IICI-E-IV-35, IIIC 1928-1938, Paris, UNESCO Archives.
139. The United States was a member of the Pan-American Convention on Copyright and would thus enter into a new legal relationship with Japan as a member of the Berne Convention.
140. Letter from Yamada Saburō to Foreign Minister Ugaki Kazushige, in *Kokusai Renmei Gakugei Kyōryoku Kokusai Iinkai oyobi Kokusai Gakuin kankei ikken – Gakugei Kyōryoku Kokunai Iinkai kankei* (Matters Concerning the International Committee on Intellectual Cooperation and the International Institute: Regarding Japan's National Committee on Intellectual Cooperation), July 22, 1937, DA MoFA, JACAR, Ref. B04122162900, pp. 0288-0290.
141. "Report on the Status of International Copyright Protection submitted to the Committee for the Study of Copyright of the American National Committee on International Intellectual Cooperation," JACAR, Ref. B04122522600, p. 12.
142. Tōkyō Shuppan Kyōkai, *Tōkyō Shuppan Kyōkai 25nen shi*, pp. 101, 144.
143. Tōkyō Shuppan Kyōkai, p. 144.
144. Noma Seiji died one month after this meeting took place, but Egusa Shigetada remained on the committee.
145. "Copyright Pacts' Merger Is Topic at Parley Today," *Japan Times* (September 9, 1938), p. 2.
146. "Free Translation Will be Asked by Takayanagi," *Japan Times* (6 October, 1938), p. 2; "Free Translation of Foreign Books to Be Demanded," *Japan Times* (September 10, 1938), p. 1.
147. Miyata, *Hon'yakuken no sengo-shi*, p. 296.
148. Letter from Konoe Fumimaro to the Ambassador to France, in *Bungakuteki oyobi bijutsuteki chosakubutsu hogo dōmei kaigi kankei ikken – 'Burasseru' kaigi (1935) – chosakuken tōitsu senmon iinkai kankei* (Regarding the Conference for Copyright Protection of Literary and Artistic Works: 'Brussels' Conference (1935) – Regarding the Committee of Experts for the Unification of Copyright), October 7, 1938, DA

MoFA, JACAR, Ref. B04122522500, p. 0104; Tōkyō Shuppan Kyōkai, *Tōkyō Shuppan Kyōkai 25nen shi*, p. 144.
149. Miyata, *Hon'yakuken no sengo-shi*, p. 296.
150. "Chosakuken tōitsu jōyaku senmon iinkaikai hōkoku" (Report of the Committee of Experts for the Unification of the Copyright Treaties), in *Bungakuteki oyobi bijutsuteki chosakubutsu hogo dōmei kaigi kankei ikken – 'Burasseru' kaigi (1935) – chosakuken tōitsu senmon iinkai kankei* (Regarding the Conference for Copyright Protection of Literary and Artistic Works: 'Brussels' Conference (1935) – Regarding the Committee of Experts for the Unification of Copyright), late October 1938, DA MoFA, JACAR, Ref. B04122522500, pp. 1-23.
151. "Report on the Status of International Copyright Protection Submitted to the Committee for the Study of Copyright of the American National Committee on International Intellectual Cooperation," JACAR, Ref. B04122522600, pp. 14-17.
152. "Chosakuken tōitsu jōyaku senmon iinkaikai hōkoku," JACAR, Ref. B04122522500, p. 9.
153. Itō Nobuo, "Hon'yaku jiyū no riron to jissai (2)" (Theory and Practice of Translation Freedom), *Nihon hōgaku* vol. 5, no. 6 (June 1939): p. 52.
154. "Chosakuken tōitsu jōyaku senmon iinkaikai hōkoku," JACAR, Ref. B04122522500, p. 9.
155. Robert Cryer and Neil Boister, eds., *Documents of the Tokyo International Military Tribunal: Charter, Indictment and Judgments* (Oxford: Oxford University Press, 2008), p. 221.
156. Sheldon Anderson, *Politics and Culture of Modern Sports* (London: Lexington Books, 2015), p. 89.
157. "Report on the Status of International Copyright Protection Submitted to the Committee for the Study of Copyright of the American National Committee on International Intellectual Cooperation," JACAR, Ref. B04122522600, pp. 23-24.
158. "Report on the Status of International Copyright Protection," pp. 24-25.
159. Miyata, *Hon'yakuken no sengo-shi*, p. 296.
160. Itō Nobuo, "Hon'yaku jiyū no riron to jissai (3)," *Nihon hōgaku* vol. 5, no. 8 (August 1939): pp. 34-69.
161. Tōkyō Shosekishō Kumiai, *Tōkyō Shosekishō Kumiai 25nen shi*, pp. 84-89.
162. Tōkyō Shosekishō Kumiai, pp. 84-89.
163. "Gakugei Kyōryoku Kokunai Iinkait dai-13kai kaigō giji yōroku" (Protocol of the 13th Meeting of the National Committee on Intellectual Cooperation), in *Bungakuteki oyobi bijutsuteki chosakubutsu hogo dōmei kaigi kankei ikken – 'Burasseru' kaigi (1935) – chosakuken tōitsu senmon iinkai kankei* (Regarding the Conference for Copyright Protection of Literary and Artistic Works: 'Brussels' Conference (1935) – Regarding the Committee of Experts for the Unification of Copyright), January 27, 1939, DA MoFA, JACAR, Ref. B04122522500, pp. 1-4.

164. Suzuki Takeo, "Chosakuken hō tōitsu undō no genkyō" (The Current Status of the Movement for the Unification of the Copyright Law), *Hōgaku Kyōkai zasshi* vol. 57, no. 2 (February 1939): p. 110.
165. Saikawa, "From Intellectual Co-operation to International Cultural Exchange," p. 238.
166. "Gakugei Kyōryoku Kokunai Iinkai dai-13kai kaigō giji yōroku," JACAR, Ref. B04122522500, pp. 1-4.
167. This plan was realized in May 1939 when the KBS invited many publishers to a dinner at the Gakushi Kaikan. 110 publishers of the Tōkyō Shuppan Kyōkai attended the dinner. Tōkyō Shuppan Kyōkai, *Tōkyō Shuppan Kyōkai 25nen shi*, p. 106.
168. "Gakugei Kyōryoku Kokunai Iinkai dai-13kai kaigō giji yōroku," JACAR, Ref. B04122522500, pp. 1-4.
169. "Le Droit d'auteur, revue du bureau de 'union internationale pour la protection des oeuvres littéraires et artistiques, 15 Octobre 1939 – pages 119 et 120" (Copyright, Review of the Office of the Berne Union), in *Bungakuteki bijutsuteki chosakubutsu hogo dōmei kaigi kankei ikken – 'Burasseru' kaigi (1935) – chosakuken tōitsu senmon iinkai kankei* (Regarding the Conference for Copyright Protection of Literary and Artistic Works: 'Brussels' Conference (1935) – Regarding the Committee of Experts for the Unification of the Copyright Law), 1939, DA MoFA, JACAR, Ref. B04122522600, pp. 1-10.
170. "Le Droit d'auteur, revue du bureau de 'union internationale pour la protection des oeuvres littéraires et artistiques," JACAR, Ref. B04122522600, pp. 5-7.
171. Translated from French. "Le Droit d'auteur, revue du bureau de 'union internationale pour la protection des oeuvres littéraires et artistiques," JACAR, Ref. B04122522600, pp. 9-10.
172. Löhr, *Die Globalisierung geistiger Eigentumsrechte*, p. 254.
173. Various letters between the Paris Institute and Maruzen, Dépositaires des publications de l'IICI – Maruzen Co. Ltd., Tōkyō, 1932-1940, FR PUNES AG 1-IICI-H-X-11.40, IIIC 1932-1940, Paris, UNESCO Archives.
174. Okudaira Yasuhiro, ed., *Genron tōsei bunken shiryō shūsei dai-12ken: Shuppan Shintaisei no zenbō – ihon Shuppankai gaiyō* (Collection of Literary Documents on the Regulation of Freedom of Speech, vol. 12: Overview of the Publishing 'Shintaisei': Outline of the Nihon Shuppankai) (Tōkyō: Shuppan Taimususha, 1941; Reprint Tōkyō: Nihon Tosho Sentā, 1992), p. 38.
175. Okudaira, *Genron tōsei bunken shiryō shūsei dai-12ken*, pp. 100-103.

CHAPTER 5. TOWARDS INDEPENDENCE

1. Ichihara Tokurō, "Nihon Shuppankai kokusaika no ayumi to Noma Shōichi shi (1)" (The Steps toward the Internationalization of the Japanese Publishing Industry and Mr. Noma Shōichi (1)), *Shuppan Kurabu dayori* vol. 504 (February 2007): p. 1.
2. Nihon Shuppan Gakkai 35nen shi Kankō Iinkai, ed., *Shuppangaku no genzai: Nihon Shuppan Gakkai 1969-2006nen no kiseki* (The Present State of Publishing Studies: History of the Nihon Shuppan Gakkai 1969-2006) (Tōkyō: Chōyōkai, 2008), p. 25.
3. Furuya, "Postwar Publishing Trends in Japan," pp. 213-218.
4. "U.S., Communist Countries Vie in Getting Books Translated," *Japan Times* (June 14, 1953), p. 3.
5. Ichihara Tokurō, interviewed by author of this book on November 2, 2017.
6. John B. Hench, *Books as Weapons: Propaganda, Publishing, and the Battle for Global Markets in the Era of World War II* (Cornell University Press, London, 2010), p. 249.
7. An exemption of the complete interruption was America where several non-state and private associations like the FISAC, the Inter-American Bar Association, the American Scientific Congress and the Inter-American Academy of Comparative and International Law had continued to promote the unification of existing multilateral copyright treaties even during the war.
8. Löhr, *Die Globalisierung geistiger Eigentumsrechte*, pp. 255-256.
9. Löhr, p. 263.
10. French original: Sous-commission de l'information de masse.
11. Löhr, *Die Globalisierung geistiger Eigentumsrechte*, p. 256.
12. Ray A. Moore, *Partners for Democracy: Crafting the New Japanese State Under MacArthur* (Oxford: Oxford University Press, 2002); Robert E. Ward, "Conclusion," in *Democratizing Japan: The Allied Occupation*, Robert E. Ward and Sakamoto Yoshikazu, eds. (Honolulu: University of Hawaii Press, 1987), pp. 426-427.
13. T.J. Pempel, "The Tar Baby Target: 'Reform' of the Japanese Bureaucracy," in *Democratizing Japan: The Allied Occupation*, Robert E. Ward and Yoshikazu Sakamoto, eds. (Honolulu: University of Hawaii Press, 1987), p. 161.
14. "Publishing U.S. Books in Nippon Language: SCAP Outlines Procedure for Japanese to Secure Publishing Rights," *Japan Times* (January 17, 1946), p. 2.
15. Hench, *Books as Weapons*, p. 227.
16. Pempel, "The Tar Baby Target," p. 161.
17. Under the US-Japanese Copyright Treaty Japanese publishers had been free to translate works without having to ask the original author for permission or pay any royalties.
18. "Chosakuken Shinsakai iin ichiran" (Member List of the Chosakuken Shinsakai), in *Chosakuken Shinsakai kankei zakken* (Various Matters related to the Chosakuken Shinsakai), June 29, 1943, DA MoFA, JACAR, Ref: B09041816500, pp. 0668-0669.
19. Miyata, *Hon'yakuken no sengoshi*, p. 36.

20. "Chosakuken Shinsakai kondankai yōryō" (Outline of the Chosakuken Shinsakai Panel Discussion), in *Chosakuken nami dōhōki kankei zakken – Nichi-Doku hon'yakuken torikime kankei dai-2kan* (Various Matters Relating to Copyright and Copyright Law: Matters Regarding the Japanese-German Translation Right Agreement, Part 2), November 15, 1944, DA MoFA, JACAR, Ref: B09041813100.
21. *Chosakuken kankei dantai no dōkō* (Trends in Copyright Related Organizations) (Tōkyō: Kokuritsu Kokkai Toshokan Chōsa Rippō Kōsakyoku, 1950), p. 9.
22. Nakajima Kenzō, "Hon'yaku ni tsuite" (Regarding Translations), *Ningen* vol. 2, no. 12 (December 1947): pp. 39-41.
23. *Chosakuken kankei dantai no dōkō*, p. 11.
24. Rōdō Kumiai Hō, Law No. 51/1945, amended as Rōdō Kumiai Hō, Law No. 174/1949; "Go-shomei genpon, 1945, hōritsu dai-51gō, rōdō kumiai hō" (Signature Original, 1945, Law No. 51, Labor Union Law), in *Go-shomei genpon, 1945, hōritsu dai-51gō, rōdō kumiai hō* (idem), December 21, 1945, NAJ, JACAR, Ref. A04017709400.
25. "Chosakuken hō no ichibu o kaisei suru seigan ni tsuite" (On the Petition to Revise Part of the Copyright Law), in *Kōbun ruiju dai-73hen – Shōwa 23nen/dai-26kan/kokkai 14/seigan 5* (Official Document 73rd Edition -- 1948/Vol. 26t/14th National Diet/Petition No. 5), December 1, 1948, NAJ, JACAR, Ref. A13110980700, pp. 8-10; *Chosakuken kankei dantai no dōkō*, p. 14.
26. *Chosakuken kankei dantai no dōkō*, p. 15.
27. "Chosakuken hō no ichibu o kaisei suru seigan ni tsuite," JACAR, Ref. A13110980700, pp. 8-10.
28. Nihon Chosakuken Kyōgikai, "Chosakuken kyōgikai – 12nen no ayumi" (Copyright Council: The Steps of 12 Years), *Chosakuken shirīzu* 6 (May 1960), p. 9. (This publication is part of the private collection of the Nihon Shoseki Shuppan Kyōkai (Japan Book Publishers' Association) which is currently in the process of being archived by Professor Shibano Kyōko of Sophia University in Tōkyō. It was accessed in summer 2017).
29. Von Staden, *Business-Government Relations in Prewar Japan*, p. 40; Schwartz, *Advice and Consent*, p. 49.
30. United Nations Educational, Scientific, and Cultural Organization (1949, June). *Introductory Report to the Committee of Copyright Experts in Session at UNESCO House, July 4-9, 1949* (Programme and Meeting Document DA/9). Retrieved from the United Nations Educational, Scientific, and Cultural Organization website: http://unesdoc.unesco.org/images/0014/001439/143959eb.pdf.
31. United Nations Educational, Scientific, and Cultural Organization, p. 3.
32. United Nations Educational, Scientific, and Cultural Organization, p. 3.
33. United Nations Educational, Scientific, and Cultural Organization, p. 2.

34. Japanese National Commission for Unesco, *Unesco Activities in Japan* (Tōkyō: Japanese National Commission for Unesco, 1956), pp. 7-8.
35. Japanese National Commission for Unesco, pp. 7-8; Saikawa Takashi, "Returning to the International Community: UNESCO and Post-war Japan, 1945-1951," in *A History of UNESCO: Global Actions and Impacts*, Poul Duedahl, ed. (New York: Palgrave Macmillan, 2016), pp. 123-125.
36. Miyata, *Hon'yakuken no sengoshi*, p. 214.
37. United Nations Educational, Scientific, and Cultural Organization (1949, June). *Introductory Report to the Committee of Copyright Experts in Session at UNESCO House, July 4-9, 1949*; Saikawa, "Returning to the International Community," p. 120.
38. United Nations Educational, Scientific, and Cultural Organization (July 1949). *Committee of Copyright Experts on Copyright, Paris July 4-9, 1949, Recommendations* (Programme and Meeting Document DA/24, Catalog number 0000143949), 1. Retrieved from the UNESDoc Digital Library: http://unesdoc.unesco.org/images/0014/001439/143949eb.pdf.
39. United Nations Educational, Scientific, and Cultural Organization, p. 2.
40. Monbushō kanrikyoku, *Yunesuko yori hassareta 'bankoku chosakuken jōyaku ni kan suru shoseifu no kenkai yōsei' to kore ni tai suru Nihon seifu kaitō, chosakuken shiryō U.C. no. 1* (The "Request for Governmental Views Concerning a Universal Copyright Convention" Issued by UNESCO and the Reply from the Japanese Government, Copyright Documents U.C. No. 1) (September 1950), p. 1.
41. Nakajima Kenzō, "Chosakuken shōron" (A Short Essay on Copyright), *Hōritsu jihō* vol. 22, no. 6 (June 1950): pp. 58-59.
42. "Chosakuken Shinsakai kansei no ichibu o kaisei suru seirei an" (Draft Government Ordinance to Revise a Part of the Governmental Chosakuken Shinsakai), in *Kōbun ruiju dai-75hen– Shōwa 25nen/dai-25kan/kanki go/Monbushō/Kōseishō* (Official Document 75th Edition – 1950/vol. 25/Official Regulation 5/Ministry of Education/Ministry of Health and Welfare), July 31, 1950, NAJ, JACAR, Ref. A13111358700.
43. "Gov't to Revise Copyright Law: Revisions to Be Based on Int'l Convention -- Study Council to Be Set Up," *Japan Times* (August 25, 1950), 3; "Bankoku chosakuken jōyaku kyōgi" (Consultation Regarding the International Copyright Treaty), *Yomiuri shinbun* (August 4, 1950), p. 2.
44. "Gov't to Revise Copyright Law," p. 3.
45. *Chosakuken kankei dantai no dōkō*, pp. 46-47.
46. Monbushō kanrikyoku, *Yunesuko yori hassareta 'bankoku chosakuken jōyaku ni kan suru shoseifu no kenkai yōsei'*, p. 5.
47. Monbushō kanrikyoku, p. 6.
48. Monbushō kanrikyoku, p. 8; Hōki Jirō, "Bankoku chosakuken jōyaku no seiritsu" (The Establishment of the International Copyright Agreement), in *Gengai shihō no shomondai: Katsumoto Masaakira sensei kanreki kinen* (Various Problems of Modern Pri-

vate Law: In Commemoration of Professor Katsumoto Masaakira's 60th Birthday), Nakagawa Zennosuke and Uchida Shun'ichi, eds. (Tōkyō: Yūhikaku, 1959), p. 668.
49. Miyata, *Hon'yakuken no sengoshi*, p. 213.
50. "To Attend Copyright Talks," *Japan Times* (October 7, 1950), p. 7.
51. Monbushō. *Chosakuken Hō Kaiseian Kisō Shingikai Tokubetsu Iinkai, dai-1kai Tokubetsu Iinkai gijiroku: kōhon* (Special Committee of the Copyright Law Revision Draft Council, Minutes of the First Special Committee Meeting: Manuscript) (November 1950), p. 28.
52. Monbushō, *Chosakuken Hō Kaiseian Kisō Shingikai Tokubetsu Iinkai, dai-1kai Tokubetsu Iinkai gijiroku: kōhon* (Special Committee of the Copyright Law Revision Draft Council, Minutes of the First Special Committee Meeting: Manuscript) (November 20, 1950), pp. 4-5.
53. Monbushō, *Chosakuken Hō Kaiseian Kisō Shingikai dai-4kai sōkai gijiroku* (Minutes of the 4th General Meeting of the Copyright Law Revision Draft Council) (February 1951), p. 10.
54. "United Nations Educational, Scientific and Cultural Organization: Supplementary Request for Views Concerning a Universal Copyright Convention," in *Dai-3ji Yoshida naikaku jikan kaigi shiryō toji – Shōwa 26nen 6gatsu (June 11-20,1951)* (Bound Documents of the Vice Chairman's Meeting of the 3rd Yoshida Cabinet – June 1951), January 17, 1951, NAJ, JACAR, Ref. A17112229700, p. 4.
55. Hōki, "Bankoku chosakuken jōyaku no seiritsu," p. 669.
56. Letter from S.M. Lee, UNESCO representative in Japan, to Nishimura Iwao, Chief, Liaison & UNESCO Section, Ministry of Education, in *Dai-3ji Yoshida naikaku jikan kaigi shiryō toji – Shōwa 26nen 6gatsu (June 11-20, 1951)* (Bound Documents of the Vice Chairman's Meeting of the 3rd Yoshida Cabinet – June 1951), April 25, 1951, NAJ, JACAR, Ref. A17112229700, p. 126.
57. "Yunesuko kara shōkai o uketa 'bankoku chosakuken jōyaku ni kan suru kenkai tsuika yōsei' ni tai suru Nihon seifu kaitōan ni kan suru ken" (Regarding the Draft Response from the Japanese Government to a Request for Additional Views on the Universal Copyright Treaty Inquired by UNESCO), in *Kōbun ruiju dai-76hen – Shōwa 26nen/dai-96kan/gaiji 2* (Official Document 76th Edition – 1951/Vol. 96/Foreign Affairs 2), June 1951, NAJ, JACAR, Ref. A13111631300, p. 6.
58. "Yunesuko kara shōkai o uketa 'bankoku chosakuken jōyaku ni kan suru kenkai tsuika yōsei' ni tai suru Nihon seifu kaitōan ni kan suru ken," JACAR, Ref. A13111631300, pp. 3-4.
59. Hōki, "Bankoku chosakuken jōyaku no seiritsu," p. 670.
60. Hōki, 671; "Bankoku chosakuken jōyaku sōan ni kan suru kaitō an (Monbushō)" (Proposal Draft for the International Copyright Treaty (Ministry of Education), in *Jikan kaigi shiryō toji – Shōwa 26nen 12gatsu (December 3-27, 1951)* (Bound Documents of the Vice Minister's Meeting December 1951), December 1951, NAJ, JACAR, Ref. A17112393200, p. 0163.

61. No author, "Tokushū: chosakuken hō 100nen" (Special Edition: 100 Years of Copyright Law), *Kopiraito* vol. 39, no. 459 (June 1999): pp. 105-106. pp. 105-106.
62. Monbushō, *Chosakuken Hō Kaiseian Kisō Shingikai Tokubetsu Iinkai, dai-1kai Tokubetsu Iinkai gijiroku: kōhon* (Special Committee of the Copyright Law Revision Draft Council, Minutes of the First Special Committee Meeting: Manuscript) (November 20, 1950), pp. 4-5.
63. The House of Councillors succeeded the prewar House of Peers in 1947.
64. Kokkai Kaigiroku, *Sangiin Monbu Iinkai kaigiroku dai-25gō* (Records of Proceedings of the House of Councillors Educational Committee Session 25), April 15, 1952, NDL.
65. Kokkai Kaigiroku, *Shūgiin Monbu Iinkai kaigiroku dai-19gō* (Records of Proceedings of the House of Representatives' Educational Committee Session 19), April 22, 1952, NDL.
66. Kokkai Kaigiroku, *Sangiin Monbu Iinkai kaigiroku dai-27gō* (Records of Proceedings of the House of Councillors' Educational Committee Session 27), April 24, 1952, p. 2, NDL.
67. Kokkai Kaigiroku, *Shūgiin Monbu Iinkai kaigiroku dai-8gō* (Records of Proceedings of the House of Representatives' Educational Committee Session 8), March 25, 1952, NDL.
68. "Chosakuken Kyōgikai ga seimei" (Copyright Council Makes an Announcement), *Yomiuri shinbun* (April 25, 1952, morning issue), p. 3.
69. Kokkai Kaigiroku, *Sangiin Naikaku-Monbu Rengō Iinkai kaigiroku dai-1gō* (Records of Proceedings of the House of Councillors Joint Session of the Cabinet Committee and the Educational Committee Session 1), May 9, 1952, NDL.
70. "Chosakuken Shingikai rei (Monbushō)" (Copyright Council Ordinance (Ministry of Education), in *Kakugi shiryō toji – Shōwa 27 6gatsu 3nichi (3-13 June 1952)* (Bound Documents of the Cabinet Sessions – June 3, 1952), June 1952, NAJ, JACAR, Ref. A17112631600.
71. Kokkai Kaigiroku, *Sangiin Monbu Iinkai kaigiroku dai-29gō* (Records of Proceedings of the House of Councillors Educational Committee Session 29), May 9, 1952, p. 5, NDL.
72. Nihon Chosakuken Kyōgikai, "Chosakuken kyōgikai – 12nen no ayumi," p. 30.
73. Nihon Chosakuken Kyōgikai, *50nen no ayumi: sōritsu 50shūnen kinenshi* (The Steps of 50 Years: A 50-Year Anniversary History) (Tōkyō: Nihon Chosakuken Kyōgikai, 2000), p. 14.
74. Hōki, "Bankoku chosakuken jōyaku no seiritsu," p. 653.
75. Bannerman, *International Copyright and Access to Knowledge*, p. 106, quoted from *Records of the Inter-Governmental Copyright Conference, Geneva, August 18 – September 6, 1952* (Paris: UNESCO, 1955), p. 123, item 62.
76. Hōki, "Bankoku chosakuken jōyaku no seiritsu," pp. 674-677.
77. Bannerman, *International Copyright and Access to Knowledge*, p. 109.

78. Harari, "The Institutionalisation of Policy Consultation in Japan," p. 150.
79. Ōichi Tobitarō, "Chosakuken hanrei yawa" (Tales about judicial precedents concerning copyright), *Kopiraito* vol. 5, no. 2 (May 1961): p. 2.
80. Nunokawa Kakuzaemon, Suzuki Takeo, Miyazawa Toshiyoshi, Wagatsuma Sakae, "Jurisuto no me: Chosakuken hō no kaisei" (Jurist Eyes: Amendment of the Copyright Law), *Jurisuto* vol. 363 (February 1967): p. 20.
81. "Copyright Pact Ends," *Japan Times* (April 28, 1953), p. 3.
82. Uchida Susumu, "Yunesuko jōyaku o meguru chosakuken mondai" (Copyright Problems Over the UNESCO Treaty), *Refarensu* vol. 49 (December 1955): p. 69.
83. Miyata, *Hon'yakuken no sengoshi*, p. 232, quoted from "Chosakuken mondai no genjō," *Tōkyō shinbun* (June 11, 1955), page number unknown.
84. "Yunesuko jōyaku o megutte chūmoku sareru chosakuken mondai" (Copyright Problems Brought to Attention by the UNESCO Treaty), *Asahi shinbun* (September 3, 1955 morning issue), p. 5; "Yunesuko jōyaku ni sanpi sontoku no wakareme, hon'yakuken" (Translation Rights, a Turning Point in the Pros and Cons of the UNESCO Treaty), *Asahi shinbun* (November 12, 1955), p. 3.
85. "Yunesuko jōyaku o megutte chūmoku sareru chosakuken mondai," *Asahi shinbun* (September 3, 1955 morning issue), p. 5.
86. "Yunesuko jōyaku," p. 5.
87. "Yunesuko jōyaku," p. 5.
88. Takemae Eiji, "Early Postwar Reformist Parties," in *Democratizing Japan: The Allied Occupation*, ed. Robert E. Ward and Sakamoto Yoshikazu (Honolulu: University of Hawai'i Press, 1987), p. 361.
89. Azuma Suehiko, "Chosakuken hō no kaisei to gakujutsuteki chosakubutsu no hogo" (The Revision of the Copyright Law and the Protection of Academic Works), *Shihō* vol. 29 (October 1967): p. 375.
90. Miyata, *Hon'yakuken no sengoshi*, p. 233.
91. Miyata, p. 233.
92. United Nations Educational, Scientific, and Cultural Organization (1956, July). *Intergovernmental Copyright Committee: Report on the First Session, Paris June 11-15, 1956* (Programme and Meeting Document CUA/78). Retrieved from the UNESDoc Digital Library: https://unesdoc.unesco.org/ark:/48223/pf0000127366.
93. Nihon Chosakuken Kyōgikai, "Chosakuken kyōgikai – 12nen no ayumi," p. 24.
94. Nihon Chosakuken Kyōgikai, pp. 26-27, 41.
95. Nihon Chosakuken Kyōgikai, p. 19.
96. Nihon Chosakuken Kyōgikai, p. 19.
97. Ichihara Tokurō, "Noma Shōichi no tenki to ketsudan (part 1) (On Noma Shōichi's Turning Point and his Decisions)," (Kōdansha) *Shayūkai kaihō* (November 2004): p. 11.
98. Ichihara, "Noma Shōichi no tenki to ketsudan (1)," pp. 11-13.

99. Ichihara Tokurō, "Noma Shōichi no tenki to ketsudan (2)," (Kōdansha) *Shayūkai kaihō* (December 2004): pp. 16-18.
100. Nihon Shoseki Shuppan Kyōkai, ed., *Nihon Shoseki Shuppan Kyōkai 10nen shi* (10-Year History of the Japan Publishers' Association) (Tōkyō: Nihon Shoseki Shuppan Kyōkai, 1967), p. 8.
101. Takeda Tetsuji, "Shuppan bunka kōryū wa heiwa e no suishinryoku" (Exchanges Between Publishing Cultures Are a Driving Force of Peace), in *Tsuitō Noma Shōichi* (In Mourning of Nōma Shōichi), Noma Shōichi Tsuitōshū Kankō Iinkai, ed. (Tōkyō: Kōdansha, 1985), p. 417.
102. Ichihara Tokurō, "Nihon Shuppankai kokusaika no ayumi to Noma Shōichi shi (3)" (Steps Toward the Internationalization of the Japanese Publishing Industry and Mr. Noma Shōichi (3), *Shuppan Kurabu dayori* vol. 506 (April 2007): p. 4.
103. The doyen of the involved ministerial bureaucrats, Mizuno Rentarō, had already died in 1949.
104. "Chosakuken zenmen tenaoshi – Shingikai iin 30shi kimaru" (Complete Copyright Revision: Decision Made on 30 Shingikai Members), *Asahi shinbun* (May 2, 1962, morning issue), p. 1.
105. Miyata, *Hon'yakuken no sengoshi*, p. 270.
106. Miyata, pp. 272-274.
107. Nihon Shoseki Shuppan Kyōkai, *Nihon Shoseki Shuppan Kyōkai 10nen shi*, pp. 87-89.
108. Nihon Shoseki Shuppan Kyōkai, ed., *Kokumin bunka to 'hon'yakuken'* (The People's Culture and Translation Rights) (Tōkyō: Nihon Shoseki Shuppan Kyōkai, 1966).
109. Nihon Shoseki Shuppan Kyōkai, pp. 5-6.
110. Nihon Shoseki Shuppan Kyōkai, p. 5.
111. Nihon Shoseki Shuppan Kyōkai, p. 10.
112. Nihon Shoseki Shuppan Kyōkai, p. 16.
113. Nihon Shoseki Shuppan Kyōkai, p. 16.
114. Miyata, *Hon'yakuken no sengoshi*, p. 275.
115. "Tokushū: chosakuken hō 100nen," p. 107.
116. Hemmungs Wirtén, *Cosmopolitan Copyright*, p. 46, quoted from UNESCO, "The Administrative Obstacles to the Universal Free Flow of Culture, Deriving from the Existence of Copyright," Free Flow Com./14, October 13, 1947.
117. Bannerman, *International Copyright and Access to Knowledge*, pp. 205-207.
118. Hemmungs Wirtén, *Cosmopolitan Copyright*, p. 50.
119. Hemmungs Wirtén, p. 54.
120. Hemmungs Wirtén, p. 53.
121. Nunokawa et al., "Jurisuto no me: chosakuken hō no kaisei," p. 19.
122. Nunokawa et al., pp. 14-20.
123. Miyata, *Hon'yakuken no sengoshi*, pp. 278-279.

124. In Japanese, the name of this conference was the Ajia Chiiki Shuppan Senmonka Kaigi.
125. Ichihara Tokurō, "Nihon Shuppankai kokusaika no ayumi to Noma Shōichi shi (2)" (The Steps Toward the Internationalization of the Japanese Publishing Industry and Mr. Noma Shōichi (2)), *Shuppan Kurabu dayori* vol. 505 (March 2007): pp. 4-5.
126. Ichihara Tokurō, interviewed by the author of this book on November 2, 2017; Ichihara, "Nihon Shuppankai kokusaika no ayumi to Noma Shōichi shi (2)," p. 4.
127. Nihon Yunesuko Kokunai Iinkai Bunkaka Kariyaku, *Ajia chiiki shuppan senmonka kaigi hōkokusho sōan: Yunesuko shusai* (Draft Report for the Asian Regional Publishing Expert Conference: organized by UNESCO) (Tōkyō: Nihon Shoseki Shuppan Kyōkai, 1966).
128. Nihon Yunesuko Kokunai Iinkai Bunkaka Kariyaku, pp. 45-46.
129. Ichihara Tokurō, "Noma Shōichi no tenki to ketsudan (3)," (Kōdansha) *Shayūkai kaihō* (January 2005): p. 15.
130. "UNESCO Official Hails Japan's Publishing Role," *Japan Times* (October 23, 1969), p. 3.
131. World Intellectual Property Organization (WIPO), *Records of the Intellectual Property Conference of Stockholm (June 11 – July 14, 1967)*, Vol. 1 (Geneva: WIPO, 1971), pp. 589 and 594.
132. Hemmungs Wirtén, *Cosmopolitan Copyright*, p. 72.
133. Hemmungs Wirtén, p. 50.
134. World Intellectual Property Organization, *Records of the Intellectual Property Conference of Stockholm*, p. 649.
135. Irwin A. Olian, "International Copyright and the Needs of Developing Countries: The Awakening at Stockholm and Paris," *Cornell International Law Journal* vol. 7, no. 2 (May 1974): p. 101.
136. "New Copyright Law," *Japan Times* (May 7, 1970), p. 14.
137. "New Copyright Law," p. 14.
138. China acceded to the Berne Convention in 1992 and joined the WTO in 2001. The Russian Federation joined the Berne Convention in 1994 with the treaty entering into force a year later. In 2008, Russia acceded to the WIPO Copyright Treaty and in 2012, the country became part of the WTO and thereby a member of the TRIPS Agreement.

CONCLUSION

1. Carayannis and Weiss, *The "Third" United Nations*, 2021.
2. Fukui Kensaku gives an overview of the newer discussions within Japan and response to the challenges facing the copyright landscape like digital archives, public domain or the extension of copyright protection is given in *Chosakuken no seiki: kawaru 'jōhō*

no dokusen seido' (The Century of Copyright: The Changing 'Information Monopoly System') (Tōkyō: Shūeisha, 2010).
3. "Hogo kikan 'enchōha' 'shinchōha' sore zore no wake" (The Protection Period 'Extension Faction' and the 'Cautious Faction' and Their Respective Reasoning), Chosakuken Hogo Kikan no Enchō Mondai o Kangaeru Fōramu, accessed June 15, 2023, http://thinkcopyright.org/reason.html.
4. "Bijutsu, bungei, ongaku chosakuken, 30nichi kara shigo 70nen ni enchō" (Art, Literature and Music Copyrights, Extended to 70 Years After Death from the 30th), *Asahi shinbun* (December 24, 2018, morning issue), p. 25; "Japan to Extend Copyright Period on Works Including Novels and Paintings to 70 Years on Dec. 30," *Japan Times* (December 10, 2018), accessed on November 13, 2019, https://www.japantimes.co.jp/news/2018/12/10/national/japan-extend-copyright-period-works-including-novels-paintings-70-years-dec-30/#.Xa8QXi_5zUr; "Rationale for Extending Japan's Copyright Protections Unclear," *Japan Times* (December 22, 2018), accessed November 13, 2019, https://www.japantimes.co.jp/news/2018/12/22/national/media-national/rationale-extending-japans-copyright-protections-unclear/#.Xa2w1S_5zUo.
5. Löhr, *Die Globalisierung geistiger Eigentumsrechte*, p. 276.
6. Sebastian Conrad and Andreas Eckert, "Globalgeschichte, Globalisierung, multiple Modernen: Zur Geschichtsschreibung der modernen Welt" (Global History, Globalization, Multiple Modernities: On the Historiography of the Modern World), in *Globalgeschichte – Theorien, Ansätze, Themen* (Global History: Theories, Approaches, Themes), Sebastian Conrad, Andreas Eckert, Ulrike Freitag, eds. (Frankfurt: Campus, 2007), p. 21.
7. Ian Clark, *Globalization and Fragmentation: International Relations in the Twentieth Century* (Oxford: Oxford University Press, 1997), pp. 31, 197.

BIBLIOGRAPHY

ARCHIVAL HOLDINGS

Gaimushō Gaikō Shiryōkan (Diplomatic Archives of the Ministry of Foreign Affairs, DA MoFA)

Kokuritsu Kōbunshokan (National Archives of Japan, NAJ)

League of Nations Archives (Geneva)
League of Nations Secretariat

Mohr Siebeck Publishing Archive (Berlin)

Kokuritsu Kokkai Toshokan (National Diet Library Japan, NDL)
Kensei shiryōshitsu (Archival Collections of Materials for the Constitutional History of Japan)
Kokkai Kaigiroku (National Diet Records)

The Archive of British Publishing and Printing Reading Sources
Collection of George Allen & Unwin Ltd.

The National Archives of England, Wales and the United Kingdom (TNA)
Foreign Office and Foreign and Commonwealth Office

Tōkyō Shōkō Kaigijo (keizai shiryō sentā) (Tōkyō Chambers of Commerce and Industry (Economic Research Center)

UNESCO Archives
International Institute of Intellectual Co-operation

PERIODICALS

Articles from before 1950 are referenced in the footnotes only. Newspapers are not listed.

Educational Survey
Gaiji ihō
Hōgaku Kyōkai zasshi
Hōritsu jihō
Jitsugyō no sekai
Kanpō
Keisatsu Kyōkai zasshi
Kokka Gakkai zasshi
Kokusai chishiki
Nihon hōgaku
Nihon Shuppan Kyōkai
Ningen
Shinchō
Shuppan Kurabu dayori
The Lancet

LITERATURE AND PRINTED PRIMARY SOURCES

Abel, Jonathan E. *Redacted: The Archives of Censorship in Transwar Japan.* Berkeley: University of California Press, 2012.
Abel, Jessamyn. *The International Minimum: Creativity and Contradiction in Japan's Global Engagement, 1933-1964.* Honolulu: University of Hawaii Press, 2015.
Actes de la conférence de Rome 7 mai – 2 juin 1928. Berne: Bureau de l'Union Internationale Littéraire et Artistique, 1929.
Actes de la conférence réunie à Berlin du 14 octobre au 14 novembre 1908. Berne: Bureau de l'Union Internationale Littéraire et Artistique, 1909.
Akami, Tomoko. "A Quest to be Global: The League of Nations Health Organization and Inter-Colonial Regional Governing Agendas of the Far Eastern Association of Tropical Medicine 1910-25." *The International History Review* vol. 38, no. 1 (2016): pp. 1-23.
Anderson, Sheldon. *Politics and Culture of Modern Sports.* London: Lexington Books, 2015.
Association Littéraire et Artistique Internationale, son histoire, ses travaux, 1878-1889. Paris: Bibliothèque Chacornac, 1889.
Azuma Suehiko. "Chosakuken hō no kaisei gakujutsuteki chosakubutsu no hogo." *Shihō* vol. 29 (October 1967): pp. 366-377.

Bannerman, Sara. *International Copyright and Access to Knowledge*. Cambridge: Cambridge University Press, 2016.

Bennett, A. LeRoy. *International Organizations: Principles and Issues*, 5th edition. New Jersey: Prentice Hall, 1991.

Berger, Gordon M. "Politics and Mobilization in Japan, 1931-45." In *The Twentieth Century*, vol. 6 of *The Cambridge History of Japan*, Peter Duus, ed., pp. 99-153. Cambridge: Cambridge University Press, 1988.

Bowry, Kathy. "Who's Writing Copyright's History?" *European Intellectual Property Review* vol. 18, no. 6 (1996): pp. 322-329.

Brown, Roger H. "(The Other) Yoshida Shigeru and the Expansion of Bureaucratic Power in Prewar Japan." *Monumenta Nipponica* vol. 67, no. 2 (2012): pp. 283-327.

Burkman, Thomas W. *Japan and the League of Nations: Empire and World Order, 1914-1938*. Honolulu: University of Hawai'i Press, 2008.

Carayannis, Tatiana and Thomas G. Weiss. *The "Third" United Nations: How a Knowledge Ecology Helps the UN Think*. Oxford: Oxford University Press, 2021.

Chosakuken kankei dantai no dōkō. Tōkyō: Kokuritsu Kokkai Toshokan Chōsa Rippō Kōsakyoku, 1950.

Clark, Ian. *Globalization and Fragmentation: International Relations in the Twentieth Century*. Oxford: Oxford University Press, 1997.

Clavin, Patricia. "Defining Transnationalism." *Contemporary European History* vol. 14, no. 4 (2005): pp. 421-439.

Cobble, Dorothy Sue. "Who Speaks for Workers? Japan and the 1919 ILO Debates over Rights and Global Labor Standards." *International Labor and Working-Class History* vol. 87 (2015): pp. 213-234.

Conférence de Bruxelles – tableau des voeux émis par divers congrès et assembles. Berne: Bureau de l'Union Internationale Littéraire et Artistique, 1935.

Conférence de Bruxelles – propositions, contre-propositions et observations présentées par les administrations des pays de l'Union. Berne: Bureau de l'Union Internationale Littéraire et Artistique, 1936.

Coox, Alvin D. "The Pacific War." In *The Twentieth Century*, vol. 6 of *The Cambridge History of Japan*, Peter Duus, ed., pp. 315-382. Cambridge: Cambridge University Press, 1989.

Cryer, Robert and Neil Boister, eds. *Documents of the Tokyo International Military Tribunal: Charter, Indictment and Judgments*. Oxford: Oxford University Press, 2008.

Drahos, Peter. *A Philosophy of Intellectual Property*. Applied Legal Philosophy. Aldershot: Dartmouth, 1996.

Duedahl, Poul, ed. *A History of UNESCO: Global Actions and Impacts*. New York: Palgrave Macmillan, 2016.

Fletcher, William Miles. *The Search for a New Order: Intellectuals and Fascism in Prewar Japan*. Chapel Hill: University of North Carolina Press, 1982.

Foucher, Victor. *Le Congrès de la propriété littéraire et artistique tenu à Bruxelles en 1858*. Paris: Librairie de Michel Lévy Frères, 1858.

Fukui Kensaku. *Chosakuken no seiki: kawaru 'jōhō no dokusen seido'*. Tōkyō: Shūeisha, 2010.

Fukui Yūsuke. "Shuppan kanren giin to seiron media no hensen – zasshi no senmonka to shōgyōka." In *Kindai Nihon no media giin: 'seiji no mediaka' no rekishi shakaigaku*, Satō Takumi and Kawasaki Yoshinori, ed., pp. 169-201. Ōsaka: Sōgensha, 2018.

Fujii Shōtō. "Oyaizu Kaname-shi." *Shin Nihon* vol. 6, no. 11 (November 1913): p. 39.

Furuya Natsuko. "Postwar Publishing Trends in Japan." *The Library Quarterly: Information, Community, Policy* vol. 32, no. 3 (July 1962): pp. 208-222.

Ganea, Peter. "Copyright History." In *Japanese Copyright Law: Writings in Honour of Gerhard Schricker*, Peter Ganea, Christopher Heath, and Hiroshi Saitō, eds., pp. 1-10. The Hague: Kluwer Law International, 2005.

—— and Sadao Nagaoka. "Japan." In *Intellectual Property in Asia: Law, Economics, History and Politics*, Paul Goldstein and Joseph Straus, eds., pp. 129-152. Munich: Springer 2009.

Garon, Sheldon. *Molding Japanese Minds: The State in Everyday Life*. Princeton: Princeton University Press, 1997.

——. "From Meiji to Heisei: The State and Civil Society in Japan." In *The State of Civil Society in Japan*, Frank J. Schwartz and Susan J. Pharr, eds., pp. 42-62. Cambridge: Cambridge University Press, 2003.

—— and Mike Mochizuki. "Negotiating Social Contracts." In *Postwar Japan as History*, Andrew Gordon, ed., pp. 145-166. Oxford: University of California Press, 1993.

Gluck, Carol. "The End of Elsewhere: Writing Modernity Now." *The American Historical Review* vol. 116, no. 3 (June 2011): pp. 676-687.

——. *Japan's Modern Myths: Ideology in the Late Meiji Period*. Princeton: Princeton University Press, 1985.

Giddens, Anthony. *Capitalism and Modern Social Theory: An Analysis of the Writings of Marx, Durkheim and Max Weber*. Cambridge University Press, 1971.

Goto-Shibata Harumi. *The League of Nations and the East Asian Imperial Order, 1920-1946*. Singapore: Palgrave Macmillan, 2020.

Greaves, Harold. *The League Committees and World Order: A Study of the Permanent Expert Committees of the League of Nations as an Instrument of International Government*. London: Oxford University Press, 1931.

Haas, Peter M. "Introduction: Epistemic Communities and International Policy Coordination." *International Organization* vol. 46, no. 1 (Winter 1992): pp. 1-35.

Harari, Ehud. "The Institutionalisation of Policy Consultation in Japan: Public Advisory Bodies." In *Japan and the World: Essays on Japanese History and Politics in Honour of Ishida Takeshi*, Gail Lee Bernstein and Haruhiro Fukui, eds., pp. 144-57. London: Macmillan, 1988.

Hartmann, Maj. "Matsumoto Gaku: A Bureaucrat between Culture and Politics in the Beginning of the 1930s." *New Ideas in East Asian Studies* vol. 1 (2017): pp. 1-10.

Hemmungs Wirtén, Eva. *Cosmopolitan Copyright: Law and Language in the Translation Zone.* Uppsala: Uppsala Universitet, Institutionen för ABM, 2011.

——. *No Trespassing: Authorship, Intellectual Property Rights, and the Boundaries of Globalization.* London: University of Toronto Press, 2004.

Hench, John B. *Books as Weapons: Propaganda, Publishing, and the Battle for Global Markets in the Era of World War II.* Cornell University Press, London, 2010.

Herren, Madeleine. "Governmental Internationalism and the Beginning of a New World Order in the Late Nineteenth Century." In *The Mechanics of Internationalism*, Martin H. Geyer and Johannes Paulmann, eds., pp. 121-144. London: Oxford University Press.

——. "Towards a Global History of International Organization." In *Networking the International System: Global Histories of International Organizations*, Madeleine Herren, ed., pp. 1-12. Heidelberg: Springer, 2014.

High, Peter B. *The Imperial Screen: Japanese Film Culture in The Fifteen Years War, 1931-1945.* Madison: The University of Wisconsin Press, 2003.

Hunter, Janet. "'Extreme Confusion and Disorder'? The Japanese Economy in the Great Kantō Earthquake of 1923." *The Journal of Asian Studies* vol. 73, no. 3 (August 2014): pp. 753-773.

Hirobe Izumi. "Kokusai Renmei Chiteki Kyōryoku Kokusai Iinkai no sōsetsu to Nitobe Inazō." *Bungaku kenkyūka kiyō* vol. 121 (February 2007): pp. 1-20.

Hirschmeier, Johannes. *The Origins of Entrepreneurship in Meiji Japan.* Cambridge MA: Harvard University Press, 1968.

Hōki Jirō. "Bankoku chosakuken jōyaku no seiritsu." In *Gengai shihō no shomondai: Katsumoto Masaakira sensei kanreki kinen*, Nakagawa Zennosuke and Uchida Shun'ichi, eds., pp. 652-681. Tōkyō: Yūhikaku, 1959.

Hudson, Valerie M. "Foreign Policy Analysis: Actor-Specific Theory and the Ground of International Relations." *Foreign Policy Analysis* vol. 1, no. 1 (March 2005): pp. 1-30.

Huffman, James L. *Creating a Public: People and Press in Meiji Japan.* Honolulu: University of Hawai'i Press, 1997.

Hughes, Christopher and Shinohara Hatsue. *East Asians in the League of Nations: Actors, Empires and Regions in Early Global Politics.* Singapore: Palgrave Macmillan, 2023.

Ichihara Tokurō. "Nihon Shuppankai kokusaika no ayumi to Noma Shōichi shi (1)." *Shuppan Kurabu dayori* vol. 504 (February 2007): pp. 1-3.

——. "Nihon Shuppankai kokusaika no ayumi to Noma Shōichi shi (2). *Shuppan Kurabu dayori* vol. 505 (March 2007): pp. 4-5.

——. "Nihon Shuppankai kokusaika no ayumi to Noma Shōichi shi (3)." *Shuppan Kurabu dayori* vol. 506 (April 2007): pp. 4-5.

Ikei Masaru. "Nihon Kokusai Renmei Kyōkai – sono seiritsu to henshitsu." *Hōgaku kenkyū* vol. 68, no. 2 (February 1995): pp. 23-48.

International Convention for the Protection of Literary and Artistic Works – Rome, June 2, 1928, Treaty Series No. 12. London: H.M. Stationary Office, 1932.

Iriye, Akira. *Cultural Internationalism and World Order*. London: The Johns Hopkins University Press, 1997.

——. *Global Community: The Role of International Organizations in the Making of the Contemporary World*. Berkeley: University of California Press, 2002.

Itō Nobuo. "Mizuno Rentarō to Chosakuken Shinsakai." *Kopiraito* vol. 13, no. 2/146 (May 1973): pp. 8-10.

Japanese National Commission for Unesco. *Unesco Activities in Japan*. Tōkyō: Japanese National Commission for Unesco, 1956.

Johns, Adrian. *Piracy: The Intellectual Property Wars from Gutenberg to Gates*. Chicago: University of Chicago Press, 2011.

Johnson, Chalmers. *Japan: Who Governs? The Rise of the Developmental State*. New York: Norton, 1995.

Jönsson, Christer and Jonas Tallberg, eds. *Transnational Actors in Global Governance: Patterns, Explanations, and Implications*. New York: Palgrave Macmillan, 2010.

Josephson, Harold. *James T. Shotwell and the Rise of Internationalism in America*. London: Associated University Presses, 1975.

Kasza, Gregory J. *The State and the Mass Media in Japan, 1918-1945*. London: University of California Press, 1988.

Katō Atsushi. "Nihon – Berunu jōyaku to chosakuken hō no keisei." In *Gurōbaruka no naka no kindai Nihon – kijuku to tenkai*, Hidemasa Kokaze and Yoshiya Suetake, eds., pp. 201-231. Tōkyō: Yūshisha, 2015.

Kawakami Tarō. "Nihon ni okeru kokusai shihō 70nen – toku ni Yamada Saburō oyobi Egawa Eibun o chūshin toshite." *Kokusaihō gaibun zasshi* vol. 65, no. 4 (October 1966): pp. 5-22.

Keppel, Frederick P. "The International Chamber of Commerce." *Documents of the American Association for International Conciliation* (1922): pp. 187-210.

Kingdon, John W. *Agendas, Alternatives, and Public Policies*, 2nd edition. Boston: Little, Brown & Company, 1995.

Kinmoth, Earl H. "Fukuzawa Reconsidered: Gakumon no Susume and Its Audience." *The Journal of Asian Studies* vol. 37, no. 4 (August 1978): pp. 677-696.

Kobayashi Hiroji. *Genkō chosakuken hō no rippō riyū to kaishaku– chosakuken hō senbun kaisei no shiryō toshite*. 1958; Reprint Tōkyō: Daiichi Shobō, 2012.

Kohlrausch, Martin, Steffen, Kathrin, and Stefan Wiederkehr. "Expert Cultures in Central Eastern Europe: Introduction." In *Expert Cultures in Central Eastern Europe: The Internationalization of Knowledge and the Transformation of Nation States since World War I*, Martin Kohlrausch, Kathrin Steffen, Stefan Wiederkehr, eds., pp. 9-30. Osnabrück: fibre Verlag, 2010.

Kornicki, Peter. *The Book in Japan: A Cultural History from the Beginnings to the Nineteenth Century*. Leiden: E. J. Brill, 1998.

Koskenniemi, Martti. *The Gentle Civilizer of Nations: The Rise and Fall of International Law, 1870-1960*. Cambridge: Cambridge University Press, 2002.

Kretschmer, Martin, Lionel A. F. Bently, and Ronan Deazley. "Introduction: The History of Copyright History." In *Privilege and Property: Essays on the History of Copyright*, R. Deazley, M. Kretschmer and L. Bently, eds., pp. 1-20. Cambridge: Open Book Publishers, 2010.

Kudō Eiichi. "Jitsugyōka toshite no Sakuma Teiichi – Meiji-ki jitsugyōka-zō no ichi ruikei." *Meiji Gakuin ronsō* vol. 127 (June 1967): pp. 15-40.

Kuniyuki, Terada. *Actors of International Cooperation in Prewar Japan: The Discourse on International Migration and the League of Nations Association of Japan*. Baden-Baden: Nomos, 2018.

Kurata Yoshihiro. *Chosakuken shiwa (rekishi sensho 11)* (The True History of Copyright (History Anthology 11)). Tōkyō: Senjinsha, 1980.

Kurozawa Fumitaka. "Das System von 1940 und das Problem der politischen Führung in Japan." *Zeitschrift für Geschichtswissenschaft* vol. 47, no 2. (1999): pp. 130-152.

Lachenmann, Frauke and Rüdiger Wolfrum, eds. *The Law of Armed Conflict and the Use of Force: The Max Planck Encyclopedia of Public International Law*. Oxford: Oxford University Press, 2017.

Laqua, Daniel, ed. *Internationalism Reconfigured: Transnational Ideas and Movements Between the World Wars*. London: I.B. Tauris & Co Ltd, 2011.

——, Wouter Van Acker and Christophe Verbruggen, eds. *International Organizations and Global Civil Society. Histories of the Union of International Associations*. London: Bloomsbury Academic, 2019.

Lee, Alan J. *The Origins of the Popular Press in England, 1855-1914*. London: Croom Helm, 1976.

Lloyd, Amy J. "Education, Literacy and the Reading Public." *British Library Newspapers* Detroit: Gale, 2007.

Löhr, Isabella. *Die Globalisierung geistiger Eigentumsrechte – Neue Strukturen internationaler Zusammenarbeit 1886-1952*. Göttingen: Vandenhoeck & Ruprecht, 2010.

Lorca, Arnulf Becker. "Eurocentrism in the History of International Law." In *The Oxford Handbook of the History of International Law*, Bardo Fassbender and Anne Peters, eds., pp. 1034-1057 (2012).

Mabire, Jean-Christophe. *L'Exposition Universelle de 1900*. Paris: L'Harmattan, 2000.

Mack, Edward. *Manufacturing Modern Japanese Literature: Publishing, Prizes, and the Ascription of Literary Value*. Durham: Duke University Press, 2010.

Manning, Patrick. *Navigating World History*. New York: Palgrave Macmillan, 2003.

Mathias, Regine. "Reading for Culture." *Senri Ethnological Studies* vol. 28 (1990): pp. 110-126.

Matsumoto Takanori, ed. *Senzenki Nihon no bōeki to soshiki-kan kankei – jōhō, chōsei, kyōchō*. Tōkyō: Shinhyōron, 1996.

Marshall, Byron K. "Professors and Politics: The Meiji Academic Elite." *The Journal of Japanese Studies* vol. 3, no. 1 (Winter 1977): pp. 71-97.

Maruzen kabushiki-gaisha, ed. *Maruzen 100nen shi: Nihon kindaika no ayumi to tomo ni* vol. 1-3. Tōkyō: Maruzen, 1980/1981.

McDermot, John. "Trading with the Enemy: British Business and the Law During the First World War." *Canadian Journal of History* vol. 32, no. 2 (August 1997): pp. 201-219.

Minichiello, Sharon A. "Introduction." In *Japan's Competing Modernities: Issues in Culture and Democracy 1900-1930*, Sharon A. Minichiello, ed., pp. 1-21. Honolulu: University of Hawai'i Press, 1998.

Mintrom, Michael and Phillipa Norman. "Policy Entrepreneurship and Policy Change." *Policy Studies Journal* vol. 37, no. 4 (2009): pp. 649-667.

Mitani Taichirō. *Taishō demokurashī ron – Yoshino Sakuzō no jidai*. Tōkyō: Tōkyō Daigaku Shuppankai, 1995.

Mitchell, Richard. *Censorship in Imperial Japan*. Princeton: Princeton University Press, 1983.

Miyata Noboru. *Hon'yakuken no sengoshi*. Tōkyō: Misuzu Shobō, 1999.

Monbushō. *Chosakuken Hō Kaiseian Kisō Shingikai Tokubetsu Iinkai, dai-1kai Tokubetsu Iinkai gijiroku: kōhon*. November 20, 1950.

——. *Chosakuken Hō Kaiseian Kisō Shingikai dai-4kai sōkai gijiroku*. February 1951.

Monbushō kanrikyoku, ed. *Yunesuko yori hasserareta 'bankoku chosakuken jōyaku ni kan suru shoseifu no kenkai yōsei' to kore ni tai suru Nihon seifu kaitō, chosakuken shiryō U.C. no. 1*. September 1950.

Moore, Ray A. *Partners for Democracy: Crafting the New Japanese State Under MacArthur*. Oxford: Oxford University Press, 2002.

Morohashi Eiichi. "Daiichiji Sekai Taisen ki no taiteki torihiki kinshi seisaku to Nihon." *Kokusai buki iten shi* vol. 4 (July 2017): pp. 117-140.

——. "Daiichiji Sekai Taisen to zeizaisei seisaku: sōryokusen ni okeru senji ritokusei no dōnyū to sono igi." *Shigaku zasshi* vol. 125, no. 8 (2016): pp. 1395-1419.

Müller, Simone. "The 'Debate on the Literature of Action' and Its Legacy: Ideological Struggles in 1930s Japan and the 'Rebirth' of the Intellectual." *The Journal of Japanese Studies* vol. 41, no. 1 (Winter 2015): pp. 9-44.

Nagao Teruhiko, ed. *Nitobe Inazo: From Bushido to the League of Nations*. Sapporo: Hokkaido University Press, 2006.

Naiseishi Kenkyūkai, ed. *Tsuchiya Shōzō shi danwa sokkiroku. Naiseishi kenkyū shiryō* vol. 59-60. Tōkyō: Naiseishi Kenkyūkai, 1967.

Nara Katsuji. *Meiji Ishin to sekai ninshiki taikei: Bakumatsu no Tokugawa seiken shingi to seii no aida*. Tōkyō: Yūshisha, 2010.

Naraoka Sōchi. *Taika 21kajō yōkyu to wa nan datta no ka. Daiichiji Sekai Taisen to Nitchū tairitsu no genten.* Nagoya: Nagoya Daigaku Shuppankai, 2015.

Natsukawa Kiyomaru. *Shuppanjin no yokogao.* Tōkyō: Shuppan Dōmei Shinbunsha, 1942.

Nihon Chosakuken Kyōgikai. "Chosakuken kyōgikai – 12nen no ayumi." *Chosakuken shirīzu* vol. 6 (May 1960).

Nihon Chosakuken Kyōgikai. *50nen no ayumi: sōritsu 50shūnen kinenshi.* Tōkyō: Nihon Chosakuken Kyōgikai, 2000.

Nihon Shoseki Shuppan Kyōkai, ed. *Kokumin bunka to 'hon'yakuken'.* Tōkyō: Nihon Shoseki Shuppan Kyōkai, 1966.

——. *Nihon shuppan 100nen shi nenpyō.* Tōkyō: Nihon Shoseki Shuppan Kyōkai, 1968.

——. *Nihon Shoseki Shuppan Kyōkai 10nen shi.* Tōkyō: Nihon Shoseki Shuppan Kyōkai, 1967.

Nihon Shuppan Gakkai 35nen shi Kankō Iinkai, ed., *Shuppangaku no genzai: Nihon Shuppan Gakkai 1969-2006nen no kiseki.* Tōkyō: Chōyōkai, 2008.

Nihon Yunesuko Kokunai Iinkai Bunkaka Kariyaku. *Ajia chiiki shuppan senmonka kaigi hōkokusho sōan: Yunesuko shusai.* Tōkyō: Nihon Shoseki Shuppan Kyōkai, 1966.

Nishio Rintarō, ed. *Mizuno Rentarō kaisōroku – kankei bunsho.* Tōkyō: Yamagawa Shuppansha, 1999.

Nitobe Inazō. *Bushido: The Soul of Japan.* Philadelphia: Leeds and Biddle, 1900; Reprint Tōkyō: Kodansha International, 2002.

No Author. "Tokushū: chosakuken hō 100nen" (Special Edition: 100 Years of Copyright Law). *Kopiraito* vol. 39, no. 459 (June 1999): pp. 105-106.

Nunokawa Kakuzaemon, Suzuki Takeo, Miyazawa Toshiyoshi and Wagatsuma Sakae. "Jurisuto no me: Chosakuken hō no kaisei." *Jurisuto* vol. 363 (February 1967): pp. 14-20.

Ogata Sadako. "The Role of Liberal Nongovernmental Organizations in Japan." In *Pearl Harbor as History: Japanese-American Relations 1931-1941*, Dorothy Borg and Shunpei Okamoto, eds., pp. 459-486. New York: Columbia University Press, 1973.

Ōhashi Otowa. *Ōbei shōkan.* Tōkyō: Hakubunkan, 1901.

Ōichi Tobitarō. "Chosakuken hanrei yawa." *Kopiraito* vol. 5, no. 2 (May 1961): pp. 2-3.

Okano Takeo. *Nihon shuppan bunka-shi.* Tōkyō: Shunpodō, 1962.

Ōkubo Hisao, ed. *Senzen Tōkyō-Ōsaka shuppan gyōshi dai-1kan.* Kanazawa: Kanazawa Bunpokaku, 2008; Reprint of Tōkyō Shuppan Kyōkai. *Tōkyō Shuppan Kyōkai 15nen shi.* Tōkyō: Shuppan Kyōkai Jimusho, 1929.

Ōkubo Hisao. *Shuppan – Shosekishō jinbutsu jōhō taikan: Shōwa shoki.* Kanazawa: Kanazawa Bunpokaku, 2008; Reprint of *Nihon shuppan taikan.* Tōkyō: Shuppan Taimususha, 1930.

Okuda Shirō. "Genron no jōkei – 1918nen." *20c.21c. Masukomi jānarizumu ronshū* (1994): pp. 46-67.

Okudaira Yasuhiro, ed. *Genron tōsei bunken shiryō shūsei dai-12ken: Shuppan shintaisei no zenbō – Nihon Shuppankai gaiyō*. Tōkyō: Shuppan Taimususha, 1941. Reprint, Tōkyō: Nihon Tosho Sentā, 1992.

Ōkuma Shigenobu. *Fifty Years of New Japan*, translated by Marcus B. Huish. London: Smith, Elder & Co, 1909.

Olian, Irwin A. "International Copyright and the Needs of Developing Countries: The Awakening at Stockholmn and Paris." *Cornell International Law Journal* vol. 7, no. 2 (May 1974): pp. 81-112.

Ōichi Tobitarō. "Chosakuken hanrei yawa." *Kopiraito* vol. 5, no. 2 (May 1961): pp. 2-3.

Ōie Shigeo. *Chosakuken o kakuritsu shita hitobito*. Tōkyō: Seibundō, 2004.

——. *Nippon chosakuken monogatari – Purāge hakase no tekihatsu roku*. 1981. Reprint, Sagamihara: Seizansha, 1999.

Ōnuma Yasuaki. "Harukanaru jinshu byōdō no risō – Kokusai Renmei jōyaku e no jinshu byōdō jōkō teian to Nihon no kokusaihō kan." In *Kokusaihō, Kokusai Rengō to Nihon: Takano Yūichi sensei koki kinen bunshū*, Ōnuma Yasuaki, ed., pp. 427-480. Tōkyō: Kōbundō, 1987.

Oppenheim, Lassa. *International Law: A Treatise, vol. 1 – Peace*. New York: Longmans, Green and Co., 1920.

Orii Yoshimi. "The Dispersion of Jesuit Books Printed in Japan: Trends in Bibliographical Research and in Intellectual History." *Journal of Jesuit Studies* vol. 2, no. 2 (April 2015): pp. 189-207.

Pan, Liang. "National Internationalism in Japan and China." In *Internationalisms: A Twentieth Century History*, Glenda Sluga and Patricia Clavin, eds., pp. 170-190. Cambridge University Press, 2016.

Parry, Clive, ed. *The Consolidated Treaty Series* vol. 180. New York: Oceana 1979.

Passin, Herbert. "Intellectuals in the Decision-Making Process." In *Modern Japanese Organization and Decision-Making*, Ezra F. Vogel, ed., pp. 251-283. Tōkyō: Tuttle, 1980.

Pempel, T.J. "The Tar Baby Target: 'Reform' of the Japanese Bureaucracy." In *Democratizing Japan: The Allied Occupation*, Robert E. Ward and Yoshikazu Sakamoto, eds., pp. 159-187. Honolulu: University of Hawaii Press, 1987.

Potter, Simon. *News and the British World: The Emergence of an Imperial Press System, 1876-1922*. Oxford: Clarendon Press, 2003.

Pyle, Kenneth. *Japan Rising: The Resurgence of Japanese Power and Purpose*. New York: Public Affairs, 2007.

Renoliet, Jean-Jacques. *L'Unesco oubliée: La societé des nations et la coopération intellectuelle (1919-1945)*. Paris: Publications de la Sorbonne, 1999.

Richter, Giles. "Marketing the Word: Publishing Entrepreneurs in Meiji Japan, 1870-1912." Ph.D. diss., Colombia University, 1999.

———. "Entrepreneurship and Culture: The Hakubunkan Publishing Empire in Meiji Japan." In *New Directions in the Study of Meiji Japan,* Helen Hardacre, ed., pp. 590-602. Leiden: E. J. Brill, 1997.

Ricketson, Sam. *The Berne Convention for the Protection of Literary and Artistic Works: 1886-1986.* Deventer: Kluwer law and taxation, 1987.

———. "The Public International Law of Copyright and Related Rights." In *Research Handbook on the History of Copyright Law,* Isabella Alexander and H. Tomás Gómez-Arostegui, eds., pp. 288-312. Cheltenham: Edward Elgar Publishing, 2016.

Rimner, Steffen. *Opium's Long Shadow: From Asian Revolt to Global Drug Control.* Harvard University Press, 2018.

Saikawa Takashi. "Kokusai bunka kōryū no nashonarizumu – senzenki Nihon ni okeru 'gakugei kyōryoku' jigyō o chūshin ni." *Jisedai Ajia ronshū* vol. 1 (March 2008): pp. 11-30.

———. "Kokusai bunka kōryū ni okeru kokka to chishikijin." In *Kokusai bunka kankeishi kenkyū,* Ken'ichirō Hirano, Kazuko Furuta, Akio Tsuchida et al., eds., pp. 431-453. Tōkyō: University of Tōkyō Press, 2013.

———. "From Intellectual Co-operation to International Cultural Exchange: Japan and China in the International Committee on Intellectual Cooperation of the League of Nations, 1922-1939". Ph.D. diss., Universität Heidelberg, 2014.

———. "Returning to the International Community: UNESCO and Post-war Japan, 1945-1951." In *A History of UNESCO: Global Actions and Impacts,* Poul Duedahl, ed., pp. 116-130. New York: Palgrave Macmillan, 2016.

Satō Junzō. "Kokusai Renmei to gakugei kyōryoku." *Gakugei Kōen Tsūshinsha panfuretto* vol. 48 (1927): pp. 1-15.

Schmidt, Jan. *Nach dem Krieg ist vor dem Krieg – Medialisierte Erfahrungen des Ersten Weltkriegs und Nachkriegsdiskurse in Japan (1914-1919).* Frankfurt: Campus, 2020.

——— and Katja Schmidtpott, eds. *The East Asian Dimension of the First World War: Global Entanglements and Japan, China, and Korea 1914-1919.* Frankfurt/New York: Campus, 2020.

Schwartz, Frank J. *Advice and Consent: The Politics of Consultation in Japan.* Cambridge: Cambridge University Press, 1998.

Sell, Susan and Christopher May. "Moments in Law: Contestation and Settlement in the History of Intellectual Property." *Review of International Political Economy* vol. 8, no. 3 (2001): pp. 467-500.

Shep, Sydney J. "Books without Borders: The Transnational Turn in Book History." In *Books without Borders Vol. 1 – The Cross-National Dimension in Print Culture,* Robert Fraser and Mary Hammond, eds., pp. 13-37. New York: Palgrave Macmillan, 2008.

Shepherdson-Scott, Kari. "Conflicting Politics and Contesting Borders: Exhibiting (Japanese) Manchuria at the Chicago World's Fair, 1933–34." *The Journal of Asian Studies* vol. 74, no. 3 (August 2015): pp. 539-564.

Shibasaki Atsushi. *Kindai Nihon to kokusai bunka kōryū – Kokusai Bunka Shinkōkai no setsuritsu to tenkai*. Tōkyō: Yūshindōkōbunsha, 1999.

Shimazu, Naoko. *Japan, Race and Equality: The Racial Equality Proposal of 1919*. London/New York: Routledge, 1998.

Shimizu Yu'ichirō. *Kindai Nihon no kanryō*. Tōkyō: Chūō Kōron Shinsha, 2013.

———. *The Origins of the Modern Japanese Bureaucracy*, translated by Amin Ghadimi. London: Bloomsbury Academic, 2019.

———. "Lessons Learned: Japanese Bureaucrats and the First World War," translated by Angelika Koch. In *The East Asian Dimension of the First World War: Global Entanglements and Japan, China, and Korea 1914-1919*, Jan Schmidt and Katja Schmidtpott, eds., pp. 271-289. Frankfurt/New York: Campus, 2020.

Sho Konishi. *Anarchist Modernity: Cooperatism and Japanese-Russian intellectual relations in modern Japan*. Cambridge: Harvard University Asia Center, 2013.

———. "Translingual World Order: Language without Culture in Post-Russo-Japanese War Japan." *The Journal of Asian Studies* vol. 72, no. 1 (February 2013): pp. 91-114.

Silberman, Bernard S. "Bureaucratic Development and the Structure of Decision-Making in the Meiji Period: The Case of the Genrō." *The Journal of Asian Studies* vol. 27, no. 1 (November 1967): pp. 81-94.

Snyder, Richard C., H.W. Bruck and Burton Sapin. "Decision-Making as an Approach to the Study of International Politics." In *Foreign Policy Decision-Making*, Richard C. Snyder, H.W. Bruck and Burton Sapin, eds., pp. 14-185. The Free Press of Glencoe, 1962.

———, H.W. Bruck and Burton Sapin. *Foreign Policy Decision-Making* (Revisited). New York: Palgrave Macmillan, 2002.

Suekawa Hiroshi. "Egusa Shirō." In *Gendai no shuppanjin 50nin shū*. Tōkyō: Shuppan Nyūsusha, 1956.

Takeda Tetsuji. "Shuppan bunka kōryū wa heiwa e no suishinryoku." In *Tsuitō Noma Shōichi* (hibaihin), Noma Shōichi Tsuitōshū Kankō Iinkai, eds., pp. 417-420. Tōkyō: Kōdansha, 1985.

Takemae Eiji. "Early Postwar Reformist Parties." In *Democratizing Japan: The Allied Occupation*, Robert E. Ward and Sakamoto Yoshikazu, eds., pp. 338-362. Honolulu: University of Hawai'i Press, 1987.

The Intimate Papers of Colonel House, arranged as a narrative by Charles Seymour, Sterling Professor of History, Yale University, vol. 1 and 2. Boston: Houghton Mifflin Company, 1926.

Tōkyō Shoseki Kabushikigaisha, ed. *Bukkō yakuin nami kōrōsha tsuitō kinen*. Tōkyō: Tōkyō Shoseki, 1931.

Tōkyō Shosekishō Kumiai, ed. *Tōkyō Shosekishō Kumiai 50nen shi*. Tōkyō: Tōkyō Shosekishō Kumiai, 1937.

———. *Tōkyō Shosekishō denki shūran*. 1912. Reprint, Tōkyō: Seishōdō Shoten, 1978.

Tōkyō Suppan Kyōkai, ed. *Tōkyō Shuppan Kyōkai 25nen shi*. Tōkyō: Tōkyō Shuppan Kyōkai, 1939.

Tomizawa Yoshiko, ed. *Oyaizu Kaname tsuien*. Tōkyō: Tomizawa Yoshiko, 1978.

Toyoda Tetsuya. "Japan's Early Challenge to Eurocentrism and the World Court." In *Modern Japanese Thought and International Relations*, Felix Rösch and Atsuko Watanabe, eds., pp. 43-55. London: Rowman & Littlefield, 2018.

Tsubouchi Yūzō. "Henshūsha Ōhashi Otowa." In *Zasshi 'Taiyō' to kokumin bunka no keisei*, Suzuki Sadami, ed., pp. 153-167. Kyōto: Shibunkaku, 2001.

Tsujinaka Yutaka and Robert Pekkanen. "Civil Society and Interest Groups in Contemporary Japan." *Pacific Affairs* vol. 80, no. 3 (Fall 2007): pp. 419-437.

Tsurumi Shunsuke. *An Intellectual History of Wartime Japan: 1931-1945*. London: Routledge, 2010.

Tsuruoka Satoshi. "Inoue-ki jōyaku kaisei kōshō to chiteki zaisanken – Mondai teiki to gōi keisei." *Hōgaku kenkyū* vol. 89, no. 5 (May 2016): pp. 79-115.

Uchida Susumu. "Yunesuko jōyaku o meguru chosakuken mondai." *Refarensu* vol. 49 (December 1955): pp. 62-69.

Unnō Fukuju, "1930 nendai no bungei tōsei – Matsumoto Gaku to bungei konwakai." *Sundai Shigakkai* vol. 52 (March 1981): pp. 1-38.

Vertovec, Steven. *Transnationalism*. London/New York: Routledge, 2009.

Von Staden, Peter. *Business-Government Relations in Prewar Japan*. New York: Routledge, 2008.

Weiss, Thomas G., Tatiana Carayannis and Richard Jolly. "The 'Third' United Nations." *Global Governance* vol. 15 (2009): pp. 123-142.

Ward, Robert E. "Conclusion." In *Democratizing Japan: The Allied Occupation*, Robert E. Ward and Sakamoto Yoshikazu, eds., pp. 390-438. Honolulu: University of Hawaii Press, 1987.

Wheatley, Natasha. *The Life and Death of States: Central Europe and the Transformation of Modern Sovereignty*. Princeton: Princeton University Press, 2023.

Wheaton, Henry. *Elements of International Law*. London: Sampson Low, Son, and Company 1866; Reprint Oxford: At the Clarendon Press, 1936.

World Intellectual Property Organization (WIPO). *Records of the Intellectual Property Conference of Stockholm (June 11 – July 14, 1967)*, vol. 1. Geneva: WIPO, 1971.

Yahagi Katsumi. *Yūhikaku 100nen shi*. Tōkyō: Yūhikaku, 1980.

Yamada Saburō. *Kaikoroku*. Tōkyō: Yamada Saburō Sensei Beiju Shukugakai, 1957.

Yamamoto Taketoshi. *Kindai Nihon no shinbun dokusha-sō*. Tōkyō: Hōsei Daigaku Shuppankyoku, 1981.

Yasar, Kerim. *Electrified Voices: How the Telephone, Phonograph, and Radio shaped Modern Japan, 1868-1945*. New York: Columbia University Press, 2018.

Yokota Fuyuhiko, ed. *Shuppan to ryūtsū – Hon no bunka-shi* vol. 4. Tōkyō: Heibonsha, 2016.

Yoshimura Tamotsu. "Kyū-chosakuken hō o meguru hitobito." *Copyright: Chosakuken hō 100nen kinengo* vol. 39, no. 459 (June 1999): 44-53.

Young, Louise. *Japan's Total Empire: Manchuria and the Culture of Wartime Imperialism.* London: University of California Press, 1998.

Zenkoku Shosekigyō Rengōkai, ed. *Zenkoku Shosekigyō Rengōkai shi.* Tōkyō: Zenkoku Shosekigyō Rengōkai, 1941.

ONLINE SOURCE

"Hogo kikan 'enchōha' 'shinchōha' sore zore no wake," Chosakuken Hogo Kikan no Enchō Mondai o Kangaeru Fōramu, accessed October 22, 2019, http://thinkcopyright.org/reason.html.

INDEX

Abe Isao, 167
advisory body/council, 24, 25, 41, 43, 44, 89-91, 113, 115, 146, 156-158, 163, 183
Advisory Council for Drafting a Revised Bill of the Copyright Law (Chosakuken Hō Kaiseian Kisō Shingikai), 156-159, 162
African Study Meeting on Copyright (Brazzaville 1962), 177
Agreement on Trade-Related Aspects of Intellectual Property Rights (TRIPS Agreement), 178
Akagi Tomoharu, 96, 97, 99, 105, 113, 149, 150, 156, 159, 164, 170
Akashi Taka'ichirō, 42
Allen & Unwin (publishing company), 65
American Booksellers' Association, 85
American Copyright Act (1976), 187
American Institute of International Law, 111
Anesaki Masaharu, 81, 108, 131, 133, 140, 141,
Anglo-Japanese Treaty for Commerce and Navigation, 80
Aoki Setsu'ichi, 105
Austria, 93, 110
  Austria-Hungary, 77
Arita Hachirō, 118, 124

Asahi shinbun (newspaper), 149; *see also* *Tōkyō asahi shinbun*
Asher & Co (bookseller), 65, 67
Association Littéraire et Artistique Internationale (ALAI), 30, 49, 55, 60, 61, 78-80, 86, 97, 105-107, 109, 112, 123, 132, 135, 153
Azuma Suehiko, 165

bakufu, 31, 32, 37
Behrstock, Julian, 175, 176
Beijing, 130
Belgium, 30, 48, 49, 75, 135, 162, 163
Berlin, 18, 51, 55, 56, 58, 59, 61, 98, 185, 109, 126, 133
  Berlin Act, 60
  Revision Conference (1908), 26, 55, 83, 99, 110, 132
Berne Bureau, 14, 19, 20, 35, 40, 48, 49, 51, 53-55, 60, 62, 63, 69, 71, 73, 77-79, 82-85, 87, 88, 91, 98, 112, 116, 121, 123, 124, 132, 135, 141, 148, 154, 167, 178, 181, 186, 187
BIRPI, *see* Bureaux Internationaux Réunis pour la Protection de la Propriété Intellectuelle
Bonnet, Henri, 126, 133
Boutet, Marcel, 122, 123
Brazzaville, 177

Brazil, 75, 101, 135, 162
Brussels, 18, 26, 30, 76, 77, 78, 111, 116, 121, 124, 135, 155
　Brussels Act, 155, 157, 166
　Brussels Revision Conference, 116, 120-123, 128, 132, 133, 153, 154, 173
Buenos Aires, 109
Bungeishunjū (publishing company), 113
Bungeika Kyōkai, *see* Writers' Association
Bunka Shingikai, *see* Culture Advisory Council
Bureaux Internationaux Réunis pour la Protection de la Propriété Intellectuelle, BIRPI, 49, 178
Bureau Internationale de l'Edition Mécanique, 109

Cabinet Deliberation Council (Naikaku Shingikai), 113
Cabinet Information Division (Naikaku Jōhobu), 142
Cabinet Legislation Bureau (Naikaku Hōseikyoku), 42
Canada, 162,
capitalist interests, 17, 185
Cartel des Sociétés d'Auteurs de Perceptions non Théatrales, 109
Chambers of Commerce, 38, 39, 61, 79, 95
　Federation of, 61, 95
　Tōkyō Chamber of Commerce, 39
Chiang Kai-shek, 107
Chile, 162
China, 52-54, 64, 72, 73, 96, 100, 107, 109, 122, 137-139, 145, 178, 184
Chosakuken Hō Kaiseian Kisō Shingikai, *see* Advisory Council for Drafting a Revised Bill of the Copyright Law
Chosakuken Hogo Kikan no Enchō Mondai o Kangaeru Fōramu, *see* Forum on the Issue of Extending Copyright Protection (thinkC)
Chosaku-Shuppanken Mondai Iinkai, *see* Committee for Copyright and Publishing Rights Issues
Chosakuken Seido Chōsakai, *see* Copyright System Investigation Committee
Chosakuken Seido Shingikai, *see* Copyright System Council
Chosakuken Shinsakai, *see* Copyright Investigation Council
Chūgai shinbun (newspaper), 115
Clark, Ian, 188
Civil Information and Educational Section (CIE), 147, 159
civilization, 35, 40, 48, 50, 52, 53, 58, 60, 61, 73, 80, 93, 96, 99, 138, 172, 183
　European/Western, 18, 35, 48, 50, 57, 58, 72, 96, 130, 170, 183
colonial clause, 173
colonial powers, 130
Committee for Copyright and Publishing Rights Issues (Chosaku-Shuppanken Mondai Iinkai), 170, *see also* publishing rights
Commission Préparatoire à la Conférence Diplomatique de Bruxelles, 123
Confédération Internationale des Sociétés d'Auteurs & Compositeurs, 123
Conrad, Sebastian, 188
Copyright Investigation Council (Chosakuken Shinsakai), 113-121, 132, 133, 135, 149-152, 156, 160, 161
Copyright System Council (Chosakuken Seido Shingikai), 171, 172
Copyright System Investigation Committee (Chosakuken Seido Chōsakai), 163
Council for Translation Rights Matters (Hon'yakuken Mondai Kyōgikai), 120
Cuba, 162

Culture Advisory Council (Bunka Shingikai), 187
cultural exchange, 18, 96, 104, 108, 109, 134, 147, 165
cultural harmony, 18, 129, 131, 144, 146, 184
Cunningham, William, 65
Czechoslovakia, 136

Dai Nihon Katsudō Shashin Kyōkai, *see* Greater Japan Motion Picture Association
Dai Tōa Kyōeiken, *see* Greater East Asia Co-Prosperity Sphere
Deak, Francis, 137, 138
decision-making, 15, 16, 22-24, 36, 59, 69, 127, 151, 172, 187
decolonization, 27, 147, 171, 173, 176, 179, 184, 185
Denmark, 162
developing countries/nations, 17, 27, 163, 171, 173, 174, 176, 177, 179, 184, 185
diplomacy, 19, 48, 59, 68, 73, 74, 81, 143
  cultural diplomacy, 18, 147
Droit d'auteur (journal), 98, 141
Drummond, James Eric, 79

Ghent, 48
Glesener, Edmond, 124, 125
Greater Japan Motion Picture Association (Dai Nihon Katsudō Shashin Kyōkai), 92
Greece, 60, 130, 162, 163

East Asia, 53, 74, 76, 81, 100, 128, 137, 138, 139, 183
Eckert, Andreas, 188
Egusa Shigetada, 92, 117, 120, 134, 135
Egusa Shirō, 118, 149, 153, 156, 157, 159, 164, 168

Einstein, Albert, 93
elite, 17, 22, 30, 38, 43, 75, 92, 119, 120, 139, 146, 175, 179
emperor, 21, 64, 147, 149
empire, 13, 17, 39, 47, 56, 60, 107
England, 15, 33, 36, 48, 59, 60; *see also* United Kingdom, UK
Estonia, 60
Eurocentrism, 15, 124, 188
expert conference/meeting, 85, 98, 125, 131, 132, 135, 140, 157, 175, 176

February 26 Incident, 103
Finland, 162
Forum on the Issue of Extending Copyright Protection (thinkC), 187
France, 15, 30, 33, 36, 48, 49, 55, 64, 72, 74, 75, 80, 85, 86, 93, 109, 130, 133, 135, 136, 173, 176, 181
Frankfurt Book Fair, 77, 145, 171
French Societé des Auteurs et Compositeurs Dramatique, 56
Fukunaga Bunnosuke, 92
Fukuzawa Yukichi, 33, 37
Fujita Tomoharu, 91, 95, 106, 110, 120

Gakugei Kyōryoku Kokunai Iinkai, *see* National Committee on Intellectual Cooperation
General Headquarters, 155, 156, 157, 169
Geneva, 75, 79, 82, 85, 105, 109, 148, 162, 167
German-Japanese Treaty of Commerce and Navigation, 35
Germany, 15, 30, 33, 36, 39, 48, 59, 60, 63, 66, 67, 68, 75, 78, 88, 93, 107, 109, 135, 142, 181
  National Socialist Germany, 115, 136, 141, 142

GHQ, *see* General Headquarters
globalization, 15, 18, 22, 30, 45, 51, 52, 58, 69, 76, 77, 101, 126, 132, 145, 146, 168, 179, 182, 186, 187, 188
global governance, 16
Gotō Fumio, 113, 115
Great Kantō Earthquake, 25, 89
Greater East Asia Co-Prosperity Sphere (Dai Tōa Kyōeiken), 137
Greaves, Harold Richard Goring, 87
Greece, 60, 130, 162, 163

Hakubunkan (publishing company), 43, 49, 61, 108
Hamaguchi Osachi, 84
Hara Ryōichirō, 43
Harbin, 169
Hashimura Sen'ichi, 92
Havana, 111, 123
    Convention, 125, 126, 132, 133, 134
Hayashi Heijirō, 92
Heibonsha (publishing company), 142, 169
Hemmungs Wirtén, Eva, 173
Henry Sotheran & Co (bookseller), 67
Hiroshima, 147
Hirota Kōki, 112, 116
Hōgaku kyōkai (journal), 35, 63, 140
Holland, 68, *see also* Netherlands, the
Home Ministry, 22, 25, 34, 44, 54-56, 58, 59, 64, 83, 84, 86, 87, 90, 94-97, 106, 113-121, 124, 126, 129, 133, 134, 149, 151, 156, 164, 168
    Book Division, 64, 85-87, 91, 94, 97, 106, 133, 149
Honda Akira, 121
Hon'yakuken Mondai Kyōgikai, *see* Council for Translation Rights Matters
House of Peers, 43, 44, 75, 90, 114, 126, 149
House of Representatives, 44, 64, 89, 90, 113

Hōri Kenkyūkai, *see* Legal Philosophy Research Association
Horiguchi Daigaku, 110, 112, 120, 121
Horiguchi Kuma'ichi, 110
Horikiri Zenjirō, 64
Hōritsu jihō (journal), 155
Huston, Cloyce K., 155

Iceland, 171
Ichihara Tokurō, 145, 169
Imperial Academy (Teikoku Gakushiin), 80, 81, 82, 96, 133, 135
Imperial Rule Assistance Association (Taisei Yokusankai), 142
imperialism/imperialist, 18, 47, 139, 144
    cultural, 53, 181
    powers, 139, 184
    Western, 47, 60, 137
India, 73, 75, 162, 176
Inoue Katsunosuke, 67
Institut de Droit International, 48
intellectual property rights, 13, 14, 22, 26, 33, 34, 63, 77-79, 83, 150, 178, 181, 187
    globalization of, 14, 15, 18, 22, 30, 101, 132, 148, 182, 186, 187, 188
Inter-American Commission of Authors' Rights, 123
interest groups, 20, 22, 23, 48, 157, 158, 161, 165, 168, 174, 179, 183, 187
Intergovernmental Copyright Committee, *see* UNESCO Intergovernmental Copyright Committee
International Committee on Intellectual Cooperation (ICIC), 20, 75-83, 85, 87, 88, 100, 103-106, 108, 109, 123, 125-128, 130-132, 140, 148, 150, 154, 181, 187
    Subcommittee on Intellectual Property Rights, 78-83, 85, 97, 103

INDEX

international cooperation, 18, 62, 68, 69, 80, 88, 96, 103, 104, 108, 137, 140, 144, 184
International Copyright Convention (Kokusai Chosakuken Kyōgikai), 121, 122, 128, 150
International Federation of Societies of Literature, 105
International law, 13, 14, 15, 34, 35, 41, 45, 48, 66, 75, 84, 98, 111, 149, 153, 182, 184
International Institute at Rome for the Unification of Private Law, 111
International Institute of Bibliography, 78
International Institute of Intellectual Cooperation (IIIC, Paris Institute), 20, 26, 51, 80-85, 87, 91, 97, 99, 103-106, 109, 122-133, 135, 140-142, 148, 150, 154, 187
International Labor Conference (1919), 72
International Labor Organization (ILO), 72, 73
International Olympic Committee, 137
international order, 16, 47, 60, 100, 181, 183, 184, *see also* New Order
international organization, 13-15, 17, 19-21, 25, 26, 29, 30, 35, 52, 71, 73, 74, 109, 125, 134, 144, 148, 181-187
International Publishers' Association (IPA), 145, 170, 174, 175
International Publishing Bureau, 76, 54
International Secretariat of the Berne Union, *see* Berne Bureau
internationalism, 18, 20, 71, 74, 75, 96, 104, 110, 117, 182, 185
    cultural, 74, 51
    governmental, 19
    Wilsonian, 96
Inukai Takeru, 119
Ireland, 60, 162

Iriye, Akira, 51, 74
Ishii Kikujirō, 86
Itagaki Taisuke, 43
Italy, 30, 36, 49, 56, 60, 72, 74-76, 97, 107, 110, 130, 136, 176
Itō Nobufumi, 106, 107
Itō Nobuo, 115, 138

Japan Authors' Association (Nihon Chosakka Kumiai), 150
Japan Book Publishers' Association (Nihon Shoseki Shuppan Kyōkai), 145, 168, 169, 170, 171, 173, 176
Japan Copyright Advisory Council (Nihon Chosakuken Shingikai), 152
Japan Copyright Council (Nihon Chosakuken Kyōgikai), 152, 153, 160, 161, 164-168, 170, 179
Japan Copyright Union (Nihon Chosakuken Renmei), 151
Japan Grammophone Trade Association (Nihon Chikuonkishō Kumiai), 92
Japan International Association (Nihon Kokusai Kyōkai), 108
Japan Magazine Association (Nihon Zasshi Kyōkai), 92, 93, 113, 117, 134
Japanese National Commission for UNESCO (Nihon Yunesuko Kokunai Iinkai), 174, *see also* UNESCO
Japan Newspaper Association (Nihon Shinbun Kyōkai), 92
Japan Publishing Association (Nihon Shuppankai), 16
Japan Publishers' Association (Nihon Shuppan Kyōkai), 149, 175
Japan Publishing Culture Association (Nihon Shuppan Bunka Kyōkai), 103
Japan Publishing Distribution Company (Nihon Shuppan Haikyū Kabushiki Kaisha), 103, 120

Japan Times (newspaper), 54, 114, 177
Japan Writers' Association (Nihon Bungeika Kyōkai), 187
Japanese Communist Party, 97
Japanese spirit (*Nihon seishin*), 114, 147
Japanese Pen Club, 120
Japanese-Soviet Non-Aggression Treaty (1941), 147
Jin'inkai, 44
Jitsugyō no Nihon Sha (publishing company), 113, 142
Jugoslavia, 162

Kabayama Aisuke, 126
Kaizōsha (publishing company), 95, 142
Katō Takaaki, 63, 64, 68
Katsudō Shashin Gyōsha Kumiai, *see* Motion Picture Traders' Association
Katsumoto Masaakira, 157, 160, 162, 164
Kawabe Hisao, 95
Kawai Hiroyuki, 85
KBS, *see* Society for International Cultural Relations
Keiho-kyoku, *see* Police Affairs Bureau
Keiho Iinkai, *see* Police Advisory Council
Kido Shirō, 149, 150, 156, 159
Kido Yoshihiko, 160
Kingdon, John, 23, 24
Kikuchi Hiroshi, 113, *see also* Kikuchi Kan
Kikuchi Kan, 113, 119, 149
Kobayashi Hiroji, 84, 91, 106, 113, 120, 121, 126, 133, 134, 135
Kobayashi Yoshinori, 39, 42
Kōdansha (publishing company), 117, 120, 133, 142, 145, 153, 169
Kokusai Bunka Shinkōkai (KBS), *see* Society for International Cultural Relations
Kokusai Chosakuken Kyōgikai, *see* International Copyright Convention

Kokusai chishiki (journal), 81
Kokusai Renmei Kyōkai, *see* League of Nations Association of Japan
Komura Jutarō, 53, 61
Konoe Fumimaro, 137, 142
Kopiraito (journal), 115
Korea, 31, 47, 72, 75, 96, 145
Kubota Fujimaro, 157
Kuji Manabu, 94
Kunishio Kōichirō, 133
Kuniyuki, Terada, 21, 96
Kusano Teishi, 116, 119, 156, 159
Kwantung Army, 107
Kyōto, 32, 145

Labour Union Law (Rōdō Kumiai Hō), 151
La Fontaine, Henri, 76
Lansing, Robert, 93
League of Nations, 14, 18, 20, 21, 26, 51, 71-76, 78, 79, 82, 87, 97, 100, 101, 103-109, 123-125, 129-131, 135, 137, 139-143, 182, 184, 186, 187, *see also* International Committee on Intellectual Cooperation (ICIC); International Institute of Intellectual Cooperation (IIIC, Paris Institute) International Federation of League of Nations Societies, 108
  withdrawal from, 107-109, 111, 115, 124, 184, 186
League of Nations Association of Japan (Kokusai Renmei Kyōkai), 74, 75, 81, 96, 107, 108
Legal Philosophy Research Association (Hōri Kenkyūkai), 63
Lee, S. M., 158
Leygues, Georges, 50
Lima, 140
Löhr, Isabella, 19, 78, 188
Luchaire, Julien, 85, 126

MacArthur, Douglas, 147
Maillard, Georges, 61, 62, 86, 106, 107, 122, 123
Makino Nobuaki, 72, 74
Manchukuo, 107
Manchuria, 107, 137, 147, *see also* Manchurian Incident
Manchurian Incident, 103, 107, 108, 109, 186
Manga taimusu (journal), 161
Masuda Giichi, 89, 113
March 15 Incident, 103, 114, 122
Marco Polo Bridge Incident, 130
Marshall, Byron, 36
Martinus Nijhoff (bookseller), 66
Maruya Shōsha (publishing company), 37, *see also* Maruzen
Maruzen (publishing company), 37, 55, 65, 67-69, 82, 120, 142
Marx, Karl, 94
Matsuda Michikazu, 97, 98, 105
Matsudaira Kōtō, 121
Matsui Keishirō, 79
Matsumoto Gaku, 114
Matsumura Giichi, 90
May 15 Incident, 103
Meguro Jinshichi, 95, 113, 117, 120
Melbourne, 109
Meiji Restoration, 31, 33, 35, 48, 146, 148
Mexico, 162
Miki Kiyoshi, 121
Ministry of Colonial Affairs, 117
Ministry of Commerce and Industry, 84, 117
  Patent Bureau 84, 87
Ministry of Communications and Transportation, 82, 87
Ministry of Education, 59, 80, 87, 96, 104, 117, 133, 142, 149, 155, 156, 157, 158, 161, 163, 166, 167, 174, 175, 187

Administration Bureau, 157
Agency for Cultural Affairs, 187
Copyright Department, 165
Cultural Affairs Bureau, 173, 176
Ministry of Foreign Affairs, 22, 25, 55, 68, 80- 84, 86, 87, 88, 106, 107, 108, 111, 116, 120, 124, 126, 132, 155, 156, 160, 161, 164, 167, 171, 175,
  Department of Cultural Affairs, 108, 133
  Trade Department, 68
  Treaties Bureau, 176
  Treaty Department, 106, 121, 125
Ministry of Justice, 84, 86, 87, 117, 171
Ministry of Railways, 106
Ministry of Trade, 142
  British, 67
Mishima Seiya, 106
Mitani Takanobu, 125, 132
Miyata Noboru, 166
Mizuno Rentarō, 34, 41, 42, 44, 48, 52, 55, 56, 63, 64, 68, 75, 86, 97, 113, 132, 133, 135, 149, 165
Mohr Siebeck (publishing company), 94
Motion Picture Traders' Association (Katsudō Shashin Gyōsha Kumiai), 92
Murray, Gilbert, 130

Nagasaki, 147
Nagata Shinnojō, 89
Naikaku Hōseikyoku, *see* Cabinet Legislation Bureau
Naikaku Jōhobu, *see* Cabinet Information Division
Naikaku Shingikai, *see* Cabinet Deliberation Council
Nakajima Kenzō, 150-153, 155, 160, 161, 164
Nakamura Shigehisa, 67, 68

nationalism/nationalist, 17, 71, *see also* ultranationalism
National Committee on Intellectual Cooperation (Gakugei Kyōryoku Kokunai Iinkai), 79, 80, 97, 100, 108, 109, 111, 125, 126, 135, 140, 141
National Federation of UNESCO Cooperative Associations in Japan (Nihon Yunesuko Kyōkai Renmei), 154, *see also* UNESCO
Netherlands, the, 56, 66, 68, 75, 162
New Culture in East Asia (Shin-Tōa Bunka), 138, 184
New Order for East Asia (Tōa Shin-Chitsujō), 137, 184
New Order, 103, 139, 142
postwar world order, 173
New York, 88, 109
NGO, *see* non-governmental organization
Nihon Bungeika Kyōkai, *see* Japan Writers' Association
Nihon Chikuonkishō Kumiai, *see* Japan Grammophone Trade Association
Nihon Chosakka Kumiai, *see* Japan Authors' Association
Nihon Chosakuken Kyōgikai, *see* Japan Copyright Council
Nihon Chosakuken Renmei, *see* Japan Copyright Union
Nihon Chosakuken Shingikai, *see* Japan Copyright Advisory Council
Nihon hōgaku (journal), 138
Nihon Kokusai Kyōkai, *see* Japan International Association
Nihon Shinbun Kyōkai, *see* Japan Newspaper Association
Nihon Shoseki Shuppan Kyōkai, *see* Japan Book Publishers' Association
Nihon Shuppankai, *see* Japan Publishing Association

Nihon Shuppan Bunka Kyōkai, *see* Japan Publishing Culture Association
Nihon Shuppan Haikyū Kabushiki Kaisha, *see* Japan Publishing Distribution Company
Nihon Shuppan Kyōkai, *see* Japan Publishers' Association
Nihon Yunesuko Kokunai Iinkai, *see* Japanese National Commission for UNESCO
Nihon Yunesuko Kyōkai Renmei, *see* National Federation of UNESCO Cooperative Associations in Japan
Nihon Zasshi Kyōkai, *see* Japan Magazine Association
NHK (Nippon Hōsō Kyōkai), 110
Ningen (journal), 151
Nishimura Iwao, 158
Nitobe Inazō, 75
Noma Seiji, 117, 133, 135, 145, 169
Noma Shōichi, 145, 153, 156, 168, 169, 171, 174, 175, 176
non-governmental organization (NGO), 15, 16, 20, 56, 175, 176, 182
North Korea, 145
Norway, 75, 162
Nunokawa Kakuzaemon, 164, 174

Ōgura Masatsune, 42
Ōhashi Otowa, 49, 50, 51
Ōhashi Shintarō, 43, 44, 56, 61, 64, 108
Okada Keisuke Cabinet, 113
Okazaki Katsuo, 160
Ōkuma Shigenobu, 66, 67, 68
Ōkura Yasugorō, 64, 88, 89, 92, 95, 110, 117
Ōnuma Yasuaki, 72
open access, 32, 41, 52
Osterrieth, Albert, 58
Ostertag, Fritz, 82, 83, 84, 112, 123

INDEX

Otlet, Paul, 76
Ozaki Saburō, 43
Oyaizu Kaname, 25, 37-39, 41- 44, 52-55, 61, 64-68, 76, 77, 88, 93, 117, 122, 139

Pacific War, 149, 169
Palace of the Academies, 135
Pan-American Convention, 101, 111, 134
Pan-American Union, 14, 20, 111, 126, 147
Paris, 48-51, 66, 72, 80, 81, 85, 97, 105, 107, 109, 122, 125, 126, 127, 133-136, 142, 158, 165, 167, 174
    Committee of Experts, 122, 123, 125, 127, 128, 133, 134, 135, 138, 155
    Convention for the Protection of Industrial Property, 34, 49, 78
    Economic Conference (1916), 68,
    Peace Conference (1919), 58, 72, 73, 131, 182
Paris Institute, *see* International Institute of Intellectual Cooperation (IIIC)
Passin, Herbert, 23, 24, 36
Patent Office, 176
Peace Treaty (1952), 159, 160, 164
    of Versailles (1919), 72, 78, 88
Permanent Court of International Justice, 58
Plage, Heinrich Max Wilhelm, 109, 110, 112, 120, 140, *see also* Whirlwind Plage
Pilotti, Massimo, 130
Poland, 130
Police Advisory Council (Keiho Iinkai), 90, 91
Police Affairs Bureau (Keiho-kyoku), 84, 85, 87, 90-92, 94, 95, 97, 104, 106, 114, 116, 120, 121, 126, 133, 149, 187

policy entrepreneurs, 23, 36, 52, 122
Pouillet, Eugène, 49, 50, 61
Potsdam Declaration, 147

Publication Law (Shuppan Hō), 34, 56, 84, 88, 90, 95
Publication Ordinance (Shuppan Jōrei), 33
publishing entrepreneurs, 22, 32, 41
publishing rights, 89, 90, 91, 106, 110, 170, 174 *see also* Committee for Copyright and Publishing Rights Issues
Press Law (Shinbunshi Hō), 84
propaganda, 24, 77, 122, 146, 147
Pyle, Kenneth, 59

racial equality proposal, 58, 182, 184
Renault, M. Louis, 99
Rīdāzu daijesuto (journal), 161
Rikken Seiyūkai, 75, 113, 119
Rikken Yōseikai, 161
Röthlisberger, Ernst, 63, 82
Rome, 26, 71, 84, 87, 91, 95, 109, 133, 137, 162
    Act, 113
    Institute, 123, 135
    Revision Conference, 18, 71, 82, 83, 87, 90, 91, 95-98, 106, 111, 113, 117, 119, 122, 129, 133, 139, 156, 157, 160, 170, 187
Romania, 49
Roosevelt, Franklin D., 136
Russia, 49, 57, 85, 145, 178, *see also* Soviet Union
Russo-Japanese War (1904-1905), 47, 118

Sakuma Teiichi, 42
Sasaki Norio, 167
Satō Junzō, 81, 111, 112, 124, 126, 133, 134, 135, 140
Scandinavia, 55
Sendai, 154
Serizawa Kōjirō, 119
Shibusawa Eiichi, 39, 74
Shidehara Kijūrō, 68

Shimazu, Naoko, 57, 58, 72
Shimizu Yu'ichirō, 43, 69
Shimojō Yasumaro, 152
Shimonaka Yasaburō, 169, 170
Shin-Tōa Bunka, *see* New Culture in East Asia
Shinchō (journal), 119
shingikai, *see* advisory body/council
Shōchiku (film production company), 149
Sho Konishi, 118
Shotwell, James Thompson, 131, 138
Siebeck, Paul, 94, *see also* Mohr Siebeck (publishing house)
Siebeck, Oskar, 94
Sino-Japanese Treaty of Commerce and Navigation, 54
Sino-Japanese War
  First, 34, 47
  Second, 103, 108, 130, 137, 141
Smith, Adam, 94
Società Italiana degli Autori ed Editori, 56
Société des Gens des Lettres, 56
Society for International Cultural Relations (Kokusai Bunka Shinkōkai, KBS), 108, 109, 124-128, 133, 140
South America, 85, 145
South Manchurian Railway Company, 168
sovereignty, 14, 139, 146, 153, 157, 158, 159, 161, 162, 168
Soviet Union, 107, 122, 176, *see also* Russia
Spain, 30, 49, 136, 173
Stockholm, 56
  Act, 177
  Revision Conference, 18, 27, 172-178
Subcommittee on Intellectual Property Rights, *see* International Committee on Intellectual Cooperation (ICIC)
Sudetenland, 136
Sugimura Yōtarō, 105
Sugiyama Naojirō, 127

Supreme Commander of the Allied Powers (SCAP), 146-150, 152, 154-156, 159, 165, 179
Suzuki Bunshirō, 149
Suzuki Kisaburō, 84, 88, 90, 91, 93, 97, 117
Suzuki Takeo, 135, 140, 174
Sweden, 40, 55, 162, 173, 176
Switzerland, 30, 93, 130, 162

Tagore, Rabindranath, 94
Taguchi Ryūzaburō, 167
Takagi Shōichi, 168, 169 *see also* Noma Shōichi
Takayanagi Kenzō, 135, 136, 140, 170, 174
Takebe Rokuzō, 94
Taisei Yokusankai, *see* Imperial Rule Assistance Association
Tanaka Giichi, 84, 85, 105
Tanakadate Aikitsu, 81
Teikoku Gakushiin, *see* Imperial Academy
Thailand, 162, 171, 172
Tōa Shin-Chitsujō, *see* New Order for East Asia
Tōkyō Book Development Centre (Tōkyō Shuppan Sentā), 175, 176
Tōkyō Book Publishing Businessmen's Assocation (Tōkyō Shoseki Shuppan Eigyōsha Kumiai), renamed Tōkyō Booksellers and Publishers' Association (Booksellers' Association) (Tōkyō Shosekishō Kumiai), 25, 38, 39, 53, 55, 61, 64, 76, 88, 89, 92-94, 119, 129, 168
Tōkyō City Council (Tōkyō Shikai), 41, 42
Tōkyō Imperial University, 22, 34-37, 42, 63, 68, 75, 80, 81, 86, 98, 127, 131, 135, 168, 182, 184
Tōkyō nichi nichi shinbun (newspaper), 114

Tōkyō Publishers' Association (Tōkyō Shuppan Kyōkai), 25, 64, 89, 93, 106, 113, 117, 118, 120, 126, 132, 134, 142, 168
Tōkyō Shikai, *see* Tōkyō City Council
Tōkyō shinbun (newspaper), 164
Tōkyō Shoseki Shuppan Eigyōsha Kumiai, renamed Tōkyō Shosekishō Kumiai, *see* Tōkyō Booksellers and Publishers' Association
Tōkyō Shuppan Kyōkai, *see* Tōkyō Publishers' Association
Tōkyō Shuppan Sentā, *see* Tōkyō Book Development Centre
Toller, Ernst, 94
Toyoda Tetsuya, 58
Trading with the Enemy Proclamation, 66
Extension Act (1915), 66, 67
transnational copyright community, 15, 17, 45, 55, 57, 123, 127, 137, 140, 146, 147, 153, 173, 179, 182, 183, 185
Transpacific Partnership Agreement (TPP), 187
TRIPS Agreement, *see* Agreement on Trade-Related Aspects of Intellectual Property Rights
Trump, Donald, 187
Tsuchiya Shōzō, 85- 87, 91, 94, 96-98
Tunesia, 176
Turkey (Türkiye), 162, 163, 171, 172

Uchida Kōsai, 111
Uehara Seiichirō, 92
Ugaki Kazushige, 134
Ume Kenjirō, 42, 43
UNESCO (United Nations Educational, Scientific and Cultural Organization), 20, 145, 147, 148, 151, 154-161, 165-168, 170, 173, 174, 175, 176, 179, 181, 185, 187

Subcommittee for Information and Mass Media, 148
Committee of Copyright Experts, 153, 155, 157
Intergovernmental Copyright Committee, 167, 169
Copyright Division of, 156
unequal treaties, 34, 44, 123
United Kingdom (UK), 29, 30, 59, 65, 66-68, 93, 109, 130, 136, 162, 173,
United Nations (UN), 14, 21, 155, 167, 175, 178, 186
Security Council, 165, 166
Third UN, 186
United States (US), 14, 20, 33, 36, 38, 40, 48, 49, 52, 54, 60, 63, 72-75, 77, 85, 88, 96, 124, 129-131, 135, 136, 139, 141, 145, 147, 149, 154, 159, 162-164, 166, 173, 176, 187
universal exhibitions, 48, 49, *see also* World's Fair
Universal Copyright Convention (UCC), 18, 20, 27, 101, 125, 132, 135, 147, 148, 153, 155, 158, 159, 160, 163-167, 173, 179, 185
Universal Manhood Suffrage Act (Futsū Senkyo Hō), 84, 97
Uraguchi Tetsuo, 161
US Occupation, 24, 27, 146, 178

Vanderlip, Frank A., 93
Vereniging van Letterkundigen, 56
Von Preußen, Wilhelm, 93

Washington, 157, 175
Wedekind, Frank, 94
Weiss, Raymond, 51, 105, 122, 125, 126, 131, 133, 134
Wells, H.G., 93

Whirlwind Plage, 109, 112, 122, 140, *see also* Plage, Heinrich Max Wilhelm
Wilson, Woodrow, 74
WIPO (World Intellectual Property Organization), 30, 178, 186
Convention, 178
World's Fair (1900), 48, 49 *see also* universal exhibitions
World Trade Organization (WTO), 178
World War I, 26, 43, 47, 48, 51, 59, 62, 64, 65, 66, 68, 69, 70, 72, 74, 77, 88, 93, 100, 184
World War II, 14, 20, 21, 26, 101, 140, 141, 145-147, 149, 175, 178, 184-186
Writers' Association (Bungeika Kyōkai), 92

Yada Chōnosuke, 88
Yamakawa Kenjirō, 68
Yamamoto Sanehiko, 95, 120
Yamaoka Mannosuke, 85, 92, 94, 96
Yamada Saburō, 35, 36, 38, 45, 48, 49, 51, 52, 62, 63, 68, 69, 75, 80, 82, 83, 91, 96, 100, 108, 109, 122, 126-136, 139, 140, 149, 150, 156, 157, 159, 163, 164, 166, 170, 174, 184
Yamanouchi Yoshio, 121
Yokohama mainichi (newspaper), 31
Yomiuri shinbun (newspaper), 114, 117, 118
Yoshida Shigeru (bureaucrat), 87
Yoshida Shigeru (diplomat and prime minister), 152
Yūhikaku (publishing company), 92, 117, 118, 149, 153
Yugoslavia, 171, 172

www.ingramcontent.com/pod-product-compliance
Lightning Source LLC
Chambersburg PA
CBHW051608230426
43668CB00013B/2025